FAMILY
Treasures

15
LESSONS,
TIPS, *and*
TRICKS *for*
Discovering Your

FAMILY
HISTORY

FAMILY *Treasures*

15 LESSONS, TIPS, *and* TRICKS *for* Discovering Your FAMILY HISTORY

BARRY J. EWELL

PLAIN SIGHT PUBLISHING
AN IMPRINT OF CEDAR FORT, INC.
SPRINGVILLE, UTAH

This is not an official publication of The Church of Jesus Christ of Latter-day Saints. The opinions and views expressed herein belong solely to the author and do not necessarily represent the opinions or views of Cedar Fort, Inc. Permission for the use of sources, graphics, and photos is also solely the responsibility of the author.

ISBN 13: 978-1-59955-948-3

Published by Plain Sight Publishing, an imprint of Cedar Fort, Inc.
2373 W. 700 S., Springville, UT 84663
Distributed by Cedar Fort, Inc., www.cedarfort.com

LIBRARY OF CONGRESS CATALOGING-IN-PUBLICATION DATA

Ewell, Barry J., author.
  Family secrets : 15 lessons, tips, and tricks of genealogy research / Barry J. Ewell.
    pages cm
  ISBN 978-1-59955-948-3
  1. Genealogy. I. Title.
  CS16.E94 2011
  929.1072--dc23
                                        2011043561

Cover design by Angela D. Olsen
Cover design © 2012 by Lyle Mortimer
Edited and typeset by Michelle Stoll

Printed in the United States of America

10 9 8 7 6 5 4 3 2 1

Printed on acid-free paper

To Colette, Melissa, Shauna, Jason, Teresa, Bryson, and Diana—in this life we are family joined by love, standing on the foundation forged by generations. It's the now as husband, father, and grandfather that I cherish, because it makes a difference in this moment of time.

Contents

Preface

Family history is a journey of discovery. It's about finding answers to the questions one ponders at one time or another.

- Who are my ancestors?
- Where did they live?
- What did they do?

The steps of the journey are guided by the questions we ask. With each answer comes another question. In time, you begin to feel a sense of connection and a bond that spans generations. Each individual ancestor contributed in some way to your very existence.

This journey will lead you to discover the names of ancestors and important events in their lives. As you uncover information from memories, objects, and resources, you are able to create and preserve a documented record.

This will not be a "how-to," but rather an expression of my journey in becoming a genealogist. The experiences will range from sacred and cherished to funny and disappointing. The focus will be to share what I have learned in hopes that it will provide assurance that you are not alone in your search for generations, and that you can do it.

Come join me in "Sharing Information to Join Generations."

Introduction

We all have many questions about those who have gone before us. The steps of the journey toward learning more about our progenitors are guided by the questions we ask. With each answer comes another question. In time, you begin to feel a sense of connection and a bond that spans generations. Each individual ancestor contributed in some way to your very existence.

This journey will lead you to discover, uncover, and recover the one-of-a-kind story of the ancestral lines whose path leads directly to yours. Your ancestors' path is forged by time, choices, and life's experiences that begin in the home and expand into the lands where they lived. It's about the people known, the places visited, the decisions made, the opportunities lost or gained; it's about the spiritual, physical, and mental exuberance and folly.

You'll learn of important events such as birth, marriage, and death. You'll understand how the story is influenced by culture, religion, political endeavors, education, and social and economic status. You'll gain a front-row seat to the historical events that surrounded members of your family, from war and migration to famine and struggles for civil rights.

Do not underestimate the value of your ancestors' story or the story you are currently living. Every story is important and unique, if for no other reason than that they lived.

My journey as a genealogist has not been easy. I wanted to quit countless times. Yet there was always a gentle and loving force that seemed to encourage—if not compel—me to find my ancestral lines. With experience and focused persistence, the journey became easier, increasingly successful, and more rewarding. I've learned how to do the following:

- ask the right questions to be led to answers;
- find, access, and explore genealogical resources quickly;
- develop, expand, and sharpen my genealogy research skills;
- recognize clues and use them to trace and explore my family ties;
- resolve genealogical "brick walls;"
- effectively use technology in research and preservation;
- learn to find and use specific country, state, and county records; and
- help others with their genealogy research.

My Journey Began on August 3, 1998

Before I say anymore, I'd like to share with you a personal experience about how I began my journey as a genealogist.

I became a genealogist on August 3, 1998. That is the day my mother died. There were three events in the ensuing six weeks that inspired me to begin a life focused on family history, sharing knowledge, and helping others.

Mom died from a horrific lymph node cancer. I had gathered with my brother and sister to discuss with my mother her desires for what we all thought would be several months of life and to help her put her affairs in order. She entered the hospital the first day of my arrival and died three days later.

Her passing was one of the more spiritual, yet ugly, experiences of my life. I was very sad to see Mom go, but grateful that her suffering was over. While at her side, I saw the manifestation of God's intervention and love for one of his children. Away from the bedside, it was contention at every turn with my sister. She knew everything about what Mom wanted and needed, yet the only opinion and decision that mattered to her was her own. Even as we sought to help Mom write her last will and testament, all that could be heard was "That's mine." It became an argument over things. As far as I was concerned, things were not important; I had all I needed and wanted. I just wanted there to be peace and an amenable resolution to helping Mom.

EXPERIENCE ONE:
PRESERVE THE RECORD.

Following Mom's passing and funeral, my brother, sister, and I met for one last time in Mom's front room. My sister's parting words were direct and expected, "You are welcome to stay the night. Whatever is left when you leave is mine." My sister pointed to a pile of things that were in the middle of the floor and instructed my brother and I that we could take what we wanted. Whatever was left would be given to the thrift store. And then she left to go back to her home.

As soon as she left, my brother and I knelt in prayer and gave thanks to our Father in Heaven for our mother and asked a blessing that relationships with our sister would heal in time. Upon conclusion of the prayer, there was a sense of serenity. We were both emotionally and physically drained. Where do you begin? I was standing in my mom's home. It was just things. Mom had been a waitress at the Las Vegas Horseshoe Club for over forty years. She raised three children by herself. I always loved coming home, just to be with her. Now here I was, standing in the middle of her front room, feeling lost and in need of direction regarding where to begin. And in almost that very moment, there was clarity. My mind filled with two thoughts: First, that this would be the last night that I would ever stand in this home and, second, that I needed to preserve the record—gather photos, certificates, letters, and other related documents that would tell the history of my mother.

I knew I needed to follow the direction I was receiving. My next thought was, where should I begin? Within seconds, the thought came. I was first led to look in a cupboard in the kitchen where Mom kept coloring books. I couldn't see anything. As I began to close the door, I felt the need to look again. In the back was a bank pouch with unused check registers. I pulled it down, and inside was an envelop with pictures from Mom's early childhood. I was next guided to a drawer in the kitchen where I found, in a plastic bag, key photos of Mom's life.

Next I was directed to a spare bedroom dresser. As I went through the drawers, I found them all empty except for a larger drawer that Mom had filled with paperback books she had read. I pulled out half the books, became frustrated, and put the books back in the drawer, thinking that there was nothing there. As I stood to leave, the thought came: *Look again.* I returned to the drawer again and removed all the books. At the bottom of the drawer was a sack filled with Mom's important papers, such as her birth certificate, marriage license, photographs, and other documents.

Throughout the night, I went from room to room, having the same experience of knowing where to look in each room. My brother and I worked and packed until just before dawn. I privately asked for the last time, where else should I look? The answer was a total sense of peace. We were done.

As the morning progressed, I became grateful that I had heeded the promptings of the night before, as my sister made it clear that my brother and I were no longer welcome in what was now her home and that we would never receive any of moms pictures or records.

EXPERIENCE TWO:
TELL THE CHILDREN ABOUT ME.

Three weeks to the day after Mom's passing, I had a dream where I heard a knock at the front door. When I opened the door, I saw my mother. She asked me to take a walk with her. We came to an outdoor café, where we sat down and ordered a soft drink. During the conversation that followed, Mom reached out and held my hand and said, "Barry, will you please tell the children about me?"

I replied by saying, "Of course, Mother, I will do that." At that very moment, I awoke. I woke my wife and told her of the experience. We both found the dream somewhat odd, since during my mother's life, whenever she was asked to tell us more about her life, she would usually respond with, "It was hard; that's all you need to know."

I pondered the dream until it was time to rise to get ready for work, trying to make some sense of what I had experienced. I had no answer, so I discarded the experience as an interesting dream with little or no meaning.

EXPERIENCE THREE:
TELL THE CHILDREN ABOUT ME—NOW.

Three more weeks passed. During the night, the same dream I'd had three weeks earlier began to unfold exactly as it had played out before. This time, however, when I was asked, "Barry, will you please tell the children about me?," I responded with irritation in my voice, "Mother, I told you I would."

Mom responded with an emphatic voice, "Tell the children about me, *now*."

This time, I awoke immediately. My mind began to fill with names, with the instruction that I should talk to and record my interview with each person. I turned on the computer and began typing the five names as they appeared. At that point, I thought, well, if I am going to talk to these people, I should also talk to . . . and I began to brainstorm other names. Then my mind went blank. I felt the most empty feeling I had ever experienced. I knew I had gone beyond the bounds of what the Spirit wanted me to do. I immediately erased what I had added to the list and then knelt in prayer, asking for forgiveness and requesting that the stream of thought return. After about twenty minutes of prayer, the first five names reappeared in my mind, followed by five new names. When I was through, I had five people I knew and five that I didn't. My instructions were to contact each person and conduct oral histories in regards to their relationship with my mother.

In the year that followed, I was able to meet with and record oral histories with each of the ten individuals. Each one of them was able to reveal a unique chapter of my mother's life that spanned the sixty-five years she had lived. In addition to the oral history, I received memorabilia that represented their relationship, such as cards, letters, photographs, documents, and more.

Oh, how I wish I had come to know the mother they described when she was still alive. I had come to know her now through the eyes and experiences of her friends and family. It was the first step in what would become a connection to the generations before me.

The Meaning of "Tell the Children about Me."

In the beginning, interviewing Mom's friends and family was the limit of my intended participation in fulfilling the solemn promise I had given my mother in my dream. Genealogy and family history were not in my vocabulary. In fact, whenever I heard the words, I would usually find a good reason to leave the room.

Since August 3, 1998, I have had countless experiences that have forged my path as a genealogist. From conducting oral histories to searching the lands of my ancestors, I have become the keeper of the record. It is much more than searching for names and connecting one generation to the next. It's realizing that I am the total sum of all those who came before. I am a chapter being written in a legacy to which I will humbly add my name.

As the keeper of the record, I seek to fulfill my role by carefully using the time I have available to record, manage, organize, extend, and expand my family tree. I have come to understand what Mother meant when she asked me to "tell the children" about her. It's simply that she and those who have tasted the end of mortality live on. The family tree is a living bond that extends beyond mortality. And no one in that link shall be forgotten.

Since that very first experience, I've learned

- about records—the information they contain, where to find them, and how to use them;
- about my ancestors—their roots, their records, and their times and seasons;
- about technology and its use in research and preservation;
- to use and preserve countless forms of data and file formats;
- to search in the field, on the Internet, and in libraries and archives;
- to conduct interviews;

- to track my family through states and counties and find their records;
- my place in the link of time; and
- each individual ancestor contributed in some way to my very existence.

I've spent countless hours researching, learning, and asking questions, all the while wishing there would be an easier way. I've read books, attended conferences, and consulted with fellow genealogists. If I've learned anything, it's that genealogy is a repeatable process. The process that makes the most sense to me is divided into the following steps:

Step 1: Select an individual or family to research
Step 2: Define research goals
Step 3: Search reliable sources
Step 4: Cite and verify each and every source
Step 5: Analyze your sources
Step 6: Resolve any conflicts created by the evidence
Step 7: Make your conclusion

I pondered at length how I might share the process with you. I could simply state each step and tell you what it means with a few examples, or I could introduce each step and provide a more in-depth account of the lessons I learned from following the process. I chose the latter.

WHAT'S TO FOLLOW?

My journey has not been a straight line between two points, but rather a zig-zag of projects and explorations that, when combined, have helped to create a rich reservoir of cherished experiences and skills.

In the pages that follow, I will share with you my journey as a genealogist, through which I hope to impart a reassurance that you too can successfully research and find ancestors while creating a connection that spans generations. I'll share my experiences, my insights, and the lessons I've learned as a student and as a mentor.

As you read each chapter, I will encourage you to do the following:

• Open your mind to ideas.
• Choose what you need.
• Use what you take.
• Share what you learn.

Whether you are a beginning genealogist or a seasoned researcher, you will find the answers to many of your questions within the pages that follow. But more important, you will learn how to ask the questions and find the answers that expand beyond the material covered. You will become a better genealogist, your research will be more focused and productive for the time you have available, and you will experience greater joy and satisfaction in your family history research.

The topics I will cover are those lessons I have learned that have been the most important in my personal journey and the thousands with whom I have collaborated and mentored.

Additional PDFs, videos, forms mentioned throughout the book, and other resources are available at www.FamilyTreasuresBook.com.

Lesson 1: Genealogy Is a Repeatable Process

Genealogy is a repeatable process. Focus your research on the one. Choose one ancestor, one objective, and one life event at a time. Start with the information you have and expand your knowledge. Learn lessons that will keep you growing as a genealogist.

Lesson 2: Start Organized, Stay Organized

Starting out organized is easier than getting organized later on. You will be introduced to color-coded paper filing systems for genealogists and learn about using forms and taking good notes.

Lesson 3: Every Record Has Value

Each type of record is unique in the information, clues, and answers it provides to the genealogist. In this section, you will learn about the records, the information you can find, which are preferred, and which can act as substitutes.

Lesson 4: Where to Find Records

Tap into vast information, tools, and experts at local, county, state genealogical or historical societies, and university or state archives and libraries to enhance and magnify your research. Learn how to plan, prepare for, and experience successful research in these record repositories.

Lesson 5: How to Search the Internet like a Genealogist

Searching the Internet is a skill. Learn how to formulate a variety of genealogy-related search queries to find what you want in minutes. In addition, you'll find the top websites to get you started in your research.

Lesson 6: Field Research Is Required

This is where the computer screen ends and shoes hit the street. Whether you are planning a genealogy research trip for a few hours, a day, a week, or a month, care and preparation in your planning will enrich and enhance your opportunities to successfully prioritize and accomplish your goals. Learn how to make your field research more productive, cost-effective, and enjoyable.

Lesson 7: Cite and Verify Every Source

Do it right the first time! What genealogical evidence do you have to prove your ancestral lines? Did you attempt to verify the genealogy you copied from the Internet? Learn about the evidence as it relates to genealogy and the steps necessary to verify and document your research.

Lesson 8: If Sherlock Holmes Were a Genealogist

Learn the secrets used by Sherlock Holmes and become a first-rate genealogist—investigator, researcher, problem-solver, and mystery-buster. Explore the main steps used by Sherlock to solve mysteries, which include observation, analysis, search, and imagination.

Lesson 9: Learn to Network

Network with family, friends, and other genealogists to tap into the knowledge reservoir of experience, resources, and research. Learn about—and how to use—blogs, message boards, mailing lists, email, social media, wikis, and other resources to aid your research ability to work with others.

Lesson 10: Stay Connected to the Network

Communication with real people is paramount. Here, I share personal examples about how networking has been instrumental in my development and success as a genealogist.

Lesson 11: Carefully Search Ancestor Writings

The writings of our ancestors are among the most valuable resources genealogists have to provide direction in their research. Learn what to look for and how to use the writings of your ancestors.

Lesson 12: Search Every Page of Hometown Newspapers

Newspapers are the journal of every community that are preserved in bound, microfilm, and digital archives. Learn effective strategies for researching, finding, and using information in newspapers about your family to substantially enrich your family history pursuits.

Lesson 13: Learn to Find the Origins of Immigrant Ancestors

Genealogists are often faced with tracing ancestors from one country to another. Sometimes there is a clear and easy-to-follow path, but often the discovery of a person's country of origin requires multiple resources and clues. Here, you'll learn easy steps that can aid in your research.

Lesson 14: The Oral Interview Is the Most Valued Research

Oral and written histories are an integral part of genealogy research. Conducting oral history interviews can become the gateway to uncovering important clues and forging relationships that will dramatically speed research. Learn how to prepare, conduct, and use oral and written histories.

Lesson 15: Write and Publish Your Story

Writing personal histories takes planning and time to stitch the research into a cohesive blend of resources to tell the story that will inspire generations to come. Learn the steps in writing, researching, and publishing your individual and family histories.

Lesson 1: Genealogy Is a Repeatable Process

My First Steps as a Genealogist

After Mom's passing, I received some of her personal effects. I remember finding photos, articles, brochures from a trip, past checks and receipts, and so forth in bottoms of drawers, tops of closets, and every place imaginable. I put those items in a sack, brought them home, and forgot about them. Because of the experiences I had with my mother in my dreams following her death, I had this longing to know more, but I just wasn't ready. I think most of my hesitation had to do with not knowing how to begin.

This longing to begin kept growing and growing until I simply had to start. Mind you, I just didn't wake up one morning and decide I wanted to be a genealogist; search court records; fly fifteen hundred miles to search out a graveyard in the middle of Kansas; and have a file collection of color-coordinated folders filled with photos, photocopies, life histories, and artifacts.

I did it because of the love I had for my mother and because I wanted to know who she was. Upon her death, I felt a longing to know more about her. What I did know about Mom—not much—was that she didn't like to talk about who she was. In a quick outline, I knew the following information about her: She was a divorced, single mom, worked graveyard at the Horseshoe Club in Las Vegas for more than thirty years, and supported three children without assistance from anyone. Mom liked movies (John Wayne was the best); enjoyed going home each summer to Spanish Fork, Utah; liked nice clothes; took us to McDonalds and to go bowling at the Showboat Hotel on Monday nights; attended church when she could; and came to my football games, always sitting in the upper-left part of the bleachers.

When I was ready to start my research, I rediscovered the sack I had put away and spread the contents out on the kitchen table. I made two spreadsheets to help me sort through the material. The spreadsheets helped me organize the early phases of my research. I was able to begin building a mental picture of Mother's activities and experiences by time periods. I began to identify people who might have insights and artifacts relating to my mother's life, come up with topics and questions I wanted to discuss with different individuals, find gaps for which I did not have information, and locate areas where I could conduct background research to help tell the story.

Once I completed the sack, I reviewed other artifacts gathered, such as our family photo album, items in shoeboxes, and so on.

In one spreadsheet, I captured the following information:

What do you have?	Describe what you have.	What clues or questions do you have? (Inscriptions, people in picture, and so on)	Are any further actions needed?

In the second spreadsheet, I created a list of the people I wanted to make contact with.

Who is the person?	What is their relationship?	Address, telephone, and email address	Notes for follow-up

With information in hand, I was able to build a list of questions and topics I wanted to learn more about. I started with a tape recorder and a list of ten people that knew my mom. One by one, I visited each person and interviewed them about their experiences with her. I uncovered, through their eyes, who my Mom was to them. Some knew her as teenager, some as a sister, some as an adult, some as a child; all knew her as a dear and beloved individual. I uncovered pictures, news articles, correspondences, genealogy, yearbooks, mementos, and—best of all—stories of who my mother was. I grew to have such a great love for her, her family, and my heritage. That love began my quest to become a genealogist. All I did for the next six years was conduct oral histories on both my mom's and my dad's side and re-gather the record that was strewn across the various family members.

As I found artifacts and records, I placed them in one central location, which for me was a plastic box. Everything I found about my parents went in one folder and everything I found about my grandparents went in another. As time when on, I organized the information about each person chronologically into six categories: Childhood (0-11), Adolescence (11-18), Early Adult (18-25), Prime Adult (25-45), Middle Adult (45-65), Senior Adult (65+).

In the chapters that follow, I will expand further on the lessons I learned about conducting oral histories and preserving the artifacts.

IT'S TIME TO START YOUR GENEALOGY RESEARCH

It was June 2004. Following church service, Ila, a good friend of our family, came up to me and asked if I could talk for moment.

"Barry, I'm not sure how begin," she started. "During the church services, I felt that I should tell you that it is time to start doing your genealogy. And that I was the one who was to be your mentor."

At first I didn't know how to respond. My life was already full of my job, my family, and church and community service. Genealogy research was not anywhere on my priority list. Since my mother's death, I had been conducting oral histories and gathering family artifacts, heirlooms, and memorabilia, but that was it. Not "real" genealogical research.

I wanted to say, "Thank you, but I really don't have time." Instead I responded, "Ila, what did you have in mind?"

She replied, "How about Tuesday at 6:00 p.m. at the local family history center? I'll meet you there and we'll start. I'll show you the steps to become a genealogist."

"Okay. What do I bring with me? I think my genealogy has been done pretty well by others in my family, such as my aunts," I replied. I still wasn't convinced that it was even worth the time to meet with Ila.

She immediate responded, "Don't you have step-fathers?"

"Yes, John Garvin and Mel Wagner." Instantly, I seemed to know that researching the family of John Garvin would be a good place to start.

Ila thought for a moment and said, "Let's start with John Garvin. Write down what you know. If you have a birth or death certificate, bring that and we'll get started."

"Okay, sounds good to me. I'll see you at 6:00 p.m.," I concluded. I went home that afternoon, searched my records, and found John's death certificate. Tuesday evening, I showed up at the appointed time and began the process of becoming a genealogy researcher. Tuesday at 6:00 p.m. become a fixed appointment on my calendar. I'm not sure I can explain the excitement that I felt. It was the right thing to do. Each week I would learn a little more and be given an easy assignment that I could do from home. Ila was there every step of the way, encouraging me, answering my questions, and challenging me to piece the puzzle together, to put myself in the shoes of my ancestors, and to see the world from their perspective.

I would now like to share with you some of the most important lessons I've learned in the pursuit of discovering my ancestors.

FIVE-STEP PROCESS TO DISCOVER YOUR ANCESTORS

As a new genealogist, it was easy to feel much like a bee jumping from one flower to the next, searching for the precious nectar. Thanks to my mentor, I was introduced to a simple but important five-step process to discover my ancestors.

Step 1. Write down what you know. What do you know about the individual or family group? Write it down. This step can take from a few hours to several weeks, depending on how thorough you want to be. I find that the more complete my understanding is of the person or family I am going to research, the easier and more productive my research will become.

Information can come from firsthand experience or documents you personally have in your possession. Look for copies of birth, marriage, and death certificates; journals; scrapbooks; old letters; family bibles; photographs; school records; military records; obituaries;

deeds; and wills. Check your genealogy software program, read through your genealogy notes, and review files you have kept on the family to determine what you already know and what you still want to learn about your ancestors. Make a record of each piece of information that you learn about your ancestor. I found it valuable to learn all I could about my ancestor and the events, circumstances, relationships, and background that pertained to their lives.

If this is the first step you have taken in learning the process, start with yourself to identify a pedigree (list of direct ancestors) and work backward in time by filling in as much information as you can, by memory, on a pedigree chart. Go back as far as you can from memory. Answer the questions from the following list that apply to your specific family members:

- What do you know about yourself?
  - State your full birth name.
  - When were you born? Include exact date and location.
  - When were you married? Include exact date and location.
- Who were your parents?
  - State the full birth name of each parent.
  - When was each parent born? Include exact date and location.
  - When were your parents married? Include exact date and location.
  - When did your parents die? Include exact date and location.
  - If needed, estimate dates and places as a starting point.
- Who were your grandparents? Start with your mother's parents, followed by your father's parents.
  - State the full birth name of each grandparent.
  - When was each grandparent born? Include exact date and location.
  - When were your grandparents married? Include exact date and location.
  - When did each grandparent die? Include exact date and location.
  - If needed, estimate dates and places as a starting point.

This exercise will immediately expose what information is missing. Don't worry if you're unable to fill in all of the information. This information will be gathered during the research process. Evidence for a person's life events is usually found in historical documents stored in a repository located near the place where a person lived sometime during that person's life. You will want to record what you know on printed or electronic forms, such as pedigree charts and family group sheets.

Pedigree charts graphically outline relationships across generations. The chart shows the direct ancestor of each individual. Each individual on the chart is identified by full name, date and place of birth, date and place of marriage, and date and place of death. Start by completing a pedigree chart with yourself on the far left and then information about your parents and grandparents on the right, writing down as much information as you already know.

Family group records show information about a single family. Each family group record includes information about the father, the mother, and all of their children. Each individual on the record is identified by name.

If the dates of birth are known, the children are listed in order of birth. If you have the names of the children's spouses, you will be able to list that information also. There is often space on the family group sheet to record birth, marriage, and death information and additional notes about the family, as needed. This can include censuses; joining or leaving churches; christenings; confirmations; burials; acquisition or sale of land; migrations; citizenship changes; jury duty; lawsuits; wills probated; paid taxes; obituaries; being mentioned in newspaper articles; new job; draft registration; military service; serving as a witness, bondsman, or godparent; working on the county road crew; jail; and much more.

I keep notes about family history on a separate sheet of paper. These notes could be biographical information such as military service; education; social or economic status; migrations; participation in community, social, religious, or historical events; or physical descriptions.

Step 2. Decide what you want to learn. Start by selecting an ancestor you would like to know more about. If you are just starting, I would suggest that you choose an ancestor for which you already have some information, preferably someone before 1920. It's been my experience that it is much easier to obtain information from family and sources such as vital records, census records, and land records.

Focus on one ancestor, one question, and one record at a time. I refer to this as the "Power of One." I would like to expand on this topic.

Conducting genealogy research means finding answers to questions. When I first started researching my ancestral lines I found myself overwhelmed with questions I wanted to learn about for each ancestor, such as the following:

- What was their name?
- When and where were they born?
- When and where did they marry?
- Who did they marry?
- How many children did they have?
- What were the names of the children?
- Where did they live?
- What type of work did they do?
- What religion did they belong to?
- Were they in the military?
- Did they belong to any other organizations?
- What did they look like?
- When and where did they die?
- What was the cause of death?
- Where were they buried?

How can you simplify your genealogy research? Start by realizing that genealogy research is a project, and a genealogy project is completed one individual, one question, and one task at time.

Below, I have outlined my first genealogy research project, which is the basis of the process I follow today:

- Choose one individual, family, or generation to focus my research on. Use pedigree charts and family group sheets to help identify problems to resolve, such as:

- Missing information: names, dates, or places are missing.
- Incomplete information: part of a name, date, or place is missing.
- Unverified information: information cannot be traced to a credible source (that is, someone who would have known the information first hand).
- Conflicting information: information from two sources does not agree.
- Develop a list of questions and tasks associated with the project.
- Review the list and pick the most important item to complete.

As I begin, I will then outline the task in detail by asking myself questions such as the following:

- What is my goal for the task?
- What information do I have already?
- What resources will provide the answers I am looking for?
- Do I have the desired information in my records already?
- Do I have the knowledge to complete the task? If not, what do I need to learn about? Where can I find the answers?
- Do I need help from others? If so, who?
- Do I need to conduct Internet research?
- Do I need to go to the library?
- Do I need to contact another family member or genealogist?

I will then work on the task until it's complete.

The most important task at hand is not necessarily the most urgent or easiest task; it's the most important task. For example, I may have as one of my tasks that I want to go to a regional library to conduct research. While going to the library is important, calling the library and finding out information such as hours of operation, collections to search, and names of staff that can help me with my specific research are my first priority over going to the library.

Essentially I was applying the 80/20 principle, which tells us that 80 percent of our results will come from 20 percent of our inputs. By picking the most important task to work on, we're making sure that it falls within the critical 20 percent. Also, by focusing 100 percent of our energies on this item, we'll accomplish it much faster than we would have if we'd allowed ourselves to be distracted by interruptions—or worse, tried to multi-task and complete two or three items at once. It's amazing how fast you can get something done if that's all you work on. Items that used to sit on my to-do list for weeks, even months, began to disappear. I found that for every hour I put into preparation and planning, I saved myself twenty hours of work and found my ancestors three times faster.

Step 3. Choose a record or source of information. Once you know what information you're looking for, ask yourself where you might find it. Then choose one source or record to focus your research on. For example, if I had the objective of to find the birth date of an ancestor, I would ask these questions: "What type of records could I find a birth date in? Where are these records kept? How do get access to the records?" And so forth. I will record all questions, thoughts, and findings in my research log.

The types of records you will search include the following:

Compiled Records. These are records of previous research on individuals and families already done by others, such as family histories, biographies, or genealogies with pedigree charts and family group records. It is best to search compiled records first. You can save a lot of time by seeing what information others have already found about your family. Though compiled records are very helpful, some information may be inaccurate or incomplete. Compiled records can usually be searched quickly and easily. Compiled records include:

- Genealogies
- Biographies
- Genealogical periodicals and indexes, such as the Periodical Source Index
- Family newsletters
- Local histories

Original Records. These are records created at the time of important events in your ancestors' lives. For example, a local church or the local government may have recorded your ancestors' births, christenings, marriages, and burials. Original records include:

- Vital records and civil registration
- Church records
- Cemetery records
- Census records
- Probate records
- Military records
- Immigration records

Other original documents include court, land, naturalization, taxation, business, medical, and school records. Be sure to check all jurisdictions (for example, town, county, state, and country) that may have kept records about your ancestor.

Background Information. These are records dealing with geographical, historical, or cultural information. They include local histories, maps, gazetteers, language dictionaries, and guidebooks. Search these records to learn more about the area where your ancestors lived and the events that may have affected their lives and the records about them.

Finding Aids. These help you find the location of records, name indexes, library catalogs, or websites.

Step 4. Obtain and search the record. Investigate the record or source for the information you are looking for. Once I have made a choice about the source I will search, I try to learn about the source and how to use the information I might find. For example, if I were going to be searching the 1880 United States Federal Census, I would search for a study guide to learn about how to research and use the information in the record. If my source was a person, I would contact the person, make a list of questions, and conduct and record my interview. I would make sure that I record or make a copy of the information I have found. This information provides the information necessary for citing and analyzing the information.

When researching a record or source, some of the common issues you will face include:

- *Name Changes.* It was common for immigrants to change or shorten their names after arriving in a new country. You may need to check for various possibilities.

- *Spelling Variations.* Many ancestor names have variant spellings. Many recorders spelled names according to sound. A person may also be listed under a nickname or abbreviation.
- *Handwriting.* Most original documents you will search are handwritten. If you cannot read a letter, look at other names in the record to see how the writer made certain letters. Some handbooks illustrate the ways letters were written in earlier times.
- *Dates.* You may want to check a range of dates for an event. It may be recorded on a different date than you expect.

Step 5. Use and record what you learned. Evaluate the results of your inquiry and share your information with others. This is a very important part of the process. I am asking myself the question, "What do I see?" Sometimes what I find is only a clue; other times, it's a goldmine. I record what I learn in my research log. At this point, based on the information I've gathered, I decide where I want to go and start with step one again.

As you evaluate your information, consider the following questions:

- Did I find the information I was looking for?
- Is the information complete?
- Does the information conflict with other information I have?
- Is the source of the information credible?

Transfer any new information you find to your pedigree charts and group records. It's important to include source of the information, which is valuable in helping you resolve problems with conflicting information. For example, you may have a birth record that provides a birth date, and an obituary gives another birth date for the same person, you will want to determine which date is the most reliable by reviewing your sources; the most reliable source is usually the source made closest to the time of the event.

You will want to organize your records for easy access. I will address this topic in more detail in a later chapter. There are a number of computer programs that can help you organize your records on your home computer. If you are just starting, consider the following tips:

- Keep pedigree charts numbered and arranged numerically
- Keep family group records in alphabetical order by the husband's name
- Keep notes, research logs, and copies of documents behind the related family group record

FAMILY AND HOME INFORMATION SOURCES

Every research project begins at home. Whether you are looking for information for the first time or searching through your personal research folders, your home is a valued source of family information.

Take time to look for records that you might have. Use the following chart as a guide to sources of information that you might find in your home or in the home of a relative.

Birth	Birth certificate Adoption record Baby book
Citizenship	Alien registration Deportment papers Naturalization papers
Civil and Legal Activity	Bonds Contracts Guardian papers Summons or subpoena
Death	Death certificate Funeral book Memorial cards Obituary Will
Divorce	Paperwork
Employment	Apprenticeship records Disability records Income tax records Pension records Retirement records Social Security card Union records

Everyday Life	Biography Journal or diary Letters Newspaper clippings Photographs Publications Scrapbooks
Family	Bibles Bulletins or newsletters Coats of arms Histories Lineages or genealogies
Health	Hospital or medical records Immunization records Insurance papers Records
Household Items	Dishes or silverware Engraved items Quilts Tapestries or needlework
Land and Property Ownership	Abstracts of title Deeds Estate records Land grants Mortgages or leases Water rights
Licenses	Business or occupation Driver or motor vehicles Firearms Hunting or fishing Passport or visas Professional
Marriage	Anniversary Announcement Wedding announcement Wedding book

Military Service	Disability records Discharge records National Guard records Pension records Selective service records Service medals or ribbons Sword or firearms Uniform
Religious Activity	Baptismal or christening record Blessing Ministerial record Ordination Confirmation record Church records
School	Awards Graduation diplomas Honor roll Report cards Transcripts Yearbooks

GENEALOGY IS A SKILL REQUIRING PREPARATION

Genealogy is a skill requiring preparation and planning; detailed and exhaustive research; and careful correlation, analysis, and reporting.

Preparation and planning. Develop a research plan based on analyzing and defining the research problem you seek to resolve. Preparation and planning requires that you place the problem in its legal and social context, identify related and associated individuals, and identify relevant resources, tools, and methods, as well as the pros and cons in the use of those resources.

Detailed and exhaustive research. Use all relevant finding aids and sources, recognizing that differences exist in each source. To be thorough, examine each record or record set for flaws, quirks, and strengths. As you identify information, create a complete citation, noting the source of the information and when you accessed it. Look for clues, placing all new information into geographic and legal context. You will extract as much relevant information from that source as you can, looking for key details that might require an immediate revision of your research plan and marking anything that needs subsequent study. You'll conduct follow-up research on all family and associates whose records might shed light on the person of interest.

Careful correlation, analysis, and reporting. Correlate all pieces of information that you find—no matter how small—looking for connections and patterns. Summarize your findings and analyze what you've learned. Does your analysis warrant a conclusion, or does the information lead you to expand your original plan? Prepare a conclusion or proof statement for ongoing research and reference.

Stay Focused on the Research You Start

Once you have a clear picture of the specific individual, couple, or family group, it's time to define your objective. Do you want to prove a statement? Do you have a question to answer? Do you have a theory or hypothesis you want to test?

It's a good idea to create a brief timeline of events for your ancestor to help you determine what questions you still need to answer and what information you hope to find (such as date of birth).

At this point, you are able to build your research plan. This plan identifies what you want to search, where you will search, and what resources you will search.

As you follow the plan you've created, keep a research log, which will keep you focused on your goals and help you document where you've been and where you want to go.

Remember the Power of One. It's very easy to start researching one line of thought, become interested in another, and change direction, all in a matter of a few minutes. Soon you're surrounded with papers, documents, names, dates, and locations and are left with a head full of swirling questions.

You will find your research more productive if you clearly identify your research goals, develop a research plan and focus on their completion. The following are a few ideas for keeping your research on track and manageable.

1. Focus on specific sections of your genealogy at a time. This can

include the following:

• A specific family line or surname,
• A specific time and place,
• A specific family unit, or
• A specific question to solve.

2. Once you have focused a specific area to research, create a log to help you develop a big picture of what you have and where you want to go. Keep the log up-to-date—it will save you time and energy. Note when and where you viewed the information. The log can include, but is not limited to, the following:

• Who you have talked to and information provided,
• Information you have found and citations,
• The questions you still seek answers to,
• Thoughts of where to research,
• The answers you have found, and
• Ideas and assumptions you are making and why.

3. Keep a to-do list—a plan as to what research you seek to perform. Organize the plan so the most important research gets done first. Often you find that when you focus on top priority research, many other items on your list are completed also.

4. Group your to-do items by the source you will use to conduct research.

5. Create a "future research" file. As you are conducting your focused research, you will always come up with ideas for research you want to conduct that is outside the focus of your current line of inquiry. Record it—whether it's an idea, a paragraph, a printed document, a photocopy, or whatever else—put it in the file, and forget about it until you are done with the task at hand. You can then go through the file at a later date, organize your notes, and start the next task. Don't be surprised if you begin doubling your accomplishments.

6. Keep track of your progress.

7. Reach out for help as you need it.

8. If you have a hard time finding time or are spending too much time doing research, schedule time with yourself to conduct your research. Make your appointments start and end on time. There is something about a deadline that helps keep you on track.

See the big picture. While focused research will help keep your genealogy work organized and streamlined, it's important not to get so focused on finding a single individual or piece of information that we don't look at extended family, neighbors, and the migration patterns of the entire community. Often the missing person (or piece of information) will pop up in someone else's family in a completely different geographic location.

Sometimes the shortest distance between two points is not a straight line. There are many instances where researchers come to a dead end on an individual and, through researching related people (siblings, aunts, uncles, and so on), are led back to the individual of interest. Think outside the box. If you're stuck, find unusual ideas and places to look for information.

Genealogy Is about Questions

Learning begins with a question. Questions and answers are the foundation for exchanging information. We have many ways to learn, but by simply asking questions, we set the stage for learning and also for sharing what we know.

Narrow the focus of your questions. It is easy to become overwhelmed by the number of questions that need answers. It's been my experience that the further back I go, the more questions I ask.

The key is to identify one person or a few individuals of the same family. You will find your research efforts move forward faster if you focus on one individual and one question at a time. Use your pedigree charts and family group sheets to help you identify those questions. Make a research plan listing the questions you want to research.

What information do you really want? It's not uncommon to read and hear questions from new genealogists that seem to be asking for the responder to provide them answers to every question they will ever need now or in the future about a given family line or individual. The questions you ask determine your research path. Know what you want to learn. Know what information you want to find. The following are examples of the questions I have created to guide my research plan development, personal skill development, and research process:

Library visit. How do I prepare for a library visit? What does the library have that will help me with my genealogy? What is a good book for beginners? How do I do research at a distance? What are some useful tips for successful genealogical research?

Searching for information. What records do I search if I want to find birth records? Death records? Immigration records? Adoption records? Maiden name? City or parish of foreign country?

Immigration. How do I locate passenger lists? Where do I find information on immigration and naturalization? What is available on the Internet? Where was my ancestor born? His parents? What language did they speak in the home? What language was their newspaper printed in? Did they immigrate? If so, what year? What language did they speak before they came to the United States? What is their status – AL (alien), PA (papered, or applied for citizenship), or NA (naturalized, or received citizenship)?

Ancestor profile. Where was my ancestor born? Was my ancestor married? Single? Widowed? Divorced? Married more than once? Where do I find vital records? Did my ancestors own a home or rent? Was it a farm or a house? Was it mortgaged or owned free and clear? Homesteaded? How much was the mortgage payment or the rent? What was their occupation, profession, or trade? Did they own their own business or employ others? Work for someone else? What was the type of business or trade?

Locating record repositories. What resources are available at the local library? The county or regional library? What about in university libraries and archives? State archives? Local, county, or state historical societies? Is there a local, county, or state genealogy society? What is available to you in the homes of family members?

Using census records. Which census enumerations were taken during the life of my ancestor? What maps exist for the period my ancestor lived? Where can I find blank census forms to help me record the information I find?

Ancestors in the community. Were there relatives in the community where my ancestor resided? With whom did my ancestor do business? Where did his children find their spouses? Was it an ethnic community? If so, what language did they speak at home? When was the community founded? What records were available? What disasters had the community weathered? How had wars affected the community and its records? What churches were in the community? Are records available?

LEARN TO RECOGNIZE AND USE SOURCES IN YOUR RESEARCH

You have many sources available to you in your genealogical research. Sources are considered people, documents, publications (all media), artifacts, and so forth. We find sources in the original or derivative forms. Derivative forms include abstracts, transcripts, and narrative histories, as well as any other secondhand account of information. Sources provide information from which we select evidence for analysis that leads a sound conclusion, which we refer to as proof. Information is considered to be the words (oral or written) used by the sources, which can be either primary (firsthand) or secondary (secondhand). Evidence is information that is relevant to resolving a research question. Direct information explicitly states an answer to our question while indirect information does not explicitly state an answer to a question but can be combined with other information to build a case.

Tip: Are document copies okay to use? Image copies are derivatives but are acceptable evidence when originals are not available and the images are made by authoritative agencies. Record copies made by civil and clerical authorities are derivatives but are considered "best evidence" when originals are destroyed or not open for public examination. Both original and derivative works can have errors. Derivatives have a higher margin of error.

Tip: How do you determine the quality of information? Information's quality cannot be determined unless you can identify the informant and the nature of their involvement with events. Both firsthand and secondhand information can contain errors. Firsthand information is generally more reliable.

Tip: What if the direct evidence does not completely answer my question? Direct evidence does not have to answer all aspects of a question. It's not uncommon to have direct evidence answer only part of a question. The key point is that it does make a direct statement in answer to the question. Keep in mind that indirect evidence, when it's assembled well, can be more accurate than direct evidence.

Build an Identity Profile about Ancestors' Lives

The identity of the ancestor is more than a name. It is every known detail of a human life, which includes information about the individual, their relationships, and their origin. Begin by targeting your research location. Search for any document created during the time your ancestor lived. Make sure you understand the circumstances under which every document was created, continually comparing, contrasting, and questioning details. From this analysis you will be able to do the following:

Build a profile about the individual. This is not just about collecting birth, marriage, and death data. Consider all aspects of their life that make them unique such as their name, education, occupation, religious and civic associations, social and financial status, precise locations of residences, personality traits, and signature. Next, place the individual in his or her family, neighborhood, and cultural context. Search for and identify individuals from the same place and time who have the same name and sort out their identities.

Learn about their relationships. Relationships are proven by linking people through known interaction, proximity of where they lived, common ownership, and patterns of migration, naming, and so forth. Knowing these things will give you a fuller picture of the life your ancestor lived and provide ideas for sources to find additional records.

Determine their origin. Origin can be established from statements and documents associated with the person, as well as by identifying migration patterns of associates and family.

Learn to Analyze the Documents You Find

The first time I searched my mother's vital records (birth, marriage, divorce, and death records), I copied names and dates and put the records aside. Several years later when I re-examined her vital records, I found over fifty data points that were instrumental in learning about my ancestral lines. I've learned a series of questions that helps me analyze and extract available source information. The questions include the following:

- What is the source citation of this document?
- Is this an original document or a derivative?
- Where did the document originate?
- When was the document written?
- Who is the primary individual listed in the document?
- Who are the other individuals named in the document? What are their roles?
- What relationships are stated?
- What is the purpose of the document?
- What information is directly stated within the document (such as dates or places)?
- What information is implied (indirect) by this document?
- What information is not stated, (name of wife, names of children, and so on)?
- When was the document recorded?
- Who had jurisdiction over the document then? Who has current jurisdiction over the document?
- What other document(s) partner with this one?
- What hints are contained within the document, suggesting additional research?

Learn about and Use the
Genealogical Proof Standard

The Genealogical Proof Standard is a principle associated with information found in direct evidence as well as cases built upon multiple pieces of diverse or contradictory evidence. By following this standard, you will substantially reduce costly mistakes of connecting family and generations. To comply with the Genealogical Proof standard, your research must include the following features:

Reasonably exhaustive research. Identify and use all relevant sources, including finding aids. The key word here is "all." It requires you to search beyond what is conveniently at hand or published online. It is more than finding just three pieces of evidence that "say the same thing." Without searching all documents, you will miss key clues and opportunities for verification.

Complete and accurate source identification. Record all details necessary to relocate the source. Abstract analytical and descriptive details necessary to evaluate the reliability of the information you've taken from the source.

Skilled analysis and correlation of data. Start by learning about the nature of the record and the conditions under which it was created. Make sure you understand the language of the record based on the meaning from the time period. Learn about the relevant laws of the place and time as well as the cultural context of the community. Compare and contrast minute details to establish the meaning of the entire document and the information contained. Then select which facts you will consider as evidence.

Resolution of any conflicts in evidence. Don't overlook any evidence that contradicts what you feel is the appropriate conclusion. Take all the time necessary to sort out this issue. I spent several years researching the wrong line because I jumped to a conclusion without taking the conflicting evidence seriously.

A soundly reasoned conclusion or "proof argument." This is a formal statement of evidence you have gathered to prove a point. Statements are written for both corresponding direct evidence and complex or contradictory evidence. A proof argument for corresponding direct evidence includes citations to multiple sources that are independently created and proof summary that identifies a source or sources of direct evidence and discusses the factors that support its credibility. A proof argument for complex or contradictory evidence provides a thorough discussion of the problem (such as the available resources, the methodology used, the evidence found, any contradictions that exist, and how those contradictions are resolved) and a concise, clearly expressed, convincing conclusion. This includes the reasoning that supports the conclusion and thorough citations for each and every piece of evidence.

ANCESTOR PHOTOGRAPHS ARE IMPORTANT LINKS TO THE PAST

One day, I was looking through a series of photographs of my ancestors taken in the early 1900s. For the first time, I noticed the writing on the window behind the row of carriages. I took out my magnifying glass and looked closer to find the name of the company (Spanish Fork Co-op), date it was established, and related information. I took time to learn more about the co-op and found that my great-great-grandfather was president. That piece of information was just the beginning of the stories and documents that helped me build my knowledge of that generation and their place in my history.

Now as I look at photographs of my ancestors, I see important clues that are so prominently displayed but so innocently overlooked. Next time you look at your ancestors' photographs, search for the following clues to help in your research:

Photographer's imprint. Photographers placed imprints in different places, depending on the type of image. The imprint can be on the front cardboard mount, the back of the image, or in the lower right corner of some images. Imprints include the photographer's surname and sometimes the location where they operated their business. Try these resources for additional help researching photographers. With this information, you can do a Google or other online search. On one of the photographs in my collection, I saw the imprint of George Anderson. I did a Google search on the name and included the location of Utah County, Utah. My search results included a listing for the BYU archives, which housed over 12,000 images taken by George Edward Anderson. As I searched the database, I found over 200 images relating to my family, most of which were not in the possession of anyone in my family.

Military uniforms. Pay attention to the hats, braiding, patches, shape and style of pants and jackets, and any props included in a military uniform. Consult one of the many encyclopedias for military dress. With the help of a shoulder patch from a WWI photo, I was able to secure details about the individual's unit and military records.

Work or trade dress. Throughout the 1800s and 1900s, uniforms were an important part of defining individuals and who they were the world over. Even today in many countries, the uniform is as important as the job itself. In many of the photos I've seen, men wore loose shirts, work pants, and sometimes hats. Tradesmen were known to wear more distinctive clothing that identified their occupation, which can help place them in a geographic context. Look for individuals who posed for portraits with the tools of their trade.

- **Ethnic or regional variations.** Many ancestors were proud of their heritage. Look for ethnic and regional dress reflecting the local culture. Pay attention to any details in a person's dress that does not reflect contemporary fashion.

- **Postal clues.** Family pictures were often used as postcards. I've used the postmark and stamps to define time periods and location. Don't forget to check the back of the card for a message.

- **Props.** Many photographs of ancestors include props. A prop can tell you where a picture was taken. Interior scenes can reveal products, furniture, and even religious beliefs.

- **Location.** Outdoor pictures contain scenery, signage, and buildings. These can all be helpful in determining where the picture was taken.

- **Celebrations.** Since families document their history in photographs of events like weddings, baptisms, holidays, and even deaths, look carefully for extra clues that give clues to location and ethnic roots.

Include photograph information in your timelines. I have used clues found on the photographs to help trace my ancestors' immigration and migration.

One of my main objectives as a genealogist has been to re-gather the record from generations past, which includes many precious and one-of-a-kind photographs, which I preserved, documented, and shared with members of my immediate and extended family. Look for photographs by asking relatives. Re-examine your research and see if documents and histories contain photographs. For instance, starting in 1929, all Declarations of Intentions required a picture of the individual seeking citizenship. Alien registration cards and passports also contain images of your ancestors. Make sure you search library, archive, genealogical, and historical society collections. Once you learn who the friends of your ancestors were, contact the genealogist of the family and request to see if there are documents or photographs that document the relationship between families.

As a matter of practice when you look at ancestral photographs, ask yourself these questions to recognize available information:

- What do you know about the image?
- Who was its previous owner?
- How did it come to be in your possession?
- Are there any stories associated with it?
- Why it was taken?
- When it was taken?
- Do you know any of the people in the picture?
- Did a family member supply the identification?

When you can't identify the photograph on your own, show the picture to as many relatives as possible. You don't know when someone will have an identical copy. Post it on your website or someone else's. There are a number of sites that help to identify photographs or reconnect people with lost family photographs.

Identifying photographs. Now that you have located

photographs, the next step is properly identifying the images. Treat the photos with great care. *Do not* turn the photo over and start writing. That will damage the photo. The method I use is to scan the photo and name the image. I will then enter the following data into a photo log:

- Date (exact or approximate) of the photograph.
- Names of individuals in the photograph, in the order they appear, recorded in such a way as to not confuse anyone at a later date. ("From left to right . . ." or "In the top row, second from right . . .").
- The ages of the individuals.
- The circumstances around which the picture was taken.
- Who took the photograph, if known.
- If there is an original negative, where it is located.
- If the photograph is a copy of an original, where the original is located.

The above information is true for images that have been captured from tombstones, newspapers, and so on. Add any other information to help find where the photo came from, such as the cemetery and lot number, the name of the newspaper and issue and page numbers.

Expect the Unexpected

One of the first lessons I learned in genealogy was to count on surprises, to "expect the unexpected." Life is all about the unexpected—the good, the bad, and the crazy. I have found many unexpected bits of information in my own research, such as the following examples:

Shortly after my Mom's death in 1997, I was interviewing one of her childhood friends. At the end of the interview, I was presented with a scrapbook she had kept on her friendship with my mother over the years. It included cards, photos, news articles, and much more.

When I was researching the life of a step-father, I uncovered the fact that, at one time, he had been a member of the New Jersey mafia and was forced to leave the state when a contract was placed on his life. One clue led to another, and I finally found family connections in New Jersey.

I had been told of a family rift over the "stealing" of land and water rights during the 1920s. After investigation, I found the land was lost due to taxes not being paid. Another family member bought the land for the cost of the taxes.

In a diary of a relative, I found accounts of abuse and deep sorrow that were never discussed openly or known by anyone other than in the lines of the journal.

Managing the unexpected. When you find the unexpected, it may take some getting use to. The unexpected usually happens when we move beyond the dates and explore court and land records, newspaper clippings, journals, letters, and other, more personal records.

In today's world, it's hard to imagine keeping a marriage, birth of a child, serving a prison sentence, or some other major life event a secret in the family. But remember: in the past, family members lived far apart and were unaware of day-to-day happenings miles away. Personal lives were more private than in today's wide-open, anything-goes world. Whatever news was passed on to the rest of the family went through a sort of "public relations" clean-up to make it sound better.

The basics of handling the unexpected are simple: Sometimes the information will be used to help you in your research or to tell a story, but sometimes it may be best kept a secret. Be respectful of the living and their wishes, especially if the information is sensitive. In my own case, I can only think of one unexpected piece of information that I chose to leave a secret. It had no value to the living or the dead, to genealogy or a good story. So enjoy your research and the unexpected information that will turn up along the way!

Lesson 2: Start Organized, Stay Organized

Starting out organized is easier than getting organized later on. It didn't take long before my own research became weighed down with pedigree charts, family group records, to-do lists, research logs, documents, notes, and research tools. I was robbing myself of the precious research time because I spent hours looking for what I knew I had and duplicating research I had already done. When I became organized, I was able to

- know exactly what information I had for each ancestor,
- have a complete list of information I was missing for each ancestor,
- know exactly what resources I had checked and results of my research,
- know every book I had ever searched,
- remember who I had contacted and the response I had received, and
- easily file new research findings.

Choose an organization system that genealogists use. Several popular organization systems exist for genealogy. Research these systems and use the one that fits your style and that you will actually use.

My recommendation. I have evaluated, started, and subsequently abandoned several filing systems. I took a class from Mary E. V. Hill on a filing system, and I reorganized my genealogy using her color-coded filing system. It is extremely flexible—the more ancestors you find, the more expandable and flexible the system

28

becomes. It can be multi-generational and strictly linear at the same time. The system is simple to set up, simple to maintain, well organized, and inexpensive. It is easy to understand for the researcher and the mildly interested relatives alike. I can find anything in just a few seconds.

I have used the concepts to organize my paper files, computer files, and oral and personal history files. I would like to share with you the step-by-step instructions for helping you become organized using the color-coded genealogy research filling system.

Color-Coded Genealogy Research Filing System

Getting Started

The following four steps will help you begin to organize your family records and documents.

Step 1. Gather items that have genealogical information. Place a box in the middle of the floor or somewhere that will catch your attention. Start gathering together items you already have that give genealogical information—documents, newspaper clippings, pictures, letters, and so forth. This is not the time to decide what does or does not have value to you as a genealogist. Whatever you find around the house, place it in the box.

Step 2. Fill in a pedigree chart. Write down your name and the names of your parents and grandparents. Include birth, marriage, and death dates and places if you know them. Take special note of the four surnames that you listed on the pedigree from both sets of your grandparents. You will use these surnames in Step 3. For example, the names of my parents and grandparents are:

Father: James Ewell
Father's parents: Arthur Ewell and Robera Jolley

Mother: Mary Jones
Mother's parents: Ora Jones and Vera Dearing

I used the surnames of Ewell, Jolley, Jones, and Dearing in step 3.

Step 3. Separate the items found in Step 1 into boxes labeled with those four surnames. It's now time to temporarily divide the items you found in Step 1 into four separate boxes, each labeled with one of the surnames (last names) of your grandparents. I like to use containers that are the size of apple boxes. Sort what you have gathered, putting items belonging to the family or ancestors of one of the surnames into the container labeled with that surname.

Step 4. Create and expand pedigree charts and family group records. Look at the items in each container and see if you have information about births, marriages, and deaths of your ancestors. Using the information you find, add new names, dates, and places to your pedigree chart. Make family group records for each family on your pedigree chart. If you use a computer genealogy program, such as PAF, RootsMagic, or Legacy, enter your family information into the program. Don't worry if you can't fill in all the names and dates. Just start with what you know.

SETTING UP THE COLOR-CODED FILING SYSTEM

There are thirteen steps for setting up the color-coded filing system. The system is time-tested and proven to be the organization resource that will grow with you as you expand your research.

This system sets up file folders for the families on your pedigree lines and also shows you how to file information about cousins and other relatives. Pedigree charts and corresponding family group folders are divided into four colors, based on the lines of your four grandparents. Dividing your pedigree by color helps make it clear which line a family belongs to. For each family on your pedigree, a family file folder holds documents and a copy of that family's group record. Don't think you have to do all the steps outlined in one day. Pace yourself. Check each step off as you do it. This system will keep your genealogy records organized for your own benefit and to hand on to your posterity.

Step 1. Gather supplies for your filing system.

This system works best if you gather together the following basic supplies:

- **Two file boxes with lids.** The boxes need to be strong, preferably made of plastic, and with inner ridges or grooves for hanging letter-size hanging files.
- **Hanging files, colored.** Letter-size hanging files in blue, green, red, and yellow. They come with 1/3 and 1/5 cut slots, which has to do with the size of the plastic tab. Choose the 1/5 cut, which works best with this system. Hanging files keep the manila folders from slipping down in the file box.
- **Hanging files, standard green.** Letter-size hanging files in generic standard green color, 1/5 cut.
- **Manila folders.** 1/3 cut tabs assorted, with reinforced tops to last through heavy use. Start with fifty folders.
- **Pens.** Pen with an ultra-fine point, felt tip and permanent black ink.
- **Highlighters.** Highlighters colored light blue, light green, yellow, and pink (don't use red because it is too dark). Colored pencils also work.
- **Labels for file folders.** Labels with blue, green, red, and yellow strips along the top and permanent adhesive on the back.
- **Dots.** Dots colored blue, green, red, and yellow. These are not usually available with permanent adhesive, but the non-permanent adhesive will work just fine for this.
- **Prong bases, clips, punch.** If you want to clip papers into manila folders, these tools are useful. The two-hole punch is the one you need.
- **Acid-free paper.** Paper that is acid free extends the life of your notes. Good quality photocopy paper is almost always acid free, but be sure to check the packaging.
- **Other file boxes.** For expanding your files, as needed.
- **Carrying case.** Letter-size carrying case with a handle, to take with you when researching.

Tip: What type of highlighters should I use? I would recommend that you find the type of markers you use to highlight in a book because they won't absorb through your paper and make a mess.

Tip: Why am I buying boxes when I have a filing cabinet? You can use a filing cabinet if you want, but I have found it very convenient to use boxes. I can pick up the box and take it over by my computer or put it on the dining room table when I'm working with my research and stay organized.

Step 2. Put pedigree charts of your lineage at the front of your file box.

Label the tab of a standard green hanging file "Pedigree Charts." Put a copy or printout of your pedigree charts, starting with yourself, in the file. Hang the file in the front of the file box. This set of your pedigree charts will act as a map for your family files. PAF Companion and Legacy will print pedigree charts in the four colors—blue, green, red, and yellow. Add more charts as you find the information.

Step 3. Study the Circled Five-Generation Pedigree Chart.

Study the Circled Five-Generation Pedigree Chart. It is a crucial key to understanding how the color-coding of family files works in the filing system using the five-generation pedigree chart. Each of the circles on the chart represents a family, and each circle has a color. In the steps that follow, you will learn to use those colors to set up your filing system.

See Figure 1 and Figure 2 for an example of five generations converted to a color-coded system.

Tip: Do I really need to use a five-generation chart? Experience has shown that this system is set up most easily based on a five-generation chart. The four-generation chart does not work and confuses people. As your research progresses, you will be able to expand this system and go way beyond the five-generation chart.

Tip: Can I use the same five-generation chart for myself and my spouse's line? When I set up my system, I used a five-generation pedigree chart for my direct ancestors and a separate one for my wife and her ancestors. It is possible to start with one of your children as #1 on the chart. However, then you only have two colors for the husband's lines and two for the wife's lines. I prefer the advantage of having the four colors for my own four grandparents.

Tip: Who should be in the #1 position on the pedigree chart? The real purpose of the filing system is to help you do genealogy research, and if you are really going to concentrate on doing your own lines, you probably want to start with yourself as #1. It will make using the color-coded system easy to follow when you are sorting the blue, green, red, and yellow sections for your four grandparents. Because I was working with two pedigree charts, I put myself as #1 for my family line and my wife was #1 for her family line.

Step 4. Separate the lines of your four grandparents by color.

Print a copy of your own five-generation pedigree chart from genealogy software, or print out and then manually fill in a blank form, starting with yourself as #1. You are the first generation; your sixteen great-great-grandparents are the fifth generation. Using the Example of Five Generations Converted to a Color-coded Filing System (available for download on my website) as a guide, draw colored circles around each family on your five-generation pedigree chart. Color-code the lines as follows:

- **Blue:** Circle all families who are ancestors of your father's father in blue.
- **Green:** Circle all families who are ancestors of your father's mother in green.
- **Red:** Circle all families who are ancestors of your mother's father in red.
- **Yellow:** Circle all families who are ancestors of your mother's mother in yellow.

Allow me to explain in further detail how to relate the chart to your own pedigree chart. I have created the following exercise to walk you through mapping your pedigree chart into blue, green, red, and yellow. Look at your pedigree chart. Notice the numbers that are associated with different names. You are #1, your father is #2, and your mother is number #3. I will refer to these numbers throughout the exercise.

Start with the blue highlighter. Place a blue line under your name (#1), your father's name (#2), and your grandfather's name (#4). Put the blue highlighter away and open the green.

Highlight your father's mother (#5) with green. Now pick up the blue and put a circle around the number 4/5 family (your father's parents). Are you beginning to see how this works? The grandmother introduces the green family line, but it is a blue family. Why is it blue? In this filing system, we file information under the name of the father. It is blue because the father in this situation is highlighted with blue.

Let's now use the pink highlighter for red (if you actually use a red highlighter, it will block out the name. Draw a pink line under your mother's name (#3) and your mother's father (#6).

Now we are ready for the yellow highlighter. Underline your mother's mother (#7) with the yellow marker. She introduces the yellow line.

Take your pink highlighter again and draw a circle around the number 6/7 family (your mother's parents). This family unit will be red because the father is red.

Pick up the blue highlighter again and draw a circle around your family unit (such as yourself #1, father #2, and mother #3). With the blue still in your hand, circle the family units of numbers 8/9, 16/17, and 18/19. Your father and all his ancestors as far back as you discover them will be blue.

Take the green highlighter and circle the family units of 10/11, 20/21, and 22/23. Your father's mother and all her ancestors will be green.

Use the pink highlighter to circle the family units of 12/13, 24/25, and 26/27. Your mother's father and all his ancestors will be red.

You have now filled out your own personal five-generation pedigree chart and circled each family. In the steps that follow, you are going to see just how important the chart really is. It is the map to the rest of your genealogy research. I recommend purchasing a sheet protector and putting your circled five-generation chart back to back with the sample chart.

When I finished this exercise for the first time, I understood the logic of the color system—me as the child with blue for my father and his parents; green for my father's mother and her parents; red for my mother and her parents; yellow for my mother's mother and her parents. As I get information, I have colors in my mind attached to the names of the people that I am working with, and with those colors, I can quickly remember where to put it and where to find it, and it gives me a sense of direction that I didn't have before.

Tip: What if I can't do everything exactly as explained? I've found that it's important to not get too bogged down by the details. If you run into a snag and you can't do it exactly the way the instructions say, do the best you can with what you have. Feel free to experiment. Try it and see if it works. Nothing that you do is going to be set in stone. You can redo it if you need to, and if you find something works, great; if you find that it doesn't, you can go back and make changes.

Step 5. Put sixteen hanging files into your box.

Place four blue, four green, four red, and four yellow hanging files in your box, in that order.

Step 6. Label the colored hanging files with your family surnames.

Label each colored hanging file with the surname of one of your sixteen great-great-grandparents. There will be four surnames in each color. Use the sixteen surnames that go down the right side of your five-generation pedigree chart to know which surnames to put within each color.

Place all the tabs on the left side of the colored hanging files.

Write one surname on each hanging file tab (plastic tabs come with the colored hanging files). Use a permanent, black-ink, ultra-fine-point pen for writing names. Rather than write the names by hand, I chose to print labels from my computer with color-coded labels.

Hang the files in alphabetical order within a color. Put the blues alphabetically in one group, the greens in another, the reds in a third, and the yellows in a fourth group, so you can separate out one color group into a new box if the original box gets too full with all your documents and research.

It's okay if you don't know the last name of some of your sixteen great-great-grandparents. Label as many of the files as you can and leave the other blank-tabbed files in the box for future use.

Tip: Where are my great-great-grandparents located on the five-generation chart? Your great-great-grandparents are the people who are listed with the numbers 16 to 31 on your five-generation pedigree chart. For example, the surnames for my blue files will come from the lines 16, 17, 18, and 19 (for me, those names are Ewell, Weech, Thompson, and Frisby). The surnames for the green files will come from lines 20, 21, 22, and 23 (Jolley, Spriggs, Boyter, Niell). The surnames for the red files will come from lines 24, 25, 26, and 27 (Jones, Dahle, Jones, Bevan). The surnames for yellow files will come from the lines 28, 29, 30, and 31(Dearing, Parkin, Hickman, Carrel).

Tip: Why are the tabs placed on the left side? Putting surnames on the left-hand side is something that developed over time by people using the system. The files on the left are the surname hanging files for the pedigree charts. It's the front piece of the surnames that go behind that particular folder. So if it's the Ewell folder, it's going to have Ewell pedigree charts in the front folder, and it's going to have Ewell families behind it. It makes it very easy to quickly locate these files. In the steps that follow, you will learn about the positioning of the other files.

Tip: What surname do you use on the label if you find it spelled multiple ways? In one of my family lines I have the German name, Diehl. I have five different ways that name can be spelled, and I have tried writing on my tab all of those variations—Diehl/Deal/Dill/Deel/Dehl. That was a hassle, so I chose to use the most common spelling that was used in the United States—Diehl. I then placed a note in the file explaining my decision along with a list of the various spellings.

Step 7. Put a highlighted copy of your five-generation pedigree chart in each of the colored folders.

Print sixteen more copies of your five-generation pedigree chart, with you as #1 on the chart. On one of the pedigree charts, highlight the names of all persons with the same surname, using the color assigned to that surname. File the highlighted pedigree chart in its surname hanging file.

Repeat the process of highlighting a surname line and filing the pedigree chart in its surname hanging file for each of the sixteen surnames. These charts will be used as guides or maps for each of the surname folders. Highlighting the surname on the pedigree chart makes it quick and easy to see how that surname fits into your complete family pedigree.

Tip: What if your research goes one or more generations beyond the five-generations? You may want to print all the pedigree charts for one surname, starting from the first person with that surname on your five-generation pedigree chart. Staple together and file these pedigree charts in the front hanging file of that surname, together with the highlighted five-generation pedigree chart.

Tip: What if I have two persons with the same grandparent on my pedigree lines? (This situation happens when cousins marry.) If two persons on your pedigree lines prove to have the same grandparent, put a note in one of their files saying that that particular line will be continued in the file of the other person. Name the other person, so the charts are easy to find. From then on, just follow the one pedigree line because they will be identical.

Step 8. Set up a manila file folder for each family on your five-generation pedigree chart.

This is a really exciting moment in the creation of your filing system. You are now going to identify and pick out each family as a unit. Each family gets their own manila folder in which you can begin to organize your research. Start by printing or writing a family group record for each of the families on your five-generation pedigree chart. If you can identify all of these families, including the parents of your great-great-grandmothers, you will be setting up a total of twenty-three manila family folders. These third great-grandparents will not be on the five-generation pedigree chart. You will have to go to the next chart to find their names.

Once the system is set up, you can add additional family folders as you find more information.

Using your five-generation pedigree chart as a guide, decide what color each of the families should be filed under. Mark the color on the top of the family group record or print with PAF, Roots-Magic, or Legacy. Set up manila folders for each of the families by putting a colored label on the file folder tab. Match the label color to the color of each family group record. Be sure to use labels with permanent adhesive. The manila folders of parents should all be right-tabbed folders. Fold left-tabbed manila folders inside-out to make them right-tabbed, as needed.

On the label, write the following information, as shown below:

- The surnames of the husband and wife followed by their first names.
- A small "b." (for "birth") and the year of their birth.
- If one of them was married more than once, label which marriage this is—for example, "m2" would denote this as the second marriage.

Colored strip
JONES, Paul b. 1841 m2 SMITH, Jane b. 1845

The label only gives enough information to identify this family. Other information about them can be found on their family group record in the file folder.

Tip: Why do I want to set up family file folders for the parents of my great-great-grandmothers now? If you are going to have a family file folder for each of the sixteen surnames in the fifth generation on your five-generation pedigree chart, you are going to have to find the names of the parents of your great-great-grandmothers. Then set up file folders for these eight families. Your eight great-great-grandmothers will appear as daughters in these families. If you want to, you can do the same for your eight great-great-grandfathers now. If you also do the parents of your eight great-great-grandfathers, you will have a total of thirty-one family file folders in your system.

Tip: Where do I find the information to make family file folders for the parents of my great-great-grandmothers? To find the parents of your great-great-grandmothers (numbers 17, 19, 21, 23, 25, 27, 29 and 31 on your pedigree chart), go to the pedigree charts you printed and filed in the standard green hanging file at the front of your box. If you have the information about the sixth generation in your database program already, find the pedigree chart that shows the sixth generation for a great-great-grandmother. That pedigree chart will give you the names of the parents of that great-great-grandmother.

Step 9. File the manila family folders.

Put a new colored hanging folder behind each surname hanging file, matching the color of that surname. Place the manila family folders in these newly added hanging folders. Group the manila family folders by color and then by surname—all the "red" Smith's together, all the "yellow" Jones families together, and so on. You can now arrange the family folders in alphabetical order by the husband's first name or by the generation.

Tip: How do you manage patronymics? For those of you who have Scandinavian, Asian, Polynesian, or American Indian ancestry—any situation where the surname changes every generation—it can be a challenge. In this situation, I prefer to file family members by location. In other words, these people tended to live for generations in the same parish and on the same farm, and I have found it easiest to keep them by generation going back, by location. Another option you may consider is to file each of the families by the name that they're known by in alphabetical order and then by date. I encourage you to look at the various options in patronymic filing and realize that it is possible to keep track of these people either by location or alphabetically and by date. See my website for more details about patronymics.

Tip: How do you organize the files by generation? I chose to organize my family files by generation. Folder 1 would be the first generation, the second folder would be the second generation and so forth. I will align the family folder labels on the right side of the container. The following is an example of the first five generational family folders behind the Ewell surname (blue folders):

Generation Sequence in Box	Family Label
Generation 1:	Barry J. Ewell and spouse
Generation 2:	EWELL, James N. b. 1932 m1 JONES, Mary E. b. 1933
	EWELL, James N. b. 1932 m2 READY, Linda M b. 1941
Generation 3:	EWELL, Arthur E. b. 1901 JOLLEY, Robera b. 1902
Generation 4:	EWELL, Franklin M. b. 1862 THOMPSON, Kate b. 1871
Generation 5:	EWELL, Francis M. b. 1834 WEECH, Frances Mary b. 1838

Step 10. Start filling your family folders.

Include the following things in a family folder:

- The family group record of the family. If there was more than one marriage, make a separate folder with a family group record for each marriage. Do the non-direct line marriages in center-tab folders.
- Documents you have already gathered that belong with this family.
- Add the following items to a family folder, as you need them:

- To-do list of questions about this family that you want to find answers for.
- Research log for keeping a record of sources you look at about this family.
- Timeline for a chronology of this family's life events.
- Maps pertaining to where this family lived.
- Research notes.
- New documents you find.

Include all documents from the time of a couple's marriage. Documents that pertain to events prior to their marriage can be filed in the folders of their parents, such as birth certificates and baptism certificates.

These are all valuable tools, and as you add these tools to each of the manila folders, you'll find that you'll be able to systematically move forward—identify this family, document this family, and have the feeling that you are really creating a good, strong, and accurate genealogy. I encourage you to understand what to do with the to-do list, how to use a research log, how to keep track of where you've been researching, and how to use a timeline to be sure that you're not combining generations when they should be, for example, a junior and a senior.

Tip: Is there a way that I can include folders about the individual children of a family unit? Using center-tab manila folders, create a file for each child, as the parent of a family. Include his or her spouse and their children. File these center-tab manila folders behind the direct line parent's folder.

Use center-tabbed manila folders for the children. This includes collateral line (aunts and uncles) families.

File the children's folders right behind their parents', in birth date order of the related children (not the birth date of the spouse).

Put a colored star on the upper right corner of your direct ancestor. The color of the star should be the same as the parent's line.

Put a colored dot in the upper right hand corner of the family group records of non-direct line children so that you can quickly see they are non-direct line. The color of the dot should be the same as the color of the parent's line.

When I am filing papers about a direct descendant (folders with the star), I place all the information about a person in the years prior to marriage (birth certificate, baptismal record, and so on) in the "child" folder behind the parent. All information associated with the direct descendent following their marriage, I place in their family folder (marriage certificate, death certificate).

When I am filing papers associated with siblings of my direct ancestor (aunts and uncles) and their families, I will place any information I find (birth certificate, marriage certificate, or death certificate) in the child's folder.

When I create children's folders, I will include the child's spouse on the label. This is a personal preference of mine, so do what works best for your own filing.

The following is an example of how the children folders are organized for my great-great-grandparents:

Family Folder Sequence	Folder Label	
Parents	EWELL, Francis M. WEECH, Frances Mary	b. 1834 b. 1838
Child 1	Teancum Pratt Sarah Eliza Ewell	b. 1900 b. 1860
Child 2	* Franklin Marion Ewell Kate Thompson	b. 1862 b. 1871
Child 3	Lorenzo Hyrum Ewell Mary Jane Dennis	b. 1865 b. 1867
Child 4	John Young Bigelow Mary Elizabeth Ewell	b. 1866 b. 1868
Child 5	William Walter Ewell Elvira Lillian Bigelow	b. 1870 b. 1877
Child 6	Daniel Joseph Dennis Laura Ann Ewell	 b. 1872
Child 7	Either Ewell	b. 1877
Child 8	Purmitt Samuel Ewell Ethel Jan Savage	b. 1879

Step 11. Set up other useful files.

The files that we are going to talk about in this step are as important as any of the previous files we have previously set up. It would be nice if we could always get our genealogy to fit into surname files that we have set up, but that is not a reality. The Holding, Locality, and Help files are used when you find information that is useful for researching more than one family group such as a group of cemetery records for that surname in the same locality where your ancestor lived.

1. Holding Files

Set up surname Holding Files to store items with information about that surname that includes more than one family of that surname.

Place the Holding File right behind the surname hanging file with the pedigree charts and before the family files. Do this for any surname where you see the need.

When you have a large number of documents for a surname, it helps to create two Holding Files for that surname. Set up one folder as a temporary storage file, and the other to permanently store documents that have a great deal of family information in them. An example might be the parish registers of a church where your ancestors of that surname lived for two hundred years. Be sure to go back and use the documents stored in the Holding Files!

Tip: How do I store photographs in folders? Photographs should be stored in archival quality holders in three-ring binders for long term preservation.

Tip: How do you use the holding files? The most helpful part of this system for me when I first started was the holding files, because I took my piles of information and broke it down into big groups of surnames, and then they became actually very manageable. I could then go refine and organize as I had time. There are two kinds of holding files that I find useful. For example, I have a temporary holding place for the Ewell family. There are times when I come home from research and for one reason or another I don't have time to sort my research. I just put them in a temporary holding file right behind the Ewell surname. When I have the time, I will sort the documents into the appropriate family and individual folders. When I have documents that pertain to several Ewell families (such as they were all going to the same church, buried in the same cemetery, or went to the same school), I will put this document into a permanent Ewell holding file that will go right behind the Ewell pedigree chart file.

2. Locality Files

Set up Locality Files for locations you are researching. Documents are often found which contain information about more than one family from the same place. Records such as a census index of your family surnames, a map, a list of marriages from a town or county, an index to the wills in an area, or a local history can be stored in a file named for that locality. Information from these documents should be added to your computer database—such as PAF, RootsMagic, or Legacy—with a source reference and notes taken from the documents filed in your Locality File. Add Locality Files as you need them. Set up Locality Files for countries, states or provinces, counties, cities, parishes, or towns, as you find the need.

Use standard green hanging files for Locality Files. Put these hanging files in the second file box you purchased.

The following are several scenarios of the organization structure of a locality box for different countries showing the sequence in which the files and folders will appear:

Brazil	Canada	France	Germany	United States
State	Province	Old province or new department	Province	State
City or town	County, when one exists	City or town	District (Kreis)	County
	City or town		City or town	City or town

What do you put in each folder? Available records vary depending on the location. In a state, province, or department file folder, put the following kinds of items:

- Guide to the state, province, or department archives.
- A will index for the whole state, province, or department for the surnames you are interested in.
- Census index for the state, province, or department for the surnames you are interested in.
- History of the state, province, or department.
- County boundary changes for the whole state, province, or department.

In a county file folder, put the following kinds of items:

- Printouts from the Family History Library Catalog.
- Index to the county court records for surnames you are interested in.
- Index to county land records: grantor and grantee indexes for surnames you are interested in.
- Pages from a book of marriages in the county for the surnames you are interested in.
- Tax lists for certain years in the county.

In a city or town file folder, put the following kinds of items:

- Cemetery records.
- School census.
- City map.
- Map of ward or parish boundaries within the city.
- Church records from churches in the city or town.

Tip: Can you provide an example for setting up locality files? Anyone who does family history gets into places fairly heavily, and so you end up getting records about many people, not just your direct line. You need to create files that deal with county records, census records, all kinds of different things about the place. When I started using locality files, I was researching ancestors from the state of Kansas. I set up a totally separate container with the label "Kansas." The first folder in the container was set up for maps (road maps, period maps). The second folder was labeled "Kansas" and included genealogical and historical publications from Kansas. Following the Kansas folder, I set up a series of folders with the names of the counties I was researching. These folders are alphabetically organized. I then have the ability to add folders as I need them behind each county. For example, when I was researching the city of Otis, Kansas, (in Rush County) I secured cemetery records from a Methodist and a Lutheran cemetery. Behind the Rush County file, I added a file for each cemetery and dropped the records associated with each cemetery into each folder.

Tip: When do I create a holding file rather than a locality file? Someday you're going to run across a list of cemetery records, and you're going to look at it and say "There were six of my families with six different surnames in this cemetery. Which one of my family folders am I going to put this cemetery record in?" And then you will ask, "Do I need a holding file or a locality file?" A locality file works if that cemetery is in a specific county (such as Rush County) and all six of those families were in Rush County. That's a locality file. A holding file is created if you have lots of information about one surname (such as Wagner family) but you have the Wagner family getting land in ten different places. You can't simply put that one list of deeds in one Wagner family because it belongs with lots of Wagner families, and so you put it in a holding file.

3. Help Files

Set up Help Files, as needed, for tools such as language aids, religious information, or handwriting guides. Group Help Files together in the front of the Locality box.

Step 12. Expand to other boxes, as needed.

When one of your color sections gets too big for your box, move all files of that color into another box. As you find more information, you will eventually end up with boxes for each color—sometimes with several boxes for a color!

Tip: Do binders have a place in the color-coded organization system? Three ring binders do have a place. I will share several experiences with you.

There were times when I was researching a complicated "brick wall" type problem in which I included a to-do list, maps, pedigree chart, family group records with research logs for the various families, copies of documents, and so forth. Once I resolved the problem, I wrote a case summary explaining my research and findings and put it in the binder. Then I stored the binder on its side in the box next to the family folder and continue to use the family folders for research. Label the binder with the name of the person you researched in that binder such as "Smith, John." Why did I keep the research in the binder? Because I wanted the research, documentation, and analysis to stay together to review as needed and for future researchers.

There are times when I have very precious, one-of-a-kind artifacts that I do not want to go in the filing system. I will use archival supplies and a binder to help preserve the artifacts.

Once, we took a month-long research trip back to Virginia, Tennessee, Pennsylvania, North Carolina, and Washington, DC. I created binders with information I needed for each of the counties I was going to visit. The binder kept the research organized and together. Using folders in this type of research experience tends to get messy and shuffled. I had a binder for each person on the trip. When I came home, I transferred the information back into appropriate folders.

There is a purpose for binders, but I am convinced that for your overall filing system, you will do better with manila folders.

Tip: Do you ever use any other colors besides blue, green, red, and yellow? Yes. Remember that the system is very flexible to expand to your research needs. When I began research on the ancestral lines of my step-parents, I chose to use the color purple to separate my research. I set the files up exactly as I had done for my ancestors in a separate box.

Tip: What are your thoughts about including (living) descendents' files? The system is very flexible to help you keep track of family in both directions, so feel free to include living descendents' files in your system as well. I use the system to record and organize information about my wife and I, our children, and our grandchildren. I set up the family file for my wife and I. I then created a folder for each of our children and their spouses and placed them in the order of their birth. As grandchildren are born to each family, we add a folder and place it behind their parents' folder. It makes it very easy for me to keep track of the precious documents and memories we share with our family. I chose to create these files and folders in blue, but it would be really easy to create a descendant's box with another color, such as orange.

Step 13. How do I keep the basic file folder system updated and useful?

Once you get your basic file folder system set up, it is important to realize that it will continue to mature as you continue your research. The following are suggestions on how to do so:

- Set up a simple "in box." Any basket you have will do. Place new documents, emails, correspondence, and so on into the in box until you have time to file the items in Holding Files, Family Folders, or Locality Files.

- Take time regularly to decide where each item needs to be filed. Write the name of the family or locality the document pertains to in the upper right hand corner of the document—"Smith, John" or "Cumberland, New Jersey." Set aside time to file it in the proper box.

- Work on researching one family line at a time. Pick one family line. Make a to-do list of questions you want to find answers for. Do the research needed to answer the questions on your to-do list.

- Record on research logs the records you search and whether the record had information.

- Label the documents you find with the name (such as Smith John) or locality and file the documents.

- Enter the information you found into computer programs such as PAF, RootsMagic, or Legacy. Enter documentation into the "sources" field and make explanations in the "notes" field.

How to Add New Surnames

It is simple to add new families to your filing system as you find new information.

Let's say you have a line where you know that Jeremiah Perry, b. 1748, Cumberland County, New Jersey, has a wife, Sarah. You know nothing more about her so you have her entered as Mrs. Sarah Perry.

One day while searching on the Internet, you find a reference to a Sarah Harris who was married first to a John Miller in about 1767 in Cumberland County, New Jersey. They had one child, and then John Miller died. Sarah Harris was then married to Jeremiah Perry in 1769 and had a son, Jeremiah Perry, b. 1770. That matches the family bible records you have perfectly!

The website goes on to give you three generations of Sarah Harris's ancestors with good documentation. After verifying the information, you want to add these new families to your filing system. Jeremiah Perry and Sarah Harris are in your yellow line.

To add this information to the file, simply follow these steps:

- Make new yellow hanging surname folders for: Harris, Crosley, James, Hand, and Johnson—the five new surnames you have now identified. Add highlighted pedigree charts to the folders to see how these people are related to you.
- Make family groups for Sarah Harris as a child with her father, Jacob Harris, and her mother, Rachel Crosley.
- Then continue making other family groups and filing them for each of these new families.

USING THE COLOR-CODED FILING SYSTEM FOR PATRONYMICS

The same basic filing system can also be used for families that did not have fixed surnames, but it requires some additional considerations. The example described here is from Scandinavian countries where, prior to the period 1860–1900, a child took his father's given name and the suffix -sen/-sson or -datter/-dotter, depending on whether it was a boy or girl. Similar patronymic systems were used in the Netherlands, Slavic countries, and northern Germany. They can be handled differently. Patronymic systems used in Latin American countries may require a different organization.

Instead of using a surname to organize your family files, for countries with patronymics you will need to use the name of the farm or village where the family lived. As Scandinavian and European societies were based on a feudal system and most people were farmers, the place where the family was living becomes very critical in identifying and distinguishing the family from others with the same names. In Norway and parts of Sweden and Finland, every farm had a name. Larger farming districts also had names. Not every farm in Denmark and some parts of Sweden had a name, but the village or farming community would have had a name.

As property generally stayed in the same family from one generation to another, you can use the place name and family name as identifiers rather than the surname.

COLOR CODING

The color-coding system is used to distinguish different branches of your family. Just as you can distinguish your four grandparents' lineages using four colors, you can also identify each of your Scandinavian lineages with a different color. If you have two Danish ancestors and one Swedish ancestor who all came to America from different parts of Denmark and Sweden, you should use a separate color for each line. This will help you keep the three lines distinct and keep you from getting them confused. Mark each file according to the color of the emigrant ancestor whose lineage it belongs to.

The filing system for these patronymic families will have a file with pedigree charts at the front showing the ancestry of the emigrant ancestor. It will then have general information and records about the county where the emigrant was from, the parish where the family was from, and the farm where the family was from. These general and locality-based files will have a tab in the center of the file, so they can easily be distinguished from the family files, which will have tab labels on the left or right side. The farm file might include copies of census records that list all those living on a farm or in a village for different census years. The county file might have extracts from records that include more information than just one farm.

Behind the file with information from the farm will be a file for each generation of the family, listed from most recent generation back to the earliest generation. For example, if your first ancestor from Denmark was Iver Bendtsen, born 1822, from the Skårup farm, his file will be listed first. The files for his father Bendt Knudsen (born 1802) and grandfather Knud Madsen (born 1769), who raised their families on the Skårup farm, will be listed next.

In some cases, the property may have been inherited from a mother's line rather than from the father's line, in which case the father would be from another farm. The mother's line will then be followed under that farm and the father's lineage will be listed under the farm where his family was from. In this example, Knud Madsen's wife Kirsten Bendtsdatter was born on the Skårup farm, so her father's file (Bendt Nielsen, born 1725) will be listed next. Knud Madsen was born in the village of Højmark in Lem Parish. After all the direct line ancestors from the Skårup farm have been filed, a place file with a center tab for Lem Parish and one for Højmark village will be next. Then the file for Mads Andersen will be the next file.

The pedigree chart at the beginning file will be a key to the system and pedigree charts showing the ancestors who extend back in each locality should be included in the locality files. You should have one copy of this pedigree chart with the farm where the family is filed listed next to the male ancestor's name and highlighted. This will make it easy to find a particular ancestor's file.

This example is shown in the diagram on page 52, with the files (each square represents a file folder) at the front of the filing box at the bottom of the diagram.

DESCRIPTION OF FOLDERS

The left and right tabs can both be used for family files. The purpose is to distinguish the place files from the family files by having the place files in the middle. If you are researching families other than

Anders Hojmark Hojmark (unknown) c. 1695		
Mads Andersen Hojmark Else Knudsdatter c. 1727		
Knud Madsen Skarup Kirsten Bendsdatter 1769	Hojmark Village	
Bendt Knudsen Skarup Ane Kirstine Iversdatter 1802	Lem Parrish	
Iver Bendsten Skarup Johanna Marie Christensd. 1825 [Includes all documents, biographies, photographs, and other family history materials about this family]		Bendt Nielsen Skarup Karen Jensdatter 1725
	Skarup Village [Includes copies of pedigree charts showing the direct line ancestors who lived on this farm and extracts of census and other documents that include all those living in this village.]	
	Hanning Parish [Contains maps, historical information, and extracts of records.]	
	Ringkobing County [Several parishes in this county.]	
	General Denmark File [Contains general information about Denmark, handwriting guide, word lists, and pedigree charts showing the ancestry of Iver Bendsten.}	

direct ancestors (collateral lines), you could put all the direct line ancestors in left tab files and all non-direct lineages in right tabbed files.

The information listed on the tab includes the name of the husband and wife on the left and the farm where the family lived and the husband's year of birth. If you have not color coded the files, you might also include an abbreviation to indicate this is the ancestry of Iver Bendtsen. If a family lived at more than one farm during their married and later life, try to find the place where they lived for the most time or where the majority of the children were born and file the family under that farm. Color-code the files for the ancestors of Iver Bendtsen red.

Important Practices and Tools to Keep You Organized

Regularly merge and purge files. Once you have set up your filing system, you need to periodically purge duplicate items, remove unnecessary documents, make decisions about the contents, and move some items to another type of folder or container. After reviewing, sorting, and purging information in the file folder, I make it a practice to ask myself, "What is missing that would help me be a better researcher?"

Keep source citation. Try to maintain a source citation for each document or item in the file so that you can verify the trail of your research. Make it a habit to have the citation available when writing the family history or when sharing this information with others. It will eliminate the time-consuming extra steps of going back to the original book, document, film, or website to secure the source.

Include your handwritten notes. Over the years, I have had the opportunity to interview many family members, some of whom are no longer living. I've made it a practice to include the interview notes (original or scanned) in the filing folders. You will find these notes to be pertinent to future research. If you have recorded an interview, include a transcript in the folder. All of these sources are important family documents.

Include five-generation group sheets. Genealogical computer programs provide many options for charts and reports. A good five-generation chart will quickly outline the relationship between family members. When I first started research, I had many family group sheets that had been hand-written. I took the time to enter the information into my genealogy software.

Keep photocopies and digital images. As you conduct research, make it a practice to make photocopies or digital images (with your camera or scanner) of the key sources of your research. It provides proof, citation, and clues for future research. Make it a practice to include the title page of your source. If the title page is missing, substitute the library catalog printout. As your research progresses, some of the images are no longer pertinent (not the right family) and should be purged.

Photographs require their own storage place. Genealogical file folders are not a good location to store family photographs. Take the time to learn about how to preserve and archive photos properly. After I scan or duplicate images, I have made it a practice to catalog and file the images so I can actively use them in my research. Where appropriate, I will place a copy of an image in the file folder. Because a large portion of my photographs are digital images, I have created a digital catalog, which is cross referenced to the individuals, locations, and the original.

Keep original documents in a safe place. Whenever possible, store original documents such as birth, marriage, and death certificates under archival safe conditions. I have found that archival sleeves or file folders stored in an archival box are the best storage method. I place a reference photocopy in the appropriate folder of my filing system. I make it a practice to always scan these documents, which allows me to share this information with other family members and to use the digital image in family history research.

Create and file a cross-reference guide. For ease of access, I have created a cross-reference guide indicating which documents pertaining to this person or family are available in other folders. There is no reason to duplicate documents within the paper files, such as a marriage certificate or a census page. However, these documents and many others include multiple names.

Use forms to gather, manage, and guide your research. It doesn't take long for new genealogists to get out of control when it comes to miscellaneous scraps of paper with undecipherable notes, orphaned photocopies with no identifying marks, lecture and class handouts, copies of emails, bibliographic references, post-it notes, scribbled messages, and torn bits of magazine or newspaper articles. I use a variety of forms to help me stay organized in all phases of my research, and I regularly file these forms for later review and use. The following is a list and description of the most common forms I use in my research. These forms are available for download at my website.

1. Timelines. It is important to draft regular summaries of your findings. Two of the forms that summaries can take are the timeline and the narrative. The timeline is a chronological listing of events in the life of a particular person or a span of time in the existence of a family. The timeline should reflect the research principle that you should work from the present to the past. Thus, a timeline on a particular person should begin with his or her death and then progress back in time. It may prove helpful to introduce historical events into the timeline, particularly those of regional significance, which may dictate the availability of records (a tornado that destroyed a courthouse, for example).

2. Narratives. A narrative can be as simple as an informal collection of paragraphs about an ancestor or as elaborate as a multi-generational family history suitable for publication. For most researchers, the simpler paragraph narrative is the precursor to publication. You need not be an award-winning author to present your findings in this manner. Simply compose an accurate and concise summary of your research steps and a condensed version of your findings. Consider such a narrative to be a research status report that can help you to spot inconsistencies in your evaluations as it highlights potential pursuit opportunities.

3. Research activity logs. The research activity log, used in conjunction with the timeline, is an efficient way to keep track of the origins of information provided on the family group sheet and in a chronological account. A well-kept research activity log will serve as a quick reference for sources of information, allowing you to see at a glance what work remains to be done. The source numbers serve as a cross-reference to the sources used in entering information on the family group sheet and the timeline.

4. To-do list. Periodically, I will review each folder in a filing system and make a list of items that need further attention or research. I will make one to-do list per folder. On the list, be very specific about the items needed. Also include any clues about the names, time frame, and place. Use this list to search websites and take it on research trips. Include item(s) to search, pertinent dates and names, and film or book numbers.

5. Cemetery log. A worksheet to take with you when researching cemetery records or visiting a cemetery in person can be very helpful. Cemetery logs can also show families, collateral lines, and friends, since many people were buried in clusters.

Your cemetery log form should look something like this example:

Name of Cemetery: _____

Town or County: _____

Physical Address: _____

Age	Date of Birth	Date of Death	Inscription	Location in Cemetery

6. Research logs. The research log, also called a calendar, is a running list of sources checked; annotations can indicate whether a particular source revealed anything. The log shows all sources checked and acts as a table of contents to the research notes.

7. Correspondence log. The correspondence log lists all the letters and emails you send and receive. It includes who the correspondence was to and from, the topic, and next steps I want to take in the process. Create an electronic or hardcopy file so you easily retrieve letters as needed.

Date	Name, Address, email	Information Requested	Information Received	Correspondence Research Notes

8. Pedigree charts. Pedigree charts provide an overview of the family and enable you to track research progress. All information recorded on the sheet (names, dates, and places) should be accompanied by a notation showing how that information was obtained. If names, dates, or places indicated on a pedigree chart are a product of speculation (unproven or undocumented), that fact should be indicated in some way on the chart.

9. Family group sheets. Family group sheets organize what is known about a couple and their children. Researchers usually use family group sheets—which include spaces for names, parents, dates and places of events, children, spouses, sources, and other information—to help identify members of a particular family. Sources can be entered on the back of the sheet if room is limited on the front. Blank sheets can be used as worksheets when researching.

10. Index to notes and handouts. If you attend many society meetings, classes, or lectures, you probably receive lots of handouts. Since most handouts don't apply to any specific family, remembering what handouts and notes you have can be difficult. An index, organized alphabetically (if possible), will give you an "at a glance" reference to what sources of information you have.

11. Marriage log. A marriage log displays information about the bride and groom for a specific location. You can adapt the form to your needs if you wish to cover more than one location on a form.

Town/County/State: _____

Courthouse Address: _____

Name of Groom	Age	Name of Bride	Age	Book	Page	Date of Wedding

12. Migration trail map. Migration trail maps display every place your ancestors lived, which is useful when trying to locate specific locality resources. A migration trail can also lead you to further information about the forces that drove the families to move (war, land opportunities, crop failures, or simply a desire to change locations). You should be sure to check out each stop for collateral lines and extended families.

13. Relationship chart. If you are confused about how one

individual is related to another person or group of people, a relationship chart will tell you their relationship. There are several relationship (cousinship) charts available online, but for multiple relationships, use a genealogy database program to generate a chart. Relationship charts can be very helpful when you have two ancestral lines that inter-marry.

14. Research log. Research logs can be divided by individual or surname, as you desire. Logs should be taken with you when you research, and every item you search should be entered. This may seem like a lot of work (especially for those resources in which you find no information), but a detailed research log can be used as a roadmap to show you what resources you've checked and what results you found there. You may adapt a research log for use on the Internet as well; notations of what websites, indexes, and databases you've searched can be helpful, as can listing those sites and newsgroups to which you have submitted a query.

Ancestor's Name _____

Family Group or Chart # _____

Information Needed:

Location:

Date of Search	Location or Call No.	Source	Comments	Document Number

15. Abstract forms for deeds and wills. An abstract form walks you through the task of extracting vital information from deeds and wills by prompting you to note the important information found on these legal documents. An abstract form is worth its weight in gold when you find yourself in a dusty, dimly-lit courthouse basement with a huge deed book on your lap.

16. Census extract forms. It is easy to miss information after you've worn out your eyes staring at census microfilm—hence the creation of census extract forms. These forms (available for all census years from 1790-1940) allow you to make notes of the important information and show families and neighbors as they occur on the microfilm. Any notes or comments you may wish to make can be entered on the back of the form.

17. Problem worksheet. A problem worksheet can be created for all the research on an individual or for a specific problem. If you need to find the birth and marriage records for a person, you can create a worksheet outlining the two problems and possible avenues of research. A problem worksheet is your place to brainstorm—put down any ideas you have where you might look for answers. Note the results, and be sure to include the specifics in your research log.

Transcribe and abstract documents. In order to fully understand all of the clues, details, and actual facts included in documents, transcribe and abstract those documents. A transcript should include verbatim the content contained in the original document. An abstract should minimize the words used, yet maintain the pertinent facts and the integrity of the document. Transcriptions and abstracts are helpful in documents such as deeds, interviews, journals, letters, pension papers, and wills. The transcription helps to identify all facts contained within the document, understand each word used, and simplify subsequent readings. The abstract helps to summarize the pertinent facts, list the names, and remove the confusion with language terms used.

Consistently conduct evidence analysis. Always be asking, "Does my research provide the evidence to prove the relationship from one generation to the next?" Analyze your sources. You need to determine how much weight or validity to give to each source.

I have found that genealogy research involves more than just examining records. It involves understanding the difference between primary and secondary information, original and derivative sources, and direct and indirect evidence. I learned about and use the Genealogical Proof Standard to measure the credibility of genealogical statements. I've learned to do the following in my research:

Carefully consider the source. Sources are anything or anybody that provides data. Sources vary in terms of reliability. Original sources are most reliable, but derivative sources can also contain helpful and accurate information. An original source is one that is still in its initial form, such as a birth, marriage, or death certificate. A derivative source is one that has been modified from an earlier form, such as someone transcribed the information from the original record. More reliable sources are generally given more weight; thus, original sources usually carry more weight than derivative sources. But be careful and make sure to double-check the information provided from any source, since even reliable sources can provide erroneous information.

Always ask, "Who provided the information?" Information is the data provided by sources. The reliability of information depends on the credibility of the person who provided it. Primary information—which comes from someone with firsthand knowledge—is generally more reliable than secondary information—which comes from someone who learned it from somewhere or someone else. Primary information usually carries more weight than secondary information. An informant's credibility depends on the way in which the information was obtained; how soon after the event the details were recorded; and circumstances such as age, illness, or bias.

Turn information into evidence. Sources are carefully analyzed to extract relevant information. Relevant information from different sources is compared to establish similarities and inconsistencies. Data analysis and correlation turns relevant information to evidence. Evidence may be direct or indirect. Direct evidence provides an answer to a research question on its own. Indirect evidence doesn't provide an answer on its own, but when combined with other evidence it can help establish a solution.

Prove your conclusions. Information obtained from sources is analyzed and correlated to develop a body of evidence for the given genealogical problem. "Proof" consists of a well-reasoned conclusion based on the sum of the evidence. Genealogical Proof Standard (GPS) requires that five criteria be met before a genealogical statement is considered credible:

- Conduct a reasonably exhaustive search for all information that is pertinent.
- Include an accurate source citation for each item of information.

- Analyze and correlate the collected information to assess its quality.
- Resolve any conflicts of evidence that contradict each other.
- Write a soundly reasoned coherent conclusion.

All proven genealogical conclusions are subject to re-evaluation if new evidence is discovered or if an error in reasoning can be demonstrated.

Create proof summaries of your research. As a genealogist, I don't know of any document that directly says John Jones or Maxcey Ewell is my ancestor. It has taken a combination of clues and other documents to lead to those conclusions. After I conducted my research on a particular family line, it's not uncommon for me to have to take a week and sometimes months before I am able to resume my research. It's easy to forget the steps taken and the current conclusions, thus making it necessary to start all over again. While all of the facts are fresh, write down the theory in a proof summary that states what you have researched and why you have drawn the conclusions about your family. In the future, you may find new supporting or conflicting information that will alter the theory, but you have a proof summary to review and make necessary adjustments.

Lesson 3: Every Record Has Value

O nce you have had a chance to discover and organize records you have found at home, you are now ready to expand your search. Be prepared to conduct an exhaustive search. Look in reliable sources. Make it a practice to track each key piece of information back to its original source. Be prepared to search documents that are photocopied, digital images, and handwritten. Documents will be full or partial transcripts, condensed abstracts, or partial abstracts.

Events create records. The most important concept I learned about searching for records is to think of events, not records. Rather than searching only for birth or death certificates, ask yourself what other types of records the event would generate in the time period the event took place.

For example in the case of my birth, there was an announcement in the paper, a baby shower, a baby book, a birth certificate, a record of my Church blessing, hospital records, and, later, a one-year-old picture in the local paper.

In the case of my mother's death, there were cemetery and sexton records, a funeral book, funeral home records, hospital records, memorial cards, an obituary, video of the funeral services, and her will.

The next important concept I learned was to search the records of siblings. Think about the families. When I have not been able to find any information in the vital (birth, marriage, divorce, death) records of my family, I have usually been able to find the information clues needed in the vital records of the siblings of the ancestor I am researching.

Use multiple sources to correlate information. Never take any-thing at face value. Finding your ancestor's name does not guaran-tee that you've found the right ancestor. Remember that nothing is truly fact until you can back it up using more than one resource. When searching multiple sources, I have found the records I need in the same location or area in which my ancestor lived. Always ask yourself, what records were created in this location during the time that my ancestor lived here?

Learn what resources contain the needed data to further your research (or to document data) and where they are available such as in societies (genealogy and historical) and libraries (public, col-lege, private, and governmental). Census, birth, marriage, divorce, death, probate, land, school, military, fraternal, and obituaries are all records that can contain similar data—names, dates, places, family structure, and names of family members. Some might be easily found and available. Others might require travel costs or other fees. Start with the closest and most economically available records.

Searching multiple resources often reveals family relationships and personal information that, when viewed collectively, provide a more complete picture of the family and its members. For example, when I go to cemeteries, I always take a camera and a tape or digital recorder. Many times, I have found places where there are graves of children who may have only lived a few days or months and were never listed in census records or perhaps other family members did not know of or forgot about. Sometimes the child will be buried by parents but not listed in family records, and visiting the cemeteries is the only way you would know of their existence.

Search the US Census, vital records, and other records. US Census records are available for the years 1790–1940 and can include names, dates, locations, and occupations. You can also discover and verify vital information through the Social Security Death Index and birth, marriage, and divorce records. Additional life information can be found in immigration, naturalization, and military records.

I like to start with the most recent event of the individual I am researching, which is usually their death. Death certificates are usually the first source in which an official written account will reveal an exact place and date of death. The record also includes additional genealogical details, such as the date and place of birth, name of father, maiden name of mother, name of spouse, social security number, name of cemetery, funeral director, and the name of the informant (often a relative of the deceased).

The clues found in the death record usually provide ideas for my next steps. These clues often include the following:

- Exact place and date of death known for a person
- Funeral record
- Cemetery record
- Newspaper obituary
- Social security death record
- Place where birth, marriage, church, military, occupation, or court records can be found

The first United States census was taken in 1790. Since then, census records have become a major source for locating the place where an ancestor lived, which opens the door to many more discoveries. After 1840, census records also list age, place of birth, occupation, personal wealth, education, spouse, children, hired hands, and even immigration information. To protect individual privacy, the government doesn't release census data for seventy-two years after the census is taken. The 1940 census is the latest census to be made available.

Search in county and state records. If you've located an ancestor on a census, you know their county of residence. Now you're ready to search for the records at the state and county level to find written evidence of that person's life. Documents may include newspapers, county histories, special genealogy collections, tax lists, voter registrations, court records, probates, wills, estate papers, and much more.

Use the Genealogical Records Selection Table on the following pages to help you decide which records will help you fill in missing pieces in your pedigree chart and family group sheet. This table is most helpful for searching post-1800 records.

GENEALOGY RECORDS SELECTION TABLE

When looking for this information	Look for these records first	Look for these records second
Age	**Church:** Parish records, membership records **Family:** Bible records Government: Vital records	**Government:** Census **Newspaper:** Obituaries **Other:** Cemeteries
Birth	**Church:** Parish records, membership records **Family:** Bible records **Government:** Vital records **Other:** Cemeteries	**Government:** Census, military, taxation **Newspaper:** Obituaries
Birth, foreign	**Family:** Bible, biography, genealogy **Government:** Census, emigration, immigration, naturalization, citizenship	**Church:** Parish records, membership records **Library:** Histories, maps, gazetteers **Newspaper:** Obituaries
Death	**Church:** Parish records, membership records **Government:** Death, probate **Newspaper:** Obituaries **Other:** Cemeteries, funeral homes, hospitals	**Government:** Military, court, land and property **Newspaper:** Articles
Divorce	**Government:** Court records, divorce records	**Government:** Vital records **Newspaper:** Articles
Religion	**Church:** Parish records, membership records **Government:** Civil registration **Library:** History, biography	**Family or library:** Bible records, genealogy **Newspaper:** Obituaries **Other:** Cemeteries
Family members	**Church:** parish records, membership records **Government:** Vital records, census, probate **Newspaper:** Obituaries	**Family:** Bible **Government:** Immigration, emigration, land and property
Immigration, emigration	**Government:** Immigration, emigration, naturalization, citizenship **Family/library:** Genealogy	**Church:** Membership records **Government:** Census **Library:** Biography **Newspaper:** Articles
Living relatives and adoptions	**Family:** Bible records, court records **Government:** Vital records **Newspapers:** Obituaries	**Church:** Parish records, membership records **Government:** Census, probate records

Maiden name	**Church:** Parish records, membership records **Family:** Bible records, genealogy **Government:** Vital records **Newspaper:** Announcements, obituaries	**Family or library:** Biography, genealogy **Government:** Military, probate, land and property, nobility, naturalization, citizenship **Other:** Cemeteries
Marriage	**Church:** Parish records, membership records **Family:** Bible records, genealogy **Government:** Vital records **Newspaper:** Announcements, obituaries	**Family or library:** Biography, genealogy **Government:** Military, probate, land and property, nobility, naturalization, citizenship **Other:** Cemeteries
Occupation	**Government:** Census, immigration, emigration **Other:** Directories	**Government:** Court records **Library:** Newspaper
Physical description	**Government:** Military records **Other:** Biography	**Family:** Genealogy **Government:** Vital records, naturalization, citizenship, emigration, immigration
Place finding aids	**Library:** Gazetteers, maps	**Library:** History, periodicals
Place of residence	**Church:** parish records, membership records **Family or library:** History, genealogy **Government:** Census, land and property, military, vital records **Other:** Directories	**Government:** Taxation **Newspaper:** Obituaries
Places family has lived	**Family:** Genealogy **Government:** Census (indexed), military, vital records, statewide indices	**Government:** Military, taxation, obituaries
Prior research (genealogy)	**Family or library:** Periodicals Other: Societies	**Library:** History, biography
Social activities	**Church:** Parish records membership records **Community:** Societies **Library:** History, biography, newspapers	**Government:** Town records, court records **Newspaper:** Obituaries **Other:** Cemeteries, directories

Expect the unexpected. One of the first lessons I learned in genealogy was to expect surprises—to "expect the unexpected." Life is all about the unexpected—the good, the bad, and the crazy. I have found many instances of "unexpectedness" in my own research.

The basics of expecting the unexpected are simple: sometimes the information will be used to help you in your research, to tell a story, or it may be best kept a secret. Be respectful of the living and their wishes, especially if the information is sensitive. In my own case, I can only think of one unexpected, that I chose to leave a secret. It had no value to the living or the dead, to genealogy or a good story. Enjoy your research and the unexpected.

Learn about the time period and locality of your ancestors. Knowing the time period and locality (including boundary changes) of your ancestors helps you find records. Become familiar with the towns, counties, states, and countries where your ancestors lived. Look for timelines of this period for the town, county, state, and country.

Read the history of countries, states, counties, cities, towns, and villages. Gain a feel for the areas where your ancestors lived. Search the Internet, libraries, and bookstores for histories written about the locations and time periods your ancestors lived in.

Maps provide help for tracking facts about ancestors. Old and new maps can help track down facts about ancestors. In the United States, birth, death, property, and some other kinds of records are normally kept by the county governments. If you can name the place where an ancestor lived, new or old maps of that place may also show the county seat where useful data about your kin can be obtained.

Old maps can be particularly useful in this regard because pinpointing the name of the place where an ancestor lived can be like trying to hit a moving target. Many towns, counties, cities, and even countries have experienced numerous name changes over the years.

Expand your knowledge of the place(s) where your ancestor lived. Learn about the "community"—the everyday life during the time of your ancestor. Answer questions such as the following:

- What is the ethnic makeup of the community?
- What is the influence of the ethnic group on the community?
- What is the history of the ethnic group in town, county, and state?
- What are the surnames associated with the community?
- Where did your ancestors come from?
- What is the primary location in the town?

Much of this information about your ancestor may have already been compiled or published, including in online databases, books, and periodicals. The Library of Congress (LOC) catalog is an excellent place to search for published books.

I have found periodical articles that have been instrumental in helping me resolve research issues and open my eyes to new possibilities. I have used journals such as the New England Historic Genealogical Register, the National Genealogical Society Quarterly (NGSQ), and regional genealogical and historical journals to find articles that outline and discuss research methodology, provide case studies, list published genealogies, detail repository resources, focus on local research issues, and much more.

Using genealogy and historical periodicals is a must as a researcher. I suggest you use the Periodical Source Index (PERSI) to search for periodicals, such as journals, magazines, and quarterlies of genealogical and historical societies. PERSI is a subject index to genealogical and local history periodicals. It covers over 11,000 genealogy and local history periodicals written in English and French and published in the United States, Canada, Britain, and Ireland.

PERSI is available on CD from many public libraries. You can also find PERSI online from the following sources: 1) Heritage Quest Online, available in many public libraries (and available remotely using a library card from the participating library) and from family history centers of The Church of Jesus Christ of Latter-day Saints. Heritage Quest provides four options for beginning a search: People, Places, How-tos, and Periodicals. 2) Ancestry. com, through personal subscription, or is free at subscribing libraries and some LDS family history centers. From the Ancestry.com main page, click the "Search" tab and then, under "Dictionaries, Encyclopedias & Reference," select "Periodical Source Index."

Search out historical resources. History associated with our ancestors is easily found. Pick a topic and begin your search. Some of the most common sources for historical information include the following:

- Archived newspapers
- Chambers of commerce
- Historical societies and associations
- Company histories
- History networks
- Libraries (university, state, regional, and local)
- Internet
- Living history museums (for example, Plymouth Plantation shows Plymouth as it was in the seventeenth century: a centuries-old Wampanoag home site, a welcoming bench covered in furs, bluefish roasting slowly over a bed of hot coals, and a man dressed in traditional deerskin clothing.)
- Historic sites (state and national parks, monuments)
- Museums
- Personal journals

Study drawings, paintings, and photographs of the time period. Images of our ancestors and their times give us clues to the lives of our families. A simple exercise would be to take a photograph of your family from the early 1900s, study the image, and record your thoughts and observations.

Consider clues the photograph has to offer. What time period was the photo taken in? Look at the physical aspect of the photo (house, people, clothes, animals, surroundings); what does it tell you? (Family economic status, priorities, relationships, expressions, emotions, and so on.) Look for identifiers such as house numbers, license numbers, and types of uniforms. They can give clues about where to look, such as the license bureau or occupation or employment records. What is the name and location of the photographer or studio? (This information is usually printed on the front or back of the photo.) The location of the photographer or studio does not necessarily mean your ancestor lived in that town. Photographers had traveling studios and would often travel around taking photographs, which were pasted on cards with their studio information. Your ancestor may have made a trip to a larger community to shop or attend a function and had photographs taken while there. Certainly the studio name and location is a good clue for beginning your research in those areas.

What Records Can You Expect to Find?

The following is an overview of the type of resources that I have found constantly valuable in my genealogy research, in addition to hundreds of other resources I have learned to research and use through the years. When I mastered researching these resources, I was able to easily expand my research to other records to help me connect the pieces of my genealogy puzzle.

In my profile of each resource, I have included what you will find, how to use the resource, and research insights for each resource. I would encourage you to use this section as a starting point from which you can search out and find other genealogical tutorials, guides, and helps to provide deeper insights.

While the resources discussed will be mostly relevant to United States research, be aware that resources will vary in information and availability based on the time and place in which the resource was created. Resources can be found in a variety of locations, such as online, in libraries and archives, and from societies, museums, and courthouses. Keep in mind that each repository acquires and manages artifacts that are very specific to the community, county, region, and state they serve. While some items may be duplicated across collections, many items are unique and can only be found in specific locations. It then becomes very important that you gain a comprehensive understanding of all the resources that are available to you collectively. Many state organizations provide reference guides, brochures, or leaflets (in print and online) that discuss specific aspects of their collections and how to use them or how to conduct research in a particular state, region, or locale. Look for guides such as the following:

- A Guide to Genealogical Research at the (State) Historical Society
- Population Census Records at the (State) Historical Society
- Index to Naturalizations in (State)
- List of Basic Sources on (State) History

CEMETERY RECORDS

The most common cemetery records can include sexton or care-taker records, church records, and tombstones and gravestones.

What you will find. Cemetery records usually include birth and death information. You will often find other information and clues that will lead you to other records. This information can include address of deceased; age at death; cause of death; cost of the plot or burial; date of death; full name, including maiden name for women; birthplace; full dates of birth and death; information linking the plot owner to other plots (in cases of disinterment, reburial, and so on); information about military service, such as unit; inscription (poem, Bible quote) providing insight into the ancestor or those left behind; logo of organization that the deceased belonged to (ethnic, religious, military, or other organizations); name of doctor or hospital; name of officiating minister; names of other involved (funeral home, officiating clergyman, memorial company); owner of the plot; relationship clues ("Beloved wife of . . .", list of children, or who else is buried in plot); marriage date (rare); where deceased died, if other than where he or she lived; and photos, favorite saying, writings, music, or images that relate to a hobby or profession.

Research insights. In order to find tombstone and sexton records, you will need to know the ancestor's name and where he or she was buried. Search all available sources of cemetery records to build as complete a profile as you can for your ancestor. Tombstone inscriptions are as different as the individuals they commemorate. In most cases, you will find some element of value. You will most likely find the true given name of the person or even a nickname that can help you find information. Many cemeteries have paper records of persons who are buried there, which are kept with the sexton. These records come in many formats. Some churches keep what is known as burial records.

Also keep in mind that there are several types of cemeteries.

1) Religious Cemeteries. These cemeteries were often located next to the religious group's church or synagogue. Qualification for burial was often reserved for burial of the members of the congregation or faith. The records of burials in religious cemeteries are most likely to be found with that religious group, rather than with a sexton.

2) Community Cemeteries. If you suspect your ancestor was buried in a community cemetery, contact the sexton. The sexton's job is to coordinate, and often actually handle, the burial duties (usually in concert with a mortuary and church) and keep the records of burials in that cemetery.

3) Private Cemeteries. Some of the earliest cemeteries in North America were private, family cemeteries. These are especially common in the southern states and in some New England areas, although they may appear in any locality. Private cemeteries can also include cemetery associations and fraternal or social groups, such as the Mason or Old Fellows. These cemeteries are usually located in very rural areas where there were no other options.

4) Commercial Cemeteries. Commercial cemeteries are among the most common cemeteries today and have taken the place of community cemeteries. These cemeteries are run by a local mortuary or company and usually found in larger communities. Ancestors are not likely to be found in such cemeteries unless they lived in the 1900s.

5) Military Cemeteries. There are over thirty-seven cemeteries and memorials overseas for soldiers who died during the service of their country.

Where to find cemeteries. Locating a burial site can be difficult, but people are usually buried where they die. Begin your search for a cemetery where your ancestor drops out of the records. In any given area, there are usually many cemeteries. The records of these various cemeteries are often in many different places and may not be easily accessible. The records are often organized in chronological order or by plot, and therefore, are not usually alphabetical. If public records exist for your ancestor, they will usually denote where the burial occurred. For deaths occurring after 1870, the community may have required a burial permit from the local health department (these are not death certificates), which would identify the cemetery the person was buried in.

The first place to find sexton's records is the cemetery itself. If you come across a cemetery that is "inactive" or "full" because there is no more room for additional burials, contact the local sexton to begin your search to see if they have records.

There are many directories to assist you in locating a specific cemetery or even a list of all possible cemeteries in a certain locality. In large cities, begin with the city directory for the time period your ancestor died. There are also online record directories, such as Interment.net, Cemetery Junction, African American Cemeteries Online, FindAGrave, Obituary Central's Cemetery Search, and the Political Graveyard. You may also want to check with local mortuaries in the area your ancestor died, as they will be aware of at least the active cemeteries of that time and may be able to refer you to a local cemetery association.

Other resources I have used include maps, GPS, land records (deeds), obituaries, death certificates, mortuary records, local and regional government, church officials, genealogy and historical societies, community residents, and local historians.

CENSUS RECORDS

A census is a government-sponsored enumeration of the population in a particular area and contains a variety of information—names, heads of household (or all household members), ages, citizenship status, ethnic background, and so on. Below, I've discussed some different types of census records you are likely to come across in your research.

Federal Census: Population Schedule. Federal census records provide the building blocks of your research, allowing you to both confirm information, and to learn more. Compiled every decade since 1790, census "population schedules" are comprehensive, detailed records of the federal government's decennial survey of American households. Information from the schedules is used by the federal government for timely demographic analysis. The schedules themselves, of interest primarily to genealogists, contain the personal information of the survey respondents. To protect the privacy of the people whose names appear in each schedule, census records are restricted for seventy-two years after the census is taken and are not available to researchers during that time.

What you will find. The earliest census records contain information on people born well before the American Revolution, while the 1940 schedules—the most recent ones open to public inspection—contain information on many people who are still living. Using these records, a researcher might conceivably trace a family line from a living person down to an ancestor born more than 250 years ago.

From 1790–1840, only the head of household is listed, along with the number of household members in selected age groups. Beginning in 1850, the name of every household member was recorded, along with their age, color, occupation, and place of birth. As other censuses were taken, additional questions were added.

From the 1850 census on, the names, ages, occupations, and birthplaces (country or state only) of each member of a household were included.

The 1870 census gave, in addition to previous information, the month of birth if born during the year, the month of marriage if married within the year, and whether the father or mother of each individual was foreign born.

The 1880 census (and later censuses) added two valuable pieces of information: the relationship of each person to the head of the household and the birthplace of the father and mother of each person.

The 1885 census was a special census, with population and mortality schedules conducted by the federal government to help five states or territories—Colorado, Florida, Nebraska, New Mexico, and Dakota Territory.

The 1890 census was largely destroyed by fire in 1921 and only fragments of it are available.

1900 and 1910 censuses ask the questions on the 1880 census, but also include the age of each individual, how many years he had been married, his year of immigration, and his citizenship status. The 1900 census also gives the month and year of birth. For mothers it lists the number of children born and surviving. The 1910 census identifies Civil War veterans.

The 1920 census includes the same information as was found on the 1910 census. It gives ages but not the month and year of birth. It also lists the year of naturalization, the only census to do so.

The 1930 census asks questions on the 1920 census and also asks for marital status and, if married, age at first marriage. If the individual was an American Indian, it asks whether he or she is full blooded or mixed blood and for tribal affiliation.

The 1940 census included several standard questions, such as name, age, gender, race, education, and place of birth. But the census also introduced some new questions. The instructions ask the enumerator to enter a circled x after the name of the person furnishing the information about the family. It also asked whether the person worked for the CCC, WPA, or NYA the week of March 24–30, 1940; and asked for their income for the twelve months ending December 31, 1939. The 1940 census also has a supplemental schedule for two names on each page. The supplemental schedule asks the place of birth of the person's father and mother; the person's usual occupation, not just what they were doing the week of March 24–30, 1940; and for all women who are or have been married, whether this woman had been married more than once and age at first marriage.

Be aware that in addition to population schedules, there were other schedules taken usually at the same time. There are resources online and in print that provide more detail on these schedules and how to use them in genealogy research. These other schedules include the following:

- Mortality Schedule: conducted from 1850 to 1885, provides information about persons who died during the twelve months prior to the census.
- Veterans Schedule: conducted in 1840 and 1890, provides information about Union veterans and their widows.
- Slaves Schedule: conducted in 1850 and 1860, shows slave owners and the number of slaves they owned. Slave schedules play a very important role in identifying the person who owned the slaves.
- Agricultural Schedule: conducted in 1850 to 1880, provides data on farms and the names of the farmers.
- Manufacturing Schedule: conducted in 1810 (fragments only), 1820, and 1850–1880, provides information on businesses and industries.
- Defective, Dependent, and Delinquent Schedule: conducted in 1880, focuses on handicapped, paupers, or criminals.
- Indian Schedules: conducted in 1910. Indian schedules are found at the end of the regular population schedules for each county. The Indian schedules are similar to regular population schedules but have some slightly different questions. They are not to be confused with the Indian census rolls.
- Institutions Schedule: usually follows the county population schedules and include jails, hospitals, poor houses, or asylums.
- Merchant Seamen Schedule: conducted on United States flag merchant vessels in 1930.
- Military and Naval Forces Schedule: conducted from 1900 to 1930 on forts, bases, and Navy ships, and is usually found after the population schedule.
- Social Statistics Schedule: conducted from 1850 to 1870, includes information about real estate, annual taxes, cemeteries, school statistics, libraries, newspapers, and churches.

Research insight. Use the census records to track your ancestors' movement over time, find names and rough birth years, determine relationships, learn birthplaces, find clues to the previous generation (such as their birthplace), learn street addresses, learn whether ancestors were slaves or slave owners, learn occupations, learn other country of birth, learn of other children who likely died young, learn year of immigration or naturalization, note naming patterns in your family, find clues to your family's economic status, find some clues to education, find some clues to military service, find some clues to medical conditions, narrow year and place of marriage, learn about employment status, learn about exceptional circumstances (such as convicts and homeless children), learn native tongue, narrow death dates, and identify other potential branches of your family living nearby.

Using maps in conjunction with the census schedules is important. State and county boundaries have changed over the years, so an ancestor may have lived in the same place for years, but have been enumerated in several different counties. This is also important for urban dwellers, since city precincts also changed with time. Use of city directories and books such as those listed in guidebooks will help provide clues to possible localities.

Where to find censuses. There are several resources for the finding the United States Federal Census, including the following:

- United States Censuses 1850-1930—Free Internet census indexes and images of the 1850, 1860, 1870, 1880 (index only), 1890, 1900, 1910, 1920, and 1930 censuses can be viewed on the FamilySearch Record Search.

- Ancestry.com, a subscription Internet site, has online images and indexes for all available 1790-1940 population schedules, 1850 and 1860 slave schedules, most 1850 to 1885 mortality schedules, surviving 1890 veteran's schedules (except Ohio and Pennsylvania), and the 1930 merchant seamen schedules.

- Heritage Quest, a subscription Internet site, has online images for all available 1790 to 1940 federal population schedules, and 1850 and 1860 slave schedules. They also have indexes for some years.

Other Census or Enumeration Schedules

Below is an outline of other censuses and enumeration schedules that may be helpful in your research.

State censuses. In addition to the decennial censuses of the federal government, many states also produced their own censuses in the intervening years. State census records vary greatly from state to state based on what the code required and when the state thought it was important to enumerate its citizens. The state and local enumerations can fill in gaps for when federal census do not exist and when you "just know" the people were in a particular area but the federal census records don't show them. Many researchers have used state and local enumerations to fill in for the 1890 Federal census.

Local enumerations. Many cities, towns, and counties conducted special censuses. Some of these local enumerations are found under such titles as school censuses, sheriff's censuses, and a variety of ethnic censuses.

Church records. Church registers are often the only way to determine birth, marriage, and death dates in the years before states started to keep vital records. They are a valuable substitute when vital records do not exist. Most churches keep their own records, but libraries usually have a number of books, copies of church records, a few manuscript volumes of original records, and microfilmed church records.

What You Will Find

Each denomination will have different types of records that they keep. The types of church records you will find include records they kept in accordance with their theology. Some types of church records that can be found include christenings or baptisms, marriages, burials, confirmations, communion, admissions and removals, financial records, Sunday school lists, church censuses, and church related newsletters. The actual information found in each type of record varies also. For example, when I have researched christenings or baptisms records I have often found the birth information of a child, parents of the child, and witnesses or godparents, who were often relatives.

Research insight. When you search church records, look for records of the entire family and relatives. As a general rule, the more individuals that were served by a church, the more information you'll get about the individuals. In order of priority, search the following church records:

Burial. From these records you can learn ancestor's death date and place, find ancestor's last residence, find the date or at least year of birth, find names of surviving relatives, learn the maiden name of a woman, learn the cemetery of burial for further research or visit, and determine death date for obituary or death notice search.

Wedding. If you are able to find a public record of an ancestor's marriage, you will note who performed the marriage. If you see the title of officiator as Pastor, Reverend, Father, or listed as minister of the gospel, your ancestors probably had a church wedding. You can determine the church the individual belonged to and search for records there. From these records you can find ancestors' marriage date and place, find ancestors' place(s) of residence, determine a year of birth for the bride and groom, learn of previous marriages, learn groom's occupation, find clues to family relationships (usually through names of witnesses), discover the names of the preceding generation, correctly ascribe children to appropriate marriage if a parent has married more than once, learn of other possible religious affiliations, see the handwriting of an ancestor, narrow the time period for the death of the first spouse in the case of the widow(er) remarrying, and learn of other family connections through dispensation remarks.

Baptism. From these records you can find an ancestor's birth date, discover the names of the preceding generation, find a family's place of residence, find clues to family relationships (through names of sponsors), learn about previously unknown children who died young, learn the parental association in the case of multiple marriages by one of the parents (to determine which one a particular child came from), and learn about changes in church affiliation.

Confirmation. Most church records simply list those that were confirmed on a specific day. On rare occasions you might find information such as their birth dates, parents' names, and place of birth. Information will vary somewhat by religion, with Scandinavian and Lutheran, for instance, generally providing more details.

Minutes or Communicant Lists. These records can be helpful in reconstructing family history. The disappearance of a couple from the list may signify their departure from the community. The disappearance of one but not the other may indicate death, an important clue if the death records no longer exist. These lists may also provide insight as to where persons have moved. These records also help to build a picture of what your ancestors were like and how they worshiped.

Be aware that church affiliation can change from within a generation and from one generation to the next. If you are not sure of the church affiliation of your ancestors, note the location where they lived for possible churches to research. Look for names of clergymen who performed the marriage and burial. Often the obituary includes church membership. Check the state, regional, and local historical and genealogy societies for church records they might have. Some churches have archives of their records.

Our immigrant ancestors as a whole were religiously devout and connected closely with one another through church. If you know your ancestor's country of origin and you don't know their religious denomination, use the following table as a clue of where to start. The table also provides the name of the American name for the church.

Country of Origin	Prominent Church	Church in United States
Denmark	Lutheran	Lutheran
Finland	Lutheran	Lutheran
France	Roman Catholic	Roman Catholic
Germany	Roman Catholic	Roman Catholic
Italy	Roman Catholic	Roman Catholic
Latin Countries	Roman Catholic	Roman Catholic
Norway	Lutheran	Lutheran

Poland	Roman Catholic	Roman Catholic
Scotland	Church of Scotland	Presbyterian
Sweden	Lutheran	Lutheran
England	Church of England or Anglicans	Protestant Episcopal

Where to find church records. If you know the church an ancestor attended, contact the current minister to ask about record availability. When a church closes, or sometimes by practice, the records may be transferred to denominations archive. The following are locations for finding the archives for major United States religious denominations:

- Adventists: Washington, DC
- Adventists: Washington, DC
- American Baptists: Rochester, NY
- Southern Baptists: Nashville, TN
- Brethren in Christ Church: Grantham, PA
- Church of Christ, Scientist: Boston, MA
- The Church of Jesus Christ of Latter-day Saints (Mormons): Salt Lake City, UT
- Churches of Christ: Memphis, TN
- Congregational: Boston, MA
- Disciples of Christ: Nashville, TN
- Greek Orthodox: New York, NY
- Jewish: Cincinnati, OH; Waltham, MA
- Evangelical Lutherans: Chicago, IL
- Missouri Synod Lutherans: St. Louis, MO
- United Methodists: Madison, NJ
- Pentecostal: Tulsa, okay
- Presbyterians: Philadelphia, PA; Montreat, NC
- Episcopalian: check local parishes
- Reformed Church: New Brunswick, NJ
- Roman Catholic: Notre Dame University, South Bend, IN; Catholic University, Washington, DC
- Quakers (Society of Friends): Swarthmore, PA, for Hicksite

records; Haverford, PA, for Orthodox records
- United Church of Christ: Boston, MA; Lancaster, PA
- Unitarian and Universalist: Harvard Divinity School, Cambridge, MA

Make sure you check FamilySearch.org to see what has been microfilmed and can be accessed through the Family History Library system. These include records of many denominations, particularly the Society of Friends (Quaker), Presbyterian, Congregational, Lutheran, Reformed, and Roman Catholic churches. Some churches have donated their records to local genealogical and historical societies. Many local universities and public libraries have copies of church records. Most libraries and societies have websites and list their holdings online.

CIVIL VITAL RECORDS (BIRTH, DEATH, MARRIAGES, AND DIVORCES)

Civil vital records—for births, deaths, marriages, and, sometimes, divorces—denote the key milestones of our lives and are the cornerstone of family history research. Vital records can offer details often found through no other genealogical resource. Adoption records are also considered to be vital records but will not be covered in this section.

What you will find. The following is a brief overview of what you will find in vital records.

Birth records. Birth records are considered primary source records because they are completed at, or close to, the time of the birth by someone who was present at the birth. Birth records generally give the child's name, sex, date and place of birth, and the names of the parent. Additional information can include the name of the hospital, birthplace of parents, occupation of the parents, marital status of the mother, and the number of other children born to the mother.

Marriage records. Marriage records are primary source records because they are completed at, or close to, the time of the marriage by someone who was present at the marriage. A marriage record can provide the age at time of marriage, church of marriage ceremony, county where the marriage took place, date or place of birth for bride and groom, date of the marriage, full names of bride and groom, name of minister or priest, names and birthplaces of the bride's and groom's parents, names of the witnesses to the marriage (often relatives), occupation, residence of the parties, and whether single, widowed, or divorced prior to the marriage.

Marriages are usually filed with each county court. Some counties may have given their early marriage records to the historical society.

Death records. Death records are especially helpful because they are the most recent record available about an ancestor and may often exist for persons who have no birth or marriage records. Keep in mind that most of the information on the death certificate is provided by a person who knew the deceased, thus it is considered a secondary source for information such as the birthplace, birth date, and parents' names of the deceased.

The death certificate can provide information such as age at death, cause of death, date or place of birth, date or place of burial, details about the length of illness (if applicable), disposition of cremated remains, exact time of death, how long they lived in that country or location, maiden name (for deceased woman), marital status at the time of death (single, married, widowed or divorced), name of surviving spouse, name (and sometimes address) of informant (frequently a surviving spouse, child, or other close relative), name and location of mortuary, names of parents, occupation or name of employer, residence of the deceased, religious affiliation, signature of attending physician, and witnesses at the time of death.

Divorce records. Divorces before the twentieth century were uncommon and in some places illegal. Records of divorces contain data on family members, their marital history, their property, residences, and dates of other important events such as the children's births. Divorce records are primary source records for the information on property, living children, age of husband and wife, and date of divorce, and they are secondary source records for information on the marriage, birth dates of children, and so on. Divorce records are often open to the public and can be obtained by contacting the clerk of the court.

Research insight. It is important to know that vital record searches are most useful for finding relatively recent information. Most US states did not assume legal responsibility for vital records until around 1900. The first state to start keeping vital records was Massachusetts in 1841, and the last was New Mexico in 1920.

One of the most important details about a birth, marriage, or death record is the person providing the information. This person varies, and, therefore, the accuracy of the information varies. A parent may give the information on their child's birth record. A bride or groom will usually provide the information for the marriage record, and the widow or nearest family member may give information on a death record. It is also possible for non-related persons to give information on any and all of these types of records. Many records will provide the name of the informant toward the bottom of the form.

Always start your vital record search with the death-related records. It's the most recent event in your ancestor's life. You usually learn where your ancestor last lived, which provides a starting point for where to look for other records. Death records also include birth and marriage information. Other key death-related records include burial and probate records. As a practice, also search the death records of your ancestor's siblings if available. I have found key pieces of information in them that was lacking in my ancestor's records.

I make it a practice to ask myself the following questions to make the most of the information I find when reviewing vital records:

- What dates does this record provide?
- What ages are given?
- What places are mentioned in this record?
- Are parents or a spouse named?
- Are witnesses to the event related to the family?
- Who provided the information? Was that person someone who knew the family well?

- Does the death record give the name of the cemetery or funeral home? If yes, see if cemetery records are available to search for more information.
- Does the information from the record fit with what you know about the family from other records? If not, it may have been miscopied by a clerk. Check the sources.

Where to find civil vital records. Each state has the equivalent of a bureau of vital records. It's generally called the "Bureau of Vital Statistics," "Division of Records and Statistics," "Division of Public Health," "Vital Records Division," or some similar title. No matter the name, the state agency is where you go to obtain birth, marriage, and death certificate. Historical and genealogical societies are an important resource for vital records prior to the state's date of taking legal responsibility for vital records.

Diaries and Journals

The terms diary and journal are used interchangeably today. No matter what you call them, these accounts are the autobiographies of ordinary people like your ancestors, and these may be the only existing records of their personal lives. Along with genealogical data, diaries give you a wonderful glimpse into someone's daily life, thoughts, and attitudes. A diarist may also record feelings on national events, such as a war or its impact on family and the community.

Directories

Directories and member lists are the predecessors of the modern-day phone book. They listed the inhabitants of a locality with their addresses and occupation (and sometimes business address).

What you will find and research insights. The types of directories you will find and their value to you as a genealogist include the following:

Alumni Directory. Alumni directories contain a listing of individuals who attended a particular university, the year that they graduated, and their degree. If you can find information about your ancestor in one of these directories, you may be able to locate other records within the organization that can provide insight into the life of your ancestor.

Business Directory. Business directories are listings of businesses in the community and usually contain personal information about the owner such as dates and places of birth, dates of marriage, names of children, length of residence in the town, and other valuable information. They are usually organized by county and, depending on the time period, vary in the amount of information they contain. Often, you'll find advertisements for certain businesses in these directories.

Professional Directories. Includes directories for people such as doctors and lawyers. They will most often include information relating to that individual's history in the profession, as well as other biographical information.

City Directory. City directories help you locate where and when a person lived. You will also find a publisher's introduction, history of the city, a street directory, ward boundaries, a map of the city, abbreviations, a directory of churches, a directory of cemeteries, a list of city officials, classified lists of businesses, a list of fraternal and social organizations, city laws or ordinances, a calendar of events, and more. A city directory can often guide you to other records such as censuses, death and probate records, naturalization records, land records, and church records.

Telephone Directory. Most people are familiar with the common telephone directory; they contain addresses and phone numbers. These directories can be quite helpful in locating living relatives or possible relatives with the same surname or a similar surname. The phone company in each city in the United States publishes a directory of everyone in that area who has a phone number.

Where to find directories. The first place to look for a book or microfilm copy of directories is the public library of the town you are conducting research about. State libraries and larger regional libraries may also have city directories for towns in that state or area. State and academic libraries also have sets of city directories followed by genealogical and historical societies. Online resources include DistantCousin, United States Online Historical Directories, and US City Directories.

IMMIGRATION RECORDS

Naturalization Records. Naturalization is the legal procedure by which an alien becomes a citizen of a state or country. Records of naturalization were not required to be reported to the United States government until the Basic Naturalization Act of 1906, after which naturalization forms became standardized and were sent to the US Bureau of Immigration (later the Immigration and Naturalization Service [INS]). Prior to that, federal, state, and local courts could naturalize citizens. The records are kept by each court or, in some cases, sent to be stored elsewhere. Immigrants often filed their first application for naturalization as soon as they came off the boat or other places on their journey to their final destination.

The formalized process required that a prospective citizen file a declaration of intention in which he or she renounced allegiance to foreign sovereignties. Following a waiting period of five years, an immigrant could then petition a federal court for formal citizenship.

What you will find. There were three steps to the naturalization process, which are detailed below.

Declarations of Intention (or First Papers). Normally the first papers were completed soon after arrival in the United States, depending on the laws in effect at the time. Certain groups, such as women and children, were exempt in early years.

Prior to September 1906, Declaration of Intention forms usually requested relatively minimal information about the applicant, including name of the person requesting citizenship, year and country of birth, port of entry, month and year of entry into the United States, name of foreign sovereign, signature, and date of request.

After September 1906, Declaration of Intention forms requested increasingly more detailed information about the applicant, including name, age, occupation, personal description, place and date of birth, current address, country of emigration, name of vessel, last foreign residence, name of foreign sovereign, port of entry, month and year of entry into the United States, signature, and date of request.

Beginning in the late 1920s, Declaration of Intention forms also requested information about other family members.

Petition (Second or Final Papers). Naturalization petitions were formal applications submitted to the court by individuals who had met the residency requirements and who had declared their intention to become citizens. As with the declarations of intention, the information they contained varied dramatically from one court to another.

Prior to September 1906, information on the Petition for Naturalization was often limited to the petitioner's name, address, occupation, date and country of birth, and port and date of arrival in the United States.

After September 1906, subsequent versions of the Petition for Naturalization required increasingly more detailed information, including petitioner's name, residence, occupation, date and place of birth, race, date and place of Declaration of Intention, marital status, name of spouse, date and place of marriage, date and place of spouse's birth, date and place where spouse entered the United States (if applicable), and residence of spouse. It also required the names, dates of birth, and place of residence of children; last foreign residence; port of emigration; port and date of entry; petitioner's name at time of arrival; name of vessel or other conveyance; name of foreign sovereign, length of time, dates, and places of residency in the United States; signature; and date of document.

Part of the Petition for Naturalization also includes a place for signed and dated affidavits of two witnesses, Certificate of Arrival file number, and Declaration of Intention file number. After 1930, the Petition for Naturalization often includes a photograph of the petitioner.

Certificates of Naturalization. Most certificates of naturalization contain only the name of the individual, the name of the court, and the date of issue. Certificates were issued to naturalized citizens upon completion of all citizenship requirements. The Certificate of Naturalization includes name, address, birthplace or nationality, country from which they emigrated, birth date or age, personal description, marital status, name of spouse, age (or birth date) and address of spouse, information about children (including names, ages, and addresses), and date of document.

Certificate of Citizenship. This document granted the individual United States citizenship.

Oath of Allegiance. This document was used to renounce an immigrant's allegiance to a foreign country and declare his or her allegiance to the United States. The Oath of Allegiance includes the petitioner's signature and date of document.

Where to find immigration records. Begin by looking for naturalization records in the courts of the county or city where the immigrant lived. Look first for the petition (second papers), because they are usually easier to find in courts near where the immigrant eventually settled. After 1906, the declaration can be filed with the petition as the immigrant was required to submit a copy when he submitted the petition. Online resources include Fold3.com, Ancestry.com, Olive Tree Genealogy Naturalizations, and United States Citizenship and Immigrations Services. Also check regional branches of the National Archives.

Land Records

One of the major factors influencing our ancestors coming to America was the availability of land. There is a high likelihood that your ancestor can be found in land records. It is estimated that by the mid-1800s, as many as ninety percent of all adult white males owned land in the United States.

There are many types of land records—title abstracts, land purchases, grants, and more. Land records are typically one of the records kept from the very early days of settlement in an area and may be available when other records are not. These records provide information on relationships between individuals, approximate relocation dates, and the financial state of a family.

What you will find. Use the land records to find death date and place; find residence; find names (and addresses) of descendants; learn details to search for land records; discover other places where the ancestor may have held property; discover relationships; get a feel for an ancestor's economic standing; look for clues about an ancestor's feelings toward family members; find clues to the deaths of other family members; sort out adoptions, guardianships, and other unclear relationships; learn names of stores and vendors frequented by your ancestor; and find your ancestor's signature, occupation, citizenship, and marital status. The following is a brief overview of some of the land records you will find.

Deeds. Deed books record the ownership and transfer of property, usually real estate.

Bounty-land Warrants. The federal government provided bounty land for those who served in the Revolutionary War, the War of 1812, the Mexican War, and Indian wars between 1775 and 1855. Bounty lands were offered as incentive to serve and as a reward for service. Bounty land was claimed by veterans or their heirs. The federal government reserved tracts of land for this purpose. The states of New York, Pennsylvania, and Virginia also set aside tracts of bounty land for their Revolutionary War veterans. Federal bounty land applications and warrants for the Revolutionary War have been microfilmed. They are available at the National Archives, its regional branches, and through the Family History Library system.

Donation Land Records. In 1850, in an attempt to lure settlers to the new western lands, the government gave lands to would-be settlers in Florida, New Mexico, and Oregon and Washington Territories. These land grants were known as donation lands. Settlers were required to reside on and improve the land by cultivation for four years before receiving a patent. Unique to the donation lands was the limits placed on the time of arrival rather than time of application. Young children who came with their families between 1850 and 1855 could claim their land when they became adults.

Homestead Records. The first homestead law was enacted in 1862 and was intended to encourage settlement in the west. As with the Donation Lands, the only requirement was to live on and improve the land through cultivation. Only a small filing fee was required. Although only an estimated 780,000 people received patents under the Homestead Law, two million applications were made, dispersing approximately 285 million acres.

Research insights. Start by determining the time and place your family might have owned property. Begin your search at the smallest jurisdictional level—usually the county (except in Connecticut, Rhode Island, and Vermont, where town clerks have kept the records). First look in the indexes. You will want to check both the grantor or direct (seller) and grantee or indirect (buyer) indexes for all possible entries of the ancestor you are searching. Once you find them, copy the references, which you will then use to look up land transitions in the appropriate books or volumes and page numbers. When you find the transaction, review every detail, which includes dates, names, relationships, and property description. Make a handwritten, photo, or digital copy of the full entry.

TOWNSHIP, CITY, COUNTY, AND STATE HISTORIES AND BIOGRAPHIES

Local, county, and state histories detail the events that occurred and the people who played a part. These histories detail the early settlements, who held what offices, who founded various towns, including when different churches were started and other valuable information. It is common to find histories that were written between 1870 and 1920 with biographical sketches of the individuals and families. The majority of these histories were written in the west and those states bordering the Great Lakes or Midwest states. These histories give insight and are helpful to the researcher since this is the region where most of the immigrants settled.

What you will find. The following are the type of histories you can expect to find:

Local History. The overwhelming majority of local histories address how a particular region and its citizens handled and reacted to every major state and national happening. In these compilations, you can find how a community handled everything from wars, waves of immigrants, and depressions to changing political scenery, taxation, trade, and commerce. Each of these events affects what people do, where they live, what organizations they belong to, how they earn income, and how they dispose of that income. Knowing what neighborhoods developed during a particular time period, realizing when certain organizations came into and went out of business, being aware of various laws and codes, as well as local customs and ceremonies, all provide the researcher with the ability to uncover more information.

Biography. A biographical sketch can include almost any aspect of a person's life, but generally contains information about the individual's family, education, and occupation. Thus, biographical sketches usually tell the subject's date of birth, parent's names, and wife's and children's names and often their birth dates. Usually there is some information about where they were born. Even if we are not fortunate enough to find a biographical sketch of the subject of our interest, there are other things to consider. Even if your ancestor wasn't prominent enough to get a mention, there may be other clues to his personality in these books. Also, you may want to consider whether the subject of a biographical sketch was related to the family in some way. Frequently, groups emigrated from the "old country" together, and by learning more about one member of a pioneer group, we can also find valuable clues to others.

Institutional Histories. Look for histories of the institutions that may have relevance to your family: churches, orphanages, charitable institutions, schools, hospitals and dispensaries, cultural institutions, cemeteries, or businesses.

Research insights. Start by determining when your ancestor lived. As you look for the local, county, and state histories, also look for books or volumes that focus solely on biographical sketches of many from the locality. Most of the sketches are written about men and generally include information about the family, education, and occupation. These sketches will also tell the subject's date of birth, parent's names, wife's and children's names. Usually there is some comment about where they were born.

Where to find these records. Genealogy and historical societies are usually great sources for finding histories, which are invaluable as you discover the roots of your ancestors. Also search libraries and archives.

FAMILY HISTORY

A family history is a book or document that gives facts and information about one or more generations of a family. Published family histories are sometimes referred to as genealogies. They represent a compilation of a family historian's research, in which all the family information they gathered is compiled into a publishable volume. For many family historians and genealogists, publishing a complete history of their family is their ultimate goal. Many of these family historians then sell their work to the general public or to other family members, or perhaps donate it to a local library. A good family history—one that is well researched, well documented, and contains information relevant to a number of families—can achieve widespread distribution.

Make sure you look in the notes section of family and personal histories. As a genealogist, the family and personal histories will provide clear documentation for statements made; footnotes and bibliographies can provide key data if you engage in a process known as citation analysis. This process involves taking a critical look at all notes and bibliographic references with an eye toward analyzing them for evidence of previously unknown record groups, publications, court records, and other papers that might document the life of an ancestor.

Genealogy and historical societies are usually great sources for finding histories, which are invaluable as you discover the roots of your ancestors. Also search libraries and archives. Many can also be found at the Family History Library and local family history centers.

Military Records

Military records kept by the United States government about soldiers and sailors who served their country are a major source of information about individuals. The four major wars of interest to genealogists are the following:

- American Revolution (1775–1783). Approximately one out of every seven Americans fought in the American Revolution.
- Civil War (1861–1865). Approximately one out of every ten Americans fought in the Civil War.
- World War I (1918–1919). Over 4.8 million served in World War I

- World War II (1942–1945). Over 16 million served in World War II.

Because of these statistics, it is worthwhile to investigate the possibility that adult males (age 13 and up) who were alive during these wars may have fought in them. Many smaller wars have occurred in United States history, and there are records of genealogical value for those conflicts, which can be found at the state level. These wars and conflicts include the War of 1812, the Mexican-American War, the Spanish American War, and Plains Indian Wars.

Military records provide basic information about a soldier, including the unit in which he or she served, dates of military service, and sometimes a date of death. There are three types of military records: Service Records, Pension Records, and History Records.

Service Records. Service records cover the time an ancestor was actually in the service. These records almost always include a name; dates of enlistment, attendance, and discharge; beginning and ending rank; and military unit.

Use service records to learn about an ancestor's military service, find the necessary details to locate a pension file or military history; learn place or date of birth (secondary source for this information); learn other details such as residence, occupation, or citizenship; find a physical description; find death or burial information; find medical information; find insights into the ancestor's personality and performance (promotions, AWOL notations, and so on); and see if and where the ancestor was held as a prisoner of war (POW).

Pension Records. Pension records cover the post-service period when your ancestor (or their next-of-kin) may have received benefits. They usually include a name, dates of enlistment and discharge, beginning and ending rank, and military unit.

Use pension records to learn about an ancestor's military service, find the necessary details to locate a military history, learn place or date of birth (secondary source for this information), learn of dates and places of other life events, learn names of spouse or children (and sometimes their birth dates), learn other details (such as residence, occupation, or citizenship), find a physical description, find death or burial information, find medical information, gain insights into ancestor's personality and performance (through his letters, affidavits filed by others who knew him, and so on), learn of ancestor's literacy, see ancestor's signature, and learn more about ancestor's post-war years and life.

Military History. Military histories (often referred to as regimental or unit histories) can add historical background to help you understand the conflict and your ancestor's participation in it. They usually include a roster of those who served in the unit and dates of major engagements.

Use military history records to more fully appreciate the military experience of your ancestor, learn who he or she served with, learn which engagements he or she was involved in, and see what he or she looked like.

NEWSPAPERS

Newspapers can contain a multitude of genealogical information—obituaries; notices of births, marriages, and deaths; legal notices; estate transactions; biographies; military service; and immigration. They provide insight into life as it was at a given moment in time. It answers questions like, What world events shaped their lives? What neighborhood happenings occurred? What fashions were being advertised, and what was their cost? What were the brands of food and other household items used and their cost? What were the forms of entertainment on a Saturday night? What opportunities were there in the want ads? Was there a letter waiting at the post office?

Many current newspapers are online and an increasing number of older newspapers are being digitized or portions transcribed and put on line. If you can't find what you need online you stand a good chance of finding a microfilmed copy that can be obtained through interlibrary loan.

PERIODICALS

Through periodicals, researchers can begin to gain access to data contained in vital records, court records, maps, family bibles and day books, declarations of intention and naturalization certificates, local census and tax lists, church records and cemetery inscriptions, as well as the dozens of unique local items.

Genealogical Society Publications. City, county, regional, and state genealogical societies write and publish journals, newsletters, and quarterlies that focus on the area of interest to the genealogical organization. These periodicals are published monthly, quarterly, and annually and range from a few pages to hundreds of pages. They tend to index, abstract, and transcribe the records of the region where they are published. The types of articles you will find include the following:

- Genealogical sources and resources in specific geographic areas.
- Indexes and abstracts of source materials.
- Ancestor charts and group sheets of members.
- Lists of upcoming seminars significant to family historians.
- Acquisition lists and holding statements of area libraries and archives.
- Names of officers and directors of the organizations who can be used as research contacts.
- Unique and forgotten sources of information.
- Important research tips for the area.
- Such items as genealogies, transcripts and abstracts of local records, probate records, church records, and cemetery records.

Historical Society Publications. Society publications can be a significant aspect of immigrant research. Any local record may be the subject of publication by a local society. Whenever you contact a genealogical or ethnic society, be certain to inquire about their publications. Even when such publications do not identify an immigrant's hometown, they may provide further identification about your immigrant, or may instruct you on additional sources specific to a locality or ethnic group.

City, county, and regional historical society publications document the local geographic area, the activities of organizations and institutions, the lives of the leaders of the community, the impact of major events such as war and depression, and the impact of major trends such as migration and settlement patterns. You will also find indexes and abstracts of records found in the area.

State historical society publications contain articles that chronicle the lives of the rich and famous, unusual scientific or religious movement, or detailing a Civil War regiment.

Ethnic society publications provide an excellent resource of articles that are focused on the ethnic culture (e.g., Historical Society of Germans from Russia). They help trace and discuss ancestry, share sources of data, and common findings across the group.

Society Conference Syllabi. Historical societies hold annual conferences that usually publish a syllabus. These provide insights, tips, and research strategies specific to the area of interest.

Special interest publications focus on groups that have a common experience or shared interest among the group of patriotic, military, and heraldic society publications (for example, the B-26 Marauder Historical Society, United Daughters of the Confederacy, Daughters of the American Revolution, and Daughters of the Utah Pioneers.) They provide data on individuals that participated in the common or shared experience, a rich profile of records available from local to national levels, genealogies, profiles of units and groups, and insights into daily life.

Family publications, also known as surname publications, focus specifically on a family and are full of family group sheets, individual histories, details of family reunions, photographs, documented genealogies, and lists of publications that contain family information. These types of publications include the following:

- Help to set research in the proper historical context.
- Useful information for citation analysis (for example, constructing the widest possible data pool in which to look for ancestors.)

- In-depth information of individuals, communities, and so on to which our ancestor belonged.
- Items such as genealogies, transcripts and abstracts of local records, probate records, church records, and cemetery records.
- Unique and forgotten sources of information.
- Important research tips for the area.
- Indexes and abstracts source materials.
- Help to focus on the articles that will have the greatest value.

PROBATE RECORDS

Probate records (which document the process of passing property, both land and various goods, on to one's heirs) are one of the major types of records used in genealogical research. Heirs may be anybody the testator (the person who made the will) chooses to name, including servants, in-laws, friends, and others. Wills and other papers created during the probate process are often the best possible source to document relationships between family members, particularly parent to child. Persons often identified themselves according to the place (often a town) they came from or were born in.

When a person left a will (referred to as testate), the probate process documents the will's validity and completes the wishes of the deceased by the executor or executrix who was named in the will. If the individual did not leave a will (referred to as intestate), the court used the probate to appoint an administrator or administratrix to decide the distribution of assets to heirs and relationships according to the laws of the jurisdiction.

Probate packets or files may include wills, estate inventories or lists of assets, appointments of executors or administrator, administrations or documentation of the distribution of assets, petitions for guardianship of minor children, lists of heirs, and lists of creditors or accounts of debts.

Probate records can be found at the county courthouse. In some cases, older probate records may have been transferred to archives. You can request probate records from the courts. When requesting the record from the courthouse, make sure you order the complete packet or jacket that holds all the papers.

Societies and libraries will have older probate records for some counties. In addition, the Family History Library in Salt Lake City has filmed many probate records.

Use probate records to find date and place of death, residence, names (and addresses) of descendants, and details to search for land records, and to discover other places where the ancestor may have held property, discover relationships, get a feel for ancestor's economic standing, look for clues about ancestor's feelings toward family members, find clues to the deaths of other family members, sort out adoptions, guardianships and other unclear relationships, learn names of stores and vendors frequented by your ancestor, find your ancestor's signature, find occupation, find citizenship, and find marital status.

LEARN ABOUT THE RECORDS

Throughout my research experiences, I have made it a cardinal rule that before I begin to research any record type, I will take the time to learn about the records, how to research the record, where to find the records, what information is contained in the record, and how I can use the information in my research. It doesn't matter whether it's the first time I have researched the record type or the hundredth time, it is important to me to refresh my knowledge so that I am keen and sharp on what I am searching, so as not to miss important details.

Simply being aware of the various records gives me options of how to connect the generations. No one record has all the answers, but combined they give me the ability to resolve my family's genealogy puzzle through the clues and answers the records offer.

Lesson 4: Where to Find Records

The history of a family over many generations lies buried in different sources and places. Like a good detective, the genealogist must search for the pieces of a family's past in those many sources such as books, documents, and manuscripts. The genealogist must also be patient and imaginative, because the search can take years and involve a string of clues that lead to new sources. The facts—names, dates, events—that a genealogist gathers through the years are like pieces of a puzzle. Gradually those pieces can be fitted together to make a picture of a family, its many members, and its unique history.

PERSONAL EXPERIENCE: INTERWOVEN HISTORICAL AND GENEALOGICAL RESOURCES.

As a beginning genealogist, I had focused much of the research on records available online, in microfilm, and in the local family history center. Naïvely, I thought I had reached most of the available resources that pertained to my family. Then my perception changed with a trip to the roots of my family—Kentucky, North Carolina, Pennsylvania, Tennessee, and Virginia. What started out to be a ten-day trip ended up being a month-long experience of personal and genealogical discovery that literally changed the way I approached ancestral research.

My focus for the trip was to visit areas in which my family lived and to search a few libraries for whatever I could find. Prior to my trip, I thought I had done extensive preparation—I had searched online at the Library of Virginia, spoken with and made arrangements to visit a few county historical societies, and identified where my family lived. I searched my own records to see what information I had and collaborated with fellow family genealogists.

By the end of my trip I had traveled 2,500 miles, taken 24,000 digital images, identified more than 300,000 ancestors from direct and collateral lines, and visited and researched university archives and special collections; public and regional libraries; state, regional, and local historical and ethnic societies; and state, county, and local government agencies.

I had also spoken and counseled extensively with subject matter experts, walked the land of my family, visited the graves and cemeteries of my ancestors, found previously unknown records, and met cousins both of Anglo- and African-American descent.

The result of this experience came about because of interwoven historical and genealogical resources that were dedicated to collection, preservation, and interpretation of artifacts and documents. They included college and university archives and special collections; corporate archives; federal, state, and local government; state, county, local, and ethnic historical societies; and regional and community public libraries

If I learned one thing, it was simply that every record repository had information and resources that would help me learn about and tell the story of my ancestors. I found that each of the organizations had information that was shared by more than one organization; I also found that each had unique and precious elements of my past. Finally, and probably most important, I found a deep appreciation for the resources of individuals who freely gave of their time, expertise, and donations to acquire collections and make them available. I was also grateful to institutions and organizations for their dreams and vision to coordinate, collect, preserve, and manage the history.

For many genealogists, historical societies and university and state libraries are a vast reservoir of information, tools, and experts that will enhance and magnify your research by leaps and bounds.

As a genealogist, I found it necessary to learn as much as I could about the various record repositories and how I could be more productive in accessing available records and resources. I began by asking and answering the following questions:

- What is the role and mission of the societies and libraries?
- What resources do they provide genealogists?
- How can I, as a genealogist, give back to societies and libraries?

Historical Societies

The mission of historical societies is to nurture and promote awareness and appreciation of state, regional, and local history and culture. This is done through the identification, collection, study, and preservation of materials (common, rare, and unique) that include printed, manuscript, map, and photographic collections that are made available to the public, researchers, and genealogists. Societies receive over 75 percent of inquiries from genealogists.

Societies can be private or operated as a government agency. If they are managed through government, they will be required to follow all state government rules, regulations, and statutes.

Many historical societies make these collections available through on-site, online, and inter-library loan resources. Every society is different, but the types of services you will typically see historical societies provide include the following:

- Public lectures
- Seminars
- Conferences
- Consulting services
- Arranging school and general group tours
- Supporting scholarly research
- Maintaining museums of changing, permanent, and traveling exhibitions
- Operating a research library
- Publishing books, magazines, and newsletters

In addition to historical societies, there are other categories of "societies" that can provide a wealth of knowledge and information to the genealogist. Below, I've listed and described some of the most common types of societies that are useful for genealogy research.

Lineage or Hereditary Societies. A lineage society is an organization whose membership is limited to persons who can prove lineal, documented descent from a qualifying ancestor. Hundreds of such organizations exist in America, such as for descendants of those who fought in the American Revolutionary War (Daughters of the American Revolution, DAR), who came across the plains as Mormon Pioneers (Daughters of the Utah Pioneers, DUP), or who arrived on the Mayflower.

Many lineage societies publish books that are of interest to their members and to other researchers. These books are found in most major genealogical libraries and can help you determine if a society might have information about a possible ancestor.

Immigrant and Early Settler Societies. Dozens of societies have been established focusing on specific immigrant groups or early settlers of a particular locality. While these societies have an interest in immigrants, they do not always know where any particular immigrant came from in the old country. Their objectives do not include establishing the immigrant or settler's ancestry, only their descent to current persons. Examples of these societies include the following:

- Society of the Descendants of the Founders of Hartford (Connecticut)—requires the ancestor be living in Hartford by early 1640.
- Order of Descendants of Ancient Planters—those persons who arrived in Virginia before 1616.
- General Society of Mayflower Descendants—descendants of the Mayflower passengers.
- The Order of the Founders and Patriots of America—pre-1657 founders who established families in America, among whose descendants, of the same surname line, were persons who fought for American independence in the Revolutionary War.

Some examples of immigration collections include the following two organizations:

- The Balch Institute for Ethnic Studies at Temple University in Philadelphia transcribes many of the passenger arrival lists of ethnic immigrants.
- The Immigration History Society at the University of Minnesota has collected thousands of ethnic newspapers and other sources dealing with eastern European ethnic groups. Their "Immigration History Research Center" is one of the most significant repositories of research materials for those groups in North America.

European Ancestry Societies. Some lineage societies focus on ancestors who were notable long before the American colonies were established. Therefore, descendants who wish to join need to trace their ancestry back to the immigrant (called the "gateway" ancestor), and then trace that immigrant's ancestry back to the qualifying ancestor in the old country. Usually the qualifying ancestor was part of British royalty or nobility. Examples include the Order of the Crown of Charlemagne in the United States of America (which requires documented descent from that early emperor; this means tracing your ancestry back more than 1,000 years) and the Descendants of the Illegitimate Sons and Daughters of the Kings of Britain.

Nationality or Ethnic Lineage Societies. These are societies that focus on an entire ethnic group. They gather information, teach their members, and publish stories, findings, and sources about that group. A small number of such societies, and actually the oldest such societies in America, are true lineage societies. Membership is limited to those persons who can prove descent from an early settler of a specific ethnic group. Examples include the Dutch in New York, Germans in Pennsylvania, and the Scots-Irish in the Carolinas.

Special Interest Societies. These societies focus on research and archives focusing on specific areas of interest where generally large groups of individuals have interest. For example, the B-26 Marauder Historical Society is the nation's largest organization dedicated to preserving the memory of the accomplishments and importance made by the B-26 Martin Marauder and the nearly 300,000 service personnel during World War II.

GENEALOGICAL SOCIETIES

Genealogical societies exist throughout the United States and Canada in every state or province, most counties, and many major cities. The people in these societies share the same interest you do: individually discovering a heritage. They meet together, usually monthly, to learn from each other about how to trace their ancestry. They recognize that together they have much more knowledge about family history research than they do individually.

UNIVERSITY AND STATE LIBRARY ARCHIVES AND SPECIAL COLLECTIONS

The mission of library archives and special collections is to grow, organize, care for, and manage collections of records that are of local, regional, state, and national interest—many of which date back to the early colonial period. They are responsible for those items that are especially rare and unique in the library's collections, including rare books, broadsides, sheet music, photographic images, and fine art. These collections are made available to researchers from across the country and the world on-site, online, and through inter-library loan. In addition to managing and preserving its collections, the libraries provide the following services:

- Research and reference assistance
- Consulting services
- Administration of numerous federal, state, and local grant programs
- Publication of books, magazines, and newsletters
- Public exhibitions, lectures, and other educational programs

COUNTY, STATE, PROVINCE, REGION, AND LOCAL ONLINE RESOURCES

As a genealogist, some of the most important online resources you have are those that focus on county, state or province, regional, and local levels. For many genealogists, historical societies and university and state libraries are a vast reservoir of information, tools, and experts that will enhance and magnify your research by leaps and bounds.

The online sources provide resources of varying degrees of value, which can include the following:

- **Databases and lists:** Whether it's a list of persons buried in a local cemetery, transcribed census records and family trees, or searchable databases of civil vital records, many state-level resources hold vast collections of data that can easily be searched by the genealogists. Many organizations actively research, transcribe, and publish genealogical information to the web.

- **Links to other databases and resources:** Each organization usually has an extensive understanding of the information available online specific to their charter and will provide links to databases and resources that will help further your research. Links will range from commercial sites like Ancestry.com to hard-to-find resources such as an individual who provides a list of cemetery transcriptions of small town cemetery. By reviewing these links, you will find much of the Internet search already done for you.

- **Resource catalogs:** When the information you seek is not online, it is probably available via microfilm, book, or another hard-copy source. Many libraries and archives have online catalogs that provide you an instant review of what is available at that library or archive. In many cases these materials are available via inter-library loan. When they are not available, then it becomes a matter of deciding whether the organization or library has what you need, asking the librarian to review the desired resource for information you seek, or even planning a fieldtrip.

- **Email address of experts:** Consider the librarians, officers, and volunteers to be experts in their collections and areas of focus. If you are focusing on a particular county, there will be people who know details about the part of the county you seek to review, what materials are located in the bookshelves and vertical files, or who is researching a particular family surname. The librarian knows their collections and where best to find what you seek or where to find what you need in other collections in their region or state. A phone call, email, or personal visit will often yield helpful insight into finding valuable genealogical data.

- **Lists of available resources:** Many websites, particularly those of libraries, will outline and list details of the information that is available in their collection and how to access the information.

- **Research Guides:** Many websites will also include outlines of how to conduct research for their collections, or for local or particular types of records. These research guides provide valuable insights and often list available resources.

STRATEGY FOR SEARCHING SOCIETIES AND LIBRARIES

Societies and libraries collect books, manuscripts, reference files, maps, newspapers, photographs, and all other items of historical value. The following is an outline of steps that are helpful in searching these resources to unlock and find your family's history and genealogy.

Consult handbooks on genealogical research. Handbooks on genealogical research offer instruction, advice, and information useful to both beginning and advanced genealogists. Topics covered by these books include getting started, types of records to consult, research in other states and foreign countries, and record keeping. Of particular value are those reference books that are focused on research in the locale of your interest. Look under the headings such as "Genealogy-Handbooks, Manuals" and other similar headings.

Check genealogy surname card files. This physical or online card file is arranged alphabetically by surname and contains references to births, baptisms, marriages, and deaths. These cards were compiled over the years from newspapers printed before 1850, books, journals, church records, and other sources.

Search family history files and published biographies and genealogies. Family history files contain unpublished notes and charts on lineages specific to the state, region, or locality and are compiled by other genealogists.

Published genealogies are part of the library's book collection and are listed by author, title, and family name in the book catalog. Books giving information on more than one family are cross-referenced under all the important surnames.

Biographical encyclopedias, often published during the nineteenth century to flatter prominent businessmen and politicians, also contain valuable genealogical information.

Check books on state and local history. A wealth of genealogical information is contained in books on state and local history.

Search journals and periodicals. Often bits and pieces of family history can be found in articles in historical and genealogical journals. These are in bound volumes on the library shelves, which are sometimes microfilmed or put online. A name index often appears at the end of each volume. There are thousands of local, county, regional, state, and national periodicals currently published. The task of finding specific geographic and surname data may, at first, appear daunting. The following are several good and reliable sources.

- **Worldcat**—WorldCat is a catalog of the holdings of thousands of libraries worldwide. Many of these libraries have cataloged their periodical holdings, and WorldCat can be searched by family name or geographic location. Other things you can do on WorldCat include the following:
  - Search many libraries at once for an item and then locate it in a library nearby
  - Find books, music, and videos to check out
  - Find research articles and digital items (like audio books) that can be directly viewed or downloaded
  - Link to "Ask a Librarian" and other services at your library
  - Post your review of an item, or contribute factual information about it

- **PERSI**—The Periodical Source Index, or PERSI, is the largest subject index to genealogical and historical periodical articles in the world and is widely recognized as being a vital source for genealogical researchers.

  Although PERSI does not index every name in periodical articles, it is the most comprehensive of the indexes to American genealogical periodicals. Beginning and experienced researchers should make full use of this reference tool. Researchers can use PERSI to locate references to personal names and locality records. If articles of interest are located, the researcher may request a photocopy of them through inter-library loan or obtain a copy for a fee by contacting the Allen County Public Library Foundation (P.O. Box 2270, Fort Wayne, IN 46801-2270) or another library that holds the periodicals of interest. A form is available online for requesting copies of articles.

- **Regional Indexes**—Check to see if the state or region you are focusing on publishes indexes, such as the Virginia Historical Index or the Worcester Area Union List of Serials (WAULS) in Massachusetts.

Trace footnotes and endnotes. Tracing footnote and endnote tracing means using footnotes or endnotes found in books or articles to identify other relevant material. The advantage of using footnotes to locate materials is that they often provide a citation to a specific primary source within a larger collection. Sometimes citations even offer commentary on the cited work. Finally, the use of material in a scholarly work provides a way of judging the usefulness of the material.

Search original source material. Original source collections include books, manuscripts, reference files, maps, newspapers, and photographs on all aspects of history and people. Not all of the collections are indexed or reproduced online. Contact the library or archive for research assistance if you don't find what you are looking for. What follows is a detailed overview of the type of source material you can expect to find in your discovery of societies and libraries, as well as definitions of what these terms mean.

- **Archives.** Archives are usually an unpublished, primary source material that documents the activities of an individual or organization. These unique materials are preserved in an archival setting because the information contained therein has enduring value or because they provide evidence of the role and activities of the individual or organization that created them. Archival materials that document the activities of an individual are often referred to as manuscripts.

- **Archivist.** Archivist is a title that is used to describe a person who may be responsible for the management of archival and manuscript collections. An archivist's job may include activities such as appraising, acquiring, arranging, describing, preserving, and providing access to primary sources. By carrying out these activities, archivists serve to protect the authenticity and context of the materials in their care. An archivist is often the best person to approach for in-depth information about the collections he or she oversees. The terms *archivist* and *curator* are often used interchangeably. Archivists may also have additional descriptors in their titles to explain specific areas of responsibility. For example, the University Archivist is the person who cares for the permanent records of the university. A project archivist has been hired to work in a concentrated subject area or on a specific collection.

- **Finding aids.** Finding aids are tools that assist researchers in locating items in a special collection. A finding aid can be as simple as a listing of folders (often called an inventory or preliminary inventory) or as intricate as a complex document that places special collections materials in context by consolidating information about the collection (such as a history or biographical note and a description of the arrangement of the collection).

- **Manuscripts.** Manuscripts are usually an unpublished, primary source material that documents the activities of an individual. These unique materials are preserved in an archival setting because the information contained therein has enduring value or because they provide evidence of the role and activities of the individual. In modern usage, the term *archives* can also refer to the papers of an individual. *Personal papers* is another term used to describe manuscript material. In the broad sense, a manuscript can refer to any unpublished document. *MSS* is a common abbreviation for *manuscripts*.

- **Primary sources.** Primary sources are usually defined as accounts or artifacts generated by an eyewitness or participant in events. Interpretation and evaluation of these primary sources becomes the basis for historical narrative. Evaluating whether something can be used as a primary source depends on two things: proximity to the source and the questions asked.
  - *Proximity to the source.* Ideally the best type of source material comes from a person or process that is closest in time or proximity to the event, person or place under study. Usually the creator of this type of primary source is an eyewitness who left a record for personal or procedural purposes. Reliability of sources declines as one gets farther away in time and proximity.
  - *Questions asked.* Determining whether a source is a primary source often depends on the questions asked of it by the researcher.
- **Rare books.** Rare books are usually either old or unusual and considered valuable due to unique qualities. A book that is old is not necessarily considered a rare book.
- **Secondary sources.** Secondary sources are completely removed in proximity from the original event, person, or place but seek to provide an interpretation based on primary sources. There is a continuum from primary to secondary sources, and many sources show elements of both.
- **Special collections.** Special collections have characteristics that set them apart from other types of collections in libraries. These special aspects may include the following:

- *Rarity:* books, manuscripts, and other materials that are old, scarce, or unique.
- *Format:* photographs, slides, films, audio recordings, maps, artworks, artifacts, and other objects that need special handling.
- *Comprehensiveness:* accumulation of materials that individually are not unique but collectively make up an important resource because of their relevance to a particular topic or individual.

These characteristics also mean that special collections are not readily replaceable and require a higher level of security and special preservation to insure their survival. In contrast to museum collections assembled for visual display, special collections focus on research as their primary mission. Thus, they complement general research collections and are often located in institutions that house both kinds of collections.

Here are a few more tips on how to further your research using libraries, societies, and archives:

Research other libraries. Become aware of all the resources in the state, region, and local area that might have collections for you to research. By simply asking the society and library reference staff, you will be able to secure a list of resources to consult for your research.

Make your research available to others. Societies and libraries are glad to accept gifts of published books as well as notes and charts relating to research on families from their locale. You can help future researchers by donating copies of your work.

Talk to scholars or other experts. Talking to people who have already done work in your field of interest is another way of locating relevant primary sources. Within their area of specialization, experts are likely to be familiar with a majority of the material written about a given topic as well as the major collections of primary sources that support their research.

As a researcher, you will find many experts on topics of local and regional research. These individuals will help you locate and find material. I have had experiences where local experts have been the key to unlock doors. For example, I was searching in one town for the land of an ancestor. While searching for the property and gravesite, I was referred to a local historian that lived in a remote area. After I found the historian, he took me directly to the property and gravesite, which was little more than a field with stones on edge for the headstones. Upon inviting me back to his home, he answered key questions I had been searching for. He also had several rare books of local history and genealogies that had been out of print for more than seventy-five years that he allowed me to digitally photograph. I couldn't have found any of this precious information without his help.

Another experience I had with experts is also worth sharing here. I made an appointment with a county historical society several weeks ahead of my arrival, and corresponded via email about my research priorities. Upon my arrival, I found that the staff had pulled multiple books they had in their personal library and had the information I was seeking already marked. They had also set out several "family" vertical files on surnames and topics related to my search. This particular society had on duty a member of the society that was knowledgeable about my particular area of the county, who answered my questions and had suggestions of other areas I should research and people with whom I should speak. The society also had a seventeen-page, unpublished, extensively documented historical society research paper on the formation of a specific church and congregation that my ancestors helped form. The efforts of these local experts saved me hours of research and years of searching for information that was only known to the local experts. An expert can also be other professors, historians, or the author of a book or article on a certain topic.

Talk to librarians, curators, and archivists. Most librarians, curators, and archivists are very knowledgeable about the subject areas related to their collections. They often know of similar collections in other institutions or other people doing similar work. They are also the best source for information about materials in their repository that may not be listed in a library catalog, website, or finding aid.

When I Was Fresh Out of Ideas

As a genealogist, I have found that my research success dramatically increased when I realized that it was important for me to learn about how to work with and conduct research in various types of record repositories. During my first few years of research, I didn't think about first the repository, then looking in the catalog, and then finding my desired resource. When I was fresh out of ideas, all it took was one kind librarian to ask me the question, "Have you thought about . . . ?" From that day I have always made it a point to familiarize myself with the repository, its people, and its resources from which I can make a research plan with options.

Lesson 5: How to Search the Internet like a Genealogist

Instead of going to the library, traveling great distances to secure records, or waiting weeks and months to hear from correspondence, researchers can now use the Internet for much of their research. The Internet has opened the possibilities and created the opportunity to have research as close as your desktop. Census images are now online. You can post a query on a message board and begin a dialog with genealogists around the world within hours or instantly share research and photos with a click.

Searching databases is just one part of the research you will do. Some websites provide the following kinds of research information:

- Historical information;
- Records such as census, birth, marriage, and death records;
- Leads to books and other materials available to help with your research;
- Free courses to help you learn fundamental to advance research issues;
- Message boards where you post and view queries to genealogy questions;
- Links to free online forms, guides, publications, calendar conversion tools, translation tools, and many other useful tools that will help organize your research;
- Family trees and histories; and
- Many other useful resources.

I use search engines (such as Google) almost daily to assist in genealogy research. Whether I am conducting a surname search, looking for an address, seeking an answer to a question, or looking for a particular database, Google provides accurate and relevant search results in seconds. The key to making Google productive for your research is knowing how to use the search engine to query for results. In this chapter, I will expand on this topic and provide ideas of how to search the Internet like genealogist.

We like to think that everything found on the Internet is accurate and true. However, you should always verify any genealogy information found online, no matter what site you find the information on. The best way to verify information is to locate and research the source. Many databases include a list of sources, but sometimes you'll come across one that doesn't. In this case, look at dates and the type of information and ask yourself what type of source would provide that information.

A note about search engines: All search engines are not alike. Search engines have different talents and abilities, each searching and cataloging the Internet differently. When results show 850,000 "hits," the search engine will provide a maximum of 200 to 1,000 hits in the search results. Be aware that search engines use robot indexers to search the web for content. When a new website appears, it may be months before a search engine finds and indexes the site. That said, less than 50 percent of the visible Internet has been indexed. "Visible web" refers to the portion of the Internet that search engines can index. The reason for the invisible Internet is that there are incompatible file structures in websites that cannot be indexed by search engines. Invisible pages and specialized or authoritative indexes can only be found at the portal and only searched with a page's built-in search capability. A good example would be RootsWeb.org, where many of the pages are not indexed but can be easily found when using the search function on RootsWeb.org.

Search engines are very sophisticated. If your search is not relevant to what you are looking for, it is most likely an issue with your key word selection. If you find a webpage today, there may be a chance that you won't find it later. This is because a website may change a URL or shut down, which outdates the previous indexes and frustrates your attempts to repeat a search. A webmaster who removes or renames pages often disturbs search engine index's reliability and produce "Page Not Found" messages.

USING KEYWORDS AND CONTROLLED VOCABULARY

A search statement consists of words and punctuation that are entered in the search box of a library catalog, article database, or Internet search engine to find matching records. The simplest search statement is a single word. The first step to creating any search statement is building a list of search terms that describe your research topic as precisely as possible in language that the computer understands. Keywords and controlled vocabulary are two kinds of search terms.

FINDING AND USING KEYWORDS

Brainstorm to select the two or three most meaningful words that describe your research topic. Identify and list broader terms, narrower terms, and synonyms. A good way to select keywords is to write a sentence that describes your research topic and then select the important words to use as keywords.

Example
Research topic: Did Tyrannosaurus Rex have feathers?

Another good way to select keywords is to select words that describe the broad or generic ideas of the topic.

Example
Generic keywords: dinosaurs, birds, evolution.

Tip: You may want to try different keywords if the first keywords you try get unsatisfactory results.

QUALIFY SEARCH PARAMETERS WITH BOOLEAN OPERATORS

Google is not case-sensitive regarding the parameters of your search. A search on the uppercase *SMITH* will generate the same

40 million results as a search on the lowercase *smith*. Boolean operators define the relationships between words or groups of words and are used to broaden or narrow a search. Boolean operators used to qualify search parameters include the following:

- **AND**—Narrow search and retrieve records containing all of the words it separates.
- **OR**—Broaden search and retrieve records containing any of the words it separates. The | can be used instead of "or" (for example, *mouse | mice | rat* is equivalent to *mouse OR mice OR rat*).
- **NOT**—Narrow search and retrieve records that do not contain the term following it.
- **Parenthesis ( )**—Group words or phrases within parentheses when combining Boolean phrases and also to show the order in which relationships should be considered: for example, *(mouse OR mice) and (gene OR pseudogene)*.

Using Boolean Operators in a String. Search queries containing several operators should use the operators in the following order:

( )
NEAR
NOT
AND
OR

To ensure that a search containing different operators performs as you intend, use parentheses: *calder AND (painting NOT (sculpture OR mobiles))*.

Examples of when to use Boolean Operators. Consider using Boolean Opearators as follows:

- **Too many records on your topic.** If you are retrieving too many records on your topic, try adding another search term with the connector *AND*.
- **Too many records on unrelated topic.** If you are retrieving too many records on an unrelated topic, try eliminating a word with the connector *NOT*.

- **Too few records on your topic.** If you are retrieving too few records on your topic, try adding another, related search term with the connector *OR.*

Maximizing Website Searches among Database Record Collections

As you search the web, much of the data you seek will be gathered into websites like Ancestry.com and RootsWeb.com. These websites incorporate their own search engines to help you effectively explore their various database collections and assets. As you enter a website, our instinct is to type in the surname or individual you seek and hope you find a match. Take the time to find and review search query outlines that have been provided to help maximize their collections. Be aware that most websites have aspects of their organization and design that are unique to searching their collections and would not be effective in a Google search. The following are some tips to help you navigate searching websites that provide genealogical data:

1. **Review the contents of the databases.** Throughout the Internet, you will find many websites that promote and offer data collections with the same category headings. If you were to compare the collections side by side, you would find portions of collections that are the same and others that are unique to that website. Sometimes you will find the website does not have any data but merely has a search engine that goes out to other websites and searches their databases.

Whatever the case, it is important to take time to review what makes up the content of the database and where the sources come from so that you can better understand the value of the databases to you—especially if you are getting ready to order a subscription, such as with Ancestry.com. By looking around, you may be able to find exactly what you are looking for on a free site.

2. **Start broad and narrow your search.** Whenever I start my search, I will usually start with a general, broad search. Based on what I receive in my search results, I will then use the search logic

associated with the particular website search engine to narrow my search.

3. Starting with a name. The search engine will first look for an exact name match, followed by common variants, misspellings, and nicknames. For example, a search for *Bill Smith* might return "William Smith," "Wm Smith," "Bill Smith," and "B. Smith."

4. Filling in the blanks. When you are entering the data for your search, you must have at least the last name. The other fields can be blank. You don't have to fill in all the fields of your query.

5. Be careful with abbreviations. Search engines find only exact matches. If you have used abbreviations, retype your search string using alternatives—for example, *PA*, then *Penn.*, then *Pennsylvania*. Avoid abbreviations for descriptive terms (such as *Sgt.*, *Co.*, *Reg't.*, *Dr.*, or *Jr.*). Do not enter titles (like *Dr.*, *Earl*, or *Queen*) or suffixes (*3rd*, *III*, or *Jr.*). Just search for the name without the title and then check the results for the ones you want.

6. Use of quotation marks " ". Quotation marks are used in searches to denote that you are specifically looking for these words in this order. For example, you are looking for John Lee in Florida, then in your query you would enter *John Lee Florida*. Chances are, you would receive all the Johns in Lee County, Florida. By using quotations, you are able to make the search more targeted and avoid a lot of unwanted search results. The query now becomes *"John Lee" Florida*. The search will include results that include both John Lee and Florida.

By using quotation marks, you tell the search engine that you want the words surrounded in quotations to be in exactly the order you have them.

7. Advanced Search. Whenever possible, use the "advanced search" option. The more information you are able to enter in the search criteria, the better results you are likely to receive. For example, by adding a date to your search you will help to narrow the scope. Even if you don't know the exact year, an educated guess in the "date" field will improve your results. The following are a few suggestions of how to improve the advance search:

- Add a middle name, if you know of one
- Add a birth or death year
- Add a birth or death place

8. Focus on specific databases. Every time a website like Ancestry.com adds a collection of data—be it records of Mt. Carmel Cemetery, Adams County Census, or a state's marriage records—the new information is being grouped with similar records. Sometimes the collections are kept as separate databases, and sometimes they are folded in with other data. In either case, you are given the opportunity to search within or among databases. After you complete your initial search, you may feel it prudent to narrow your search by focusing on one of these categories. Usually you can choose by clicking on a radio button or choosing from a dropdown box. The type of category groupings you will see include the following:

- Ancestry Name Search
- Census Records
- Birth, Marriage, and Death Records
- Social Security Death Index
- Surname Indexes
- Passenger and Immigration Records
- Military Records
- Directories and Members Lists
- Family and Local Histories
- Newspapers and Periodicals
- Family and Local Histories
- Photos and Maps
- Court, Land, and Probate Records

9. Advanced search special features. Within the advanced search option in genealogy websites, you will be presented with unique features that will help provide greater control in your search. The following are some of the options you might see:

- **+/- Years.** This feature allows you to control the time frame in years to search for an ancestor. For example, you have entered "John Jones" and you know that he died approximately in 1861. You can enter *1861* and then check the *+/- years* box in increments of 1, 2, 5, or 10 year spreads (the exact increments will vary between sites). If you choose 10 years, the search engine would look for "John Jones" from 1851 to 1871.

- **Exact Matches Only.** You will usually find this feature as a check box. By checking this box, you will only be presented with results that match your criteria exactly.
- **Location.** Some website search engines allow you to narrow your search within location options such as in FamilySearch .org. The location option allows you to focus on a region and narrow in depending upon your knowledge. For example, start with the geographical region, narrow to country, and narrow to state, county, and city.
- **Soundex Search.** It is rare to find a surname spelled the same way as we go back in historical records. Soundex becomes a good tool to search for names that sound like the one you are seeking. For example, by entering *Smith* and using the soundex option, you would receive results that included *Smithe, Smyth,* and *Smythe*.
- **Wildcard search using the asterisk and the question mark.** Many website search engines have incorporated the use of the asterisk (*) and the question mark (?) for queries. These wildcards are effective when you are searching for names with alternate spellings.
- **Asterisk (*):** Usually represents 0 to 6 characters. For example, *john** could return "John," "Johnson," "Johnsen," "Johnathon," or "Johns."

Anytime you use the asterisk, you must have at least three letters as part of your query. For example:

Correct: *Joh**
Incorrect: *Jo**

Searches on www.AltaVista.com are different; this site considers an asterisk (*) to be a wildcard character, so *cemeter** yields *cemetery* and *cemeteries*.

For genealogy searches, the asterisk (*) is one way to

search for a name that has a middle name or initial. An example of one query using the asterisk is *Ora * Jones*. This search sting returns pages containing Ora Jones separated by one or more words:

Ora W. Jones

Ora W Jones

Ora William Jones

Ora; Murphy, Jones

Ora Lee Jones

Ora G. Jones

It will not return results for Ora Jones with no middle name or initial.

To search for web pages containing his name with a middle name or initial and his name with no middle name or initial, use this query: *"Ora * Jones" OR "Ora Jones"*

- **Question mark (?):** Represents looking for alternate spellings where one letter may make the difference. For example, a search for *sm?th* could return "Smith," "Smyth,", "Smoth," and "Smath."

  Your query cannot start with a question mark. For example:

  Correct: *Sm?th*

  Incorrect: *?Smith*

10. Things search engines don't care about. Search engines are not case sensitive. Whether you put in *John Jones* or *john jones*, the results will be the same. Search engines are also not concerned with punctuation.

11. Back versus Refresh. If you complete a search and use your browser's "Back" button to return to the previous page, you may have to use your browser's "Refresh" or "Reset" button to remove all of the previous query data.

12. Check your spelling. If you don't find results using both the first and last name, double-check your spelling and typing accuracy. Try only the surname; maybe the given name is shown incorrectly online. Use alternative spelling variations. Use a Soundex search if available.

If you don't get the desired results using geographic criteria, again double check your spelling and typing accuracy. Use the word processor spellchecker and paste the location in the search engine. Reduce your number of locations and try your search again. Rather than *seattle, wa*, try *WA* by itself.

QUERY EXAMPLES

John Smith
- Finds files that contain the word "John" or the word "Smith" (or both)

"John Smith"
- Finds files where the word "John" immediately precedes "Smith"

"John Smith"~1
- Finds files where the word "John" precedes "Smith" by at most one word
- For example: John Smith, John Q. Smith, John Wesley Smith.
- Use *~2* for a maximum of two words between John and Smith

"Smith John"
- Finds files where Smith immediately precedes John

"Smith John" not state:TN
- Finds all files where Smith precedes John EXCEPT those in the Tennessee directory

"Smith John" not (state:TN and county:Roan)
- Finds all files where Smith precedes John EXCEPT those in the Roan County, Tennessee, directory

    Notice the use of parentheses to indicate that both conditions have to be met to exclude the file. Also notice the colons and the two-letter code for the state

Smith and (lawyer or attorney)
- Finds all files containing the word "Smith" and either the word "lawyer" or "attorney" or both

"john smith" "mary jones"A3

- Use *A* to assign priorities. This search finds files containing John Smith or Mary Jones and assigns a higher priority to Mary Jones. The higher the number, the higher priority.

GOOGLE QUICK REFERENCE FOR GENEALOGISTS

If you want a quick reference for conducting a specific type of Internet search, the following list provides the most common searches to use as a genealogist:

Search Google for ancestral village. Be as specific as possible about location. Be sure to try Google for the country as well—for example, google.ca for Canada and google.sk for Slovakia. See Google Language Tools or Google Translate, which is an application that will let users translate between different languages. Simply type in your text in any language and then hit the "translate" button. Google Language Tools offers translation services between 149 different languages

Search Google Books. Looking for a book? Try searching Google Books at books.google.com. This amazing resource contains thousands of entire digitized books that are in the public domain and selected pages of many books that are still under copyright.

Search in lower case. Google doesn't care, but some search engines are case sensitive: The search terms "ed james" gives results such as the following:

- Edjames
- Ed James
- Ed JAMES
- ED JAMES
- eD jAmEs

Don't sweat the punctuation. Google mostly ignores punctuation (commas, semicolons, periods, and hyphens). Your search for *tampa, florida* (with the comma) and your search for *tampa florida* (without the coma) produce the same results. One exception—Google includes punctuation when searching for an exact phrase using quotation marks.

View "cached" images of pages no longer available. Have you ever received an "Error 404—This Page Not Found" message? Click the "Back" button to return to Google's search results list. Then click on the unavailable item's "cached" link to view Google's archived snapshot of the page. Then copy and paste any useful content to a file on your computer.

Quickly search whole web pages. Stop manually reading through long web pages trying to find where your surnames are hiding. Use your web browser's "Find" function—Crtl+F (Cmd+F for Mac users)—to efficiently search an entire page by jumping from occurrence to occurrence of the term you want to select. PDF documents also have a find feature (binocular icon).

Search for genealogy surname websites. Google can provide a list of genealogy web sites whose titles include your surname by using the "All in Title" phrase *allintitle.genealogy "Isaac Winston"* finds sites with the word *genealogy* in the title (across the website's top band) and in which the name Isaac Winston appears on any page.

Quickly search entire websites. If a promising website lacks a search box on its home page, you don't have to manually search each page for ancestors. Google can look at all the pages of a web site in a single search. For example, a search for *"Maxcey Ewell" site:www.rootsweb.com* will search RootsWeb.com for any page that references Maxcey Ewell. This kind of search only works for the visible web.

Search phrases, not just words. Search for a phrase using quotation marks (" "). Quotation marks are used in searches to denote that you are looking for these words in a specific order. For example, if you are searching for *"ebenezer jones"*, you will have results of pages containing the exact quoted phrase "ebenezer jones".

Search synonyms. Search synonyms using the tilde character (~). For example, *~tombstone* gets the same results as searching *tombstone, gravestone, headstone, monument,* or *marker*.

Other helpful search terms for genealogy research include the following:

- *~genealogy*

- *~index*
- *~biography*
- *~surname*

Search for missing text strings. Searching for *janesville-wi* produces results with any number of missing words, including the following:

- Janesville, WI,
- Janesville, Rock, WI
- Janesville, Rock Co., WI,
- Janesville, Rock County, WI

Target timeframes. Set a date range for your searches to exclude recent events. Example: *1750..1899* produces a list of websites that include years (numbers, actually) between 1750 and 1899, inclusive, but omits sites mentioning only the 1900s.

Search for names—both forward and backward. Search names as phrases; search them "forward" (given name first) and "backward" (surname first) to also find reverse name listings. Example: search "mary sims" and also "sims, mary" to find additional relevant results.

Force Google to include "ignored" words within results. For speed, Google automatically ignores many common words like a, the, he, she, how, when, where, and if. Ordinarily this is okay, but *I* and *will* can be meaningful to genealogists. The solution: enclose *I* in quotes: "arthur darrah I" or precede *will* with a plus sign (+): *dunning +will.*

Search for all likely aliases. Don't stop with a search for "hiram h. goode" He may have been indexed as

- Hiram Goode
- H. Goode
- H. H. Goode
- Hiram Howard Goode
- Howard H. Goode

For common surnames, add geographic or time restrictions. For example, search using this single long search string of all the variations at once: *"ira smith" OR "ira a. smith" OR "i. a. smith" OR "i.aaron smith" OR "aaron smith" chicago 1874..1938*

Use minus sign "-" to exclude unwanted results (same as "NOT"). Exclude irrelevant results that crowd out desired results by using the minus sign (-). For example, adding *-ulysses* to a search for *grant* removes most of the original results. Be careful, though: *-texas* will exclude all sites with the word Texas, including sites that elsewhere contain your ancestors.

Try the marriage "combo plate." Search husband and wife surnames together to increase relevant results. For example, search *"ora jones" AND Dearing*. Understand that *"ora jones"* alone retreives thousands of hits, but by adding *Dearing*, you eliminate 99.7 percent of the initial results; the remaining 0.3 percent of results emphasize the Jones marriage and family that you are specifically searching for.

Use genealogical key words in your searches. Add genealogical terms to your surname search string and search repeatedly with different emphases. The following is a list of suggested key terms to include in your searches:

- Born
- Birth
- Died
- Death
- Married
- Marriage
- Buried
- Burial
- Cemetery
- List index
- Roster
- Genealogy
- Family
- History
- Surname
- Will
- Probate

The order of search terms is important. Search engines apply priority to early words in your search string. Example: *smith tombstone rock New Jersey* produces somewhat different results than *rock tombstone New Jersey smith.*

Don't forget the invisible Internet. Search Engines can see only the "visible Internet." Most web sites that require you to use their own search box (Ancestry.com, FamilySearch.org, and RootsWeb.com, for example) are considered the "invisible Internet" and must be searched individually.

Repeat your searches using variations of your search terms. This is important: Searching the web is hard work; missing ancestors are often inaccessible, buried on page two hundred of your search results. So continuously revise and refine your search terms and re-search (repeat) with the aim of fewer than 200 hits with highly relevant sites in the top ten to twenty results.

Repeat your searches using different search engines. No search engine has a complete index of the Internet. It pays to use more than one Search Engine. In addition to Google, consider trying AltaVista.com, AllTheWeb.com, Ask.com, and Vivismo.com.

Try searching with a meta-search engine. These are like search engines on steroids—they automate the simultaneous search of multiple search engines. The advantage of using a meta-search engine is breadth of results, but the downside is their inability to manage complex searches, because different search engines use different syntax and punctuation rules. Try Yippy.com or DogPile.com.

Find links to a relevant site. Often, a productive site will have other valuable sites linked to it. Use Google to find a list of sites that link to a good site. Example: link:www.danishgenealogy.com.

Target ancestors hiding in (.GED) files. Most genealogy programs for computers export files as GEDCOMs (.ged file format), so ask Google to look for ancestors inside highly relevant .ged files. For example: "Maxcey ewell" filetype:ged.

Let Google find (and translate) foreign language websites. In the Google search page, change your preferences (under the gear menu in the upper right corner) to include non-English language sites among your results and click save preferences. Then go to the Google Translation Tool web site to download a button for your browser that translates thirty-four languages to English at the touch of a button.

Search Google Books to find text from out-of-print books. Google is digitizing millions of books—many of which are no longer copyright protected and can be searched and read online for free at books.google.com. Use a surname and qualifier in the search box. For example, *bennet "king county, Washington"* or *"anna larsen" -genealogy.*

Let Google know your most important search terms. Google often produces results that match some but not all of your search terms. Using a plus sign immediately before your most crucial terms or phrase requires its inclusion in results. For example, a search for *+"benjamin rosenbaum" chicago OR "cook county" Illinois* makes sure Benjamin is in each search result, even if he's in Toledo rather than Chicago.

Don't let an imprecise location spoil a good search. When using a geographic search term, use all forms of the location, because the person who posted your information may have used abbreviations. Example: *"mary norwood" hollywood, "los angeles co" OR "los angeles county" OR "los angeles" AND ca OR cal OR calif OR California.* Remember: if you don't search them all, you don't get all the possible results.

Use Google blog search to meet other researchers. Online blogs can be viewed for free at http://blogsearch.google.com. Use a surname, location limiter, and genealogy synonyms in the search box. Example: *Ewell Charlottesville -genealogy.*

Use Google Image search to find photos, postcards, and maps. A Google search of images indexed from websites can find research gold. Online images can be searched at images.google.com. Use a surname, location, or qualifier like postcard in the search box. Example: *"albemarle county, virginia" lithograph.*

Try a Google Scholar search. Search historical society papers, journal articles, and college theses for ancestors. Scholarly searches are free at scholar.google.com. Use a name and location in the search box. Example: *"ann mullins" golden Colorado.*

Try a Google News archives search. Search historical newspapers for ancestors' announcements, ships, companies, crimes, and events. Limited searches of OCR (computer aided transcriptions) are free at news.google.com/archivesearch. Try a name, location, and date restriction in the search box. Example: *larsen, atlanta, georgia 1860..1890.*

Use Google to define antiquated occupations, diseases, or terminology. Google allows Define (define:) to identify the meanings of words and phrases. Example: search define: ague to discover that Uncle Cyrus died of an illness with fever and shaking chills, or define: lapidary to learn that Cyrus worked as a cutter and polisher of stones into gems.

Use Google's residential phonebook to find possible cousins. Use Google's Residential Phonebook (rphonebook) to locate phone numbers, addresses, maps, and even aerial and street-level photos of homes of the people who share your surname in a geographic area. Example: *rphonebook: walter, ames, iowa, or rphonebook: morrison 89121.*

Use Google's business phonebook to find non-residential contact info. Use Google's Business Phonebook (bphonebook) to locate phone numbers, addresses, maps, and even aerial and street-level photos of businesses that relate to your ancestors in a geographic area. Example: *bphonebook: baptist, boise, idaho.*

Use Google Maps' address location and driving directions. Enter a complete address (like 3760 n central st miami fl) into www.Maps.Google.com to get a detailed map (including a high resolution satellite option). Then, in the search terms field, add the phrase "to 3413 nevada ave madison wi" to get detailed driving directions. This type of search is great for locating cemeteries.

Use Google Street View to get snapshots of ancestral homes. As you may know, Google's camera-equipped cars are circling the United States and western Europe, taking continuous 360-degree photos of neighborhoods. Use www.Maps.Google.com to locate an address, then click Street View to call up the photo image of the home.

Let Google Alerts search while you sleep. Alerts are a neat service. Google Alerts (www.Google.com/alerts) is an automated, online tool that lets you build complex Google searches and run them continuously to look for new additions to the Internet. You are periodically alerted by email of new web info about your favorite sports team or your great-aunt.

Try Google video search to find tutorials, travelogues, and family stories. Use video.google.com to search for short videos of interest.

Setting up Advanced Searches. The following is a series of pre-formatted searches that offer new ways to research your family. Let's start with an example for a particular individual. His family information is listed here:

Randy Johnson
> Father: Richard Johnson
> Mother: Amy Bradshaw
> Spouse: Sandy Green
> Place of birth: Nashville, Tennessee
> Place of death: Kansas City, Kansas

The searches (below) are shown in the order that will often provide the best search results. Each of the searches checks for the terms genealogy and ancestry, along with similar terms, in an attempt to focus on genealogy websites. Also, each search will pick up websites that might use the common misspelling of genealogy: *geneology*.

Search for Randy Johnson with Spouse's Names. Often, searching for the spouse's names along with the primary person's names is the best way to look for an ancestor. This is because a spouse's name is more likely to be known than, for example, a mother's maiden name. So you are more likely to have good search results than with other searches.

1. This search uses the three name formats for Randy Johnson with the spouse's first and last name:
   - *"Randy Johnson" OR "Randy * Johnson" OR "Johnson, Randy" "Sandy Green" -genealogy OR -ancestry*

2. This search uses the three name formats for Randy Johnson with the spouse's first name, middle name or initial, and last name:

- *"Randy Johnson" OR "Randy * Johnson" OR "Johnson, Randy" "Sandy * Green" -genealogy OR -ancestry*

3. This search uses the three name formats for Randy Johnson with the spouse's last name, followed by a comma and the spouse's first name:

- *"Randy Johnson" OR "Randy * Johnson" OR "Johnson, Randy" "Green, Sandy" -genealogy OR -ancestry*

Search for Randy Johnson with Father's First and Last Names. Searching with the parents' names could pick up websites that have information about siblings of your ancestor and their parents. This would be the case if someone had already researched a sibling's ancestry but was, for some reason, unaware of your ancestor. Searching for the father's names along with the primary person's names might be useful, because fathers' names are more likely to be recorded in older records than mothers' names. In turn then, fathers' names are more likely to be found on websites.

1. This search uses the three name formats for Randy Johnson with the father's first and last name:

- *"Randy Johnson" OR "Randy * Johnson" OR "Johnson, Randy" "Richard Johnson" -genealogy OR -ancestry*

2. This search uses the three name formats for Randy Johnson with the father's first name, middle name or initial, and last name:

- *"Randy Johnson" OR "Randy * Johnson" OR "Johnson, Randy" "Richard Johnson" -genealogy OR -ancestry*

3. This search uses the three name formats for Randy Johnson with the father's first name, middle name or initial, and last name:

- *"Randy Johnson" OR "Randy * Johnson" OR "Johnson, Randy" "Richard * Johnson" -genealogy OR -ancestry*

Search for Randy Johnson with Mother's Names. Searching for the mother's names along with the primary person's names is not the best possible search, but it might be worth a try if you are unable to find your ancestor by searching with other names.

1. This search uses the three name formats for Randy Johnson with the mother's first and last name:
   - *"Randy Johnson" OR "Randy * Johnson" OR "Johnson, Randy" "Amy Bradshaw" -genealogy OR -ancestry*

2. This search uses the three name formats for Randy Johnson with the mother's first name, middle name or initial, and last name:
   - *"Randy Johnson" OR "Randy * Johnson" OR "Johnson, Randy" "Amy * Bradshaw" -genealogy OR -ancestry*

3. This search uses the three name formats for Randy Johnson with the mother's last name, followed by a comma and the mother's first name:
   - *"Randy Johnson" OR "Randy * Johnson" OR "Johnson, Randy" "Bradshaw, Amy " -genealogy OR -ancestry*

Search for First and Last Names of Randy Johnson and No Other Names.

1. First and Last Names with "Genealogy." This search uses the primary person's first and last names and checks for the terms genealogy and ancestry, along with similar terms, in an attempt to focus on genealogy websites.
   - *"Randy Johnson" OR "Randy * Johnson" OR "Johnson, Randy" -genealogy OR -ancestry*

2. First and Last Names with Locations. If you are getting too many results, you might want to try adding the place of birth or death to the search. This might, however, cause you to overlook websites that have your ancestor information, but with no place of birth or death given. Nevertheless, this is a way to reduce the search results to a more manageable number. If you do not have too many results at this point, you can skip these searches.
   - *"Randy Johnson" OR "Randy * Johnson" OR "Johnson, Randy" -genealogy OR -ancestry Tennessee OR +TN*

Search for Johnson Websites.

1. This first search will look for websites related to the name Johnson when the name appears in the title of the website
   - *allintitle: Johnson -genealogy OR -ancestry*

2. This second search will look for websites related to the name Johnson when the name appears anywhere in the website. This is a much broader search than the one above. Use this search if you found few websites in the previous search. If you think the name you're searching is an uncommon name, you might have useful search results with the search below. On the other hand, if it is a common name, you will most likely have an overwhelming number of results. If that is the case, you are probably better off searching on first and last names for the primary person along with the first and last names of the father, mother, and spouse.
   - *Johnson -genealogy OR -ancestry*

MAJOR DATABASES ARE AS CLOSE AS YOUR LIBRARY CARD

Many libraries also offer remote access to their various electronic offerings, such as Ancestry.com and HeritageQuest Online.

"Remote access" is a process in which you can stay at home, at school, or at any other location of your choice, use a computer with an Internet connection, and connect to the library's website. Once logged in and verified, you can access databases that the library offers. In effect, the library's website works as a "gateway." It verifies you as a library patron and tells the various subscriptions that you are a patron of that library. You can then access exactly the same screens of information from home that you would see if you were seated in the library. You can also print the same information to your own printer.

Lesson 6: Field Research Is Required

This is where the computer screen ends and shoes hit the street. It doesn't take long to realize there comes a point when computers reach the limits of their capabilities in genealogy research. If someone hasn't digitized, abstracted, or electronically captured an image and put it on the Internet, put it on a CD, or sent it to you in an email, you are going to have to conduct field research, and you will need to leave the house.

It has been my experience that most of the documentation I need doesn't exist on the Internet, and of course, that is changing daily. I need to get out and spend time in libraries and archives at the local, state, and national level.

When I conduct field research, I most often use genealogical and historical societies and local and university libraries and archives. Most of the documentation you'll need is not on the Internet, but at libraries and archives. State and local libraries have genealogy guides, local history books, and newspaper archives that are unavailable anywhere else.

To my delight and amazement, I have found books, records, and documents, from the late and early 1900s that helped to clear up and extend our family history.

As I visited the land of my family and saw firsthand what they may have experienced, I understood better why they may have made decisions to live one place versus another. Field research helps me build a mental picture that brings clarity to research that a computer screen can't and extends the research I'm able to do online.

I'd like to share a few experiences that provide insight into the value of field research and planning.

JOHN LEE IN KNOXVILLE, TENNESSEE

It was 9:00 a.m. on a Sunday in Knoxville, Tennessee. I had driven just under five hundred miles from Washington, DC, the day before in order to meet John, a distant cousin. We were both descendents of Permitt Lee, who had lived in the 1700s. I descended through his daughter Sarah, and John descended through his son Sam. We had corresponded over the previous three months and agreed to meet.

Upon meeting each other, I presented John with a binder of all the research I had on the Lee family, and John provided his research on the Lee's that stayed in the Knoxville area. Following a few minutes of discussion, we spent the next several hours touring the area, learning more about the Lee family's presence in the area then and now. The first stop was a street named Sam Lee. As we drove around the area, we saw that many of the mailboxes had the Lee name on them. We viewed a small cemetery behind a very simplistic white church. In the cemetery, John showed me family headstones. He also indicated that almost all of the persons in the graveyard were family members who had married into the Lee family. When Permitt left Knoxville, several of his sons stayed in Knoxville and had posterity spanning two hundred years of history in Knoxville.

We took photos of some of the gravestones. I felt the need to see if we could locate a plot map for the cemetery showing who was buried where. Where to begin? There were a few cars next to the church, so we started there. We went into the church, followed the fresh smell of brewed coffee, and found the pastor and others in a prayer meeting. I interrupted the meeting and learned that the church was no longer involved with the cemetery but they did give us directions to the home of the cemetery sexton and caretaker.

We drove about a mile from the church to Coon Lane and found the caretaker of the cemetery. He allowed us to photograph the plot map, which was little more than a paper with hand-drawn squares and names within the squares. Upon returning to the cemetery,

I was able to use the map to find family graves and identify graves where there was no headstone. With the knowledge that many of those who were buried in the cemetery had intermarried with the Lee family, I chose to take pictures of all headstones and later use census records to help tie family connections. John and I spent the next two hours seeing the land and exploring the area.

As the day progressed, we visited lands once owned by Permitt Lee and discussed family history and hearsay. As I left, John provided me with what would later become an important clue in searching Permitt Lee—namely that his grandmother had told him that she had always been told that the Lees were from Shropshire, England.

Lessons learned:

• Cemetery plot maps are key to understanding who is buried where.

Otis, Kansas

Following the passing of my stepfather, Mel Wagner, I desired to learn more about his family and lineage. It took six months to locate a daughter from a previous marriage. She shared with me that she had heard that an "Aunt Katie" somewhere in Kansas had records of the family, but she wasn't sure how to locate her.

With another three months of searching, I was finally able to locate her and set up a telephone interview. In the telephone interview, Aunt Katie shared with me that she was living in a nursing home, that she was in her late eighties and the last living survivor of her generation, and that her son had the record she had created about the family. I made contact with the son and other family members to discuss the records and see if I could get copies, which were promised several times in a nine-month period but never sent. After my last call with one of the Wagner family members, I felt the need to travel to Kansas and see if I could secure the records. At this point, I didn't even know what the records were, what they contained, or even their actual value as a genealogy record. It was a most unusual feeling, similar to when I have left home and know that I forgot something and needed to go back. I knew from experience that when those feelings come, I needed to act now and make arrangements to visit Kansas within that very month.

Of all Mel's family members I had spoken with, his cousin Dwight had been the only one who had been willing to help me learn more about the family. I made travel arrangements and flew into Wichita, Kansas, followed by a three-hour drive to Rush County to meet with Dwight at 10:00 a.m that Saturday. Upon arrival, I was greeted by Mary, Dwight's wife, who told me that her husband had an emergency and needed to help their son fix his car.

For the next five hours, Mary shared with me some of the family history work. We ate fresh-baked cookies and watched TV. I began to wonder whether I had done the right thing by coming to Kansas. About 4:00 p.m., Dwight came home and offered to show me the family homestead in Otis, Kansas—population just under four hundred people, settled by Germans from Russia in the late 1800s.

When we arrived in Otis, we went to the cemetery. It was a very simple cemetery surrounded by wheat fields that seemed to roll on for miles. Overhead you could hear hundreds of geese honking as they made their way to their winter homes. We got out of the car and began to find family members' gravesites. Dwight shared with me an experience he had in the early 1980s when he was feeling very depressed and lonely. He sought professional counseling, at which time he was given direction to resolve feelings of loss that were not resolved since he was a boy. The suggestion he received was to go to the gravesite of his grandfather and father and speak out his heart. Just as he reached that point, there was break in his voice and tear from his eye. Then I felt a warm presence, as if we had others in our presence that we could not see. I looked at Dwight and asked, "What are you feeling right now?" His response was, "My family, they are here with us." The family was there. The purpose of why I came was very clear; I knew I had done the right thing by coming to Kansas. I knew that I would leave with the record.

Upon leaving the Otis Lutheran Cemetery, Dwight took me to tour the fields the family had farmed for 150 years. After that was scheduled a first-time meeting with Aunt Katie and her son at a restaurant in a neighboring town. Upon greeting Aunt Katie, I received the warmest hug, as if I were her own flesh and blood. Her son, courteous at best, wasn't much warmer than a Kansas blizzard. During dinner, Aunt Katie talked about Mel, her family, and roots of generations past. Several times during the dinner, the son suggested that it was getting late and he needed to return Aunt Katie to her home.

My chance to see the record was slipping away. There wasn't going to be a "right" time to ask, so I reached out and gently held Aunt Katie's hand and said, "It's been wonderful to meet you and learn about the family. Would you be willing to show me the record about the family you have prepared?" Just as I finished, Aunt Katie's son started to speak up at which point, she replied, "Yes, it's at my son's home. Let's go there now." Her son just gave me a look that let me know he wasn't happy.

At the home, I was allowed to view the record I had heard about. It was a simple, spiral-bound notebook that a student would use in school. It contained a hand-written record of each family and family members, including names, birth dates, death dates, and notes about family members. It was a labor of love. Katie told me that she had spent many hours searching out gravestones and making calls to put the record together. In addition, Aunt Katie showed me five scrapbooks she had kept about her family during her life.

I was overwhelmed with the magnitude of what was before me—a family record that might all be thrown away at her death. It was in my hands. I then looked Aunt Katie in the eye and asked if I could be permitted to copy the record before I returned home. She responded by asking, "Why do you want the record? You are not a member of our family."

I thought for moment, then responded, "Aunt Katie, Mel is a kind and gentle man. He is the type of father I wish I had growing up. He played an important role in the life of my mother and made a difference in my life."

She smiled and said, "Welcome to the family. We are glad you came. We are glad that we got to know you. You can copy the record." Her son spoke up immediately and said, "No, you are not getting the record."

Aunt Katie, spoke to her son directly and firmly. "Yes, he is going to get the record. And if you want to stay in my will, you will let him have the record." Her son looked at me and said curtly, "There's a Safeway around the corner. They have a copier. Let's go now."

It was 9:30 p.m. The store closed at 10:00 p.m. The copier was out of toner and it only took dimes. During my copying, the son made it clear that this was the only chance I would have to copy the record, because the very next day he was going to have power of attorney with his mom and would not allow any further information to be given. At 10:02, 150 pages later, the copying was complete. The record contained 500 names and has been the foundation for linking Mel's family back nine generations to Russia and Germany.

Lessons learned:

- Field research is required.
- If one member of the family won't help, find family who will.
- When prompted to search or act on a family line, do it.

ARIZONA WAR MEMORIAL

During a family trip to visit Hawaii, we took the opportunity to visit the Arizona Memorial. We learned from others that it would be wise to start early if we were going to beat the crowds to the Memorial. We arrived at 8:30 and were able to get tickets for the 9:45 a.m. program. During our hour wait we took the opportunity to review the many exhibits throughout the courtyard. The highlight of the wait was listening to a volunteer who had been at Pearl Harbor. He told us of his experience that morning of the attack and what it was like to have been there. During the attack, he had been part of the Island defense. He mentioned that the very day before the attack, his outfit along with several other groups, had conducted anti-aircraft drills. When the drills were over, they put the guns away. If only the Japanese had come the day before. He brought to life the experience of Pearl Harbor and the hours shortly after the attack.

Visiting the memorial was a somber experience. At the start of the show, we watched a twenty-minute movie that set the stage for the attack and highlighted the details of the attack in film. Following the film, our group climbed aboard a boat that took us out to the Memorial, where we spent fifteen minutes. Over 1,100 men were entombed within the Arizona. On the list of names of persons killed on the Arizona, we found the name A.A. Ewell. My first thoughts were that it was not a member of our family.

Upon returning home, my son continued to inquire whether A. A. Ewell was related. As a research exercise, I suggested that the two of us research exactly who he was. We researched census and military records and consulted other genealogists. Yes, A. A. Ewell was a relative—in fact, his was a branch of the family for which we were not able to find connections. One clue on a wall was the link to a missing branch.

Nebraska and Kansas Trip Number Two

On an earlier field research trip, I had come to Kansas in search of a record that had been prepared by my stepfather's aunt. This trip was scheduled for Nebraska and Kansas to expand on the information and research I had done during my previous trip. I had spent two months setting up appointments and learning about where I could expand my research.

My first stop was Lincoln, Nebraska, to visit with the Germans from a Russian society. While there, I was introduced to an extensive library of research—compiled by members of the society since its founding—that is only accessible by visiting the library in person. With the aid of the librarian, I was able to find documented research that greatly expanded my own research. I was also able to receive recommendations of other genealogists that I could collaborate with. Prior to coming to the society headquarters, I had searched their website extensively and made contact with others, but coming to Nebraska revealed that there's nothing like doing research in person.

That night, I drove several hundred miles to Russell, Kansas, to be in position to have a full day of work achieving the other goals I had for Nebraska and Kansas.

On Saturday morning, my first priority was to go to Otis, Kansas, and film the gravestones of the Methodist and Lutheran cemeteries. In my research, I learned that sixteen families had immigrated from Russia, all of which were related to each other. As I reviewed the family names in the Lutheran Cemetery, 85 percent of the names were related to original immigrants. Only 25 percent of the Methodist cemetery were related to the surnames. I spent about six hours filming the gravestones.

Later that day I was scheduled to meet the Schweins from Ness County, learning about my stepfather's mother's side of the family and learned the history of the family; where they farmed, lived, went to church; and where they were buried. This trip was well planned. From the information I found, I was able to extend and expand my research, saving hundreds of hours of work.

Lessons learned:

- Return to the original source, place, or person only after you've had a chance to understand what you found the first time.
- Society websites only post a small portion of available resources.

Whether you are planning a half-day, day, week, or month-long genealogy research trip, care and preparation in your planning will enrich and enhance your opportunities to successfully prioritize and accomplish your goals.

ORGANIZE YOUR RESEARCH

Before you travel ten or even hundreds of miles to find the library or archive in the hometown of your ancestors, make sure the records you seek aren't as close as your computer or down the street at your local library.

I had planned one research trip to New England and had extensively researched the various libraries and record repositories to find what I was looking for. One of my stops was to the regional library. I spent half a day looking through their microfilmed church records. When I arrived home, I learned that the records I sought could be viewed on microfilm from the local LDS family history center or acquired by interlibrary loan.

Searching for family records in your ancestor's origins should only be undertaken after you are sure you cannot acquire the records through readily accessible means. You won't want to spend hours and hours in an old church or archive and find out later that the records you needed were just minutes away. Try to identify which records, books, and histories have not been microfilmed or are not open for interlibrary loan.

Okay, you have done your homework and confirmed that you want or need to conduct field research. Now what?

Review your records before you go on your trip. It's important to go over your records very carefully. Review every printout, photocopy, note, and Internet record. Know what you have and what you don't have, and make a to-do list of what to find. The basic genealogical advice is to work from what you know to what you don't know. Please do not take your entire notebook; rather, take key notes that will aide in your search during the trip. If you are bringing your laptop, you may already have all the details electronically.

Remember there are records available in the United States (such as parish records at the Family History Library in Salt Lake City, Utah). Concentrate on what's not available here.

What kind of records can't be found at home? It's been mentioned several times to focus on those records you can't find in your homeland. The following is a good example of what to look for. A fellow genealogist had been hunting for a particular ancestor for twenty-eight years. All he knew about the person is that he might have worked aboard ships as a young man. Prior to his trip, he became aware of a Mariner Library in that ancestor's country. While at the library, he found a letter written in the hand of the ancestor in what was known as the Marine Board correspondence. He also found meal lists from the 1850s and myriad other documents that related to his family. This is the type of information you won't find in microfilm or online. It takes visiting the ancestral lands to accomplish such research.

Questions to ask that can yield treasures. Remember you're conducting this research because you're not able to acquire these records from home. Make sure you ask your libraries, archivists, and clerks questions such as the following:

- What indexes or collections are unique to your facility?
- Do you have card files, newspapers, original records, computer databases, networks, or compact discs that can only be searched at your repository?
- Have your records been microfilmed? If yes, where else are they located?
- Are any of your collections accessible online?
- Does your collection have records such as church records that have not been microfilmed?
- Do you have records from (time period)? If not, do you know where can I find them? Note that many countries are consolidating rare records to a common depository.

Determine what resources are available in that area. Before you start your trip, do research to determine the places that have information or materials you can use. Resources can include libraries, archives, genealogical societies, historical societies, courthouses, vital record offices, churches, funeral homes, chambers of commerce, cemeteries, schools, and fraternal organizations.

Don't just concentrate on libraries, courthouses, and cemeteries. Frequently, genealogists ignore regional archives or regional libraries that may contain useful records.

Determine what type of information you seek. Know what you are looking for and what you need. Do your homework before leaving so you know where you want to go and what to look at when you get there.

I like to begin by writing down questions to the answers I am looking for. This gives me a start to my research plan. For example:

- Who are the great-grandparents?
- What was the name of my dad's brother who died as an infant?
- Where is the house my mom grew up in?

On one of my business trips to the New York City area, I made arrangements to take a few days of vacation and conduct research in the Jersey City, New Jersey, area concerning my stepfather's line. Prior to this trip, I prepared extensively so that my short time in New Jersey would be most useful. I researched and located the available resources in the city and county. I made notes about my family and printed off all the information I had about the family from my genealogy database program. I asked myself questions about what I wanted to find out about the family and made a list of the types of information I wanted to locate, the possible types of records that might satisfy the needs, and where I might find the records. Then I listed, by location, the people and record types I wanted to find. For example, if I was going to the courthouse, I would have a list of each individual and each of the types of records I would hope to find there for each person (birth, marriage, and death records; property tax records; wills; and so on).

I contacted each resource, discussed my needs, and confirmed the types of records that were available, the hours of operation, key persons to contact, any special requirements for viewing or acquiring records, the availability of copy machines and if there were any associated costs, and whether there were fees to enter the facility if any. I also asked about what types of personal documents they had to prove lineage (if needed), the availability of people to help me, guidelines for using cameras, types of facilities to do research in, opportunity to do the research online versus in person, and if I needed to make a special appointment to meet with key people.

Be specific in your inquiries. For example, when I contacted the local Catholic Cemetery, I wanted to know if they had sexton records on site and how they were organized and whether I could get access to the records. When I contacted the local library and genealogical society, I inquired about the records they had and who in the organization might know the most about records I wanted to research, how to reach the person, and when he might be able to meet with him or her. Where appropriate, I sent key contacts a detailed summary of information I had and clearly outlined the information I was seeking. This gave the person a few days or weeks to begin preparing for my arrival.

Conducting research prior to my trip helps me become more focused on goals and better utilizes my limited time. If you aren't well prepared, you could end up running around unnecessarily, looking for things in the wrong place. I learned early on that if I didn't prepare for a trip, I could spend precious hours chasing records that may or may not exist.

Make advance contact—establish a rapport. Once you have identified the available resources, make the effort to contact each source directly by mail, telephone, or email. You will save yourself many, many hours by making advance contacts.

When you make these personal contacts in advance, introduce yourself and explain that you are conducting genealogy research. Let them know what you are seeking, and try to establish a rapport. You are making new friends, and they can open doors for you while you are on-site and smooth your way.

Once, a person I'd contacted in advance helped me find the curator to a local museum that was only open a few hours a week from whom I made special arrangements to have a private opening. This was done on a moment's notice, a task that would have taken me hours in an unfamiliar town.

Whenever possible, let people know you are coming and when. Of all the hints I can provide about traveling and doing on-site research, this may be the most important. Let people know you're coming and when. Make sure the people you need to see will be there. Based on my needs, I have been willing to rearrange my schedule to be at a library when the prime resource would be there. Don't leave this to chance. Remember, you have come a long way. Don't arrive at the church only to find that Wednesday was the archivist's day off or that there was a local holiday for which all public facilities were closed.

Don't forget to confirm your appointment or even simply give a courtesy call to let them know you are excited to come. I have had the local contact with whom I was going to meet have many of the records and books I needed pulled from the shelves, all ready for me to review. At the request of my key contact, unbeknownst to me, I have had persons travel many miles to visit with me because they were an expert on my family line.

If your schedule changes and you can't make the agreed-upon time, be courteous—call and let them know so they can reschedule with you.

Make sure they have your contact information—email, cell phone number, and so on—so they can get hold of you should their circumstances change or they need to clarify your research needs.

Know the times of operation. Remember to contact county courthouses, libraries, and other record repositories you plan to visit to determine their office hours. There's nothing more frustrating than getting to a destination and finding it closed for whatever reason.

Be patient when requesting records. If you are planning to receive specific records before you leave for your trip, give yourself at least a four-month window. Why? Many libraries and archives have more requests than staff to manage them. Sometimes it will take several weeks for the staff to even begin research, let alone send you the requested information.

Planning to visit the library or archive. Check to see if the library has a website. Most library websites provide the basic information associated with hours of operation.

Larger libraries, like the Library of Virginia, and state or country archives have an online catalog. Search the catalog before you go. I have usually been able to locate specific books, microfilm, papers, photographs, and so on that will be available for my specific research. Make sure you print out the details from your catalog search.

Check out the Library of Congress Card Catalog to determine what books have been published about the county or area you're planning to visit so that you can look them up in the local library you'll be visiting.

Write to or email the libraries that don't have online information to find out about their genealogical collection, location such as floor or level, building, and hours of operation. Some collections in libraries can only be seen at specific times or may have special restrictions.

I have also found it helpful to call the library and talk with a librarian to see if there are staff researchers that can help if I have questions. Learn about the expertise of the staff. In some cases, I have planned to visit a library when the librarian with the expertise I needed was going to be working.

There may be local researchers who are available as volunteers and for hire who know the library and are willing to work with you to quickly get information you seek.

Make sure you make time to concentrate on using indexes, manuscript collections, unpublished records, rare books, photographs, and sources unique to the library or archives where you are researching before you get to the more distributed information that other facilities will have.

If the library doesn't seem to have what you are looking for, make sure you ask the library for recommendations of where to go.

Also be aware of local traditions. One genealogist tells of an experience when they visited archives located in Glasgow, Scotland. When the genealogist arrived at the archives at the prearranged time, the primary archivist left for her daily two-hour tea and lunch break. The supporting staff was unable to assist the genealogist. Upon the archivist's return, she was able to locate in a matter of minutes records of local cemeteries that the genealogist had been told by the staff did not exist.

Where is the best place to get information? As you start uncovering where to find the records, you may find out that the same records are available in different locations. Make sure you ask the cost of acquiring such records. In a recent trip, I found that a marriage record from the early 1800s would have cost me $10.00 at a university library. The same information was available at the state archive for the cost of a photocopy.

Family History Library, Salt Lake City, Utah. Anyone who has done research in Salt Lake City at the Family History Library will find foreign record offices quite a bit different. You won't be looking at original documents, but you can go and take as many films as you want out of the cases, copy anything you like yourself and return the films. You can cover a lot of territory in a short span of days, especially since it is open from 8:00 a.m. to 5:00 p.m. Mondays and 8:00 a.m. to 9:00 p.m. Tuesday–Saturday (closed some holidays). Groups of people come to Salt Lake from around the world to do research because so many records have been gathered in one place. It is so much more efficient than running around to different archives in their native countries. If you decide that you want to go to Salt Lake City, make sure you check out the online catalog to help you find exactly what you are looking for before you come. The following is the contact information for the library:

Family History Library
35 North West Temple Street
Salt Lake City, Utah, 84150-3400
Public phone number: (801)-240-2584 or (866)-406-1830
FAX: 801-240-3718
Email: fhl@ldsfs.net
Website: www.FamilySearch.org

Planning for an Extended Research Trip

The 50-50 Rule. The best counsel anyone gave me about planning a genealogy trip was: "Plan 50 percent of your trip before you go. Plan the other 50 percent when you get there."

It's important to know where you will be each day of your trip, but don't plan it so tightly that you can't take advantage of opportunities to do things that interest you. If you are going to be doing research in libraries and archives while on your trip, a rule of thumb that many genealogists have stated was to allow one day of research for every three days of your trip.

Don't forget to stop and smell the flowers, even if they're in a churchyard! See, hear, breathe, and smell the place. Maybe you won't get to take in the concert at the local cathedral, but maybe you can worship in your ancestral church (and walk the cemetery after the services), walk the docks, hike the mountains, eat with locals, and watch the sun rise and set. Try to see the country through the eyes of your ancestors.

It's not uncommon for many to have ancestors who come from

several countries. If this is your first genealogy trip, you will have a tendency to want to visit every country and place related to your ancestors. Simply said, *don't!* Narrow your focus. Based on my own experience I would recommend the following:

If your vacation is one or two weeks, focus on one country. If it is three or more weeks, focus on two countries maximum.

If this is your once-in-a-lifetime trip, I would still recommend spending more time in fewer places rather than pushing your schedule to the brink of exhaustion. You will significantly increase your chances of achieving your genealogy goals and having a great experience.

Setting realistic goals for your genealogy research trip. If you are going to spend a half-day traveling across town to interview a family member, a full day traveling to a cemetery two hundred miles away to take pictures of family headstones, or several weeks abroad searching your family roots, having clearly defined goals will help you focus on desired outcomes for your research. Being able to state your goals will require research, preparation, and prioritization.

I had been asked by a fellow genealogist to provide a little assistance in helping them for a genealogy trip abroad. When I asked what their goals were for the trip, they replied with one goal, "We want to visit the village where our family lived in Wales."

For the next couple of hours, we spend time taking inventory of what they knew, what they wanted to know, and what else they might want to do while in Wales. We discussed questions such as the following:

1. Where did the family live in Wales? When?
2. What do you know about
   - Wales?
   - The region where your family lived?
   - The village where your family lived?
3. When did the family come to America?
4. Who in the family came to America?
5. When and where were they born?
6. Where and when did family members die?

7. Did they leave any family in Wales?

8. What did the father do for a living?

9. What was the religion of the family?

10. What brought the family to America?

11. Where were the parents married?

12. What ship did they come on and from what port?

13. What do you wish to know about your family?

The couple pulled out family histories, family group sheets, and other documents that would help answer the questions. We did an Internet search on Wales and related topics. When we were done, we had a few more ideas of what they might like to do on their trip. For example, together we created the following list of goals for their trip to Wales:

- Visit the city of Swansea in Wales.
- Visit the church where our family attended church.
- Find where members of our family are buried.
- Learn about the history of Swansea.
- Find out if the family had other children or family that stayed in Wales.
- Find out who the parents and family of the wife were.
- Learn about coal mining in Swansea and the area.
- Learn about the culture in Swansea in the 1840s.
- Learn what would have caused family to leave Wales.
- Learn about common foods of Wales and Swansea.
- Take a tour of Glamorganshire.

Of course, like any good genealogy researcher, they found that one answer often leads to several more questions that needed answers before they could finalize their plans for a genealogy trip to Wales. Their pre-trip preparation would range from conducting further genealogy research in the United States to identifying research resources in Wales. They would be learning more about Wales and its history, identifying places to see and visit, evaluating options to participate in organized tours, and discovering Wales on their own.

As part of their preparation, I showed the couple how they could post a short message on one of the genealogical message boards seeking help in planning their forthcoming trip. The message introduced the couple, listed the surnames they were researching, and asked questions, such as the following:

- Where was the best place to locate their base of operations?
- Which of the local libraries was best to find specific types of information?
- What sites were must-see destinations?
- Who could they contact (such as a country genealogist) to help them, possibly for hire?
- What libraries, archives, and historical societies were important to contact?

Within hours—and over the next week—they received very insightful hints and direction from people who lived in the area or who had gone before on similar trips. Some people replied directly to the message boards, while others sent an email directly to the family. Thoughts shared included where to conduct research, where to stay and eat, where they would most likely find graves of family, and insights on personal genealogy.

Travel agent versus do-it-yourself planning. If your question is whether you should use a travel agent or plan your trip yourself, the answer is both. Planning a genealogy trip is a very customized process, and unless you've been to the location you are traveling at least once, you are more than likely going to need the help and services of a travel agent.

A good place to start your search is online. Almost every country, state, county or province, and city has a website providing insights to services, places to see, and how to start your research. You will also come across sites dedicated to promoting travel that are very helpful. You will find special events, festivals, hours and days of operation, and so forth that will help define your schedule.

One of the more helpful web searches I have found is to look for package trips run by tour operators in countries and regions where I have an interest. I see the hotels, sites, and so on that they include in their trips. It helps me see what the "highlights" are in the area.

Genealogy travel is a growing business in the travel industry. It's worth your time to check to see if there are websites dedicated to organizing genealogy-related travel to your area of focus. These sites usually have experienced genealogists who support and lead trips.

Once I get a sense of what to expect from my trip, I then make an inquiry of several travel agents who specialize in travel or genealogy in that country or region. I tell them what I am seeking to do and the areas I would like to visit. I start with email and then phone for follow-up discussions. These exchanges help me to organize how I want to approach my itinerary—from establishing a "base of operations" to choosing which tourist sites I want to see. I have found the travel agent to be very helpful in working with me to sort out how best to use their services and what to do on my own.

It only pays to use a travel agent if you use a good one. A good travel agent will know when a small change in your schedule can save you a lot of money. If you buy directly from the airline, you may not find out such information, since they will only quote you the rates for the times you ask. So if you're going to use a travel agent, make sure that you find one who is willing (and able) to search through the morass of fares and restrictions to find a good deal for you. A travel agent who just punches your data into the computer and tells you the prices is no better than the airline's 800 number. A good travel agent can probably save you 10–15 percent.

If you want a travel agent to work hard and well for you, you need to explain to them that you are indeed seriously committed to dealing with them and their agency, and that their time and effort spent researching travel products for you will indeed be rewarded by your subsequent purchase of travel through them.

These days, travel agents can spot a "shopper" a mile away—a person that picks their brains for free advice but doesn't reward the free advice with their business.

Expect to pay a good travel agent for their time, advice, and assistance.

I usually end up using the travel agent to book important cornerstones of my trip such as flights, hotel rooms, and cars or travel passes for rail. The little extra cost I may pay for working with the travel agent is well worth their expertise and service helping me to organize and manage my trip. If you run into problems with any aspect of your travel before, during, and after your trip (and it will happen), you have one number to call and a person or team who is there to help you. What problems, you ask? For starters, flights are delayed, your hotel is under renovation, or you choose to extend your stay in a specific city. The travel agent has all your key information, including credit card numbers, phone numbers, preferences in hotels, seat selection on airlines, and general itinerary in case someone should need to get in touch with you.

Choosing a travel agent. Approach the selection of a travel agent with the same care you'd exercise when you choose your doctor, lawyer, or any other long-term professional adviser. After all, the right travel agent should know both your financial wherewithal and your physical abilities and also share your tastes and sensibilities. The expert travel agent should even have an in-depth knowledge of your favorite destinations. Consider the following:

- Make a list of your own travel preferences and the services you expect from a travel agent. Do you want an adviser who will give you personal recommendations? Or would you prefer a clerk who follows your instruction and then processes your tickets and reservations?

- Interview any travel agent you're considering (see suggestions below). If possible, visit the offices, and talk with the agent you'd use. Ask specific questions to help formulate your opinion about an agent's judgment and expertise. For example, solicit comments on a hotel or a destination you know well.

- Check out the agency: does it have a reservations computer to search out the lowest airfares? Does it have preferred relationships with particular suppliers and tour operators, and do you like doing business with those suppliers? Does the agency work with hotel or airline consolidators? Does it have an after-hours help line?

- Before deciding, ask the agency to price and package a vacation for you. Then do some comparison shopping. How do the agency's recommendations and prices stack up against the competition's? And how fast did the agency work? The agent who offers the best combination of quality, price, and service is probably the one you should use.

The best way to find a good travel agent is by word-of-mouth recommendation. Solicit references from friends and family who know your desires and from travelers whose tastes and judgment are similar to yours. Ask how they use their travel agent and in what capacity. Ask the secretaries where you work for recommendations. Note that most people will recommend a particular agent—don't assume that every agent who works at that travel agency is as good. Don't be afraid to ask for the recommended agent by name. Most people tend to use the travel agent that is closest to where they work or live. If you don't like the service you're getting, try a different agent.

If you are interested in reviewing travel agents that specialize in genealogy trips, start your Google search with the words "Genealogy Travel."

Even if you need an agent only to write a ticket you've booked yourself, it helps to have one with whom you can communicate.

Be aware that travel agents specialize on either a type of customer or a type of travel. The major areas of specialization are business and leisure travel. While every accredited agency has the authority to book any kind of travel, leisure agencies specialize in cruises, charters, low airfares, or up-scale resorts. The advertising in local media reveals much about an agency's area of expertise.

A good travel agent will become familiar with your travel preferences and keep track of your frequent flyer numbers and any special requirements, such as special meals, seat selection (window versus aisle), and so on. They'll let you know if changing your itinerary slightly will result in a lower fare. They'll also advise you of any changes made by the airline on your tickets, either by calling you or, if they can't reach you, by mail.

What do people do on genealogy trips? The genealogy trip is about you, your family, and learning about your roots. It's about being free to explore and discover.

Most genealogy trips include activities such as visiting and taking pictures of the places where ancestors lived, looking up the addresses or farms, visiting churches and graveyards, exploring the history and culture of the people, searching libraries and archives for family records or information, and finding and meeting family. Trips also include visiting the tourist spots, joining tour groups for a day or longer excursions, exploring the countryside, finding an out-of-the-way café and ordering cuisine unique to the area, ordering an ice cream and taking a stroll in the local gardens, and getting an invitation to join a new acquaintance for lunch.

Let each day be a new adventure. Have just enough planning to accomplish the goals you have set, but also have enough freedom to take advantage of the unexpected opportunities that might come your way.

Plan to have a base of operations. If you have done any level of travel you have learned that not every town has the same level or type of services to accommodate your desired expectations. I usually try to identify a base of operations if I am going to be in a specific area for two or more days. It simplifies the need of packing and unpacking, checking in and checking out. During my first trip, I spent most evenings trying to find a hotel that I could afford or had vacancies. At the end of a long day of research, you just want a place to sleep. Now, I don't waste my time trying to find a place to eat and become familiar with where the basics such as gas stations, transportation hubs, ATMs, copy centers, and so on are located.

Start scheduling reservations for your trip 3–4 months in advance. Preparing for a genealogy trip requires several months of preparation and planning. Book your first and last night bed and breakfast, hotel room, guest house, or other accommodations from your home country before you leave for your trip. The last thing you want to do when you land is to scramble for a place to stay.

Whether working with a travel agent or contacting persons directly, make reservations at least 2–3 months before departure to book a room and give a deposit, if necessary.

Don't leave anything to chance when it comes to accommodations. It's helpful to book a B&B or hotel room near the airport on your last night's stay. That way, you don't have to travel for miles and miles to reach the airport to be on time for your flight home.

If you like B&Bs, booking ahead of time is especially important if you are traveling in the summer, as B&Bs—especially in cities—may be booked months in advance because tourism in the summer increases. Summer is the peak travel time in most countries. Book car and flight arrangements months ahead of time as well. In addition, find a B&B with en-suite accommodations. That is, the bathroom and shower are in the bedroom. I don't like to walk down someone's hallway looking for the bathroom in the middle of the night.

Consider hiring a researcher who speaks the local language. If you are going to be in a country where you are not familiar with the language, consider hiring a researcher that can work with you. Not only can they help with your research but they can also act as a tour guide for the area you are researching.

One acquaintance recently went to Wales and hired a Welsh-speaking researcher. The researcher did the driving. She explained what they were seeing and answered questions. Several months before arriving in Wales, the in-country researcher worked with this individual to nail down important logistics. Why hire a Welsh speaker in an English-speaking country? Welsh was commonly spoken until the late 1800s, and many of the gravestones, records, and so forth are written in Welsh.

Plan for your family when you are in the library. If you're taking your family with you on the genealogy trip, be prepared to have activities that your family can go to while you are in the library, if they won't be participating in the research work. A web search will provide many options to choose from.

Planning local transportation. Become familiar with your transportation options before you travel. Should you rent a car, take local transportation, or perhaps a combination of the two? These are questions only you can answer, but it pays to understand your options.

There is a great train system throughout Europe, where you can get a single ticket for multiple days. When I have purchased these tickets, I made sure it was all-inclusive to include bus, rail, ship, and subway. If you are going to be in the large cities, public transportation is well coordinated and rather easy to get around.

Renting a vehicle may be less expensive than a train pass. You gain the freedom of coming and going as you please. The cost of fuel is two to three times US prices. There are a few differences to be aware of. For example, if you rent a standard shift anywhere in the United Kingdom, you will save about $100 dollars over the automatic transmission. But with standard shift, keep in mind that you have to shift with your left hand, as the driver's seat is in the right-hand side of the car.

If you rent a car, set up the rental in the United States, not in the country of destination. Have the car waiting for you on a certain date at your arrival destination. But you don't actually need a car to get around in Dublin or Belfast, as public transportation is ubiquitous in those cities. For instance, if you plan to stay in Dublin for three days, set it up so that the car is waiting for you on the day you leave.

Your travel agent can be a great source for sorting out the pros and cons of different transportation options. I also rely heavily on the counsel provided by persons in the genealogy message boards about what options to make in selecting public transportation or renting a car.

Before I make any final decisions, I like to have a fairly good idea of where I am going to be and when. I have a fairly good idea of where I want my base of operations and the towns in which I want to conduct other research. For example, in planning a trip I outlined the following scenario:

Base of operations: Dundee, Scotland		
Aberdeen	2 hours	Travel by auto
Inverness	3-4 hours	Travel by auto
Perth	30 minutes	Travel by auto
St. Andrews	30 minutes	Travel by auto
Edinburgh or Glasgow	1 hour 30 mins	Travel by auto, park and take public transportation

Look through the options and determine what combination works best for your comfort levels in driving in a strange location. If you spend eight hours getting lost and finding your way, the extra expense of the train might be quite worth it.

Before leaving on your trip, purchase a Michelin Road Map of the country. These maps are usually more detailed than the maps the car rental company gives you. The drawback to these maps is that they are so large you need to stop the car to look at them. Don't throw away the maps the car rental companies give you. These tend to be a little smaller and less unwieldy in the car. These smaller maps are great for locating the major dual-carriageways (divided highways) but not for off-the-path villages.

Phone cards are a must as a backup to a cell phone. A cell phone is important to have, and it's a good idea to have a phone card as a back-up for emergencies. There are times when cell phones run out of battery and you need to make a call to confirm an appointment or other needs. The phone card is a very nice backup. In most countries, you can easily purchase a phone card in several monetary denominations, and most phones are equipped to handle these cards.

STRATEGY FOR CONDUCTING FIELD RESEARCH

Keep a travel journal during your trip.

Each day of your trip is full of research, excursions, meeting new people, taking pictures, reflecting upon your family, and unexpected happenings. Take time at the end or beginning of each day to write in your travel journal. Upon your return home, you will find that your journal will be one of the most important assets you have in furthering research and documenting the value of your trip. After just a week on the road, one day blends into the next.

I tend to write events in my travel journal in a chronological format (what happened first, second, third). For example, after I entered a library I will write details about the following aspects of my experience there:

- Who I spoke with and their role in the library, address, email, phone number, and so on.

- All discussions (no matter whom it was with) and information exchanged.
- The records I looked at and why.
- What I found and decisions I made during my search.
- All new information, carefully documenting all associated information.
- Thoughts and questions that cross my mind during the research.

I make comments about the places I visited and why they were of interest to me. I discuss what I learned. I also include brochures I may have picked up and any other information that will help me tell the story.

I find myself reviewing what I wrote several times during the trip as I ponder options and make decisions about what direction to take the research and planning my free time. The parts of my journal that are most interesting are how often I happen to meet the right person who is able to open doors to help find the place I am searching for, or the person who knows about my family name and history and will take me to the gravesite of an ancestor, or the person who knows the person who now lives in the ancestor's home, or is the person who knows where to find the record I seek.

Learn about local history. One of the most enjoyable aspects of taking a genealogy trip is learning about the history of the local area. Don't become so focused on trying to find that long-lost record that you forget that your ancestors were people with dreams, opportunities, successes, frustrations, disappointments, bills, sicknesses, and death. They may have moved more than once or cleared the land to make a new home. They lived there, so why not spend time getting to know the area's history?

Learn about the history of the area where your ancestors are from. What did they eat? Where would they have gone to church? Where is the mill they took their crops to? What sort of natural features did they encounter when farming the land? What is the city most famous for? The more you know, the more you can appreciate just what your ancestors' lives were like when you are there. If you learn that lamb and potatoes were the primary staples or that blueberries were grown in the area since the 1600s, perhaps you will take the time to order the "local" dishes when you are in town. Who knows, you might even ask for the recipe.

Searching for your ancestors' original places of residence. Like many of our ancestors, your forefathers came from tiny villages that few people have ever heard of. When they immigrated they may have simply said they were from the largest nearby town or city. If you are looking for the experience to stand exactly where Great-Great-Great-Grandpa lived or have your picture taken in front of his home, make sure you know exactly what town they came from.

Records such as birth and land records can help locate where your family lived by giving you a street address or the name of the land where they lived. With such information in hand, I have been able to ask directions from locals and gain very good directions to find what I was looking for. Don't be surprised if the information on the records gives you a different village.

You might have the right village and go to the church. However, the church may no longer have the records. It is quite possible they have been moved to the genealogical society in a larger, nearby city. In most countries, older records are being consolidated in central repositories. Always ascertain in advance where the actual records are kept.

Searching libraries and archives in the country. As I have conducted research in various countries, I have learned to expect to find the unexpected. Some of my experiences were as follows:

- Record offices will have government hours (perhaps closing for lunch).
- You may need advance reservations.
- You may need to look up your resources in a catalog and write them on a request form, which you submit to the reference librarian.
- Your request may take more than a half-hour to arrive.
- You may only be allowed to view one request at a time.
- You may or may not be allowed to take photographs of the documents. If you are not allowed to take photographs, then

you may need to fill out a request form and submit it. It may take from just a few minutes to a few hours before your request is ready.

- Sometimes you are limited to the number of copies you can make in a day.
- Remember that the person behind the desk is in charge.
- The staff may bring the requested artifacts to you and pick them up from you while you are seated.
- You may be required to stow your backpack in a locker.
- Security may ask to see the contents of your pockets or purse.
- Some record facilities are very strict about each researcher having a table or seat.
- Research under these conditions gives you the thrill of handling papers that may be over two hundred years old.

Searching graveyards during your trip. Searching graveyards can be a mixed experience of disappointment and jubilation all in the same day.

First, see if you can find a map of graveyards you intend to visit and the background about each. Check with the local historical societies and ask if there is a record of the local cemetery. If there is no documentation available, try to locate the sexton (caretaker of the graveyard) to see if there is an organizational plot chart that defines who is buried where.

Check to see if there is an old map and a new map of the graveyard. Compare them to see what differences there might be between them. In some countries, an ordinance survey (OS) reference number identifies the cemetery. Other countries have other reference systems. The key here is to realize that there may be more to graveyards and cemeteries to help find what you seek.

I enter a graveyard with reverence and anticipation. I am hoping the headstone is legible and easy to read. If the headstone is over one hundred years old, I am pleasantly surprised and grateful if the headstone is legible and not damaged by vandalism or weathered by the years. Whatever I find, it is always fun.

Take a small pocket notebook with you at all times. You'll need it to draw diagrams of graveyards and write down inscriptions.

If you have some flexibility in your trip as to the days you will be searching the graveyard, keep a close watch on the weather report. It is always better to view a graveyard on a sunny day versus an overcast, rainy day, if possible.

Are you planning on taking photographs of headstones or making headstone rubbings on your trip? If you are and you've never taken a photograph of a tombstone or made a headstone rubbing, practice on some local stones before you leave. The time to learn isn't when you're at a cemetery 2,000 miles from home on the last day of your trip.

Research Services and Fees. Many historical societies and libraries supporting genealogical research provide services to you when you are not able to come to them. These services are sometimes offered free but sometimes require a nominal fee. The fees and services cover actual costs. Each search can take from three to eight weeks depending on the backlog and available resources of the organization.

A search request is where you ask the organization to help with your research. Acceptable and unacceptable search requests are as follows:

Acceptable:

- Search for a surname in indexed county histories for one county
- Search for one family in a census
- Search for one land owner in land tract records
- Search for one obituary

Unacceptable:

- Compile your family genealogy or complete pedigree charts.
- Answer requests for "any and all" information on an individual or family.
- Speculate why an ancestor did what they did.
- Describe in detail what life in Nebraska was like for your ancestor.

- Analyze long and detailed family histories and determine what searches to do for you.

You can expect the organization to limit the number of searches you can request at one time—usually the limit is about three searches. The organization will only process one request. Requests for searches are done by mail and online. They will not initiate searches for other records not specifically requested in your letter and prepayment. The fees for research will range from $5 to $30 per search. The fee may vary, depending on if you live in the state or not. For example, $10 per search for in-state residents and members of the state historical society, or $20 per search for non-residents who are not members of the society.

In cases where you want the organization to do an extended search, you will be charged by the hour. For example, $20 per hour with a half-hour minimum.

Photocopying services. Photocopying services are available for researchers unable to visit the physical faculty. Researchers are able to request limited photocopies of portions of published works and manuscript collections. Staff are unable to copy entire published works, entire manuscript collections, bound volumes in the manuscript collection, newspapers, or any fragile or sensitive materials. Forms are available online and usually require the following information:

- A brief description of the item.
- The manuscript title or call number.
- Page numbers (if possible).

A copy order will be generated and sent to you (via email or mail—you specify on the form), explaining the procedures for ordering and payment. When the order form and payment are received, your order will receive prompt attention.

An example of fees associated with photocopying follow:

- $0.20 to $1.00 per page copied (based on size).
- $10 to $25 Service or Shipping and handling fee.
- If order exceeds 50 exposures, additional charge is added.
- 10–25 percent fee discount for members or in-state residents.

Write clear and concise queries. Whenever you are requesting information from the library or organization, you need to be very clear and concise. The following are examples of the type of information the research staff will need to complete certain types of searches:

Census:

- Exact name of the family (first and last name of head of household).
- Location of residence (county and either precinct or nearby town).

Newspapers (looking for notices of deaths, marriages, births, and other such events):

- First and last name.
- Date and place of event.
- Naturalization Records:
- Name of the individual naturalized.
- County where the person was naturalized, if known.

Probate Records:

- Individual's name.
- County where the will was probated.
- Date of death.

Consider Interlibrary Loan

Usually a portion of the library's or society's collection is available through interlibrary loan. Interlibrary loan allows you to borrow items for specific research and is transferred from library to library. **Note:** Libraries will usually not exchange information through the LDS family history centers. When you start speaking with the library or society, ask the following questions:

1. What is the interlibrary loan policy and procedure of the organization from which you will request information?
   - Are there any costs associated with the loan?
   - What is the length of time permitted for the loan?
   - How long does it take to process the loan?

- Is it possible to purchase copies?
- Are any special forms required?

2. What is the interlibrary loan policy and procedure for your local library?
   - Does the library have the equipment you need to view the requested material, such as a microfilm reader, printer, or photocopier?

The interlibrary loan comes with parameters, such as the following:

- Order 1–5 reels that can be loaned at one time.
- Orders must be received on interlibrary forms.
- Most orders will require a loan fee to be paid at the time of request. Fees range from $5 to $15 per reel.
- Cost may vary depending on if you are a state resident, non-resident, or member of the society.
- Length of time for loan is 1–4 weeks.

The types of resources that are usually exchanged through interlibrary loan include the following:

- Census (microfilm)
- Papers (microfilm)
- Original deeds, wills, tax records, vital statistics, and so forth (microfilm)
- Maps
- Books and research guides
- Photographs (microfiche)
- Military records (microfilm)

It is at the library's discretion to designate materials as non-circulating due to policy, age, condition, or special circumstances. Items that are not usually available, but can be photocopied, include the following:

- Periodicals
- Materials in the main reading rooms
- All books published before a given date (such as 1925)
- Printed local history and genealogies and regimental histories (often do not circulate out-of-state)

If you have a particular microfilm you wish to own, ask if you can purchase copies. This would be advisable if, for example, there was a unique event covering a span of months and you wanted to have detailed coverage to review and study.

Research Trip Priorities—After Your Trip

Take time to organize, catalog, and share your findings after your trip. Within hours of returning home, you will be unpacked, clothes will be in the wash, mail will be opened, and you will have spoken to family and friends about your trip.

Overall, you are very satisfied with the goals you were able to accomplish and move forward. I would recommend that within twenty-four hours of returning home, you start the process of documenting and organizing all aspects of your trip—from photographs to brochures and from photocopies to journal entries. Don't let it become another pile of genealogy "to-do's." Items easily become misplaced or forgotten, and often you forget why a record was important.

Follow your usual steps in processing, organizing, and cataloging your information. The following sequence is intended to be a recommendation, not a sequence to follow rigidly. Don't change your usual sequence if it varies from the order listed here.

1. Analyze what goals were accomplished and how.
   - What goals were moved forward and how?
   - What goals were left undone?
   - Did you find new data that requires changes or updates to genealogy records?
   - Look at your family tree and see what your next steps will be.
   - Do you continue working on the same line or do you start a new direction?
   - Start the next research to-do log.
   - Add tasks to your existing list.
   - Note any questions your research may have raised.
2. Who did you promise correspondence?
   - Why?

- By when?
- Who do you want to send a thank you to?

3. Review your journal writings.
   - Enter into computer.
   - Which people, places, and so on do you want to enter into your resource file?

4. New data that revises old data, if found
   - Update your family information (group sheets, pedigree charts).
   - In your notes, document your change (and sources) carefully so that other family members won't think you have made a mistake and change it back.
   - Record the date you made the change.
   - Make a backup of your data (clearly label) before you begin data entry of new information.
   - Make a backup of your data (clearly labeled) right after you enter data.

5. If you recorded any interviews or thoughts on tape:
   - Transcribe any interviews, noting the date, place, interviewee, and interviewer.
   - If there is a tape, videotape, photographs, or notes, be sure to indicate that on the transcription.
   - If you use exact quotes, put them in quotes, otherwise indicate that you are paraphrasing, so it is perfectly clear.
   - If you have the ability to digitize your interviews, do so for backup.

6. Carefully and safely organize documents, copies, and notes.
   - Scan documents and copies to be included in your electronic files.
   - File the acquired data (hard copies) in your files.
   - Make new files as needed.
   - If you have a database log, make notes as needed.
   - Flag files with notes to yourself if needed.
   - Clearly document data you acquired, its source, and its value to your research.
   - Make copies for your master file as needed.

7. Organize photos, postcards, brochures, and pictures.
    - Scan hardcopy or paper information to be included in your electronic files.
    - If desired, insert information into your family tree program if the software allows.
    - If you took photos, record dates, place, and reason of importance for each snapshot.
    - Edit photos as needed (cropping, color correction, and so on).
    - Develop a photo log to organize materials.
    - Develop a backup file of photos.
    - Integrate key photos with family history.
    - If you came home with rare original photos, carefully store them (in archival quality storage, acid free envelopes, low light, and so on).

8. Share information—information doesn't do any good sitting in your files.
    - Let others know what you have discovered. Let them share in your excitement.
    - Write a letter to family.
    - Include in a family newsletter.
    - Post a note on message boards of research data found with documentation.
    - Ask questions, if information you found was ambiguous or contradictory, others may be able to help you.

9. Share your resources with genealogy societies, newsgroups, and message boards.
    - In addition to what you learned about family, share what you learned about libraries and archives in the locations you visited.
    - Discuss the scope of collections and services available.

Use Your Camera to Document Your Research

Use your camera in your library, archive, or museum research.

Consider using your digital camera as a tool for documenting and capturing information you find in your research. If you have never used your camera in your library research, practice in your local library under all types of conditions, including very low light. Again, the time to learn isn't at a cemetery 2,000 miles from home.

Digital photography is all about lighting and location

The first problem you will always face when it comes to photography is lighting. I use flash less than 10 percent of the time. Instead of flash use natural lighting (near a window), light stands with diffusion screen and lights, or a self-contained photo studio (includes tripod, diffusion lights and screen, and copy stand—I like Photo Studio In-A-Box from American Recorder Technologies; you can find more information at their website, http://www.americanrecorder.com). Shooting documents with flash indoors usually creates a "hot spot" caused by using a flash too close. When you have no choice but to use a flash, use it sparingly, such as in a group setting or for a gravestone that is in a shaded area. Be aware: many libraries and research facilities prohibit flash photography, so come prepared to shoot without a flash.

Note 1: Sunlight is known as "white" light and gives what we recognize as true or natural colors. Any other type of light source has light of a different color temperature and gives off different color tones.

Note 2: Digital cameras try to automatically adjust for different kinds of lighting but sometimes need additional help. The camera's "white balance" setting provides this help. This setting "reads" the light coming into the camera lens and, by assuming the brightest area in the image is white, attempts to balance the entire image so that the bright area looks white. All other colors should then appear natural.

Photographing in libraries.

When planning to take photographs in a library, the following tips may be helpful:

- Know their policy about digital photography before you go. Eight percent of libraries have allowed me to use a digital camera with some criteria.
- Do not use flash. Using a flash is usually prohibited due to the photosensitivity of artifacts.
- Set up a photo stand or tripod.
- You may need to sign an intended uses statement.
- You may need to have one of their staff handle rare objects.
- Only take photos of intended artifacts.
- No photos are usually allowed of the building's interior or of people (especially in government buildings).
- Set up camera in a corner away from others, so as not to disturb.
- If possible, set up near a window to gain the most from natural light.

Photographing museums and archives.

When planning to take photographs in a museum or archive, the following tips may be helpful:

- Check first to see if photography is allowed. Most museums and archives will allow photography without a flash.
- Objects covered with glass or plastic are best shot at an angle. Glass and plastic will reflect a flash or act like a mirror and reflect your image under natural light, so consider photographing the object at an angle.
- Snap a separate picture of a caption or a label of the exhibit.
- Use the tripod along with your camera's self-timer and the "night" or "low light" setting. Lack of good lighting is usually the norm in museums. Use the tripod to steady your image. When you encounter very low-light situations, try putting your camera on the "night" setting and enabling your self-timer. With the steadiness of the tripod and camera settings you should be able to get some good quality photos.

- No tripod? Then brace yourself. If it is too dark and there is no tripod, leaning against a wall or a pillar or supporting your camera against a bench, a chair, or a staircase rail will be a good remedy in that situation. If a subject is important enough, by all means take an extra shot.

Photographing Microfilm.

Note: These are the backlit or rear projection readers that shine a light through the film and use a series of mirrors or lenses to display an image of the film on a vertical or flat surface. The image displayed on either style can be easily photographed.

- Depending upon your circumstances, you may or may not need to mount your camera on a tripod. I have been able to raise my camera up near the projection lens, click the shutter button, and get a clear photo with no distortion. If you choose to use a tripod, place your camera on a tripod in front of the reader screen.
- Place a white paper on the reader surface as the target area for shooting. **Note:** Try other blank sheets of colored paper (pink, blue, or yellow) to see if these colors help you with readability of the image.
- Adjust the camera or tripod position so the information you want to copy fills the LCD frame.
- Use the "macro" mode if necessary. This will depend on your camera model and how far away it is from the microfilm reader.
- Make sure the flash is turned off.
- Set the camera's self-timer, if needed.
- Gently press the shutter button halfway to lock the exposure and focus.
- Press the button completely down. If using the self-timer, move away from the camera and wait for the self-timer to trip the shutter.
- Take several shots. Consider using the "best shot selector" or auto-bracketing your shots if your camera has these features,

or use manual bracketing if it doesn't.

Photographing at the cemetery or graveyard. Over the centuries, several different types of stones have been used to create gravestones. Some of the stones are quite porous and fragile, while others are resistant to damage. Be careful when attempting to improve the readability of the inscription. The following is a brief list of types of stone used in various time periods:

- Prior to the nineteenth century: sandstone or slate.
- Nineteenth century: marble and gray granite.
- Late nineteenth century to the present: polished granite or marble.

Take photos of the cemetery entrance, sign, book of records, and church. Before you start taking photos of headstones, make sure you capture the details of the cemetery, including the name, street signs, proximity, and church adjacent to the cemetery. All these details will help you and others that follow know where you have been.

North, south, east, west—Best time of day for photographing headstones. Sunlight emphasizes imperfections in the stone and can make the carving look flat. Headstones facing west are best photographed at midday. Headstones facing north should be photographed in the late afternoon. Headstones facing south are well-lit all day. Headstones facing east are best photographed in the morning hours.

Large headstones require close-ups of inscriptions. Taking photos of large headstones alone sometimes makes the inscription too small to read. Take a photo of the large headstone and then move in close to take a photo of the inscription.

Family grave plots require group and individual photos of each headstone. A family plot constitutes two or more graves. Take a group photograph of the graves that shows the number and proximity. Take photos of each headstone separately. If you are photographing a cemetery, photograph and label all family plots the same—for example: group plot, headstones left to right, top to bottom.

Consider taking photos of all headstones in a small community cemetery. If your family came from a small town and your roots go back many generations or many decades, chances are you are related to most, if not all persons buried in the cemetery. If you have traveled a great distance to capture family graves on film, take an extra hour or two and capture the other headstones on film, you can sort out details later. You will often find direct family members buried among other families.

Look at the base, top, sides, and back of headstones. In addition to the inscription, look around the headstone for other important information that can be inscribed about the individual, family, maker of the headstone, and writings of the deceased.

Take eye-level photos of headstone inscriptions. When taking photos of headstone inscriptions, try to take the photo of the inscription at eye-level. You will find information much easier to read in the photo.

Talk to the sexton. Can't find a family member's gravesite? See if you can talk to the sexton and ask to see the cemetery plot map. The sexton may have records you can simply photograph. Some cemeteries bury several layers deep to conserve space. In these situations, the headstone on top may only be for one of the several persons buried in the plot. Sometimes headstones are not available because the family is too poor for a headstone, but the sexton will have details of who is buried where.

Take time to clear grass and other foliage away from inscription. Take time to clear any cut, dried grass away from and on top of the headstone before taking a photograph. If a branch is grown over the headstone, pull it back and take a photo. Clear overgrown grass to the edge of the marker or headstone. Important information or epitaphs may be separated from the main inscription (for example, a bronze marker denoting group or religious affiliation, service in branch of military, or that the individual fought in specific war).

Use a little chalk for the hard-to-read, old headstones. Letters on the old stones are often hardly legible. Take a little piece of white (or black or any other dark color) chalk and fill letters. Or rub the white chalk on the flat surface next to the letters.

Tilt your camera to the angle of the headstone. Older stones tend to lean or slant. Tilt the camera to the angle of the stone and your image will straighten up nicely.

Shoot black and gray polished marble at an angle. Gray or black polished headstones are sometimes hard to read or can reflect a camera's flash, making the image illegible. Shoot polished headstone at an angle and then view on LCD for clarity. Re-shoot at a different angle if needed.

Try using a flash on headstones covered with shade or on cloudy days. If the inscription you just took a picture of is hard to read, try using your flash. The light should provide you just enough extra light to fill in the dark shadows so you can read the lettering. Try using a flash from angles, if needed.

Try a soft brush or natural sponge and water to remove surface soil. Gentle brushing should remove surface dirt and bird droppings. Never use hard objects or stiff brushes to clean the stone.

Try sponge and water on light-colored stone. The stone will darken from the water and darken the inscription on the stone.

Keep a written record. Some of the items to consider as part of the written record include location, a map of the cemetery with the stones numbered, when photographed (time, date, and frame number), and transcription of the epitaph. Post your photos of headstones on family websites or sites such as Virtual Cemetery or Dead Fred.

When you take the time to adequately prepare for your field research, you will find greater success and better insight into the next steps you need to take in your research on the Internet and in the field. I have prepared additional resources that you can download from the companion website that include a suggested genealogy packing list, personal packing list, and related resources.

Lesson 7: Cite and Verify Every Source

I was given copies of genealogy for Christmas in 1990. I didn't pay to much attention to the information until 2004. As I reviewed the information, I found one line that ended in the late 1700s in North Carolina. I began the process of becoming familiar with the line and finally decided that I would like to see if I could extend the line. Within a few weeks of research, I cracked the puzzle and was able to start extending the line. Over a period of two years, I had extended it several generations. I had carefully documented my research and was quite proud of the work I had done.

On one of my genealogy field trips, I had made arrangements to visit a distant cousin and collaborate my finding with hers concerning this line. Within two minutes of looking at my research, she told me that person from whom I began my research was not the right person. With further discussion, she explained that the person I had listed was in fact in England at the time I had her marrying her husband in North Carolina. She would not arrive in American for another ten years.

Where had I gone wrong? I should have taken time to confirm the information that I had been given in 1990. I just assumed it was correct. There was no documentation. That assumption was a costly but valuable error on my part. I learned the value of analysis and hoped I would not make that mistake again.

What exactly is analysis? It's the dividing of information into its six parts: who, what, where, when, why, and how. Each of the six parts can be applied to every document or source that you acquire.

To quote Sir Conan Doyle writing as Sherlock Holmes in *The Beryl Coronet*, "When you eliminate the impossible, whatever you have left, no matter how improbable, must be the truth." Let's look at what each of the six parts means to genealogists.

- **Who.** You can define the who before you start your search by asking who created the source.

- **What.** What do you want to know? What information does the source provide?

- **Where.** "Where" is probably the most important fact after "who." Are the records in national, state, county, parish, town, or precinct records? Where did you find the records?

- **When.** Determine a timeframe or time period so you know where to search for records.

- **Why.** Why was the source created? Why did your ancestor emigrate from Germany to the United States? Why did they move from Illinois to Wyoming? Why are there so many German (or Irish, or Italian) people in the area?

- **How.** How does the information agree or conflict with information from other sources? How do I answer all these questions? How do I find the records I need?

As you analyze your data, you will be able to make good decisions about its value and accuracy. It's not necessary to write the answers to the above questions, but writing your conclusions will help to clarify your thinking and reveal any inconsistencies.

Take time to carefully review your research. Look at the sources. What is the artifact? What documents did you use? What books did you use? With whom did you speak?

Look at information gathered from oral or recorded histories. Review previous research.

Correlate unrelated information by categorizing your information. Is it primary information (participant, eyewitness) or is it secondary (non-participant)?

Look closely at the evidence. What does the evidence say to you? How relevant is the information to your research? Does it provide direct answers to the questions you are researching? Does it provide indirect answers that help answer the question but do not stand alone? Does it provide negative answers or no answer at all? Is there information missing? What are you seeing that you didn't see before? New insights? Different conclusion? Same answer? Different clues?

Ask for documentation. Never be shy about asking for documentation from another researcher when they have shared information with you. Again, without the paper records in hand, nothing is proven.

Always verify. There is never a time when you should not verify information you have received. You can go to almost any Internet search engine today and within a few minutes find hundreds of questionable "facts." I've seen the same birth recorded as happening in Florida in the 1600s and in Utah in the early 1800s. I've seen records of mothers who supposedly gave birth to children at the age of five, as well as twenty-two-year-old grandfathers. It's frustrating, to say the least.

Through the years, I have found critical errors in what I downloaded. It often appears that genealogists wanted so desperately to extend the line or make a connection that they jumped to conclusions in their research, which caused other genealogists to research someone else's family lines. Often the answers they were looking for were right before their eyes. The following are a few examples of experiences that other genealogists shared with me about the value of verifying information:

- "I verify everything for myself. I once used someone else's info and there was a huge mistake that cost me about a year of work."

- "Great-Granddad's marriage certificate had wrong occupation details on it, which caused me no end of problems with my searching."

- "Family myths are just that, myths, unless you check and double-check. I was lead to believe that my father's family was from Suffolk County in England. Everyone swore that this was right. It took me five years and a trip to Utah to find out that they were not right. In fact, the family was from the county of Essex."

- "I do not automatically accept a version of ancestry from another person—I check everything out, because people sometimes will create their ancestries to fit their own conceptions. When creating a family history, make it a masterpiece of accuracy. Inaccurate information will lead you away from where you want to go."

- "Make no assumptions. The family has always stated that my mother's family was from Germany because of the heavy accent. However, in North Carolina, an Irish or Scottish accent could also have been considered 'heavy,' as could Welsh. Don't discount anything until you've proven it can't be."

- "I learned some time ago after receiving a family CD from a genealogy company that the information was incorrect on the family line. I called the company and found that they never asked the person if all their information was documented. Today, the new genealogist seems to rely on information over the Internet."

- "Do not assume something is correct. This is a real time waster. I spent a lot of time seeking my great-grandfather who supposedly died in South Africa, when in reality he died at his home in Scotland. I have many examples of wasting time—now I'm almost too skeptical. Nothing should be taken at face value. Humans make errors."

- "Don't believe everything you read; adopt a "show me" attitude. I'd heard for years that there was a fire in the Martin County Courthouse (North Carolina) and all records were destroyed. I visited the courthouse and was informed that wasn't the case. Yes, there had been a small fire that damaged a few land records, but that was it."

Searching online presents many of the most challenging issues when it comes to verifying sources. The following are a few of the lessons I have learned from searching online:

- **Search for the source.** It would be nice if all web resources included a source. Whenever you find a record on the web that relates you to your family, look for a source of the data. This can be in the form of source citations and references (often denoted as footnotes at the bottom the page or at the end of the publication), notes or comments, or an "about this database" section for websites like Ancestry.com. You could also send an email to the author or contributor and politely ask for source citations.

- **Seek to find the referenced source.** If the website or database you are using does not have digital images of the actual source, you can search to find the source references. For example, if the source of the information is a genealogy or history book, look for a library in the area you are searching that has a copy and is willing to provide photocopies. Expect a small fee. If the source is a microfilm record, you will most likely be able to secure the original from your local family history center, where the film can be borrowed and viewed.

- **View the original online.** There is a growing trend of many online databases to provide access to scanned images of original documents. The vast majority of Internet resources have been copied, abstracted, transcribed, or summarized from previously existing, original sources. Understanding the difference between these different types of sources will help you best assess how to verify the information that you find.

  - Primary sources were created at or close to the time of the event by someone with personal knowledge of the event (for example, a birth date provided by the family doctor for the birth certificate). Primary evidence usually carries more weight than secondary evidence.
  - If the record you are seeing is a photocopy, digital copy, or microfilm copy of the original source, then it is likely to be a valid representation.
  - Compiled records (which include abstracts, transcriptions, indexes, and published family histories) are more likely to have missing information or transcription errors. If you find these records, it's in your best interest to track down the original sources.

- **Think about the possible source.** When you find information that doesn't provide you a source for the database or website, ask yourself what kind of record could have supplied the information. For example, if it's an exact date of birth, then the source is most likely a birth certificate or tombstone inscription. If it is an approximate year of birth, then it may have come from a census record or marriage record.

Use your Genealogy Software to Help Find Questionable Data

Use the "sanity checks" built into the better genealogy programs! The exact name of this feature may vary from one program to another, but all the better genealogy programs have the capability to find suspicious data within a database. These built-in quality checks help you quickly identify questionable data, such as very young girls or elderly women giving birth. When your software identifies such data, examine the evidence closely.

Whether the source provides good, limited, or no information— write it down. Citing sources gives credibility to your research, helps others understand where you have been, and aids during your analysis.

Document Your Sources. Do it right the first time! Whether the source is a newspaper, journal, court record, personal interview, letter, or church record, write everything down while you still have the source in your hands. The following are a few of the lessons I've learned about the value of documenting your sources:

1. **Sources you can rely on.** No one has a perfect memory, and some sources will have worse memories than others. The only source you can rely on is an "official" one: birth, marriage, death documents, and other confirmable databases and indices. Even if information came from a relative, list their name. You want to stay as accurate as possible and leave a clear trail for others to follow. Not only will you know you have proof of your information, but others you share the information with will know it is factual, not just speculation.

2. **Sources establish credibility.** Many genealogists pointed out that unless we are able to tell others where we obtain the information, all we are sharing is our opinion. Citing sources is essential to establishing credibility. If we have done a good job with our research, we can give others the ability to broaden and build upon the research already done and not have the same work rechecked over and over again.

3. **Write legibly.** If you handwrite any information, write legibly. It doesn't pay to hurry and then not be able to read your own handwriting later. Where possible, I try to always get a photocopy or a photo of the key information I am capturing and then enter it into my genealogical program or record database.

4. **Checking sources allows for verification.** Checking sources allows you to verify of spelling and dating and to report variations, and it also leads to more information. Relying on the expertise of others helps save time and energy. Create and maintain a record of what resource was checked, so that you don't waste time later. Likewise, some sources (books, newspapers, and so on) might be found at only a few locations. Include where these were in case you need to glean them again.

5. **How valuable is your time?** Genealogists told experiences where they tried to pick up the trail of research from undocumented records and spent weeks, months, or even years searching for the next clue, only to find out that the data they had was incorrect.

6. **Six elements of a good source citation.** The six elements of a good source citation include author, title, publisher's name and location, publication date, location of the source and identifying information (library or archive where you found the info and its call number), and specific information for the piece of data you found (page number, line number, and so on).

EXAMPLES OF CITING PUBLISHED RESOURCES

The information below is a mix of valid and fictitious data used as an example of documentation.

1. Book:

Author: Michael E. Pollock

Title: Marriage Bonds of Henrico County, Virginia, 1782-1853

Publication facts (place of publication, name of publisher, year): Baltimore Maryland, Genealogical Publishing Co., Inc, 1984

Page number: 133

Formatted:

Michael E. Pollock, Marriage Bonds of Henrico County, Virginia, 1782-1853, (Baltimore Maryland, Genealogical Publishing Co., Inc, 1984) p. 133.

2. Article:

Author: E.E. Patton

Title of the article: The Influence of the Huguenots

Name of Periodical: The Huguenot

Publication facts (place of publication, name of publisher): Vallejo, California, The Huguenot Society

Volume: 10

Month/Season and Year: 1939-41

Page Numbers: 39-45

Formatted:

E.E. Patton, "The Influence of the Huguenots." The Huguenot (Vallejo, California, The Huguenot Society), Vol. 10 (1939-41), pp. 39-45.

3. Newspaper:

Title of article: Maude Jolley Services

Place of publication: Provo, Utah

Name of Newspaper: Provo Daily Herald

Date of Publication: 12 January 1929

Page number: 1

Column Number: 2

Formatted:

"Maude Jolley Services," Provo, Utah, Provo Daily Herald, 12 January 1929, p. 1, column 2.

EXAMPLES OF CITING UNPUBLISHED SOURCES

The information below is a mix of valid and fictitious data used as an example of documentation.

1. Personal Letter

Author: Mary Jones

Description of the Letter: Letter to Barry Ewell

Date: 23 February 1977

Detail: Weekly letter from Mary Jones to Barry Ewell during his mission in Munich, Germany. Topic of letter was trip to California.

Specific Location: Original handwritten letter in possession of Barry Ewell

Form Used and Repository: Hand written

Formatted:

Mary Jones, Letter to Barry Ewell, 23 February 1977, [Original handwritten letter in possession of Barry Ewell. Weekly Letter from Mary Jones to Barry Ewell during his Mission in Munich, Germany. Topic of letter was trip to California.]

2. Oral Interview

Title of notes or tape: Oral interview with James N. Ewell

Date of interview: 21 October 2001

Interviewer: Barry Ewell

Present Owner's name and address: Recording owned by Barry Ewell, Riverton, Utah

Form used and location: James Ewell was living in Mt. Pleasant, Utah

Place of Interview: Beaver, Utah

Evaluation information: Interview focused on experiences as policeman in Las Vegas, Nevada from 1968 to 1973

Formatted:

"Oral interview with James N. Ewell," 21 October 2001, by Barry Ewell, recording owned by Barry Ewell, Riverton, Utah, James Ewell was living in Mt. Pleasant, Utah, Interview took place in Beaver, Utah, interview focused on experiences as policeman in Las Vegas, Nevada from 1968 to 1973.

3. Photograph

Description: Photograph of Francis Marion Ewell

Date of Picture: Circa 1900

Location: Spring City, Utah

Taken by: George Edward Anderson

Specific Location: Glass plates in possession of Brigham Young University, Provo, Utah

Formatted:

Photograph of Francis Marion Ewell, circa 1900, Spring City, Utah, taken by George Edward Anderson, glass plates in possession of Brigham Young University, Provo, Utah.

4. Unpublished Document

Descriptive Title of Document: Personal History of John P. Jones

Significant dates or Numbers: Written Circa 1935

Page Numbers or other Specific Designation: Original owned by Daughters of Utah Pioneers, Spanish Fork, Utah

Other Detail: 4-page history written by daughter Mary Jones Wright

Location and Form of Record: Copy received and in possession of Barry Ewell, Riverton, Utah, 7 July 1997

Formatted:

"Personal History of John P. Jones," Circa 1935, 4 pages, written by daughter Mary Jones Wright, Copy received from Daughters of Utah Pioneers, Spanish Fork Utah, 7 July 1997, in the possession of Barry Ewell, Riverton, Utah.

EXAMPLES OF CITING OFFICIAL RECORDS

The information is a mix of valid and fictitious data used as an example of documentation.

1. Vital Records

Descriptive Title of Record: Certificate of Death

Individual: James Neil Ewell

File # or other Descriptive: 20-004

Significant Dates: 8 January 2006

Location of the Record: State of Utah—Department of Health

Location and Form of Record: Certificate copy in possession of Barry Ewell, Riverton, Utah

Formatted:

Death certificate, James Neil Ewell, File No. 20-004, State of Utah—Department of Health, Certificate copy in possession of Barry Ewell, Riverton, Utah.

2. Census Record

Specific Descriptive Title: 1920 United States Census

Civil Division: Provo Ward 5, Utah, Utah

Page Numbers or other Specific Designation: p. 251, family dwelling 223, 3rd West, Enumeration District No. 209, 10B, lines 96-100, 14 January 1920

Location and form of record: Ancestry.com

Formatted:

1920 United States Census, Provo Ward 5, Utah, Utah, p. 251, family dwelling 223, 3rd West, Enumeration District No. 209, 10B, lines 96-100, 14 January 1920, Ancestry.com.

3. Legal Record

Descriptive Title: Divorce of Ann Jones vs. Ricy D. Jones

Significant Dates: 23 September 1874

Specific Location of the Records: Probate Court, Territory of Utah, Cache County, Logan City

Additional Detail or Description:

Copy of the record in the possession of Barry J. Ewell, Riverton, Utah

Formatted:

"Divorce of Ann Jones vs. Ricy D. Jones," 23 September 1874, Probate Court, Territory of Utah, Cache County, Logan City, Copy of record in possession of Barry J. Ewell, Riverton, Utah.

4. Church Records

Description Title: Baptismal Record
Individual: Soren Nielsen
Significant Dates: 27 Feb 1821
Specification Location: Ringerike, Norway, Parish Records
Form used and Repository: FHC Microfilm 0123956, p 185, number 8

Formatted:

"Baptismal Record of Soren Nielsen," 27 Feb 1821, Ringerike, Norway, Parish Records, FHC Microfilm 0123956, p 185, number 8.

5. Cemetery Records

Description Title: Headstone Inscription
Individual: Mary Jones
Significant Dates: 3 Aug 1997
Specification Location: Spanish Fork, Utah, Cemetery
Plot/Lot number: Lot 242
Form used and Repository: Barry Ewell Visit on 31 May 2002

Formatted:

Headstone inscription for Mary Jones, 3 Aug 1997, Lot 242, Spanish Fork, Utah Cemetery, (Located approximately 900 South 10th East), Barry Ewell Visit on May 31, 2002.

EXAMPLES OF CITING ONLINE SOURCES

The information is a mix of valid and fictitious data used as an example of documentation. **Note:** When possible, I include a URL or email address of the contact or source of the information and a physical address, because email addresses tend to change.

1. Scanned Image File

Description: Birth Certificate
Individual: Mary Jones
Details: Certificate # 345-289
Date: 18 Oct 1933
Location: Spanish Fork, Utah
Scan Date: 24 Nov 2005
Image File Name: JONES-Mary Jones Birth Certificate.tif
Scanned by: Barry Ewell, xxx@msn.com, Riverton, Utah
Address of person who scanned:
Image Editing: Digitally retouched by Barry Ewell, Riverton, Utah, January 2006 to provide color correction to faded document. Data was not changed.

Formatted:

Birth certificate of Mary Jones, Spanish Fork, Utah County, Utah, Certificate # 345-289, 18 Oct 1933, Image File: JONES-Mary Jones Birth Certificate.tif, scanned by Barry Ewell, [xxx@msn.com, Riverton, Utah], 20 November 2005, [Image has been digitally retouched by Barry Ewell, Riverton, Utah, January 2006 to provide color correction to faded document. Data was not changed.]

2. Email Message

Author: Igor Pleve
Email Address: xxx@mt.ixu.ru
Message Title: 1857 Schondorf Census-Wagner Surname
Description of Email: Message to Barry Ewell
Date: 6 April 2004
Specific Location: Electronic file in possession of Barry Ewell
Detail: Description of 1857 Census, Schondorf, Russia with Wagner Surname
Form Used and Repository: Located in Wagner Surname Folder, Igor Pleve Correspondence, File Name Igor Pleve-1857 Shondorf Census-Wagner Surname

Formatted:

Igor Pleve, [xxx@mt.ixu.ru], "1857 Shondorf Census-Wagner

Surname," Message to Barry Ewell, 6 April 2004, Electronic file in possession of Barry Ewell, [Description of 1857 Census, Schondorf, Russia with Wagner Surname, Located in Wagner Surname Folder>Igor Pleve Correspondence>File Name Igor Pleve-1857 Shondorf Census-Wagner Surname.]

3. Message Board:

Author: George Wright

Email address: xxx@gmail.net

Message Title: John Mullins 1789 White Hall, Virginia

Date: 23 March 2006

Message URL: http://www.genealogy.com/genealogy/17_after.html?priority=0001000

Description: John Mullins family in Whitehall, Albemarle County, Virginia. Lineage of family and children from 1750 to 1804

Form Used and Repository: Copy downloaded and in the possession of Barry Ewell, Located in Mullins surname Folder>Message Board-Mullins>John Mullins 1750-1804

Formatted:

George Wright, [xxx@gmail.net], John Mullins 1789 White Hall, Virginia, 23 March 2006, [http://www.genealogy.com/genealogy/17_after.html?priority=000100], John Mullins family in Whitehall, Albemarle County, Virginia. Lineage of family and children from 1750 to 1804], Copy downloaded and in the possession of Barry Ewell, Located in Mullins Surname Folder>Message Board-Mullins>John Mullins 1750-1804.

4. Website File

Description: Ewell Family Organization

Individual: Family line of Francis Marion Ewell

Website Address: http://www.ewellfamily.org/

Date: 29 June 2006

Detail: Downloaded Franklin Marion Ewell Gedcom. Reviewed data and includes detail and sources. Compiled by Ginger Hall

Form Used and Repository: Copy in the possession of Barry Ewell, Located in Ewell Surname Folder>Gedcoms,>Francis Marion Ewell

Formatted:

Family line of Francis Marion Ewell, Ewell Family Organization, <http://www.ewellfamily.org/>, June 29, 2006, [Downloaded Franklin Marion Ewell Gedcom. Reviewed data and includes detail and sources. Compiled by Ginger Hall], Copy in the possession of Barry Ewell, Located in Ewell Surname Folder>Gedcoms,>Francis Marion Ewell.

Lesson 8: If Sherlock Holmes Were a Genealogist

I have always been a fan of detective stories. My father was a detective for the Las Vegas police department during the 1960s. In his later years, I enjoyed listening to his stories of how he was able to crack the case after careful research and analysis.

As I read and listened to the Sherlock Holmes stories by Sir Conan Doyle, I noticed that Sherlock used the same strategies as my father.

I thought it would be fun to create a personal research project where I would use Sherlock Holmes as model. What would Sherlock Holmes do if he were a genealogist? My intent was to see if I could uncover and understand the principles and then apply them to my own genealogy research practices. The results of my project dramatically changed my approach to genealogy research. I'd like to share with you what I found.

SHERLOCK HOLMES UNDERSTOOD ANALYSIS

Analysis is a systematic approach to problem solving. Complex problems are made simpler by separating them into more understandable elements. Sherlock Holmes plainly identified analysis when he said, "When you eliminate the impossible, whatever you have left, no matter how improbable, must be the truth."

Some analysis is simply common sense. For example: You find a family record that identifies a mother to be younger than her offspring. Obviously, this cannot be true.

Other situations are cause for careful research and analysis. For example, I have an ancestor named Permitt Lee in the 1780s from Virginia. I was hoping he was related to General Robert Lee. However, there appears to be at least four Lee families in or passing through Virginia at this time. We are taking each family line one by one and seeking to "eliminate the impossible" so we can focus on the possible.

IF SHERLOCK HOLMES WERE A GENEALOGIST

Throughout the many Sherlock Holmes stories, there are four main steps followed for solving mysteries:

1. Observation—soaking up the facts
2. Search—getting to the nitty-gritty
3. Analysis—sorting through the jigsaw pieces
4. Imagination—the workshop of the mind

Much like Sherlock Holmes's approach to his cases, genealogical research methods involve beginning with a general concept and moving toward a more specific conclusion. This is also referred to as deductive reasoning. This is a process of reaching a conclusion that is guaranteed to follow if the evidence provided is true and the reasoning used to reach the conclusion is correct and logically sound.

Deductive reasoning involves using a foundation of known information and analyzing it in such a way as to make valid, objective, educated arguments for a family ancestral connection. Making such a case requires multiple pieces of information, oftentimes with supplementary resources, that logically tie personal circumstances together and consider facts that would otherwise exclude or negate the relationships in question from being established.

Deductive research is not a guessing game, a stab in the dark, or a linkage of names simply because you have found someone else with a family tree with the same surnames as yours.

As a beginning genealogist, I found my review of the facts to be either uniformed or analytically complex, trying to join too many pieces of the puzzle that didn't belong together. The following story will illustrate what I mean.

Deductive Reasoning, Dr. Watson Style!

Taking a well-earned break from the detective business, Sherlock Holmes and Watson, in *A Study in Scarlet*, were on a camping and hiking trip. They had gone to bed and were lying there, looking up at the sky.

> Holmes said, "Watson, look up. What do you see?"
> Watson replied, "Well, I see thousands of stars."
> "And what does that mean to you?"
> "Well, I suppose it means that of all the planets and suns and moons in the universe, that we are truly the one most blessed with the reason to deduce theorems to make our way in this world of criminal enterprises and blind greed. It means that we are truly small in the eyes of God but struggle each day to be worthy of the senses and spirit we have been blessed with. And, I suppose, at the very least, in the meteorological sense, it means that it is most likely that we will have another nice day tomorrow. What does it mean to you, Holmes?"
> Holmes replied, "To me, it means someone has stolen our tent."

Your research and deduction don't need to lead to a groundbreaking, intricate discovery; sometimes the simplest solution is exactly what you're looking for.

Step #1—Observation: Soaking Up the Facts

Whenever you are faced with any research situation or problem, you must first observe it. To gather the facts, we must first know what we are looking for. No matter what kind of investigation you are beginning, there are only two ways to obtain data. The first is by verbally interviewing people (taking the history). The second is by carefully scrutinizing objects (the physical examination).

Principle 1 of Observation: Genealogy observation requires the "eyes of a hawk."

Think of one of those intense, icy glares from Sherlock Holmes as he pans a room, taking in every detail.

"You see, but you do not observe," he said in *A Scandal in Bohemia*.

In *The Five Orange Pips*, Holmes said, "The observer who has thoroughly understood one link in a series of incidents, should be able accurately to state all the other ones, both before and after."

As you research any record, hear the answers to family history questions, or read the writings of your ancestors, just allow what is there to present itself to you. Open up your senses. Really listen— let the sounds affect you. Notice the smells. And look with the eyes of a hawk: sharp, precise, missing nothing. Be alert to every movement, every clue, and anything that is out of the ordinary.

Principle 2 of Observation: Do not pre-judge the situation.

When you first begin any research project, start with the assumption that you know nothing. For every genealogical problem you research, simply observe.

In looking, you are learning. When you see with fresh eyes, unclouded by what you think you know, your powers of observation become like that of a wild animal. You are far more alert. Your vision is sharper. There is no interference.

In *A Scandal in Bohemia*, Sherlock Holmes stressed the importance of not pre-judging a situation before the facts have been observed and gathered: "It is a capital mistake to theorize before one has data. Insensibly one begins to twist facts to suit theories, instead of theories to suit facts."

Evidence and Sources: What types of evidence (sources) can you expect to find in your research?

- *Primary Evidence:* Any evidence or event that is recorded at (or near) the time of the event such as a birth certificate or a will.

  "There is nothing like first-hand evidence." (Sherlock Holmes from *A Study in Scarlet*)

- *Secondary Evidence:* Any statement made by persons (or facts) that are from personal memory or any evidence recorded at any other time other than when the event occurred such as a death certificate.

- *Collateral Evidence:* Evidence that gives cause or clues to other records. The purpose of this type of evidence is an important part of the record without actually proving anything. For example, if a father speaks of his daughter in a will, land record, or deed by another surname, you would look for a marriage record for the daughter.

- *Circumstantial Evidence:* Evidence that provides an inference or hint toward a conclusion of fact. For example, a record mentions a daughter. Later he marries again and refers to the daughter as "daughter of a previous wife." This implies that he had at least one daughter by a previous marriage.

- *Reported Evidence:* Rumor, hearsay, family tradition, and so on. This type of evidence can be found in family interviews, family histories, county histories, biographies, and other such records. This information should be considered suspect until proven with primary or original evidence. For example, family tradition says Grandma was widowed young and raised her family alone, but records do not indicate a death (no probate, no change of land ownership, guardianship, and so on). When no proof appears that Grandpa died, you might suspect that he ran away from home for some reason.

Principle 3 of Observation: View your research from many different angles.

While we strive to be as objective as possible, the way a thing appears to us is always affected by the position from which we view it. To alleviate this flaw, we must try to observe our research from as many different angles as possible.

"I see no more than you, but I have trained myself to notice what I see" (Sherlock Holmes from *The Adventure of the Blanched Soldier*).

What types of resources will you find? Purists claim that in order to have confirmation of identity, you must have three independent sources of information. That is not always possible, so you must do the best with what you can get. Examples of what you'll find include the following:

- **Family**—Get as much information from people while they are still with us and still have full use of their memory.
- **Family Documents**—Bibles, prayer books, letters, photos, books, and so on can contain valuable family information.
- **Church Records**—Baptism certificates, marriage certificates, and burial records.
- **Cemetery Records**—Where specific headstones may be found. Headstone dates may be in error and reflect the assumed age, or be rounded, especially for very old people.
- **Newspapers**—May include birth announcements, wedding announcements, obituaries, and stories about family members.
- **Military Records**—Some restrictions apply to accessing these records. The individual must have been deceased for a specified period, and you may have to provide proof of this fact, especially if you are not a direct relative.
- **Genealogy Societies**—Can provide many helpful resources, such as the following:
  - Help from others on "how to" questions
  - Help searching in a particular locale
  - Cemetery headstone listings
  - Library of local publications
  - Listings of names (and addresses) of others and their families of interest
- **Historical Societies**—Good for local information.
- **Others Interested in *Your* Family**—May have limited or extensive information. May have computerized records, and may have even written a book about your family genealogy.
- **City Directories**—Tell who lived where and when; may give occupations.
- **Phone Books**—may be useful for uncommon names.
- **Books**—"How To" books may have limited information on people of interest to you; however, they point the way to other sources of information, such as local histories, which abound and may or may not have much information on individuals. The older ones tend not to be indexed.

- **Printed Genealogies**—some are available for sale at the time of publication.

Principle 4 of Observation: As you observe, you gather the facts.

You are looking to see the components of the situation or problem. You soak up everything. You ask questions of everything and everybody. You ask those questions with your senses: searching, seeking, questioning. You become totally receptive to the answers. To glean every bit of information, you learn the what and why, the when and how, and the where and who.

"There is nothing more deceptive than an obvious fact" (Sherlock Holmes from *The Boscombe Valley Mystery*).

What type of information or facts am I looking for?

Key Genealogical Data
- Full Name
- Dates and Places of
  - Birth
  - Baptism
  - Marriage
  - Divorce
  - Death (Cause)
  - Burial
- Moves (emigration or immigration)
- Names of
  - Parents
  - Siblings
  - Spouse(s)
  - Children
  - Grandparents, grandchildren, and so on
- Occupation
- Anything else of interest that may tell us what sort of people they are or were.

Principle 5 of Observation: Keep track of your observations.

As a genealogist, you will use a number of different resources in your search. Research logs are essential tools for keeping it all straight so you don't duplicate your work later. Even if you don't see the need for a research log during the beginning stages, it's a good bet that eventually you will forget some of the early records you searched. You can prevent this by indicating important facts in a research log, such as the following:

- Where the search was conducted (library, archives, family papers, and so on)
- When the search was conducted (be sure to list the full date, including the year)
- The record or other research used
- The information you did or did not find.

How can I keep track of my observations?

There are many helpful ways to keep track of all you glean from your research and observing. Here are a few ideas.

1. Personal handwritten systems
2. Computers are of great help. These may be general word processing and spreadsheet programs or specialty genealogical programs
3. Features of genealogical programs, including the following:
   - Additions, changes, and deletions should be easy
   - Help prepare index
   - Automatically link family relationships
   - Documentation of sources
   - Notes of miscellaneous information
   - Pedigree charts
   - Descendancy charts
   - Detect errors (death date earlier than birth date, for example)
   - Suggest identity among multiple records based on similar names and nearness of birth dates (for example, John b. 1834, Peter b. 1835, and John Peter b. 1833 may be the same fellow)

- Can merge records of individuals that appear more than once
- Easy to distribute copies of information
- Compatibility with other Genealogy Programs (GEDCOM)

Step #2—Search: Getting to the Nitty-Gritty

When he was on a case, Sherlock Holmes was like a bloodhound. He'd be down on his knees peering at cracks in the floorboards and then bounding through windows, over chairs, and up to the ceiling. You can picture him now with magnifying glass in hand, eyes sharply focused for clues.

> "He was out on the lawn, in through the window, round the room, and up into the bedroom, for all the world like a dashing foxhound drawing a cover" (Sherlock Holmes from *The Devil's Foot*).

This is the nitty-gritty, down-in-the-dirt aspect of problem solving. Don't be afraid of the minutiae. The solution lies in the details.

Principle 1 of Search: Search leads to clues.
Clues lead to answers.

In genealogy, you have to be willing to plunge into the details. Delve into the primary and secondary records and immerse yourself in the search for the answers.

Principle 2 of Search: Clues are found where you didn't look.

When you conduct your genealogy research, it becomes paramount to consider all your options and simply ask yourself, "Where should I look?"

> "Always look at the hands first, Watson. Then cuffs, trouser-knees, and boots" (Sherlock Holmes from *The Adventure of The Creeping Man*).

A few common mistakes we have all made in our research include the following:

- Not using forms (pedigree or lineage charts or family group records). These can be manual forms or forms produced by a genealogy software program.
- Avoiding contacting relatives and others working the same lines.
- Assuming there is no one else researching your lines.
- Not using maps for the time and area where your ancestors lived.
- Avoiding historical studies of your area or time frame of research.
- Failing to utilize family traditions when researching.
- Trying to connect to "published" or "printed" lineages.
- Avoiding using primary or original records.
- Losing control over your records (comes under the heading of organization).
- Not following through on clues.
- Ignoring spelling variants.
- Announcing you are at a brick wall or giving up. Brick walls should be considered as "rest stops" in research, not stopping places. This is a time to go back and review your data for new clues.
- Assuming the census names in one household are all one family.
- Assuming John Jr. is always the son of a John Sr.
- Not keeping an open mind to more than one marriage.
- Assuming all printed materials are correct.
- Avoiding re-analyzing your own work periodically for clues.

Principle 3 of Search: See your ancestors through the lens of the time in which they lived.

As genealogists, we often conduct our research from the point of view of today. It is important to have a knowledge of the history, geography, and social customs of the area and people being researched. Some knowledge of the history of the law and the language of an area and its people may also be necessary to understand the facts. When we take time to understand the world in which our ancestors lived, many clues will reveal themselves and open our eyes to understanding.

> "In my profession all sorts of odd knowledge comes useful, and this room of yours is a storehouse of it" (Sherlock Holmes from *The Adventure of the Three Garridebs*).

> "Have a cigarette, Mr. McFarlane. Beyond obvious facts that you are an asthmatic, I know nothing whatever about you" (Sherlock Holmes from *The Adventure of The Norwood Builder*).

> "According to my experience it is not possible to reach the platform of a Metropolitan train without exhibiting one's ticket" (Sherlock Holmes from *The Adventure of Bruce-Partington Plans*).

The following are several examples of how understanding the times and seasons can make a difference in your search.

Land records and probate records. They help to define family relationships. In order to prove facts, it was required to have land and personal tax lists include powers of attorney. You can find migration patterns through the land records. It's not uncommon to find all the persons who live in an area coming from the same place in the old country or migrating from the same area. As a genealogist, I will research the pertinent records in both places. Acknowledgment by the grantor of a deed provides evidence that the person was present at the location on that date, regardless of when the deed was recorded.

Court minutes or orders. These records define who was appointed as guardians for minors and as estate administrators. You will sometimes find acknowledgment in court of minors who attain legal age. Do not neglect looking for these records.

Combining History with Records. During the colonial period before the 1770s, an estate couldn't be divided until the youngest child became of age. When you search the Chancery court records, you can find evidence of attainment of legal age. Lawsuits were filed by lawyers on behalf of minor children naming the other children as defendants. Until a child attained legal age, a minor would first appear in the list of plaintiffs. The individual could later appear on list of defendants in subsequent actions if he had had siblings who were still minors. Look in the tax records because males became taxable at the age of sixteen.

Understanding Law. Law of primogeniture is the process through which the entire real property of the father passed to the eldest son at the death of the father. There are instances in which the eldest son isn't even mentioned in the will because the father knew that he would receive the property by law. Therefore, a genealogist cannot assume that every child is mentioned in a will during the colonial period. Similarly, the absence of an eldest daughter in a will may be explained by an examination of the land records. Her father may have given or sold her a portion of the land for a nominal price at her marriage.

Census Records. Census records are notoriously inaccurate, particularly in recording the ages of adults. Genealogists must examine a succession of census records containing the entries of the family to reveal the likely age. Birthplaces may not be indicated accurately since they're frequently representative of the childhood residence but not necessarily the birthplace.

Newspapers. Newspaper obituary accounts are based on information from persons who may not have precise information about the deceased. These accounts may be used as clues to obtain other data. When there are persons of the same name in the same locale, finding the one that is your ancestor requires careful research to eliminate each non-ancestor from consideration. This is necessary to prove that an ancestor is the only person in a particular place that could have been related to the family historian.

Principle 4 of Search: Change is constant, so sometimes *Broune* really is *Brown*

Be aware that in your research you will come across sources of trouble, but also be aware that these issues will create the opportunity for you to recognize facts and clues that you might otherwise miss. For example, be aware of the following items:

- **Vocabulary**—the way certain terms are used in older wills and other documents may not match current practice. For example, we accept "senior" and "junior" as referring to a father and son. However, years ago, it could refer to any two men in one community who happened to have the same name.

- **Dates and the Calendar**—Until 1582, the Julian calendar was used, which, over the centuries, had shifted out of sync with the seasons. To correct this discrepancy, Pope Gregory then adopted the system we use today. However, Protestant countries such as England and some German states refused to accept a "Catholic" calendar. By 1752, the Julian calendar was 11 days behind the Gregorian calendar. In that year, England decided to change over.

- **Handwriting**—Most early documents were handwritten. Some letters were written (or even printed) in a manner different from today—for example, the long S (ʃ), which was used until 1810, can be confused with F or P.

- **Names**—Family Name Spellings may change if the original spelling is not phonetic or of Anglo-Saxon origin.

- **Place Names**—May change or be repeated in different places. For example, provinces often repeat or reference the name of the founders' homeland (such as New Glasgow, Nova Scotia, Glasgow, and Prince Edward Island).

- **All Records**—All records may be suspect. Church records are probably the best, followed by civil records. Headstones are not always accurate, and census records may be off by a year or many more. Primary records (for example, record of marriage as found in the church where the event occurred) are preferred over secondary records (such as a printed county record) since there will be fewer opportunities for transcription errors.

- **Illegitimate Children**—may be attributed to others, especially grandparents.

- **Incomplete Data**—Can come from all sources. Losses (especially due to fire) years ago may leave gaps in the data.

Principle 5 of Search: Look under the chair.

Don't forget items of common use, either. Antiques that are handed down from generation to generation can substantiate your research. A chair may have been a wedding present; a piece of jewelry could have been presented to a new mother by her husband to celebrate the birth of a child. Important clues are often found by simply turning a picture over and seeing what is written.

STEP #3—ANALYSIS: SORTING THROUGH THE JIGSAW PIECES

The brilliance of Sherlock Holmes often came in the analysis of putting the jigsaw puzzle of clues and facts together to solve the mystery.

> "When you have eliminated all which is impossible, then whatever remains, however improbable, must be the truth." (Sherlock Holmes from *The Adventure of The Blanched Soldier*)

Think of a jigsaw puzzle. When you have all the pieces and they are all right-side up, you can then start to analyze where they go and how they fit together. The more pieces you have, the easier it will be to infer what the big picture will be. So the more angles you have observed a problem from and the more facts you have gathered about it, the more likely you are to be able to see the final solution. Let's take a look at how one might approach putting together a real jigsaw puzzle:

1. Take all pieces out of the box.
2. Using both hands, turn pieces face-up on the table and spread them out as you go.
3. Arrange the lid of the box so that you can see the picture.
4. Separate the edge and corner pieces and put the border together using the box lid picture as a guideline.
5. Find the edges and identify the four corners.

6. Hold each edge piece up to the picture to determine whether it's a north, south, east or west edge, then place them toward the like edge of your table in a line with the edges to the outside.
7. Divide the remaining pieces and organize them in groups such as colors, patterns, textures, and shapes.
8. Start placing similar pieces together until they fit and begin to form small parts of the larger picture.
9. Connect clusters together once you can, and keep looking at the box lid picture to find the locations of the groups of pieces.
10. Finish the puzzle, connecting all pieces together, and decide whether to glue the puzzle or take it apart and start another.

Important lessons when putting together a jigsaw puzzle:

- Use a table that you can keep a puzzle on for a few days or longer.
- Keep checking the box lid to remember what the overall picture looks like and to figure out where a certain piece might go.
- Avoid getting frustrated. Puzzles are supposed to be challenging but not overly frustrating. If you do get frustrated, walk away and come back later to try again.

How is this like genealogy? You take the pieces of the jigsaw—the facts—and you begin to think about how they fit together, how they relate to one another, how one links to the other, and what affect that has on the overall picture.

"Each fact is suggestive in itself. Together they have a cumulative force" (Sherlock Holmes from *The Adventure of the Bruce-Partington Plans*).

Principle 1 of Analysis: Study the merits of any information you receive.

To study the merits of your information, sort your information into the following categories:

- Actual Truth (proof is certain)
- Probable Truth (proof is probable, but not absolutely certain)
- Supposed Evidence (you suspect this is true, but you can't be sure). Give reasons why you suspect it to be true.
- Absolutely Ridiculous (utter nonsense, but it can't be ignored)

"It has long been an axiom of mine that the little things are infinitely the most important" (Sherlock Holmes from *A Case of Identity*).

"One drawback of an active mind is that one can always conceive alternate explanations which would make our scent a false one" (Sherlock Holmes from *The Problem of Thor Bridge*).

Use the five Ws. The "five Ws" method of analyzing can be applied to every document and source that you acquire.

- **Who?** Before you start your search define the "who." Was the surname spelled differently during different times? Was the spelling changed at the time of immigration?
- **What?** What do you want to know?
- **Where?** This is probably the most important fact, after "who." If you don't know the "where," you're not going to find anything!
- **When?** Give a time frame or time period so you know where to search for records.
- **Why?** Find the reasons behind the facts. Why did your ancestor immigrate from Germany to the United States? Why did they move from Illinois to Wyoming? Why are there so many German (or Irish, or Italian, and so on) people in the area? Why did grandma have her first child at fifteen and grandpa was thirty-two? Was he married before?
- **How?** Determine how you will go about your research. How do you answer all these questions? How will you find the records you need?

Principle 2 of Analysis: Compare all the evidence.

It's relatively easy to compare data. Get your data together, arrange it in usable form (chronological or group), and then compare and contrast the information. If there are differences, note them until you can prove the differences one way or another. I prefer to keep all of it and make the appropriate notes, such as "This is family tradition, but it was disproved by (source)."

> "Circumstantial evidence is a very tricky thing. It may seem to point very straight to one thing, but if you shift your own point of view a little, you may find it pointing in an equally uncompromising manner to something entirely different" (Sherlock Holmes from *The Boscombe Valley Mystery*).

Research that you have previously completed may contain more clues than you might think. When we are new and starting our research, we grab anything and everything we can find—and then never look at it again. Many of the answers we are looking for now may be in those records and notes. You could find useful materials that you previously missed.

When looking at the documents you so painstakingly acquired, just remember to use them, reuse them, and then use them again.

Principle 3 of Analysis: Check for warning signs.

Your research should be critically analyzed for accuracy and completeness at each phase of your search. As you analyze your records and research, be aware of the warning signs that may denote that your information is off the mark.

> "My dear Watson, you as a medical man are continually gaining light as to the tendencies of a child by the study of the parents. Don't you see that the converse is equally valid? I have frequently gained my first real insight into the character of parents by studying their children" (Sherlock Holmes from *The Adventure of the Copper Beeches*).

For example, let's consider the common warning signs we see in pedigree charts and family group sheets:

- Do you have blank lines?
- Is there incomplete information on the children?
- Is circa (CA) or "about" used too often?
- Are dates too close together or too far apart to be correct?
- Check for historical impossibilities. If a child was born in 1860, there is no way he would have served in the Civil War. On the other hand, look for historical possibilities. What war *could* he have served in? Was there a massive migration? Check the timelines to see what was happening in the world, state, or county at the time this ancestor was alive.
- Do you have wrong locations or missing locations? Is a county or town listed, or just the state?
- Is there any other missing information? Marriages of children? Second marriages?
- Each line on that form serves a purpose. Make sure all of them (or as many as possible) are filled in.

Principle 4 of Analysis: Draw your conclusions.

Once you have done the above, you are ready to make a decision. This means you have found solid, indisputable proof that will extend your pedigree. These indisputable facts are your "for sure" group. Then there are the "maybes;" you need to work on these more, but perhaps they will prove to be true. And finally, there is the "might be" category. You keep these and review them from time to time because they may fit in when you get additional information.

> "It is of the highest importance in the art of detection to be able to recognize out of a number of facts which are incidental and which vital. Otherwise your energy and attention must be dissipated instead of being concentrated." (Sherlock Holmes from *The Reigate*)

STEP #4—IMAGINATION: THE WORKSHOP OF THE MIND

Sherlock Holmes often sought seclusion to help him solve a problem; he would remove himself from all disturbances so that he could use his imagination to freely explore the problem from all angles.

As with Einstein, Holmes would take up the fiddle to help himself relax. While one part of his mind would be occupied with playing the violin, the greater part of his mind was able to roam free and form new ideas.

Holmes referred to the imagination as the mother of truth. In his times of reverie, he could allow the interplay of ideas to generate new insights into whatever case was taxing him at that time.

So there you have it. You are just as much a genius as Sherlock Holmes.

Keep an open mind when you evaluate your "evidence." The research process can be defined in five steps:

1. Gather data in order to define the problem(s) accurately.
2. Look for answers in more than one source in order to draw conclusions from all evidence.
3. Look for other alternatives.
4. Follow clues to their logical conclusions in order to make decisions based on facts.
5. Gather more data.

Your research should be critically analyzed for accuracy and completeness at each phase of your search. Remember: when looking at the documents you so painstakingly acquired, you should use them, reuse them, and then use them again. The following steps will help you glean all you can from your sources:

- Ask yourself, "What are they trying to tell me?"
- Determine what they were used for.
- Remember the time frame and the context within that time frame.
- Search for clues.
- Eliminate the impossible.
- Check out the possible to come up with the probable.
- Look for substantiating documentation.

Lesson 9: Learn to Network

If you are not networking with other genealogists, you are not being an effective genealogist. While I would like to think I am a good genealogist, I would not have found or been exposed to even a fraction of the results I have found had it not been for the willingness of other genealogists, historians, librarians, and local experts to share their knowledge and insights.

When you make contact with those who share similar interests, it's like a breath of fresh air that will renew your research. I am continually collaborating with others when I have a research question, when I am at a fork in the road and not sure of which way to turn, or simply to share my experiences.

I had been researching one of my ancestral lines in Virginia and all but lost the trail. I didn't have any leads of where to turn to next. I knew that my ancestor had attended a specific church in the community during the late 1700s. I contacted the county historical society via email to see if they had any members or projects that knew about the congregation. I explained that my research dead ends and that I was looking for others with whom I could collaborate and share research experience and knowledge.

Several weeks later, I received an email that explained that there was a group of researchers who had family who attended the church during the time period of my ancestors. If I was interested, the writer would be willing to forward my information to the other researchers. I took the opportunity to compose an email outlining what I knew, my personal contact information, the questions I would like to learn about the congregation and its members, and my desire to personally speak with the other researchers.

I received responses from two researchers with contact information. I set a time to speak with each of them. Neither of the researchers were direct links to my ancestral lines, but our ancestors did share an experience. I gained incredible insights into the members of the congregation, where they were from, what type of records exists and where they could be found, and how the group influenced the community.

Find opportunities to network. Networking can take place online, by correspondence, or in person. Opportunities for networking can happen through any and all of the following platforms:

- Blogs
- Classroom participation
- Collaborative editing
- Genealogy-specific social networks
- General social networking (such as Facebook)
- Message boards and mailing lists
- Photos and video sharing
- Podcasts
- RSS feeds
- Sharing personal libraries
- Society membership
- Virtual worlds
- Wikis
- Workshop or national conference attendance

The more information you gather about your ancestor, the more ideas you will have about who might be able to help you. Write down or list the different "groups" your ancestors fit into, classifying your ancestors by any other classification, ethnic group, fraternal or religious association, gender, military service, occupation, residence locale (local, county, state), social class, and time frame or era.

Find networking resources among family members; local, regional, and state libraries; local, regional, and state museums; university libraries and archives; genealogy societies; historical societies; message boards; mailing lists; social networks; and blogs.

Learn to use available resources to network. There are an ever-increasing number of resources and online communities where you can begin and continue to collaborate with other genealogists.

Genealogy and social networking sites. Online communities have been built as a place for individuals with common interests to build new relationships. These online services provide simple tools to generate collaborative opportunities for finding, sharing, and interacting with like-minded people. Social networking websites use networking technologies such as wikis, RSS, and mapping. Online family tree building helps people connect with family members and other researchers. Many of the sites become a platform for the family social experience. Families can produce content, preserve connections, add historical anecdotes, and communicate across a number of mediums like instant messaging and email, as well as picture and family tree viewing. You can browse by city or country to view uploaded photos of that city and names of genealogists that live in that city. Examples include Facebook, FamilyLink.com, Famiva.com, Google-plus, LinkedIn, MyFamily.com, MyHeritage. com, MySpace, and Twitter.

I actively use social networks such as Facebook and Twitter. I can reach long, long distances—even across the pond—for little or no cost at all. Usually you are contacting people who have already advertised their body of knowledge and expertise.

Facebook is the leading social networking site today and has been adopted openly by the genealogy community. Facebook has allowed me to find near and distant family. I have followed other genealogists who offer online seminars or have websites with information on genealogy and the industry.

Twitter is a messaging platform in which—just like Facebook "friends"—you gather "followers." These are people who find your messages interesting and decide to follow you. Twitter is different than simple text messaging in that you are limited to 140 characters and you have a band of followers. I actively "tweet" (the act of sending messages on Twitter) the surnames that I am searching for, especially the ones for whom I have brick walls.

Email. Writing and sending email is a quick, inexpensive, and effective means for promoting communication. Email can be sent with attached documents and photographs. A brief and polite email to a potential, newfound, or known relative is often the beginning of a wonderful exchange. When communicating via email, traditional courtesies should be observed.

Mailing lists. A mailing list is simply an email party line. Every message that a list subscriber sends to the list is distributed to all other list subscribers. Subscribing to a mailing list is one of the best ways of connecting to people who share your interests. Genealogy-related mailing lists can cover surnames, US counties and states, other countries and regions, ethnic groups, and various other topics. Many websites host mailing lists, including RootsWeb.com, Ancestry.com, and Genealogy.com.

Wikis. A wiki is a page or collection of web pages that is designed to enable anyone who accesses the wiki to contribute or modify content. The value of a wiki is that anyone can contribute. The combined efforts of several individuals usually create a better end result than any one individual could by themselves. Wikis are used to create collaborative websites where a community can work together to provide meaningful content. The most widely known wiki is Wikipedia.com. FamilySearch started the Research Wiki at wiki.familysearch.org. Be careful, though: because anyone can contribute, you must make sure to check the accuracy of information retrieved from a wiki site.

Message boards. There are message boards focusing on surnames, localities, and many other genealogy topics. By posting a message to the appropriate message board, you create a record through which other researchers can find you. You'll find message boards on Ancestry.com, RootsWeb.com, and Genealogy.com.

The message boards are a "must do" connecting point for genealogists to collaborate with one another on research topics of mutual interest in a public forum. The focuses of the boards range from surnames to locations to special topics. Depending on the board and the number of people posting queries and replies, the flow and volume of information that is exchanged is dynamic.

The majority of people using the message boards have been doing genealogy for more than ten years. There is a great pool of knowledge and experience coming together to help one another. I have used message boards to assist in the process of planning and evaluating genealogy trips to Ireland, Wales, Scotland, Norway, Germany, and Russia and which one I should do when.

I posted my queries in both the country- and county-specific boards for the focus of my research and within hours—and for the next week—I received very insightful hints and direction from people who lived in the area or who had gone on trips such as I was planning. Some people replied to the message boards, and others sent an email directly to me. Thoughts ranged from where to conduct my research to where to stay and eat to where I would most likely find graves of my family, as well as offering insights on personal genealogy.

In another case, I had posted a message in November 2005 concerning research I was conducting on the Mullins family from Goochland County, Virginia. My first reply was six months later. The individual who responded replied that he had been doing research on his line with the same name and realized that information he had gathered was not of his line and sent it to me, along with several links to review. We continued a correspondence away from the message boards for a couple of weeks, seeking to help each other with our research.

Remember: most message boards are open to the public, so anyone can view or post a query or reply. It becomes your responsibility to make sure that the information you're getting ready to post is really the information you want to share with the world. There will be no time limit as to how long the message will be posted. I have messages that have been out there for five or more years. Once you press "submit," the information is now free to be used as the public chooses to use it.

Take the time to carefully compose your message, providing the key information others will need to help you in your research. For example, the following information is usually important to provide when helping others identify family connection:

- Full name, including any middle names or initials

- Birth, marriage, and death dates
- Places where the above events occurred
- Residence and migration
- Names of their children and parents

Don't be afraid to provide detailed information. If I am looking for specific help, I need to be able to provide enough background information so that others can review it and provide quality input. It helps others understand that you have done your homework, and they will give you better answers.

Check your grammar and spelling. Think about how an error will change the response you might get, such as if you enter a date of 1962 and really meant 1926.

Rather than compose your message in the data entry window provided by the message board, compose your message in your word processing software first, run spell check, edit, and then copy and paste your message into the appropriate message window.

It is important that you use the message boards to keep track of your efforts by doing one or more of the following:

- Use a correspondence log to track your message board posts and queries. Information to track will include the date when you posted, where it was posted, and a summary of your post. As you receive the replies, track the date the reply was received and the results (positive or negative).
- Use bookmarks or favorites. Simply create a folder in your bookmarks or favorites for the explicit purpose of tracking message board queries. The program will usually allow you to add comments each time you visit the site.
- Use your genealogy software to keep track of your message board queries. Some family tree software programs include correspondence logs or to-do lists. Be sure to include the URL, copy of your post or query, the date you last checked, and so forth.

Digital sticky notes. Some websites allow you to add "digital sticky notes." Post-em is the electronic equivalent of a sticky note. These notes allow you to attach your email address, a link to another website address, and other information to the record of any individual. Search for your ancestors and leave your calling card attached to their names.

On RootsWeb.com you can add Post-em notes to the Social Security Death Index (SSDI), the WorldConnect Project, and other databases. On Ancestry.com, these notes are called "Comments and Corrections" and can be used to add alternate names to an individual's record or to add other comments about the person, both of which are viewable by other researchers.

On the Ellis Island website, you can add annotations to individual records; go to www.ellisisland.com. All of these additions to records are viewable by other researchers. Digitally sticky notes could potentially help in your research and can connect you with other researchers.

Family tree databases. Online family tree databases can help you locate others interested in the surnames you are researching. These resources include the following websites:

- Pedigree Resource File at www.familysearch.org
- Ancestry World Tree at www.ancestry.com
- WorldConnect at www.rootsweb.com

You can initiate contact through email. A number of online services also allow you to locate living individuals who may have family information to share.

Repositories and Libraries. Many libraries, archives, and societies have excellent and well-known collections of genealogical research materials. Several of these repositories—particularly the smaller ones—maintain lists of researchers and the local area families they are researching.

One of the better-known repositories is the the Family History Library (FHL), owned and maintained by The Church of Jesus Christ of Latter-day Saints and located in Salt Lake City, Utah. (For more information, visit www.familysearch.org.) It is the most widely known repository of genealogical materials. The FHL has been acquiring and preserving genealogical data since its founding in 1894. The library has collected vital information on hundreds of millions of deceased individuals. This data includes print and micro-form copies of records from all over the world. Copies of records are made available at the library in Salt Lake City and at family history centers throughout the United States and in many foreign countries as well. All are welcome to visit the FHL and its subsidiaries. A catalog of FHL sources is available online.

Societies. Hundreds of genealogical and historical societies across the country seek to preserve records and provide instruction to family historians. Most genealogists are willing to share findings, exchange ideas, and tell of their research experience. Societies work to preserve records, make records available, promote educational opportunities, and encourage participation in society activities. By tapping into the society's resources, you gain educational opportunities, instructional articles published in their periodicals, local skill-building sessions, and one- or two-day seminars featuring nationally known professionals. You will find members of the societies who know some or all of the following helpful information:

- Which records are available
- How you can access those records
- What information is online, in books, and in folders
- The experience level of members and other genealogists
- Where information is located if they don't have it
- Who to talk to if they don't know the answer—perhaps leading you to others who may be researching your surname
- History of the immigrants

Many groups form at the county level because of the research significance of local area records; organizations also exist to study a single surname or the descendants of a particular couple. Ethnic or religious origins account for many such groups, such as the Polish Genealogical Society of America and Pursuing Our Italian Names Together (P.O.I.N.T.). Other societies bring together researchers with common locales of origin—for example, groups such as The Palatines to America and Germans from Russia.

Every state has a genealogical or historical society, a state council, or both. In addition to major projects, the following is a list of the types of projects that a state-level group might coordinate with the efforts of local societies within the state:

- Their publications (newsletters and journals) supplement those produced by local societies.
- Some state organizations, such as the Ohio Genealogical Society, offer chapter membership throughout the country.
- Other state organizations operate on a less-structured basis.

At the national level, a number of organizations serve individual genealogists or societies, such as the following:

- The Federation of Genealogical Societies (FGS)—www.fgs .org.
- Umbrella organizations for genealogical and historical societies and research institutes, such as libraries and archives.
- The National Genealogical Society (NGS) comprised of individual researchers—www.ngsgenealogy.org.
- The oldest society in the United States is the New England Historic Genealogical Society (NEHGS)—www.nehgs.org.

Volunteer efforts. Most societies create and manage projects to benefit the genealogical community, such as indexing and preservation activities and producing periodicals and other publications. There are also many genealogists who work independently of societies. You will find numerous online indexes and databases created by these volunteers. Many of these projects are on the USGenWeb Project at www.usgenWeb.org. This website is full of volunteer-driven sites that publish historical information and resource material, such as a list of sites that offer cemetery indexes and newspaper abstracts.

Volunteers maintain sites and often provide important local details about an area's history, geography, and settlement. They also usually give an overview of record availability and access and research tips.

Professional groups. You can interact with professional genealogists by writing articles and books, presenting lectures that provide new information, and giving examples of methodologies to help in difficult research situations. Professionals often lead efforts to protect records in jeopardy and to make them available for wide use. Many (but not all) professionals conduct research on a contract basis for others and can assist a family historian with a quest that seems impossible. The research that professionals do ranges from an entire lineage to small but significant tasks in their field of expertise.

In the United States, there are several groups that serve the interests of professional genealogists and their clients, as well as those of the genealogical community. The following is a list of some such organizations, along with some basic information about each group:

- The Association of Professional Genealogists (APG)
  PO Box 40393, Denver, CO 80204-0393
    - Membership organization that does not administer tests, award credentials, or otherwise endorse individual researchers.
    - The association does offer arbitration in the event a dispute arises between any association member and the general public.
    - The APG website (www.apgen.org) lists members' names, contact details, and areas of expertise.

- The Board for Certification of Genealogists
  PO Box 14291, Washington, DC 20044
    - Certifying body that is not affiliated with any group.
    - BCG screens applicants through a testing process; successful candidates earn the initials CG (Certified Genealogist).
    - A roster of certified genealogists is at the BCG website: www.bcgcertification.org

- The International Commission for the Accreditation of Professional Genealogists (ICAPGen)
    - Offers independent testing without membership.
    - This program, established in 1964 (by the Family History Department of The Church of Jesus Christ of Latter-day Saints), is designed to examine and accredit researchers in specialized geographic areas.

- Those who successfully complete the program receive the initials AG (Accredited Genealogist).

- The American Society of Genealogists (ASG)
  - Founded in 1940 as an honorary society, limited to fifty lifetime members designated as Fellows (identified by the initials FASG):
  - Election to the ASG is based on a candidate's published genealogical scholarship.
  - A list of Fellows and news of the ASG Scholar Award can be found at their website (www.fasg.org).

Blogs. A blog, short for "web log," is an easy way to post new information online. When a new article or tip is posted, it is sent automatically to anyone who has subscribed to the blog. By subscribing to one or more genealogy blogs, you can keep up with the latest techniques, tips, and databases.

How can you get the most out of your blog reading time? Focus on the title. Look over the article (just a brief scan). Determine if the post is of interest or value to you. If not, carry on elsewhere.

If it is of interest, analyze who wrote the post. What are their qualifications for this topic?

Determine one or two questions that you hope to find answers to by reading the post before thoroughly reading it. This will transform you from a passive consumer of information into an active reader. Read the actual post. Reflect on the questions you asked yourself before you read the post. Were your questions answered? Take mental or written notes about the post. Summarize the post in your own words.

INCREASING THE PRODUCTIVITY OF YOUR EMAIL

Keep it simple. If this is your first genealogy-related email, consider this an introduction. Explain who you are. Briefly explain your interest in family history. Don't overwhelm the recipient with questions or your entire family tree in your first email. Tell how you're related to the person or family you are contacting them about. Consider how you found out about the person you are contacting. Was it from the relative or researcher? If appropriate, pass on a greeting from that person.

The subject line is everything. The subject will oftentimes determine whether your email is opened or directed to an email's "spam" or "trash" folder. Consider putting the full name or surname of the specific ancestor plus the word genealogy. For example, "Ewell Genealogy."

Writing to someone who speaks another language. If you're writing someone who speaks a different language than you, request help from someone who knows the language. Review a research guide from the county of the Family History Library catalog. There are usually several examples of letters in various languages with English translation. Language translation sites can help in a pinch. If you're not sure in which language to send your email, send it in both languages. Use simple words and phrases in your email, which will increase the chance that words will be translated correctly. Check (and, if needed, correct) key facts such as names and dates before you send email.

Remember that you are writing to request a favor. Once you have contacted the individual, there still may be some reservation about who you are or about sharing the requested information. Let them know it would be helpful to receive a few basic facts. Ask them what further information they may need from you. If they refuse to share information, don't press them. Ask them if there is someone else that could provide assistance.

Say "Thank you." When individuals take time to help you, write a thank-you note to them. The time to write thank-you's is the minute you finish reading their email. It is also nice to keep them posted on the progress of your research going forward.

How to write an email.

Begin by making sure that you have the correct email address of the person you are emailing. If you don't, it will come back to you as undeliverable. Type the email address into the "TO" box.

Next, determine the topic of the email. The topic is what should go in the "RE" or "Subject" box. Be specific, because the recipient may not know you; if she can't determine what the email is about, then she may simply delete your message—or worse, flag it as spam. Keep the email short and succinct. The first word of the title should be capitalized; all other words—unless proper nouns—should be in lower case.

Begin typing the message to the recipient. Use the proper rules of grammar; if in doubt, www.drgrammar.org will answer any questions. Even if the email is more casual, such as an email to a friend or family member, take the time to prevent typographical errors, use proper form, and to use spell-check. To use spell-check, click on the icon marked "Spelling" or "Check Spelling" and it will check the body of the email for errors and suggest corrections. After you have written the body of the message, read it out loud to yourself to make sure you've used proper grammar and haven't omitted any text.

Finish the email with an ending, such as "Sincerely" or "Respectfully." Under that, add your name. If this is a business email, you should always type your email address and your telephone number below your name, as well as any other pertinent information, such as your company and your title. Once you are satisfied with your email, click "Send."

How to write a personal email

- **Choose your words.** Things can get taken out of context over email, so make sure your message is clear, readable, and friendly. While you can convey discontent in an email, you should always include a warm closing statement at the end—especially if it's not the most positive email. Short phrases and one-word replies can appear snide and rude—like you're talking to something, not someone, or to someone who doesn't matter. When it comes to business, clients need to feel special and that they can talk to you even using an impersonal form of communication such as email.

- **Determine the intended recipient and include a greeting with the recipient's name.** If you're writing back and forth, try to include a greeting in each reply. A greeting will help make the email more personal. In addition, use a salutation and sign your name, even just your first name if you're comfortable enough with a client or supervisor.

- **Enable future contact.** It's very important that someone can contact you in a way other than email, so give your phone number in the signature to your message. Some people don't agree with releasing this information; however, if you're in business, you can't hide behind a computer. Giving business associates your phone number shows that they can reach you should they wish to talk instead of using email alone.

- **Chit chat.** While you don't want to recap details of your weekend, you can include a personal note. It's never bad to tell someone you hope they had a nice time on their vacation after you ramble on in a message about business. I find this often leads to more personalized email and a strong business relationship. While you may not want to get too carried away talking about personal things over email with a client or boss, I think it's okay to get to know a supervisor or customer.

Observe email etiquette. As email becomes one of the most frequently used forms of communication, it's important that you observe proper email etiquette so that you keep communications cordial and respectful. From using basic writing etiquette rules to more complex technical customs, follow these steps to observe good email etiquette:

- **Write to your audience.** Just as with letter writing or spoken communication, it's important that you write an email with your specific audience in mind. Keep the email personal, but appropriately formal or casual by starting with a greeting and a few words of courtesy. Use spaces between paragraphs and an appropriate valedictory, such as "Best regards" or "Sincerely," to end the email.

- **Keep file attachments light.** One of the most common violations of email etiquette is attaching very large files to the email. Large files literally clog the recipient's email inbox, making the download very slow. If you need to send someone an email with an attachment that is larger than one megabyte, get approval from the recipient in advance or ask if there's a better way to transfer the file.

- **Make sure the email is relevant.** An email is an address box—just like your physical mailbox at home. So flooding people you know with emails that are important to you but irrelevant to them is considered bad etiquette and sometimes is even classified as "spam," or unwanted junk mail. Before you forward someone a joke, announcement, or chain letter—make sure you know that the recipient will appreciate the email's contents.

- **Keep email addresses private.** If you need to send an email to many people simultaneously, or if you're forwarding an email from one person to another, it's very important that you protect the email addresses of your contacts. To write an email with numerous recipients, put your own name in the "To" field and then use the bcc function to hide the recipients' email addresses. When forwarding an email, remove all mentions of the sender's email address before you send the email.

- **Use online abbreviations sparingly.** Although you might love using your favorite Internet abbreviations such as "btw," or "brb," you should be careful not to overuse such language in emails. Many email users might not understand "Internet-speak," and others may find it too casual. Observe the same principle of email etiquette when using smiley faces or other emoticons.

How to organize and manage your genealogy email

A big part of keeping your inbox and your email organized is discipline, along with having a system that you consistently put into practice. There are several tasks you can put into place upon checking your email to keep ahead of your email clutter.

Put your "delete" button to work. If you do not recognize the sender, look at the subject line. Are there funny characters or alpha-numeric gibberish, or does it just not make sense? Delete it! Don't fall for tricky subject fields that say any number of enticing comments that only someone you know or do business with would say. None of these types of emails are from friends or folks you know, and they won't be from companies you do business with. They are from spammers, and the worst kind too—those who underestimate your intelligence by thinking these emails will be something you would take seriously. If you don't know the sender and the subject field looks off, send them on their way to the trash; never respond to these messages (even to request removal from their email listings) since they use your response to note an active email address, keeping you hostage to their continued invasions of unwanted mail!

Once you have deleted all irrelevant or unwanted messages, your remaining email will probably be a compilation of these types of messages, which you may need to keep on hand for future reference: several emails from the same person; email from companies who send you their information quite regularly; email that is personal business; email of a more serious nature; and so on.

Set up filters. You are now ready to determine what to do with the remaining emails that still need to be organized in an efficient manner. This is where filters come into play. Filters (or "Rules," as they are called in Outlook) are what allow you to organize your email upon download (and Send too). As you download your email, it will be sorted into email folders set up for specific topics or contacts. This is a quick and easy way to become more organized. You can have a "Mom" filter that sends all email from dear old Mom right into your Mom folder. Set up filters to have email from your banking sites go directly into their own folders. Your favorite site can have its own folder. You can even have information from your financial institutions automatically end up in a folder specifically divided into further folders (such as Annuity, CDs, Stock, Bonds). The benefit of filters is that if you organize your email to go into their own folders upon download is that your inbox will have less of your requested or expected emails—leaving only the questionable email for you to review. Filters only need to be set up once, and they stay in place until you delete them. Other benefits of using filters: You can use them to send certain email right to the trash, bypassing your inbox altogether! Filters can be configured to find certain adult or offensive terms when listed in the subject line or body text of an email message and send them right to trash on the download!

Let's go back to your inbox. You now have filters in place that organize your email upon download, so all the email you requested or expected will automatically go into their appropriate folders for you to read at your convenience. Now your inbox should only have the orphan email with nowhere to go. After following the suggestions about using your delete button, begin to review your remaining email. If you run into an email that is from a new mailing list you've subscribed to and you plan on getting regular emails from, stop and make a folder and filter to accommodate these future emails. Set up a filter to look for something specific to that email (usually an email address works best), and then all future emails from that mailing list will go directly into their own folder. Do this for any email topic or contact for which you plan to receive email on a regular basis.

Read and delete unwanted emails. Read your email as time permits and then delete any email that doesn't have content worth keeping for future reference. Having too many email files uses a ton of your system's resources, so empty your trash often. Not keeping copies of email you really will never need in the future helps remove the clutter and drain on system resources.

Prioritize. When reading your email, you can prioritize when you want to address them in the future. Many email programs allow you to label email by color when viewing a particular folder. For example, you could have labels that at a glance tell you how you have prioritized your tasks—let's say red for "urgent," blue for "later," and yellow for "maybe." By opening that specific email box, you know at a glance which email you have set to address right away and which you can get to as time permits.

Create a folder called Follow-Up, Interesting, or To-Do. This is where you will file some of the emails from your inbox that piqued your interest or that you would like to review in more detail but just don't have the time right now. Then, when time permits, you can go to that folder and check into which emails are worth keeping. Once you review them, though, either send them to another folder for safekeeping or send them to the trash.

Clear your inbox daily. To avoid email backup, be sure your inbox is cleared each day. Move email to trash, a specific folder, or your to-do folder, and then empty the trash. If email is older than ninety days in your to-do folder, send them off to trash, since most likely the information or offer is no longer current. By doing so each day, you keep your inbox clear and your email much more organized.

Take out the trash. Your "trash" folder should be emptied daily—but before doing so, be sure to take a quick look just in case any of your filters inadvertently picked up on some terms that were included in email that you didn't want to trash. This happens quite often. A quick once-over before deleting your trash will ensure legitimate email you do want to read doesn't get lost in the shuffle.

What about all these folders? Have as many folders as you need to be organized and call them whatever will intuitively work for you with a glance. This system is meant to be unique to each and every user—make sure you use terms and a system that works for you.

How to keep track of genealogy queries and emails

As a genealogist, it's not uncommon to write the same email to multiple persons or post a query in multiple locations. How do you check answers? What if you have a new email address and need to change it in the query? How do you know which persons to follow up with via email?

The following is a list of tips to help you keep track of your communication trail:

- Use a correspondence log. Place a surname at the top of the page. Record information for each letter or query sent concerning that surname.
  - For emails, keep track of the following information: Email address (name of person); physical address if you have it; a little bit about the person you are emailing; what you sent in the email to them; subject line; summary of email; date of the email; date you received response and from whom; and

note if the results were positive or negative.

- For message board queries, keep track of the following information: message board where message was posted; why you
chose this message board; subject line; summary of post;
date of the post; date you received response and from whom;
and note if the results were positive or negative.

- Bookmarks or favorites in your web browser will enhance your
organizational techniques. Create a folder in your bookmarks or
favorites for the sole purpose of keeping track of your message
board queries. If your browser allows it, add a comment with the
name of the message board and the date of your last visit. You'll
need to remember to update the comments each time you visit,
just as you would with a correspondence log.

- Genealogy software can provide unique features to help keep
you in control. Consider using a genealogy software program
to keep track of your message board queries; you can either
use an organizational program, such as Clooz, or add them to
your family tree program. Some family tree software programs
include correspondence logs or to-do lists. For programs that
do not, select a primary ancestor for each surname and add the
information to the notes field. Be sure to include not only the
URL but also a copy of your post or query (including the date
you last checked).

Lesson 10: Stay Connected to the Network

Communication with real people is of paramount importance. My research would have been impossible without the help of others. The best way for me to expound upon this concept is by sharing several experiences that have been instrumental in my development and success as a genealogist. My experiences are much like those you can expect to have if you will only reach out and request help and give help.

"Whew, That's Enough for One Evening."

Early in my marriage, my wife's parents and my parents would provide us Christmas gifts in the forms of family histories, family group sheets, and collections of pictures from our youth. Most of the gifts caught my curiosity for an hour or so, but within a day or two the gifts were neatly stowed away under the bed or in a corner of the closet. Shortly after I became interested in learning more about my Ewell heritage, I began searching for someone who could really introduce me to the Ewells. Within a few calls, I was introduced to Valene.

Our first conversation lasted about thirty minutes. I began asking her if she could help me learn more about the Ewells and where we came from. She began by asking if I knew the name of my grandfather. I drew a blank. I responded, "Grandpa Ewell," and added with an apology that I didn't know.

Valene was so reassuring and told me she had been working on the Ewell genealogy (all variations of the name) from across the United States since the late 1970s. She asked a few more questions to help her focus on my family line. That was the first five minutes.

During the next twenty-five minutes, I became excited to learn that Grandpa Ewell's name was Arthur Emanuel Ewell. Our original progenitor in America was Maxcey Ewell from Virginia in the 1750s, who fought in the Revolutionary War. Over the next hundred years, the family migrated from Virginia to Tenneessee and then on to Missouri, where William Fletcher Ewell and his family joined the Mormon church and moved to Nauvoo, Illinois. In 1847, the family joined the Mormon migration west. William and his brother John Martin joined the Mormon Battalion during the Mexican-American War. Following his service in 1848, he returned to Iowa to retrieve his family and bring them west in one of the pioneer companies. While in Missouri, he died, and his widowed wife, Mary Lee Bland, came by herself with six children and settled in Utah. Valene went on to say that Francis Marion Ewell, the son of Willam and Mary Lee, had six children. Child number two, Fanklin Marion Ewell, was my Great–Grandfather, and son number five, William Walter, was Valene's father.

Whew, that was enough for one evening, I thought. I gave Valene my contact information and concluded with a heartfelt "thank you." Six days later, I unexpectedly received a large envelope from Valene filled with family histories, photos, and several group sheets. I read and reread every page.

That was the beginning of a relationship that has turned into a close genealogy friendship. Valene has been a mentor and important influence in guiding my Ewell family research. Together we have searched records, traveled the back roads of ancestral roots in Virginia and Pennsylvania, and supported one another in preserving our shared history.

30 Days and 300,000 Ancestors

I first introduced this experience in the chapter "Learn Where to Find Records." As I began the chapter, I introduced some of the lessons I learned from one of my first extended onsite visits to my ancestral lands in Kentucky, North Carolina, Pennsylvania, Tennessee, and Virginia. These lessons formed the basis of many of my best research practices. I'd like to continue the story here by providing several of the individual experiences.

As I made my original plans for the trip, I had only planned to be there for two weeks, split between Virginia and Washington, DC. The first seven days would be spent at the Library of Virginia in Richmond, Virginia, and several historical county societies, and the other seven days I planned on searching for family homesteads in Washington, DC. By the end of my second week, I made plans to extend my trip by two more weeks. I began my trip thinking I didn't need any help with my research. I left knowing that I couldn't be successful in my genealogy research without the help of others.

Preparing for Virginia. Prior to my trip, I thought I had been very thorough in my planning and was looking forward to a very productive trip. I was going to solve all the research brick walls that other researches had failed to resolve.

As part of my planning, I spent a good deal of time research-ing the Library of Virginia online catalog for possible resources to research. I found forty resources and thought it would take four days to research them all. In addition, I had called and set appointments to visit historical societies in Albemarle, Fluvanna, and Goochland counties.

Hitting research dead ends. Upon arriving for my first day of research at the Library of Virginia, I exhausted all forty of my resources in the first four hours, only finding minimal value in two resources. Needless to say, I was feeling rather demoralized thinking that I had made a big mistake by coming to Virginia. Not knowing what else I could do, I asked the librarian on staff if I could take a few minutes of her time to help refocus my research.

I shared with her my story and what I was trying to do. All the while, she was making a few notes. When I completed my five-min-ute explanation, she asked me a few questions about the resources I had viewed and what I wanted to accomplish. As I answered, she continued to write a few more notes.

At this point, I was very curious as to what she had written. She turned the piece of paper around and began to outline seven to ten possibilities to consider in my research. She introduced ideas of collections I could research that were located in various libraries throughout the state. She suggested individual experts that knew more than she did about available resources. At this point, I was ready to try anything. When she was done, I simply asked her where I should begin. She said she would like to make a couple calls and asked me to return in a half hour.

Upon my return, she had added a few names, places, and phone numbers of librarians in other libraries. She said that she had been able to contact each of the librarians and they were willing to help me with my research goals. I gave my sincere thanks and took her advice to contact a librarian at Madison University.

Lessons learned:
- Librarians are one of genealogists' most important resources.
- Librarians know about their collections and the collections located at other libraries.
- Librarians know each other and work closely together to help patrons.

Madison University. It was now 3:00 p.m. I called Madison University library and was told the contact I wanted was going to be out until 5:00 p.m. I then made the decision to drive the two-plus hours to the library and speak with the librarian in person. When I arrived at the university, I found out that she really didn't have the answers to my questions, but she knew a retired professor who was the real resource on historical books, and he was not due back in for a week or more. I asked her if she would be willing to give the professor a call and let me speak with him, which she did.

During my conversation, we explored several options. He told me that the most important book he had that would be a good resource for me was a 500-page reference book that outlined all the family histories that the Library of Congress had on Virginia families. The book not only outlined the family histories but also the other family names that were mentioned in the family histories. I went through the book, looking for the surnames I had come to Virginia to research. I ended up copying over fifty family histories. This resource would prove to be one of the most import finds during my trip. The references I gathered included important call numbers, which I would follow up with when I got back to the Virginia Library the next morning. Most of the references I found included many important family references that were not included in the Virginia Library catalog. I later made plans to visit the Library of Congress.

Lessons learned:

- Always ask for the experts and collection resource librarians.
- Resource librarians know about every artifact in their collection.

Goochland County Historical Society. The next morning, I headed up to the Goochland County Historical Society in Goochland, Virginia, for an appointment I had made several weeks earlier. I had told the members of the historical society that I would be coming to see what information they had on the Ewell and Mullins lines. As I arrived at the Goochland Historical society building, I was greeted by the president, who said, "You won't believe what just happened. One of our members has just brought by an eighteen-page overview of the Mullin family not more than twenty minutes ago." She also added that she and members of the society had been researching their records for the family names of Ewell and Mullins.

A member of the society had heard that I might be coming this week. When I called her to thank her for her efforts, she indicated that she had gotten up that morning and felt like she should bring the information over to the office. She had been researching the foundation of what was known as Lickinghole Church—the first church of the area from the early 1700s—which no longer existed. The founding elders of the church include Maxcey Ewell, my ancestor, and John Mullins, his father-in-law. As the historical society member was researching the church, she indicated that she felt a strong need to do as much research as possible on the Ewell and Mullins families, not knowing why she needed to do it. The information she gathered included all available records (such as land and tax records) that were recorded in the county.

When I was led into the societies modest library, there was a stack of more than twenty books that, combined, had been marked with over 100 bookmarks, each denoting a reference to my family.

I learned from our discussion with the society's president that the name Mullins might be part of the group that settled in Powhatan county. These immigrants were known as the French Hugonaut Society, who came from France for religious freedom. I also learned that Maxcey Ewell was a Hugonaut last name. When I asked what that really meant for me, she explained that while it was not a hard-and-fast rule for naming in the early 1700s, it was a common practice for married couples to give the firstborn son the name of the father's father and to give the second son the name of the mother's father. Other children would be named after the surname of the mother and so forth. Based on the name Maxcey, it would be worth my time to visit the Hugonaut Society in Powhatan and explore the possibilities. She called the society and made an appointment for me to visit later that day.

Lessons learned:
- Historical societies are among the most valuable resources for genealogists.
- Historical societies have experts and resources dedicated to helping others.
- Historical societies know more about their history than I do.
- Historical societies have resources that are not posted online, so be sure to ask.

Naomi Youel Nielsen Collection of Washington and Lee. It was Friday, and I was going to spend my last four hours at the Virginia Library before I was to go to the Dulles Airport in Washington, DC, to pick up my wife and fellow family genealogists. As part of my trip, I had set goals to gather any resources that recorded a derivative of the Ewell name. Earlier in the week I had read a family history newsletter that stated Naomi Youel Nielsen had donated her genealogy research to the Washington and Lee University in Lexington, Virginia. I had already called the library three times before and was not able to find anyone who knew anything about the collection. I thought I would try one more time. This time I was able to connect with the director of the special collections. When I asked

235

him about the collection, he confirmed the collection was at the university. I then told him I was on a short time cycle and asked if he could have his assistant copy the pages of the collection. We talked back and forth, and I tried to help the director understand that if he would take the time, I would be more than happy to pay for time and copies. Then he said, "Mr. Ewell, I don't think you understand, there are thousands of pages." At that moment, I felt a strong impression that I needed to stop what I was doing and go to the university. I told the director I would be there in two hours.

When I arrived at the library, I found 140 binders, 98 of which cataloged the William Ewell/Youel family and his descendents from about 1780. Naomi Youel Nielsen had spent over twenty-five years of her life crossing America searching out her roots. The binders contained over 15,000 family members with a full backup of marriage, birth, and any other records she could find. Key pages included individual names, their lineage, and so forth. She was meticulous and showed great love for her family. I spent several hours photographing the binders until I absolutely had to travel to DC—a 3 hour trip. On the way out, I knew I needed to return and obtain the collection. I told the director I would return in seven days. I would need to extend my trip by at least one week.

Upon my return to Washington and Lee University, I was allowed to photograph the collection. The work of filming the Youel collection took over 40 hours and close to 10,000 images.

Lessons learned:
- Follow leads, no matter how small.
- University archives and special collections are repositories for many genealogy resources.

Stanton County Faubers. I had stopped in at the Stanton County Historical Society to see what information they had about the Fauber surname in that area. I didn't find very much. While I was there, I asked the librarian if she had any other resources. She pulled out the phonebook and proceeded to look for the Fauber name. I thought to myself, "I wanted books, not phone numbers from the local phonebook." When I inquired what she was thinking, she suggested that I call people with the last name Fauber and ask if they knew anyone who might be able to help. She gave me the phone book and left.

I returned to the car, put the phonebook on the passenger seat, and proceeded to leave town. For the first ten miles, I debated whether to stop and make a few calls. Finally I thought, "Why not? Make the calls and just ask people if there was a family genealogists I could talk to."

I pulled over and made five calls. No one was home, but I did leave a message on each phone telling who I was and what I was looking for and leaving my phone number. Four weeks later, after I had returned home, I received a phone call from the Fauber family genealogist, the seventy-five-year-old patriarch of the family.

The conversation began with him saying, "Hello, you called my grandson and left a message that you are a descendent of the Fauber family. Who are you, and what do you want?" I shared who I was and what my ties to the family were. We talked for twenty minutes before he ended the conversation by saying, "It's about time you returned. We have been looking for your family branch for over forty years. Give me your address and I'll send you our most recent family history." A week later I received a well-documented history of the Fauber family.

Lessons learned:
- The phonebook is a viable resource.
- Pick up the phone and call.

Search for the Mullins/Ewell Home in Goochland. The morning after I had picked up my wife and the others from the Dulles Airport, we rose to begin our search for the original lands owned by our ancestors in the 1700s in Goochland County. From my research in Salt Lake City and Goochland County, I knew the name of the town where the families of Maxcey Ewell and John Mullins had lived. The town did not exist on any map, and we were not having any luck finding our directions. We had stopped a couple times to get directions, but to no avail. As I was going down the road, I was preparing to drop into the next service station when I felt the need to stop at the Napa Auto Parts immediately on my right. I asked the four or five men inside the store if any of them were aware of the specific place we were looking for.

The men talked for several minutes, each having a different direction for us to follow. We now had a direction, but it wasn't great. One man followed me outside and proceeded to give me exact directions to where I wanted to go and told me about a mill that was located there and up for sale. When we arrived, we realized that this very out-of-the-way place could have only been known about by a few people.

Lesson learned:
- Listen and follow thoughts and promptings that come into your mind as you conduct genealogy research.

Palmyra, Fluvanna County, Virginia. Pleasant Ewell, the son of Maxcey Ewell, once lived in Fluvanna County, Virginia, in the early 1800s. I knew from my research that he and other members of the Ewell family had slaves in their household. While in Fluvanna County historical society, I asked the president of the historical society about being able to find information about black slaves. She responded by telling us that they had extensive records on slaves but that they were too fragile and had yet to be transcribed for others to research. We spoke and she agreed that she would put one of her associates on the task to help look for information related to our family but it would be at least three months before they could get to it.

When I asked if she would be willing to let me photograph the records, she responded with a "why not." The records started in 1801 and ran for over sixty years, and included lists of slaves, letters of sale, and census records. The president put on white gloves to handle the artifacts, and I took pictures. The total collection was over 300 images.

Lessons learned:
- Libraries and societies have records that are not openly publicized, but they are often willing to share and make the records available upon request.

- Always seek to learn about the society's full collection of records.

Search for Maxcey Ewell and John Mullins in Whitehall, Virginia. I was in Virginia with other family genealogists. From previous research we had done, we knew the address of land that was once owned by my progenitor Maxcey Ewell, who had moved there with his father-in-law, John Mullins, and some friends with the surname Maupin. With the help of the rental car's GPS, we were guided to a dirt-road turnoff. Now what? There wasn't an address to be found anywhere. As I proceeded up this dirt road, I crossed the path of a gray SUV. I waved the driver down, gave him our directions, and asked if he could help us. He told me he knew who could help us—Phil and Salley, the local historians. All I had to do was find their home. The SUV driver gave us directions to go up the road about a mile, turn left at the oak tree, turn right at the third fence post, and then cross the stream; Phil and Salley's home would be on the right.

As I pulled up to the home, I saw a man who I guessed was Phil in the front yard. I started the conversation with, "I understand you are the local historian?"

"Yes, who are looking for?

"Maxcey Ewell."

He crossed his arms and thought for a moment, then replied, "I know exactly where it's at. Would you like me to show you?"

"Absolutely, that would be wonderful," was my immediate reply.

Phil raised his hand and told us that he would be a few minutes. He returned with an industrial-strength weed eater and explained that there were graves on the Maxcey Ewell property that dated to the late 1700s. Within five minutes, we found the land, opened the gate, and drove onto the property. As Phil pulled the weed eater from the trunk of the car, he motioned to the rest of us to follow him up the hill. Climbing the hill, Phil explained that it was common for families to create a family burial plot on a hill that overlooked the homestead.

We followed Phil to a group of trees with knee-high grass that was cut to size in minutes. When the grass was cleared, we found three rows of fieldstones that were turned up on end. Phil pointed to the gravestones and said, "Ewell, say hello to the plot of the Maxcey and Ann Ewell family."

I was overwhelmed to think that I was standing on the very land my first progenitor owned. We had found the gravesite of Maxcey and Ann Ewell. While we were on the hill, Phil also showed us a grave marker of John Mullins and his family. The graves were no more than 150 yards apart.

The night was now coming upon us quickly. We retired to the home of Phil and Salley, where we spent the evening talking about our families and the history of Whitehall. As we spoke, we found out that Phil was a descendent of the Maupin family, who were close friends of the Ewells and Mullins. Just as we were about to leave, Phil asked us to wait while he went downstairs. He returned with five family history books that contained the genealogies, printed in the early 1900s, of the Ewells, Mullins, Maupins, and allied families. He had gathered the books from the Charlottesville Public Libraries when they were being sold as excess books over the years. I was allowed to take the books back to the hotel, where I spend the entire night photographing their pages. We returned the books the next morning, and Phil invited us into his home. He had taken the opportunity the night before to do some more research among his collection and found several more helpful books, of which I took more photographs. We shared our gratitude for the gift that Phil and Salley gave our family—finding the Ewell/Mullins homestead, burial plots, and family histories, as well as the friendship we had forged with Phil and Salley.

Lesson learned:

- Without the help of local experts, I am only marginally successful in understanding and researching local and regional resources.

SHARE YOUR TIME WITH OTHERS

Remember those who reached out to help you when you first started in genealogy? I remember when I started doing genealogy, I visited a family history center in Everett, Washington. I didn't have a clue where to start, just an interest. One of the volunteers spent an hour and helped me understand the steps in starting my family tree. Over the next six months, she helped in mentoring my development and passion for genealogy. She taught me the proper research and documentation techniques. Today, she is a dear friend whom I still call to seek counsel.

There are ways you can give back to others. For example, consider volunteering at libraries, including local family history centers. You can volunteer your time to online sites, doing work such as looking up records, taking photos of tombstones for researchers who can't make the trip to do it themselves, helping to answer questions by joining a mailing list geared toward newcomers, or answering questions in forums or chats. Alternatively, you could teach a class on genealogy through a local organization or join a historical society and help in researching local history.

Over the years, I have made it a point to give back to the genealogy community as a mentor, presenter, and researcher. I would like to share with you one experience I shared with Valene, a close friend and family line genealogist.

Research with fresh eyes. Whenever possible, I make it a practice to collaborate with other genealogists on researching specific family lines. As a team, we will review our research, analyzing documentation, notes, and logs; identify the key questions we want to research; develop a research task list for researching each question; assign tasks and deadlines; and schedule regular meetings to review, compare, and discuss projects and research.

During my collaboration with fellow genealogists on the Ewell line, I requested the opportunity to help her create a digital record that included scanning and spreadsheet catalog organization. Throughout the project, I compiled a list of seven of the family lines that seemed to dead-end (meaning no further extension of the line) in the 1750s. The surnames included Ewell, Mullins, Fauber, Rennick, Bland, Lee, and Caldwell in the states of Pennsylvania, Tennessee, Virginia, and West Virginia. During one of our scheduled project review meetings, we explored the following questions:

- Who did the original genealogy research on the family lines?
- Why were there so many dead-ends?
- Is there documentation or a research log for the research showing all the resources that were evaluated?

Most of the research, which was well documented, had been done by my collaboration partner during the 1980s and '90s but a research log no longer existed. We concluded that we would re-review the research and available resources. I took up the task of finding and reviewing available resources for the time period at The Church of Jesus Christ of Latter-day Saints Family History Library in Salt Lake City, Utah.

Over the next ten weeks, I spent my research time reviewing period resources for each and every county in Virginia, Tennessee, Pennsylvania, and West Virginia. My findings were organized by surnames into a spreadsheet that would allow us to easily review the data and look for clues that might help us answer our questions and extend the various family lines. Even though the resources were researched by other genealogists before me, I often found bits of information that may have been overlooked or dismissed that shed new light on the research.

As I researched the Rennick and Fauber lines, I was seeking to find Ann Rennick, the wife of Christen Fauber, and their children who lived in Augusta County, Virginia, in the 1700s. In my research, I came across a single notation that a Rennick from Augusta County went to Ohio to see another Rennick.

Clue 1: A Rennick from Augusta County went to Ohio to see another Rennick. My first inclination was to dismiss the clue as irrelevant. Then I thought that I should focus on researching the account of the Rennick who lived in Ohio.

Clue 2: As I searched available Ohio resources, I came across an entry in the 1959 historical society newsletter stating that they had acquired a book called Rennicks of Greenbriar, Virginia. (Greenbriar used to be a county in Virginia and later became part of Monroe County, West Virginia.)

Clue 3: I searched the Family History Library catalog and found the book in a very small collection of Greenbriar county resources. Right next to the book I was seeking was another family history book on a related branch of the Rennicks.

Clue 4: As I read the books, I came across a section that mentioned that the Rennicks also came through Lancaster County, Pennsylvania.

Clue 5: I began to search the Lancaster records for both Fauber and Rennicks. I found Christian Fauber and the Rennicks but was not able to find any Ann or Barabra Ann Rennick.

Clue 6: I decided to retrace my steps from the previous three clues to see if I had missed anything. I came to an entry of a Thomas Rennick who had four children, one named Ann. The entry for Thomas simply said, "Little is known about this family." This was the only Ann that did not have a spouse. Was this the Ann I was looking for? At least I knew that the Rennicks and Faubers were in Lancaster County at the same time.

For the next step, I went back to the Lancaster County area and began to look through the four shelves of books, looking for a Christen and Ann Fauber. I didn't find them. I went home around 4:30 in the afternoon. For an hour and a half, I pondered all of my research that day. I couldn't get rid of the feeling that I needed to return to the library that very day to find information that I knew existed. I arrived at the Library at 7:30 p.m., went back to the Lancaster shelves, and looked over the same books I had looked through earlier. As I was getting ready to close the second- to-last book on the fourth shelf, the thought entered my mind to look again. There it was—a child born to Ann and Christian Fauber. I was really excited. I didn't find a record of the wedding, but I found several births for the Fauber family.

For over twenty years, people have been looking for this family.

Lessons learned:
- Follow every clue, no matter how insignificant it may seem.
- One clue leads to another clue.
- Clues linked together form a picture.
- Research = Re-search the available resources to find overlooked clues.

- If you only search for surnames, you may miss the clues you need.
- Use spreadsheets to view all available findings.
- Follow thoughts and promptings you receive during research.

Lesson 11: Carefully Search Ancestor Writings

In reviewing the writings of my ancestors—whether they were letters, journals, postcards, notes, or email—I found interesting (and valuable) information, such as the following:

- Dates and places of events and experiences important in the life of the writer.
- Details of day-to-day life.
- Personal opinions and perspectives.
- Concerns and priorities.
- Thoughts and feelings.
- Hopes and dreams.
- Facts and dates about relatives and neighbors.
- Interesting views of historical happenings that were current events to them (wars, elections, epidemics, and so on).
- Background information about living conditions, prices, and other daily happenings.

The writings can be lively and full of energy—some fresh and intimate, some dull and non-descriptive, and most plainly spoken— simply sharing a moment in time, putting to paper something they felt needed to be said. I've found the documents in myriad places, including attics, closets, basements, bookshelves, in the homes of your known relatives, in the possession of distant cousins located through research, and in libraries, archives, genealogical and histori-cal societies, and other specialized collections. I have also found my ancestors' writings in antique shops, used book stores and flea mar-kets—especially in places near the residence of the subject—and through websites designed to reunite diaries, photos, bibles, and other memorabilia with the families from which they were separated.

I have used the information to find dates of life events to further research; to find names of family members, neighbors, and others who interacted with the family; to gain insight into the personality of the ancestor; to put the ancestor's life into context of time and history; to pull interesting details or excerpts for a family or personal history I am writing; and to find clues of medical conditions that may continue to affect family today.

Defining the Written Word of Our Ancestors

During my time as a genealogist, I have had the fortune to come across several artifacts from my ancestors, including the letters and cards of my mother, journals and poetry of my father, and myriad bits and pieces shared by others. These combined artifacts begin to tell a story of life that isn't so different from my own. Before we progress too far, I would like to outline some of the differences you will find in written communications.

Letter

A letter is a direct, written message that is usually sent some distance from one person to another, or even to a group of persons or an organization. Some of the earliest recorded letters were written about 3500 BC by the Sumerians (using picture writing), who wrote on clay tablets using long reeds.

An old term for letter is "epistle," from the Greek word *epistole*, meaning "message." Letters make up several of the books of the Bible.

Letters engage a dialogue between parties and often became objects to represent the absent person's touch and nearness. Nathaniel Hawthorne became a famous author, but he spoke like countless other correspondents when he wrote to his sweetheart Sophia Peabody in 1840, stating, "The only ray of light" in his dreary day "was when [I] opened thy letter. . . . I have folded it to my heart, and ever and anon it sends a thrill through me. . . . It seems as if thy head were leaning against my breast."

Some letters are scattered about and must be gathered to form a collection of writings.

Nowadays, letters are only widely used by companies who send out these mailings to large numbers of people (who may not have access to the Internet for email).

The term "letter" is sometimes used for email messages with a formal, letter-like format.

Journals and diaries

In 1656, John Beadle, an Essex minister, wrote an advice manual on how to keep a diary and explained the variety of types that were written in the seventeenth century. He said:

> We have our state journals, relating to national affairs. Trades-men keep their shop books. Merchants their account books. Lawyers have their books of pre[c]edents. Physitians have their experiments. Some wary husbands have kept a diary of daily dis-bursements. Travellers a Journall of all that they have seen and hath befallen them in their way. A Christian that would be more exact hath more need and may reap much more good by such a journal as this. We are all but stewards, factors here, and must give a strict account in that great day to the high Lord of all our wayes, and of all his wayes towards us.

The terms "journal" and "diary" are used interchangeably today. No matter what you call them, these accounts are the autobiographies of ordinary people like our ancestors, and these may be the only existing records of their personal lives. Along with genealogical data, diaries give us a wonderful glimpse into someone's daily life, thoughts, and attitudes. A diarist may also record feelings on national events, such as a war or its impact on family and the community. The following is an attempt to define meanings as used over the last several centuries.

Diaries (the private journal)

- Some use the words "diary" and "journal" interchangeably, while others apply strict differences to journals and diaries: dated, undated, inner focused, outer focused, forced, and so on.

- Diary is referred to as a private journal.
- The current preference (based on book and article titles) is to use the word "journal." The phrase "journaling" is often used to describe such hobby writing, similar to the term "scrapbooking."
- Diaries are relatively recent, from the 1700s in the culture of Western Europe and early America.
- Popularity of diaries stem from the Christian desire to chart one's spiritual progression toward God.
- Expanded in the 1800s to record personal feelings, self-discovery, and self-reflection.
- Diaries are found in all aspects of human life, governmental, business ledgers, and military records. Diaries run the spectrum from business notations to listings of weather and daily personal events to inner exploration of the psyche, or a place to express one's deepest self.
- Diaries or journals are often written to oneself or an imaginary person. May resemble a letter to one's self.
- There is a strong psychological effect of having an audience for one's self-expression, a personal space, or a "listener," even if the "audience" is the book one writes in, only read by oneself.
- Some diarists think of their diaries as a special friend, even going so far as to name them. For example, Anne Frank called her diary "Kitty."
- A diary is usually woven together by a single individual between its covers.
- A well-known example is "The Diary of Anne Frank," whose diary chronicled the desperation of being Jewish in Amsterdam during World War II and having to go into hiding from the Nazis. The diary is, first, a day-by-day account of the life of a Jewish family and their friends. Secondly, it is a biting commentary of the depths of suffering that men can impose on other men. A stunning website about this child and her story is at http://www.annefrank.com.

Journal (public record)

- A journal (French from late Latin diurnalis, "daily") has several related meanings:
    - A daily record of events or business; a private journal is usually referred to as a diary.
    - A newspaper or other periodical, in the literal sense of one published each day; however, some publications issued at stated intervals—such as a magazine or the record of the transactions of society such as a scientific journal or academic journals in general—are called a journal. "Journal," then, is sometimes used as a synonym for "magazine."
    - The word "journalist" (for one whose business is writing for the public press) has been in use since the end of the seventeenth century.
- Section 5 of Article I of the United States Constitution requires the Congress of the United States to keep a journal of its proceedings. This journal, the Congressional Record, is published by the Government Printing Office. Journals of this sort are also often referred to as minutes.
- A book in which an account of transactions is kept previous to a transfer to the ledger in the process of bookkeeping. For example:
    - A central book in which all financial transactions were recorded. These include the purchase of supplies, the sale of crops, the purchase and sale of livestock, and the purchase, sale, birth, marriage and death of slaves, apprentices and other servants;
    - The record of all agricultural activities from year to year, including the purchase of seed, fertilizer, cordage and wire, plows and other equipment, cost of labor, places of sale, transportation costs, and the prices obtained for the crops; or
    - A chronicle of life on the farm, including some or all of the above. Journals can provide essential clues to

African-American genealogists researching their slave ancestors. Plantation records may be the only place to ascertain names and dates necessary to prove ancestral ties.

- An equivalent to a ship's log—as a record of the daily run—such as observations, weather changes, or other events of daily importance.

Postcard

A postcard is typically a rectangular piece of thick paper or thin cardboard intended for writing and mailing without an envelope and at a lower rate than a letter.

The United States Postal Service began issuing pre-stamped postal cards in 1873. Postcards came about because the public was looking for an easier way to send quick notes. Postcards were very popular in the early 1900s. For example, in 1908, more than 677 million postcards were mailed.

The messages contained in postcards are necessarily brief and generally lighthearted, as the sender is normally on holidays and switched off from the day-to-day routines of home and work.

Greeting card

A greeting card is an illustrated, folded card, usually featuring a message of greeting or other sentiment.

The oldest known greeting card in existence is a Valentine made in the 1400s and is in the British Museum. New Year's cards can be dated back to this period as well, but the New Year greeting didn't gain popularity until the late 1700s. Cards gained their highest popularity in the late 1800s and early 1900s, offering cards with some of the most unusual art.

Greeting cards are usually given on special occasions such as birthdays, Christmas, or other holidays, but they are also sent on "non-occasions" to say hello or thank you. Ninety percent of all paper greeting cards are sold in the United States.

Greeting cards, usually packaged with an envelope, come in a variety of styles. They are manufactured or handmade by hundreds of companies big and small.

Card inscriptions can be windows to how an ancestor felt about the recipient. A card is often a token of affection that articulates the form of love and affiliation of a given time period. The messages in greeting cards are usually brief. Mostly the sender confines himself to the brevity that the form imposes and the message is cheerful and upbeat.

Written note or message

These types of messages range from a piece of paper tucked into a journal as a personal reminder to a note in the margins of a letter denoting an extra add-on thought.

Written notes can provide insight and extra meaning to what has already been written.

Email

Electronic mail, now usually called "email," is a method of composing, sending, storing, and receiving messages over electronic communication systems.

Email started in 1965 as a way for multiple users of a time-sharing mainframe computer to communicate.

Blog (Weblog)

A weblog, which is usually shortened to "blog," is a website where regular entries are made (such as in a journal or diary) and presented in reverse chronological order. Blogs often offer commentary or news on a particular subject, such as food, politics, or local news. Some function as more personal online diaries. A typical blog combines text, images, and links to other blogs, websites, and other media related to its topic.

BEFORE YOU START YOUR REVIEW

Whether you are reviewing a private collection handed down from Mom or one you find in university archives, the following are a few questions and ideas to consider:

- Is this volume the complete diary or are there other volumes or entries elsewhere?
- Is this letter a draft or "practice" letter, or is it the one actually mailed?

- Who saved the diary and why?
- Who collected the letters and why?
- Is there evidence of other readers (family members, archivists) handling or marking the text?
- Has the diarist herself added retrospective marginal notes? (Many diarists look back and criticize their younger selves or annotate their observations, scratch out passages, or even cut out pages.)
- What is the period of time covered by the text? Plan your reading to quickly scan the pages ahead to see if the number of diary entries (or letters) changes because of major historical events.
- Does the diarist clearly distinguish one day from another?
- How frequent are the entries? In one family collection, I found several hundred post cards that covered thirty years of time between family and friends. Yet in another, I found 300 separate journal entries in six months during the waning months of an individual's life.
- It is also worth a quick look ahead to see if one correspondent's letters dominate the collection or if the letters are more like a dialogue or even a full conversation among many people.
- Check out event changes, such as the place from which the communication was written. Often a writer will indicate from whence they are writing (such as Munich, Germany, or Lawrenceville, Georgia).
- Look through the collection to see if there are indications of important events. For instance, during the 19th century, deaths often were written on black-edged paper; letters announcing a marriage tend to be embossed or differently sized—both easy to spot in a sheaf of papers.

Strategies for Interpreting Writings

Whether you are reviewing a letter, journal, postcard, or other writing of an ancestor, there are several strategies for evaluating and gaining the most from the total presentation. Not only are you looking at the written word, but you are also looking at paper, images, and handwriting. All provide clues and information about your ancestor. The following represents different angles from which to view the writings of your ancestors.

Impressions by look and feel. As you hold the writings in your hands, they make an impression before you even read the words. You can glean information from the texture, condition, paper type, style of writing—which suggests the writer's care or haste—depth, surface, care of the folded sheets of a letter or the binding of the diary, and the time between inscriptions. The following clues can help you begin to make guesses about the writer, such as what their social class might have been:

- Is the paper the ordinary lined "blue" sheets of common mid-nineteenth century use or is it embossed and edged?
- Women and men were schooled to have very different handwriting.
- The document might exhibit an array of nibs (the sharpened point of a quill pen; a pen point), papers, envelopes, letter cases, letter clips, writing desks, and other objects associated with writing among well-to-do Americans of the era. Absence of these features may indicate that the writer was of a lower economic standing.

Think in terms of plot, characters, and language of the script. Think of the last article, story, or even movie you watched. Who was the main character, and who were the subordinate characters? What was the plot? How was the script written? As you review writings, you gain a feel for the individuals involved, their role, and the events of the plot.

Becoming acquainted with the characters. In a diary, we depend on the writer to introduce us to the individuals in their life. Sometimes persons are named, while other times we are left to figure them out for ourselves. When it comes to letters, the introductions to characters are hit and miss. The writer wasn't writing to us, but usually to one who knew the people being mentioned.

Try to understand who the friends and family members were,

especially if you are using unedited communications. Sometimes a family rarely uses given names in correspondence. In such cases, start out slow until you are able to determine the identity of "Dear Son" or "Your loving Daughter." The same holds true for nicknames. I know during my father's years as a youth (1930s and 40), it was common to have nicknames such as Frip, Jiggs, and Stu.

What inspired the plot? As you survey the writing, think about whether a particular circumstance inspired the writing. Is there a large-scale "story" holding the writings together? We find this type of inspiration in writings during the period of war or changes in one's life. In other cases, diaries—and especially letters—are focused on the ordinariness of the writer's life. In either case, though, surveying the text for a sense of the main narrative thread is a good way to prompt questions about the text as you begin to read more closely.

Look for unique language. Think about your use of instant messaging. In our writing we use words, phrases, and acronyms to help us communicate faster. For example, TTYL (talk to you later), :) (smile), K (okay), TY (thank you), and Ditto (I agree). Just like us, our ancestors also had interjections into their correspondence that stood for something else. For instance, many modern readers are puzzled by some correspondents' interjection of "D.V." in the midst of certain sentences expressing hope ("by now, D.V., you are safely at home") when these letters are not the recipient's initials. Then, finally, one writer solves the puzzle for us by spelling it out: *Deo Volente*, "God willing."

Such puzzles will help you to be alert to the fact that the meaning of certain words or phrases is coded. For example, to say in the mid-nineteenth-century that a woman had "taken a cold" almost always meant that she was pregnant.

How does the writer relate the experiences of their life? Personal texts are usually begun by the accounts of key events that occur over time and are important enough to write about, such as a death, a child leaving home, a marriage, a natural disaster, work, and so forth.

The story of events also reveals the interrelationships of the writers, friends, family, acquaintances, and strangers. The relationships shape our understanding of how the writer fits into the events and through which eye we see the interpretation of what is written.

Most letters are written by "news" or are rich with events, which the writer tries to describe in detail. You may see how the writer describes (or filters) the same event or news to different people in his life. For example, an experience about crossing a river and almost drowning may be written in full detail for a friend, but to a mother the description may be only that the writer became wet when crossing a river.

In letters, you will find other parties sensitive to the absence of one another. Some, however, focus on the distance apart, while other letters focus on bringing one closer together—such as in the case of lovers or parents, and children blaming each other for neglect, or praising each other for timely and satisfying letters.

Questions to Ask as You Review Writings

As you review writings of ancestors, don't conduct an in-depth analysis of every word, sentence, or meaning in every artifact. Do examine the artifacts by carefully identifying and analyzing the items. Then reflect on what you've learned.

Identify
Ask yourself about the primary source itself:
- What is the item?
- Who created it?
- Where and when was it created?
- What's the history of the item?

Analysis
Ask yourself the following questions about the primary source:
1. Creator
- Who created the primary source and why?
- What was this person's role in the event, time period, or activity?
- What was the person's perspective, point of view, opinions, interests, or motivation? How did this impact the content?

- What was the purpose for creating the source?
- Was the source intended to be public or private?
- Was the intention of the creator to inform, instruct, persuade, or deceive? How did this impact the content?
- Which events—trivial or monumental—do ancestors choose to share with each other?
- Are any events or topics ignored or skirted?
- Who among the correspondents seem the most intimate and who seem most at odds?
- How does each writer seem to value formal respect and careful language, on the one hand, and humor, exaggeration, and slang, on the other?
- Does one individual seem to be the central person in the correspondence, and, conversely, is there an individual everyone seems to regard as shy or silent?
- Which relationships seem most stable over the course of the correspondence and which most volatile, and how do events in their lives reveal these qualities?
- How do all of these relate to the identities of the various correspondents in terms of gender, class, or age?

2. Timing
- Was the item created before, during, or after an event?
- How might the timing of the creation impact the emotions, accuracy, or perspective?

3. Setting
- What is the setting of the primary source? Where was it created?
- What were the conditions or circumstances related to the creation?
- What information (such as facts and opinions) does the primary source contain?
- What details could easily be misunderstood?
- How does this resource compare to other information from the event or time period?

4. Visual information
- What story does the image tell?

- What is the perspective or point of view of the image?
- What is the setting of the image?
- What details are emphasized or missing?

5. Just for the diary and journal

- Who is the "other" the diarist seems to be writing to: a friend, a wiser self, a future self?
- What other literary forms does a given diary most resemble—a letter, a novel, a ledger?
- What kinds of events, times of the day or week, and emotional state seem to motivate the diarist to write?
- Does the diarist always write in the first person or does he sometimes distance himself by avoiding the "I"?
- Which people in the diarist's life appear most frequently in their pages, and why?
- Do any or all of these features of a given diary change over its course, and if so, in what way?

Reflection upon findings

Ask yourself the following questions about your findings:

- What information was fascinating or surprising? What would be interesting to investigate further?
- What questions do you have about the information? How could they be addressed?
- What inconsistencies or conflicting ideas did you identify? How could they be resolved?
- How does this document connect to your life? What are the relevant issues for today?

EXPANDING ON THE WRITINGS OF YOUR ANCESTORS

Writers will often make assertions about a fact that was important to them. For example, a correspondent mentions the death of a loved one due to the flu epidemic in 1917. It might be important for you to consult other sources that describe the extent of the flu in that town, state, or country. Or if a diarist makes a claim about a visit of President Kennedy on January 15, 1961, one could consult official documents, newspapers, and other observers to give perspective to what the diarist says.

Depending upon how wide you want to take your study, you can include many sources, such as census reports, government documents, photographs, maps, oral histories and other diaries and letters. For example, I read in several journals and histories that my ancestors were cattle ranchers in Utah County, Utah. I am from the city and have no clue about cattle ranching. I took the opportunity to find newspaper articles about ranching in Utah. I checked the Utah State Government Brands & Animal Identification Department to find if they had a brand. I looked for photos from the early 1900s of cattle ranching in Utah and anything else I could find that would help me understand this profession as it related to Utah ranchers. Now as I write about my great-grandfather, I can better explain and provide details about what their lives as ranchers might have been like, the jobs they performed, the trials they endured, and the satisfaction they may have felt.

The following are other ideas to use:

Chronology: Build a timeline associated with the item. In addition, create a parallel timeline that relates to local, national, and international events. Also, consider tracing the genealogy of the families associated with the item. Use this chronology to help develop an understanding of the time period.

Maps: Explore the locations discussed in the document. Consider visually tracing adventures and activities. Use maps to help develop a context for the place associated with your project.

Relationships: Explore the relationships among the people represented in the document.

Visual resources: Match visuals (such as photographs) to people, places, and events in the document.

Multimedia resources: Consider connecting the arts, books, music, movies, and other activities to the resource.

A couple of things happen when you seek to corroborate and add context to the story. You expand the "what happened" and have a greater ability to interpret what you are reading from their viewpoint. You also gain a sense of how accurate the writer was in interpreting their times as an actor and observer.

SIMPLIFYING THE ANALYSIS OF AN ANCESTOR'S WRITING

It's a great opportunity to evaluate and try to become acquainted with ancestors through their writings. Some genealogists want to find the facts and not spend much time on analysis. The following is a simplified process for reviewing an ancestor's writings:

- Identify factual information. (How is the writing, about what, and where?)
- Who are the main characters described in the letter?
- What is the plot of the letter?
- What questions do you have about the artifact? Include words you can't decode or understand.
- What research would you need to do to widen your understanding of the letter?

WHERE TO SEARCH FOR YOUR ANCESTORS' WRITINGS

Getting access to ancestors' writings that are in the possession of others. These journals, letters, and writings of our ancestors are very precious to those who own them. The owner's response to your request to access them depends a lot on how well you know each other. If they know and trust you, they may allow you to take the documents on loan for a specific time period—usually 24 to 48 hours—to scan or photograph the article.

In cases where information is a little more difficult to secure, consider the following approaches:

The insurance copy argument: If they have the original item, remind them that it could be lost or gone forever in a house fire or other disaster; by letting you copy it, the family gains a backup, security, or insurance copy.

Broker: Offer to make them a copy when you make a copy.

Trade: Offer to exchange copies of records or items that you have in return for them letting you copy their materials.

Family project: Design a family project—biography, photo

collection, newsletter—for which you need to copy and use their materials. This links your request to a family cause rather than just being personal.

Purchase: If the person's reluctance to share is because of the monetary value of the items, consider buying the material, or at least a part of it.

Take pictures: They might have an heirloom locket or Civil War uniform or other valuable items they won't let out the door. In such cases, take pictures of them and offer to share copies of your photos.

Searching the Internet for ancestors' writings. The Internet is an incredible resource in finding diaries, journals, postcards, letters, and other writings. I have found family documents on Internet sites of library collections. For example, as I was doing research for a presentation, I found thirty letters that were written between Thomas Jefferson and my ancestors in the Jefferson Papers, and fifteen journal entries relating to my ancestors' pioneer experiences in the Mormon Pioneer Overland Travel, 1847–1868 collection.

To search the Internet for ancestral writings, enter the following information:

- Names of ancestors (direct and collateral lines)
- Surnames (include various spellings)
- Names of individuals the ancestors were known to have worked with or had relationships with
- Places they lived and visited
- Important events they lived during or were a part of, such as the civil war, influenza, or pioneer treks

A note about spellings

You will find that spelling was informal and inconsistent in old records. Do not dismiss the name 'Hewes' if you are searching for 'Hughes.' In an early census enumeration, census takers reportedly spelled the surname 'Reynolds' thirty-four different ways. As you get deeper into genealogical research, you will become an expert at guessing how many ways a name may be spelled (or misspelled).

Examples of search strategies.

Keyword searches

- diar* and literature [will retrieve 'diary', 'diaries', 'diarists', and so on]
- diar* and bibliography
- Virginia and diaries [for locating many individual diaries]
- diar* and statesm*n
- memoirs and wom*n

Subject searches

- American diaries women authors
- Women United States diaries
- Women diaries
- English diaries
- Personal narratives [relating to individual events or time periods]

Searching in libraries and archives for ancestors' writings. I have found journals, diaries, and letters that have been preserved in local historical societies, universities, and other institutions where they are available to researchers. Some have been published as books, and increasingly many are available on the Internet. A good place to start is searching for writings in the areas where your family lived.

One genealogist told of an experience where she found a diary of an ancestor (who lived in Virginia) in New Mexico. The descendant who inherited the diary lived in New Mexico and gave it to a repository.

What to do when you still can't find the written word of your ancestor. My mother passed away in 1997, and I realized there was a lot I didn't know about her. I began to interview family and friends to gain their insights of her. To my joy, many of these people had kept letters, greeting cards, and postcards that she had sent them over the course of her life. The information provided insights to her feelings about her children and her pains, joys, and desires. I was allowed to scan and photograph these documents.

Strategy 1: Your first option is to contact all of your relatives and see if they saved the writings of ancestors with whom your family may have had a relationship. Letters and diaries written by your ancestor's relatives, friends, and neighbors may contain material about your ancestor. These letters and diaries will give you a glimpse into what your own ancestor's life was probably like, since relatives, friends, and neighbors probably came from the same socioeconomic background as your ancestor.

Several of my ancestors were Mormon pioneers in the mid-1800s. Although there are no surviving journals from my family of this time period, I have found journals of people who were part of the same wagon train or handcart company. I have been able to review these writings and gain a better understanding of what my ancestor may have experienced. I found an entry about my progenitor from the Dan Jones Emigrating Company, Journal 1856 May–Dec.

September 9, 1856

> Tuesday 9th[.] The remaining Waggons taken over the river[.] finished at 2 p.m. A yoke of Oxen belonging to the Church was missing. several brethren sent to search for them, and they returned to camp with them at 4.15 p.m. Bro. Elias Jones lost two gentle Cows on Sunday last <at the Loop [Loup] Fork Ferry> and up to this time they have not being found. We moved forward at 5 p.m. and camped at 8 p.m[.] travelled 7 miles along the banks of the Loup Fork.

Strategy 2: Look for writings that discuss the same time period, event, and so forth. Circumstances similar to theirs may be available in a personal account written by another person from the same area. If you can find a relationship, either through bloodlines or common bonds, you'll discover a way to understand and add depth to your family's history. Look for similarities in lifestyle, social status, profession, or neighborhood. All of these can give you a good sense of how your ancestors lived and what they experienced.

Strategy 3: Place a query online or in a genealogical magazine or message board to see if some distant relative might be in possession of an ancestor's writings. On one occasion, I had received a clue about a letter that existed from a relative in 1862. I had seen the text—a photocopy of photocopies—but I wanted to see the original. I placed a query on the message boards and, in time, received a clue of where to go. I eventually found the owner and was able to get a photograph of the letter.

Summary checklist: Where to search for ancestors' writings. The following is a recap of where to search for writings (diaries, journals, letters, or postcards) of your ancestors:

- Ask relatives if they possess any ancestors' writings.
- Put queries in genealogical magazines or message boards and online, seeking writings from distant "genealogy" cousins.
- Write to historical societies, archives, and libraries in your ancestor's locality to see if your ancestor's writings were deposited there.
- Check reference guides to help locate writings in repositories.
- Look for published writings, including anthologies.
- Look for writings of your ancestor's friends, relatives, and neighbors.
- Look for writings of people, like your ancestor, who lived in the same geographic area during the same time period and from the same socioeconomic background.

DIGITAL REPRODUCTION AND TRANSCRIPTION

As you review the writings of your ancestors, you will most likely want to transcribe the information, making it easier to read and use in multiple formats when sharing on the Internet and with others. I have found artifacts such as diaries, journals, and letters to be very fragile; it seems as though the glue, string, and paper is disintegrating before my eyes. I prefer not to work with the original when I transcribe (keeping the original safe from becoming any more worn), but rather work with a digital reproduction.

Digital reproduction. A digital reproduction is an electronic version of an artifact that is created using a scanner or digital camera.

When you are creating a digital reproduction, you will either want to reproduce the artifact—including matching colors, shading, and flaws—or have the intention to maximize the legibility of the item. I personally lean toward the side of digital reproduction for legibility while trying to preserve as much of the original. I will usually keep what I call my original file, which is the exact image of the original, and then I have the edited file, which is the original with my desired edits.

I use Adobe Photoshop Elements as my image editing software. It allows me to adjust the contrast, color, and sharpness of an image. I can edit out perceived flaws, creases, discoloration, water stains, or missing pieces.

Beginning your transcription project. Before beginning your transcription project, it is important to gather basic information that will later form the description paragraph or introduction to help others understand the project.

Provide an introduction to the project, consisting of the following elements:

- *Identification:* Provide background information about the project, including the format, length, and other physical attributes.
- *Documentation of the history:* Discuss the origin of the document and trace the history.
- *Strengths and weaknesses:* Note strengths or the unique nature of the project, along with problems encountered or concerns about accuracy or authenticity.
- *Acknowledgments:* Include credit and history of document ownership, as well as credit for digital transcription and reproduction.

Editorial transcription guidelines. Transcription is the conversion of one form of language into another, such as hand-written letters into typewritten documents. As you begin to transcribe your documents, the following set of editorial guidelines will help you maintain consistency:

1. No attempt should be made to correct spelling or perceived "mistakes."

2. Avoid the use of capital letters except in those instances where the writer used a capital letter.

3. Make educated guesses when unsure of a word; however, use square brackets [] when unsure of exact transcription. If you're unable to decipher the words, then use brackets and a note such as [illegible]. Some people choose to use colors for particular notations in a digital format.

4. Whenever possible, match the punctuation used by the author. Or you can standardize the punctuation. For example, you may choose to use commas and periods for dashes, vertical strokes, or other markings.

5. You may or may not choose to maintain the formatting of the document, such as line breaks.

6. Sometimes areas of a document are illegible. Use the following strategies to help with difficult materials:

- Examine individual letters and match them to other areas of the text.
- Scan the document at a high resolution and zoom in electronically.
- Read the sentence aloud and look for context and logical connections.
- Ask someone else to read the passage.
- Do not assume you know what the words or letters are.
- Leave the passage and come back later with a clear mind.
- If you still can't figure it out, take your best guess and put it in brackets.

The following are my personal guidelines I adopted to create a transcript from the Ohio Memory Project:

1. Create a new document in a program such as Microsoft Word, Edit Pad, or Word Pad.

- When sharing with others, save the document as ASCII or text only (.txt).

2. At the top of the page, type [page 1]

- If the first page included is not the first page of the book or document, add a second line, such as [corresponds to page 456 of John Jones' Diary].

3. Hit "return" or "enter" twice to place a blank line between the page information and the beginning of the transcribed text.

4. Copy text from the first page of the document. It is important to remember that you are creating an exact copy of the original document in typed form, not editing or interpreting the original. Each line of the transcript should follow exactly the spacing and line breaks in the original document, even if a sentence or thought ends after a line break.

Hit return twice after each line in the original to insert a blank line between the lines of text. This maintains the line breaks even if the font size of the document gets changed. Do not select double-spacing from the formatting menu. Add comments in brackets (sparingly) to describe notes or scribbles that cannot be translated. Appropriate uses of comments include the following guidelines:

- If a document has numerous pencil scribbles, type [numerous pencil scribbles] near the area where they occur on the page.
- If a word is illegible, type [illegible] in square brackets. Do this even if you can guess at part of the word.
- If text is otherwise unusual, indicate how with such notes as [crossed out words], [on back of letter], [written in pencil].
- If there is a misspelling in the original, the transcript should include the same misspelling. Make sure to turn off any auto-correct options in your word processor.

5. Following the last word or comment from page 1, type [page 2], then hit return twice and type text from second page. Repeat for remaining pages, but keep pages together in one document.

6. A good transcript should follow the same form as the written page; the same words should be on the same lines in both

the transcript and original document. Here is an example of how a transcription from an original document looks:

[Page 1]
[corresponds to page 1 of Cleveland Ordinance Banning Baseball]

An Ordinance [underlined]
For the protection of the Public Ground
Be it ordained [Be . . . ordained underlined] by the City Council of
Cleveland that from and after this dait it
Shall be unlawful for any person or
Persons to play at any game of Ball
Or at any other game or pastime [illegible]
the grass or grounds of any Public
Place or square shall be deface or
Injured, and any person or persons
who may be convicted of any of the
above offences before the Mayor shall
forefiet and pay to cit any sum
not less than five dollars at the [caret mark] discretion of the [above caret mark (Word insertion)] Mayor with the cost of prosecution
Passed Mch 5/45
Attest JB [Illegible]
W [illegible] Goodwin
City Clerk Signed Alderman

Interpreting the handwriting of your ancestors. Little time will be spent discussing interpreting handwriting other than to say that learning to read your ancestor's handwriting is an important skill to have. One resource I have referred to and find to be outstanding is *Reading Early American Handwriting* by Kip Sperry. This book is designed to teach you how to read and understand the handwriting found in documents commonly used in genealogical research.

Keeping a Journal

Think ahead to one hundred years; one of your ancestors will be seeking to better understand himself by trying to get to know you. What will you leave behind? Will there be videos to view, an oral interview to listen to, or a journal to read? Your ancestor will find your journal to be of great value. You will be one on one with him, sharing your innermost thoughts, feelings, and reflections.

Your journal is the repository of your experiences. It becomes a guide, a mirror, a confidant, and a friend. It is important to have a journal that is a statement of who you are. The following are a few ideas that will help improve your journal writing.

Your journal is a record of your life.

In your journal, you will record important experiences in your journal because they affect you. You will want to explore not only your thoughts and feelings, but also your experiences.

But a journal is not just a diary; entries you make regarding your day, events you experience, and their effects on you are only springboards to a more fulfilling activity. You will delve beyond the experiences, events, and emotions to discover what essential teachings life holds for you.

As you write your journal, cover topics from a life and chronological point of view.

Life topics can include the following:

- Economics, income, work, career
- Living arrangements
- Family developments (birth of sibling, death of grandparent, and so forth)
- Extended-family developments
- Health
- Education
- Hobbies, interests, talents
- Church or religion
- Annual holidays and vacations
- Friendships
- Current events

Chronological topics can include things such as the following:

- Roots, or the person's family heritage up to his or her birth
- Birth, including family setting into which the person was born
- Pre-school childhood
- Childhood, perhaps through grade school
- Adolescent years
- Coming of age as a young adult
- Young parenting years
- Later parenting years
- Empty-nest years and retirement
- Death and legacy

Use several writing styles when composing your journal.

How boring would it be if all you did for your journal was write the date and what you did for that day? The following are a few writing styles that you may choose (on different occasions) to help express your thoughts:

Free writing (stream of consciousness writing). Write anything and everything that comes to mind. You do not need to follow any logical formation of thoughts. You do not need to worry if grammar, spelling, or even the ideas are acceptable. Do not do anything that would interrupt the flow of thoughts from your mind to the paper.

Do not censor any thoughts. Do not concern yourself with any associations you would make. Some days, free writing will seem like an exercise in insanity, since nothing makes sense. Other days, the thoughts and ideas revealed by free writing can be astonishing.

Free writing works best if you set a time limit of ten to thirty minutes. When you reread these pages, do not edit your work, just read them and enjoy the interesting way your mind works and how thoughts can flow from your creative center.

This is a wonderful technique to remove random thoughts from your mind and focus yourself on other tasks.

Focused free writing: Focused free writing is when you start with a topic. Write down the topic at the beginning of the page. Then write down any and every association or thought that comes to mind. Soon you can take a topic without any ideas associated with it and make myriad lists, comments, and ideas. As with free writing, set a time limit and do not censor your thoughts or ideas—keep the pen moving across the page.

Brainstorming: This is a two-step process. First, write a topic at the top of the page. Make lists of all the random ideas associated with the topic. The ideas can be words, phrases, or sentences. When you have a large quantity of ideas, stop. The second step is to organize those ideas into groups. This technique helps you to see how various ideas fit together under one topic. If you group your ideas and have a list with only one or two ideas in it, brainstorm that list. This is a good way to make associations and find smaller topics under a larger heading.

Journalist questions: Who? What? When? Why? Where? How? These questions force you to approach a topic from multiple perspectives. This is a good way to approach ideas you do not understand or to sort out problems in emotional perspective entries. Write down your topic or problem at the top of the page. Then ask each question in turn about your topic. Write down your response. Soon, you will have a logical organization of thoughts about your topic.

Mapping (Webbing, Clustering): This is a visual way of brainstorming. Write down your topic in the middle of the paper and circle it. Then draw lines from the main topic to other circles and write in each major sub-topic of the original topic. With each thought, connect it to the original topic, a sub-topic, or a sub-sub-topic. Continue branching off your thoughts until you run out of ideas. This is a great way to visualize and organize thoughts similar to a flow chart and lets you see how things are connected.

Lists: This is a quick and easy way to organize thoughts. Like a shopping list, make lists of what you are happy or upset about, things you need to do, and so forth. In a short amount of time, you can have several lists of basic ideas. This is a quick way of catching up your journal writing if you have fallen behind, or an easy way to organize many thoughts before you start detail writing each one.

Prompts: These are words, quotes, or ideas that help to jump-start the imagination. If you have several favorite quotes, questions that are important to you, or ideas that you want to mull over at a later date, keep them together in a notebook or a computer file—whatever organization method you enjoy. When you cannot think of anything to write, look over your prompts and see what sparks your imagination. Another technique is to open the dictionary, encyclopedia, or thesaurus to a random page and write about the first thing you see on that page.

Perceived world: This is the most common journal-writing technique. Written from your point of view, it is how you perceive the world and events around you. Often called descriptive writing, it is putting your descriptions of events, people, and places into your journal.

Reflective writing: When you analyze the past, whether it is your journal, past events, or past thoughts, and then commit them to paper, this is reflective writing. The distance between the past and the present lends additional insight into the issue and gives clarity of sight to an event not easily interpreted.

Altered point of view: This is writing from the point of view of another person. This can often give insight into another person's emotions or decision-making. Each of us takes our own path through life, and when we walk in the shoes of another person, we can gain clarity of why a person took a different path through life.

Dialogue writing: This form of writing is an imaginary conversation between you and another person. This is a difficult method of writing. Not only must you understand your own words and why you said them, but you must also be true to the person you are speaking with, and put the proper words into their mouths (not what you want them to say). Often, you can gain insight into the actions of others as you see how your words prompt their response, or vice versa.

Dialogue is a way of interacting with others, and this is a safe method for having a private conversation or telling someone what you really think, wished, or did, without the pain or the knowledge of the other person knowing that the conversation ever took place on paper.

Unsent letter writing: Write an honest letter telling someone what you think, why an event occurred, an apology, or an explanation, but never send it. The recipient of the letter is your journal. The emotions of the letter are between you and the one who will never read your thoughts and feelings. Writing a letter adds credence to an event. This is a way of communicating with a lost friend, deceased person, or a person you never met.

A journal has many uses.

There are many "out of the box" ways that you can utilze your journal. What follows is a list of some examples:

Find personal answers: It has been said that when we are confused about a situation, we shouldn't be, because all of the answers lie within ourselves. Do you believe this to be true? Have you ever been truly puzzled about something in your life? Once it was resolved, did you feel that you knew the answers all along? Or did the answers lie elsewhere?

Write in your personal journal. If you are in the middle of a difficult time right now, try to work through it in your journal. If not, spend some time reflecting to see how you discovered the answers.

Set personal goals: The world is filled with possibilities for each of us. We can choose where to live, what job to take, what hobby to enjoy, and much more. However, sometimes we start a project and lose interest quickly because we find another project that excites us. In the end, we find we have no time to set goals—and even if we do, they are usually not accomplished.

Pick up the pen and begin to write down everything that interests you. Then take a look at all of the things you want to do. Pick two items and make them your goals. In your personal journal, write down the steps you will take to accomplish those goals and then sign the bottom. Imagine that this is your own written contract and then commit to work on those two things until they are completed.

Write about procrastination: The project you found out about weeks ago is due tomorrow and you have done little work on it. Does this sound like a familiar situation? Is this a behavior that you would like to change? Or do you find this is the best way for you to work?

Try writing in your personal journal about procrastination. If this is a pattern you would like to break, write about the steps you might take to change it. If, on the other hand, this is a good way for you to work, spend time writing about why it works for you.

Write about fear: Every person suffers from one type of fear or another in their lifetime. In order to feel truly alive, we need to face our fears. Once we do this, we step out of our inner prisons, sprout wings, and fly. Do you think this statement is true?

Spend some time journaling on the idea of fear. What is your biggest fear? Do you think it's holding you back from accomplishing all you could do in your life? Do you feel you are ready to begin to overcome it? How will you begin?

Write about a journey: Too often, as we work toward a goal we have set for ourselves, we wind up either fixating upon the obstacles along the road or focusing too hard on the goal itself. When we do this, we miss the magic and beauty of the journey.

Do you agree or disagree? Do you have a goal in your life? Are you missing all of the wonderful things you have the ability to gain along the way, including meeting new people and learning new things about yourself and others? Or do you feel it will be good to accomplish the goal but it is the journey that brings the most rewards?

Write about success: Many people in this world equate success with money. The more you have, the more successful you are.

Spend some time reflecting upon this idea in your journal. Do you agree with this statement? If so, write down the reasons why. If not, how would you define success?

Write about positive experiences: Those who keep a positive attitude will be able to achieve anything. If they reach for the stars, they will touch them. If they want the moon, it belongs to them. Do you believe that maintaining a positive attitude is the key to success? Or do you think that hard work and determination are the only keys? Think about times when you were feeling positive about something as opposed to negative—what happened?

Spend some time writing about this in your personal journal. If you find areas in your life where your thoughts take a negative turn, stay with that and try to explore the reasons why. If you want to challenge yourself, think of ways in which you can change your negative thinking into something more positive.

Write about self-reflection: Have you ever been in an argument with someone and heard them say, "Stop thinking for me"? If you think someone is angry or upset with you, do you ask them or do you just presume that they are? Do you find that you often let things build inside your head instead of talking to the person? Do you base your reactions to people on assumptions, or facts?

Spend some time writing in your personal journal about how you relate to people. Think about how you approach situations and whether or not you are upfront and honest about your feelings and concerns.

Record your day in creative new ways.

What do you write in your journal about your day? Perhaps it read something like: "Today I woke up, had Special K for breakfast and went to work where Catherine spent all day gossiping about Jenny's new haircut."

Consider some of the following ideas:

1. Lists: List parts of your day. Try writing about
   - Things that made you smile today
   - Choices you had to make today
   - People you talked to today (and what the conversation was about)
   - Conversations you overheard
   - Feelings you had over the day
2. Gather up pieces of paper in your life for one day. The possibilities are endless, and it's fun to look back on years later. The following are some examples of things you can gather:
   - Your bus ticket in the morning
   - Receipts from any shopping
   - A note from a friend left on your door

- Scribbles from your note pad at work
- A cutting from today's paper or magazine that you read.

3. Use your digital or phone camera to make a visual journal for the day.

4. Write your day as if you were telling a story about yourself. Write about your day in the third person: "BJ was tired from a restless night when she tripped over the cat on the way to the shower."

5. Write about the most ordinary parts of your day. Little ordinary details, such as the following, will be interesting reading in years to come.
   - What you ate
   - The journey to work
   - How you choose what to wear each day

6. Write to your future self. This can be a letter, words of advice, or simply explaining about your day-to-day life.

Find a comfortable place to journal.

Only you will know where you are comfortable journal writing. Will it be sitting at a desk or on the boardwalk by the ocean? Curled up in a big easy chair or sprawled out across a floor? Propped up by a comfy pillow in your bed or slouched under a shade tree at the park?

Listen to your inner voice; it will guide you to that safe, comfortable space. Once you find it, you will be able to produce the writing you want. Don't be afraid to experiment. Try everything to see what works best for you.

Find the best time of day to write.

Explore your journal writing at various times of the day to see what works best for you. Some people write when they first wake up in the morning. This way their thoughts have not been disrupted by anything yet. Some people will journal in the afternoon after lunch. Others are night writers who like to do reflective journaling to touch on things that happened throughout the day.

Personal journaling is a gift you give to yourself. Whatever time you choose, make sure that you carve out enough time for yourself to focus on your writing. I like to write at night; the nighttime is my time to unwind. However, if the mood strikes, I will journal anytime, anywhere.

Find the right journal for you.

Journaling should feel like coming home and curling up in your favorite space. So what can help you to achieve that feeling? First and foremost, find a journal that represents you.

Will you be carrying it around? If so, you will want a compact one. Do you like to fold the book back on itself? Try a wire bound journal. Do you want lined pages or blank?

Now for the fun part! Do you like colorful, floral, or textile designs? Silly characters? Black-and-white photos, or maybe even reprints of famous paintings on the covers?

Think about all of these things and then experiment to see which type suits you best. Discovering your ancestors' writings is a great way to get to know them more personally. Be sure to leave your own written legacy, as well, so that future generations can have a way to get to know you.

Lesson 12: Search Every Page of Hometown Newspapers

As a genealogist, I have found community or hometown newspapers to be valuable resources in learning about my family. The articles of hometown newspapers cover literally every aspect of life and provide insights that are rarely passed on or even remembered. Be sure to search all listings of newspapers since it's not uncommon to find more than one local newspaper. Topics will range from births and deaths to reports of travel and social gatherings.

Just as with every resource, information found in the newspapers should be evaluated and verified by primary documents where necessary. Some of the problems you will find with newspapers include the following three:

Reporter or contributor bias: Depending on the view of the reporter, political affiliation, or other opinion or bias, specific events may not have been covered or may have been viewed in light of a certain "agenda." When you are searching newspapers, make sure you are looking in other regional newspapers to see how the same events may have been reported differently.

Timeliness of reporting: Many hometown papers were printed on a weekly basis. For example, if a story happens the morning the paper is published, chances are it will be printed the following week. Depending on the timeliness or available space in the paper, the article could be delayed a couple of weeks. Sometimes the event became old news and was deemed to be not worthy of publication.

Inaccurate data: Every newspaper had deadlines, making accuracy problematic. Reporters sought as much information as possible before articles went to print; unfortunately, details were sometimes missed, such as information about relationships in an obituary. Dates published in newspapers can also prove unreliable. There is always a chance of human error.

Hometown newspapers keep the community in touch with one another. My mother's hometown newspaper was the Spanish Fork Press from Spanish Fork, Utah. Although I grew up in Las Vegas, Nevada, I looked forward each week to receiving the Spanish Fork Press. My mother always made sure she kept in touch with her roots. Once in a while, there was a story about our family—yes, our family! Even though we didn't live in the city, the city was interested in its "residents" and "family" far and wide. My point is that, even if your family lived outside targeted areas but were originally from the vicinity, it is always worth your time to search the newspaper for family-related news. Always check newspapers from nearby communities to compare reported events. It is not uncommon to find different obituaries about the same person containing slightly different information. The difference in data is often related to newer details made available at the time of the publication deadline.

How Genealogists Use the Newspaper

Genealogists commonly look in newspapers for notices related to births, deaths, and marriages. But that is just the beginning of what you can find. Newspapers provide details and clues to historical happenings: local and family news, religious notes, advertisements, probate, court, real estate, biographies, photographs, and so much more. The following are a few examples of how newspapers are used:

Features and ads

Genealogists peruse feature stories, editorials, political events, notices of sales, and want-ads to establish criteria about the life and times of your family. You will find announcements regarding settlements of estate or notices to make claims on estates prior to settlement. Advertisements can show the type of goods and services family purchased and engaged in.

Obituaries

Most of the obituaries found in hometown papers will be very detailed, providing the names of parents, siblings, and extended family. Information such as time of immigration or place of birth is common. The pre-1900 obituaries are often the only records we have of extended family and relationships. Look for more than one announcement about a family member's death. On one occasion, I found up to four accounts of a person's death in different newspapers extending over a four- to six-week period.

Neighborhood columns

Many hometown newspapers had a neighborhood column, which covered topics such as who had what social gathering, who took a trip, or news about an event. Look for names associated with your family. You may be able to contact descendants of those mentioned in news articles to find information and photos related to your family.

Photographs

Newspapers have one-of-a-kind photographs and images of events and individuals. It's not uncommon to find photos associated with obituaries from the late 1800s and early 1900s that are the only available images of family. When events such as parades and community activities took place, the newspaper is likely the only source where you can find images depicting what those occasions were like.

Local, regional, and national news

Local newspapers are not limited to local news. Many of these papers also included regional, state, and national news relevant to the time period.

Newspaper availability

Many states have taken the opportunity to microfilm newspapers. These microfilms are often located in local, regional, and state public libraries; historical societies; and archives. Many university collections will hold complete collections of all newspapers in the state. If you are unable to get to a place where you have access to these films, you will be able to (in most cases) acquire access through interlibrary loan programs. You will simply need to touch base with the source library and your local library to make arrangements. **Note:** Make sure that your local library has the necessary equipment to view the microfilm. You can also expect a nominal fee for the film.

Digitized collections

More and more newspaper collections are being indexed and digitally put online every day. Make sure you check to see what collections have been digitized and where they are located. Many local newspapers are now online starting from the late 1990s. However, the information available is limited to the time period they have been online.

If you are fortunate enough to find a historical newspaper collection that has been digitized, it will usually be indexed, allowing you to search by name, keyword, newspaper title, date, or location. Most of the indexing that is done on digital collections is performed via advanced Optical Character Recognition (OCR) technology, which automatically recognizes text within an image. The extent to which the newspaper is indexed depends on the quality of the image. If there are quality limitations to an image, the index search results for that image will not be as accurate. For this reason, you may find some results for images that do not contain the exact word for which you searched.

Check for special projects

As part of your search for newspapers, check with the local library and historical or genealogical society to see if there has been an "obituary project" (where individuals have gone through the local papers to identify the names and dates of obituaries), and if so, where they are located.

Newspapers as a Genealogy Resource

Newspapers are considered to be the journal of local communities and their inhabitants. Newspapers range in size from a few pages to over fifty pages. They are an untapped resource for genealogists and can help you with the following:

- Writing more in-depth, fact-based family histories.
- Conducting broader yet more focused genealogical research.
- Finding possible clues to your ancestors.
- Understanding the times and community in which your ancestors lived.

While newspapers are an important resource for genealogists, it is important to understand their limitations (such as inaccuracies and biased reporting). Use sound judgment and evaluate the information against that provided by other genealogical sources. As you choose to use newspaper items as evidence to support genealogical conclusions, carefully record the following information:

- Article title
- Title of the newspaper
- Place of publication
- Date of issue
- Page number

Finding Newspaper Articles

Below I've listed some of the most common places to find newspapers.

Local newspaper offices will usually have one or more copies of each edition that are bound. However, these documents are often difficult to search (fragile, faded, missing issues, out of order, articles cut out—sometimes cutting parts of the article you seek). Using files from the local newspaper office for your research often requires using a camera (digital or film) to capture the article, since photocopies might not be allowed. You are often given limited times to search and a poor-quality area in which to do your searching.

Universities and libraries will often have newspaper microfilm images organized by year, date, and page. These microfilms are cataloged and easily stored. You can order films or request them through interlibrary loan. Universities often provide equipment for copies or scans of microfilm. Scans and photocopies can include lines or scratches in film, and photos will vary in quality. Cost ranges from free use of equipment to a nominal charge per page or scan. When using microfilm records of newspapers, it is easy to pick up where you left off. The films usually include papers of the state, county, and region.

Another benefit of using microfilm from a university or library is that you can search multiple papers during your research session. You are also able to expand your search as needed.

The Family History Library in Salt Lake City, Utah, has thousands of microfilmed newspapers from around the world that can be ordered through your local family history center.

Historical and genealogical societies usually have newspaper resources for their immediate area or will know where such resources are maintained.

US state archives and libraries serve as depositories for microfilms of newspapers from across the state.

Digital online collections are constantly growing. Millions of pages are added each month for newspapers prior to 1998. These collections provide the ability to search on key words and download digital images. Examples of online collections include the following sites:

- Utah Digital Newspapers (University of Utah) http://www. lib.utah.edu/digital/unews
- Library of Congress (over 9,000 US newspapers and over 25,000 non-US newspapers) http://www.loc.gov/rr/news
- United States Newspaper Program http://www.neh.gov /projects/ndnp.html

Examples of possible search words include the following:

- "Digital newspaper"
- State you are searching, in quotes ("Utah" or "New York")
- Community you are searching, in quotes ("Provo" or "Denver" or "Charlotte", for example)

Online newspapers

Many papers have been online since the late 1990s. Most national, state, and regional newspapers are online. Some local papers are online and may be affiliated with larger newspaper agencies.

Look for the newspaper website's archive section and search by key word. After locating the information you're looking for, you will be able to save data to your hard drive, print the page, or capture the screen using on-screen imaging software (such as SnagIt from TechSmith).

Below is a list of examples of online newspaper links and resources:

Utah newspapers:
- Cedar City Review: http://www.cedarcityreview.com
- Logan Herald Journal: http://hjnews.townnews.com
- Ogden-Standard Examiner: http://www.standard.net
- Provo Herald: http://www.harktheherald.com
- Salt Lake Deseret News: http://deseretnews.com/dn
- Salt Lake Tribune: http://www.sltrib.com
- St. George Spectrum: http://www.thespectrum.com/apps /pbcs.dll/frontpage

Other Internet sources
- Hometown Free Press (links to local papers worldwide). The USA section logically organizes the links by state and then lists links alphabetically by city. The USA page also includes a link to an index of college and university websites. http:// www.hometownfreepress.com/globe.htm
- US Newspaper List: http://www.usnpl.com
- Newslink: http://newslink.org/menu.html
- RFDesk.com: http://www.refdesk.com/paper.html
- Cyndi's Newspaper List: www.cyndislist.com/newspapers

Planning the Newspaper Search

Understand the scope of your search. Consider what your search will include: A specific individual? A direct line? A collateral line? Some combination of any of the above? Are you simply looking for obituaries, or are you looking for all articles related to family? What do you know about the individuals you seek?

Learn as much as possible about the person you are going to search for. You will gain a richer understanding of possible topics to search for associated with your ancestors. For example, when I was researching the life of my wife's grandfather, I learned that he was an avid reader and helped at the community library. In the local newspaper, I found a series of articles associated with his leadership in organizing the community to build the library. At the time, the information didn't mean much to me, but it was influential in raising my level of awareness. Some of the sources from which you can gather information about your ancestor include the following:

- Verbal discussions with family, friends, acquaintances
- Written histories
- Photos
- Grave inscriptions
- Official records (such as birth and death certificates, court records, and so on)
- Printed records (such as awards, news articles, newsletters)
- Correspondence (notes, letters, postcards)
- Recorded interviews (whether on tape or video)
- News reports (from TV, radio, newspaper, or Internet news sources)

The better the search possibilities, the more information you can find. Articles in the newspaper written about every conceivable topic. Information can include, but is not limited to, the following:

- Places lived and time periods
- Birth, marriage, or death dates of individuals in your search
- Names of family, siblings, and who married (including key dates)

- Elementary, middle school or junior high, high school, college (including their interests and activities during school years, such as sports, piano, dance, or club membership)
- Awards, contests, or promotions (in religious, school, military, or club groups)
- Profession
- Places worked
- Hobbies and interests
- Dramatic events (serious illness, wreck, shutting down of plant)
- Important local, regional, and national events (depression, war)
- Favorite holidays or family traditions.
- Favorite places to visit
- Names of important friends and family
- Military service
- Organizations of affiliation
- Church/religious affiliation and service
- Organize what you know by date or time period, and place

BARRY'S PROJECTS

One project comprised the collection of obituaries of my direct lines (four generations, including their siblings and spouses). Another project entailed writing life histories of direct lines (including articles of siblings and families as found). In both of these projects, local newspapers proved to be very helpful in finding the information I sought.

Example 1: As I researched newspapers, I was able to track J. Victor Leifson (my wife's grandfather) from 1910 until his death at age eighty-nine. Newspaper finds depicted his service in WWI, run for community office, service to the Icelandic community, church service, business life, service in community organizations, and personal profiles. I gathered a total of thirty articles that included snippets of his life, thoughts, and interests; people he was involved with that were important to him; thoughts that others had about him; as well as photos at different stages of his life.

Example 2: I followed my dad's high school and college sports career from 1948 through 1952—a total of thirty-eight articles in various local newspapers.

USES OF FILES

Variant uses of files continue to expand. Here are a few "out of the box" ways newspaper files can be used:

- Developing written family histories (historical facts and stories to support and expand verbal histories collected).
- Posting articles on websites as artifacts for others to use (such as obituaries, personal family profiles, or wedding announcements).
- Creating CD or DVD slide presentations that can be viewed by others.
- Creating source CDs or DVDs to share files with other family members (which will cut down duplication of efforts).

NEWSPAPER ARTICLES THAT ARE USEFUL FOR GENEALOGY

Obituary or death listing. Information about an event, such as a death, can range from a small mention to volumes about the individual. Prior to 1940, generally, there were usually two or more accounts of persons passing: a death notice, a life sketch or obituary, and a record of funeral services. The information was printed within one to three weeks of the person's death in a local or regional newspaper. It was not uncommon to be on the front page, with the article extending to another page. Information in local and regional papers can vary (providing more information about a person). Articles were free publication and did not usually include photos. Look for a unique headline announcing a person's death.

After 1940, there were usually two or fewer accounts of death—a death notice and a life sketch or obituary. The articles did not require a fee to be published until about 1960. You will notice information in local and regional papers was standardized to include the same details. Information was located in the "deaths" or "obituary" section of a newspaper.

After 1960, death notices or obituaries usually included a photo.

Obituaries and death listings can provide place-names; place of birth; places where individuals lived during their lifetime; place of death; places where children of deceased lived; places where most relatives lived.

Death notice and place of funeral. This information is usually written and given to the newspaper by the funeral home. You may find the date of burial, place of funeral service, place of internment or burial, and name of the funeral home.

Life sketch or obituary. The life sketch is written and placed by the family, funeral home, or reporter, or a combination of any of those people. You may find a photo (sometimes more than one); date and place of birth; date and place of death; information about parents, spouses, or children; place of residence; occupation; professional organizations they belonged to; church affiliation and service; military service; hobbies and interests; significant accomplishments; funeral home; and cause of death.

Funeral proceeding or program. The program is written and placed by the family, funeral home, reporter, or a combination of those people. You may find church affiliation and service; name of pastor or church leaders; names of friends and family; pall bearers; topics of speeches; and songs sung.

Birth or christening announcement. These types of articles were not common prior to 1900. They are usually listed one to three weeks after a birth and include the parents' names and the sex of the child.

Wedding announcement. These articles were not common prior to 1940. After 1940, you can expect to find announcements of brides to be married, including a photo of the bride and limited information about the groom and family. Look in the society pages for wedding announcements. They are usually listed within eight weeks prior to marriage, but I have found them listed as much as six months—or even longer—before the wedding. The article usually exists for first marriages only. During the 1960s, wedding announcements in newspapers started including photos of couples, rather than only of the bride. Different newspapers may have different photos of the bride or couple, so check a few local newspapers.

Wedding vows. These articles are not common prior to 1940. Articles about wedding vows range from a brief mention of the license to details of the ceremony and reception. They often include a photo of the couple. Look in the society pages one to eight weeks after the marriage for wedding vow articles.

Wedding anniversary (25th, 50th). These articles are not common prior to 1940. After 1940, they include an announcement of the couple, some life details, and a photo of the couple. Look in society pages about six weeks before or after marriage date. Information can include place of celebration, date of open house, and so forth.

Birthday announcement or open house. These articles are not common prior to 1940. After 1940, you begin to see announcements for one-year-olds, which include photos and the parents' names. You also begin to see announcements for open houses for individuals who were sixty-five years old (or older) and include a photo, a short bio, and the open-house location.

Society news and local gossip. Up through 1940, these articles were common occurrence and were usually only a few lines long. The article usually includes names and relationships. Community residents would submit tidbits of interest such as travel, birthdays, parties or gatherings, illness, job promotion, and visitors.

Public announcements and advertisements. Public announcement articles provide listings of property sold at public sales—usually livestock, farm equipment, and personal property. The advertisements are related to personal or company services, insolvent debtors, forced land or sheriff's sales, runaway slaves, and missing relatives.

Time period advertisements. Look for articles about proprietors or local stores to find out more about the time period. The ads include types of goods used, styles of the period, cost of goods, and prevailing themes from ad slogans or writings.

Business and community service. These articles are usually press announcements from business and organizations covering community involvement of businesses and organizations and committees and action groups that invite community involvement.

Articles can include meeting announcements, organization highlights, plans for community programs and events, economic contribution to the community, and award ceremonies.

Legal notices. These articles can include judicial actions, land sales for payment of taxes, divorce proceedings, settlement of estates, and which parties were involved.

Unclaimed mail lists. These articles are usually found prior to 1900. They are listed infrequently. Information was usually sent by relatives to the destination of family. Useful for identifying ancestors who pulled up roots before receiving their mail.

Church-related articles. These are usually located on the front page of a small paper, but they can be located in society pages, as well. The articles were used as filler, so sometimes they can be included anywhere. Church-related newspaper articles were usually found in LDS communities and include missionary announcements (leaving and coming home); new bishoprics; Stake organizations and proceedings; athletic outcomes; stake events (such as Priesthood, Relief Society, Primary, youth groups, Seminary); ward events (such as Blue and Green Balls or youth groups); talks and doctrine; new arrivals in pioneer companies (1850–1870); church actions (such as excommunications, prior to 1890). Other church-centered articles and announcements can include new members, baptisms, confirmations, and new clergy or other appointments.

Military-related news. Usually found on front pages, society pages, or obituary pages. Articles can include photos, drawings, diagrams, and maps. You will find articles relating to increased tensions appear up to one year before war and other war-related news up to one year after war. The type of articles you will see during the war can include lists of soldiers from community; enlistment rolls; names of those wounded, missing, or killed in action; training completion announcements; assignment changes; awards, commendations, or medals earned; community drives for the war effort; letters sent home; gatherings of war veterans; and homecomings. The table on the next page lists periods of war and conflict, during which military-related newspaper articles would have increased.

United States war periods in which you will find an increased volume of newspaper articles	
American Revolution (1775–1783)	Intervention in Lebanon (1982–1984)
War of 1812 (1812–1815)	U.S. Invasion of Grenada (1983)
Mexican-American War (1846–1848)	"Desert Storm" in Persian Gulf (1991)
Civil War (1861–1865)	"No Fly Zone" Iraq (1991–2003)
Utah's Blackhawk War (Tensions: 1847–1865, (War: 1865–1873)	US Intervention in Somalia (1992–1994)
Spanish-American War (1898)	NATO Intervention in Bosnia "Operation Deliberate Force" (1994–1995)
WW I (1917–1918: American involvement only)	US Occupation of Haiti (1994)
WW II (1941–1945: American involvement only)	Terrorists acts including World Trade Center (September 11, 2001)
Korean War (1850–1853)	Afghanistan War "Operation Enduring Freedom" (2001–present)
Vietnam War (1962–1975)	"Operation Iraqi Freedom" in Persian Gulf (2003–present)

School news and activities. These type of articles include honor rolls; graduation ceremonies; class projects and programs; contest participants and winners; local and regional competitions, such as sports, clubs, band, and choir; class and club officers; school events (sports, drama, clubs); awards given to students and teachers; school board minutes; school board appointments; and new teachers. Articles often included photos, a list of children and their names, and a description of the events.

Correspondents. Small towns near communities with newspapers often had correspondents who were part-time reporters for their area. There was no timetable as to the frequency of a correspondent's reports. Correspondents often wrote for a few papers (maybe for a hometown paper and a regional paper). They usually were not trained journalists, but had some writing skills. News they reported ranged from gossip and happenings to front-page stories.

Letters to the editor. These articles were a mixture of ideas or themes for which individuals were passionate on a local, regional, national, or international level. Letters to the editor may have included thoughts about articles that had been written, personal issues an individual wished to sound off about, a public thank you or apology, "Tattle-tale" reports of happenings, and many other topics.

Articles supporting the life story. Use the newspaper to find newspaper articles that can support, explain, or expand the stories of individuals and families. This has been an important feature of newspapers for me. For example, the following table shows how newspaper findings have supported the facts that I already had about my ancestors:

Fact: Family member died of black widow bite.	Article: Story in local paper about dangers of black widow bites.
Fact: Family member fought in Utah Blackhawk War.	Articles: Ten-week series on Blackhawk War in Utah.
Fact: Family member was a cattle rancher.	Article: Story about cattle ranching in Utah.
Fact: Family picked sugar beets during depression.	Article: Importance of sugar beet industry in Utah County.
Fact: Some family members settled in Beaver, others in Spanish Fork, and so forth.	Articles: Travel logs of cities (reports by correspondents in Deseret News before 1890).
Fact: Family member involved in Icelandic community.	Article: Icelanders settling in Utah.
Fact: Family member worked at Geneva and Ironton.	Article: Construction of Geneva Steel during the time period that family member lived there.

Hometown and local newspapers can provide much useful information to supplement—or further—your genealogy research. This valuable resource should not be overlooked.

Lesson 13: Learn to Find the Origins of Immigrant Ancestors

Where are Permitt Lee and Maxcey Ewell?

As a genealogist I have experienced the frustration of coming to an ancestor (in my case, Permitt Lee and Maxcey Ewell) for which there seems to be no link to the old country or land of birth. As I have consulted with other family genealogists, I have been in awe at the lengths our family has gone to in order to find our roots, but all to no avail. I have searched online, collaborated through the message boards, and traveled to the place of our family's beginnings in Pennsylvania, Tennessee, North Carolina, Kentucky, and Virginia. I have found and developed an extensive paper trail of the family, and I did find important clues, but not close enough to where I felt I was ready to jump my search over the sea to what I believed to be my homeland.

After some thought, I decided to step away from my search and learn all I could about how to find the birthplace of my ancestors. I researched methodologies that others have used and suggested for searching for the homeland, records and artifacts that can reveal important clues that pinpoint or narrow the scope of my search, and how understanding immigration and migration patterns of my ethnic heritage at a time and place can yield rich insight not found in a document.

My search took me through hundreds of Internet sites, books, and oral discussions. I was overwhelmed by the massive amount of material that exists. When I finished, I understood how documents, immigration patterns, and research methodology would combine to help me find my ancestors. I had more clarity of how to re-evaluate what I had, I could see the gaps and opportunities for further research, and I had renewed hope that I would find the answers.

As you search for your ancestors, realize that it will take a combination of methodology, tools and resources, and knowledge about your ethnic history to find your family roots. This chapter is divided into the following sections to help you begin, continue, or renew your search:

- Methodology: How to Find the Origin of Your Immigrant Ancestors
- What Records to Search and Why: Using the Paper Trail of Your Immigrant Ancestors to Find Their Origins
- Migration Patterns: Revealing Clues to Finding the Origin of Your Immigrant Ancestors

DEFINITIONS TO REMEMBER

Assimilation. The way that someone who comes from a foreign land or culture becomes absorbed into a culture and learns to blend into the ways of its predominant, or main, society.

Colony. A group of people living as a political community in a land away from their home country but ruled by the home country.

Emigration. Leaving one's homeland to go to another country with the intention of living there.

Exiles. People who have been sent away from their homeland.

Immigration. Traveling to a country that one is not a native of, with the intention of settling there as a permanent resident.

Migration. To move from one place to another, not necessarily across national borders.

Overlanders. People traveling over land rather than by sea.

Topography. The surface features of a region, such as mountains, plateaus, or basins.

Methodology: How to Find the Origin of Your Immigrant Ancestors

Genealogy is a process, a methodology, for finding our ancestors. There are many tools available, but knowing what to use and when to use the tool makes the biggest difference.

I remember many years ago when I was a Boy Scout, a member of our troop became lost. The first thing many of us did was rush right out and start looking in the wilderness and calling out his name. We had no record of who had gone where or what—if anything—was found. Any evidence that may have been found was trampled over. When evening came, we built large bonfires, hoping he might see us in the dark. As the morning came, we gathered as a troop and discussed what we remembered and what we knew about his last whereabouts. Next, we formed ourselves into groups led by an adult, with one adult being the coordinator of our efforts. Each group was assigned a specific area or quadrant to search. When we searched each quadrant, we either found a clue of where he might be or where he wasn't. As the day wore on, we found him asleep on the trail not more than a mile from camp, a happy ending. The happy ending resulted not from our hurry and scurry of the previous day but from a systematic method of searching that began the next morning. The same principle applies in genealogy research—an organized, systematic search will yield better results than frantic, disorganized looking. This section describes an organized, useful approach to finding your ancestors through immigration records.

1. Identify important information to know about your ancestor.

What do you know about your ancestor? Gather and review all the documents you have relating to your ancestor. I like to develop a spreadsheet that allows me to record each piece of information by date. The following are a few questions to get you started on reviewing the information you currently have:

What is the full name of the ancestor? Was the name changed when they came to America? If yes, identify what the name was before it was changed.

- Name of ancestor
- Name changes—both given and surnames

What are the names of immediate family?
- Names of the parents and their birth places
- Names of siblings
- Name of spouse(s)
- Names of children
- Common names given to family members

Identify the name of friends and relatives that are associated with your ancestor in American and in the country of origin. It is a great help in making sure you have found your ancestor when you find them together with these associated people in the country from which they immigrated.
- Names of family and friends with whom they associated.

Identify an event associated with your ancestor (such as birth, christening, or marriage) which occurred in the country of origin. List the date, month, and year—be as specific as possible. I have found, especially in Scandinavian research, many individuals may have the same name, and the only way to tell them apart is by the event date.
- Birth date and locality

What was the country of origin? Do you have the name of a village, town, and county? This can be the most difficult piece of information to secure.
- Localities lived in
- Geographical clues
- Historical clues

Was the ancestor really the first one to come to America? I have found cases when my ancestor was a member of the family that came to America.

What other information do you have?
- Documents in your possession
- Information about culture and religion
- Time period of immigration

- Family stories and traditions
- Family heirlooms

2. Start a profile and timeline for your ancestor.

Take the information you know and begin a written profile and timeline. Use an existing form or create one of your own to help track your ancestor's information and what you find. Make sure you also document where you find the information you record, because the need will always arise to review at least one of your data points to confirm or search deeper for information. I believe you should record any and all information you learn about your ancestor no matter how insignificant you consider it. Not only will it help in your search but, once you find the ancestor, it will also help in writing family histories. The following are the types of information you should be looking for and recording:

- Name of ancestor
- Name changes—both given names and surnames
- Names of parents and their birth places
- Names of siblings
- Name of spouse(s)
- Names of children
- Common names given to family members
- Names of family and friends with whom they associated
- Birth date and locality
- Localities lived in
- Geographical clues
- Historical clues
- Documents in your possession
- Information about culture and religion
- Time period of immigration
- Family stories and traditions
- Family heirlooms

At this point, you should be able to clearly see some trends in your ancestor's life. The types of documents you are able to find are dependent upon where and in what time frame they lived.

Double-check that you've reviewed every document you have on your ancestor; this includes letters, diaries, and photographs in your own files and in the possession of your relatives. Check online message boards for correspondence that you may not be aware of concerning research on this family line. Your ancestor's life is recreated one event at a time.

Now that you have your information written down, develop a timeline starting from their death and moving toward their birth (reverse chronological order). What do you see? Are any trends apparent? What *don't* you see? What gaps do you see in the information? Write down all the questions you still need and want to answer. No question is too small or "off limits."

Don't forget to include items such as histories, sketches, photographs, letters, and diaries as part of your search. Documents can be online, in libraries, or in a distant cousin's file.

3. Start your document and record search in America.

Once you are fairly certain about which ancestor you are going to search for, begin in America to find records that will provide and confirm important information about your ancestor and lead you to where you should look for records from your ancestor's country of origin.

Based on the time period in which your ancestor lived, outline some of the documents that might exist for your ancestor and where they might be located. This will help fill in the gaps in your timeline and answer your questions. Start with the paper trail you already have for your ancestor. You won't be looking for a birth certificate if your ancestor's life predates civil registration. Start with the basics—birth, marriage, and death records; church documents; indentures; land records; court records; and, of course, immigration materials.

Try to find at least two records, more if possible, of your ancestors to help confirm and corroborate information provided. Throughout your search, you will be exposed to resources that range from oral discussions to information that you find in print, online, and on other types of media (such as CDs, tapes, or microfilm). It is important to always ask questions such as the following:

- What is fact? What is suspicious?
- Did I search for the entire family?
- Did I search a broad time period in this record?
- Did I search a wide enough geographical area?
- Did I search every location they lived in that is covered by this record?
- Did I search variant spellings of names in this record?
- Did I search for and record neighbors, family, and friends found in this record?
- Did I search for and use indexes?
- Do I understand this resource or record's intention, what it offers, how it's put together, and its limitation?

As you gather and review information, continue to add to your current ancestor profile and timeline. Keep a detailed log of where you have been and what sources you have used. As you continue the search, you will check off questions that have been answered and add new questions to research based on your findings. Keeping this list up-to-date is vital to keeping your research focused and helping to shed light at times when you need inspiration.

4. Review and Learn about Immigration Patterns

One of the most important factors in finding our ancestors is immigration research. Look at immigration from a historian's point of view rather than from the genealogical point of view.

As a genealogist, you wonder why your ancestors migrated. You look for clues that might direct you to their birthplace in their country of origin. As genealogists, the first thing we do is start searching through deeds, wills, bible records, and other such documents. Documents can tell that your ancestor sold his property from one person to another, but it does not tell why he moved from Virginia to Tennessee.

As a historian, you're trying to understand what your ancestors did and why. You seek to understand immigration patterns of the time and people, your chances for success expand dramatically because you begin to understand what your family was thinking—you see what other individuals were doing, where they were going, and where they came from.

By learning about the immigration patterns for the specific ethnic group your ancestor belonged to in the time period they lived, you begin to see trends that correlate to your family, such as the ports they arrived at, the counties and cities from which they came and where they settled, the reasons for decisions that were made, the types of records they left behind, and where those records might be located.

Start by answering the following questions:

- What was their ethnic background or group? Were they Puritans? Welsh? Germans?
- Why did they come?
- When did they come?
- Where did they settle?
- What were their social and work conditions?
- What was their religious background?
- Are there any clues to family naming patterns?

A few words about maps. Maps help us trace the migration paths our ancestors took. More detailed maps will show what routes were available at the time, including railroads, waterways, early roads, and so forth. It is important to trace the path our ancestors took because there may have been records created along the way. The naturalization process may have been started at the port of entry, and the records may be scattered through stops along the route to the final destination. Ethnic and religious groups often traveled together, and your ancestors' travels can be traced by tracking others in their group. Also, on the long journey west in the United States, babies were born, people married, and people died. There may have been records of events created along the way.

5. Review your data: is it time to track your ancestor in their country of origin?

Before you rush off to research in your ancestor's country of origin, review your data. At this point, you

- have confirmed the country of origin.
- can put your ancestors in historical and social context.
- have researched records and developed a timeline of your ancestor's life in the new world.
- have assigned a time period when the ancestor entered the country.
- can perhaps place your ancestor in a region, county, or city where they lived.

If you are able to provide the above information, you're ready to start your search in the country of origin. Now its time to learn about your resources and continue your search.

If you don't have what is needed, identify gaps in your information and retrace your steps to see if you missed any important clues. Often it only takes one clue to get the break you need. If you are out of clues I have found the section entitled "How to find your ancestor when you hit a 'brick wall' and you're out of clues" on page 332 to be an important step that I use to expand my options.

What Records to Search and Why: Using the Paper Trail of Your Immigrant Ancestors to Find Their Origins

The following are records and resources that genealogists find extremely helpful and full of clues to finding the birthplace of ancestors. The information provided is not listed in any particular order. It is designed to provide a quick reference and direction of where to find and search for records as probable places to find information:

Federal Census Records

Federal census records provide the building blocks of your research, allowing you to both confirm information and learn more.

The following is an outline of the type of information you may find:

From 1790 to 1840, only the head of household is listed, along with the number of household members in selected age groups.

From 1850 to 1940, details such as the following are provided for all individuals in each household:

- Names of family members
- Ages at a certain point in time
- State or country of birth
- Parent's birthplaces
- Year of immigration
- Street address
- Marriage status and years of marriage
- Occupation(s)
- Value of their home and personal belongings
- Crops that they grew (in agricultural schedules), or other occupation-related information

Census Records Reveal Naturalization Records

Census records help you to learn the following information about your ancestors:

- their movement over time
- names and rough birth years
- relationships
- birthplaces
- clues to the previous generation (such as birthplace)
- street address
- whether an ancestor was a slave or a slave owner
- occupations
- other country of birth
- other children who likely died young
- year of immigration and naturalization
- naming patterns in your family
- clues to your family's economic status
- some clues about ancestors' education level
- some clues to military service
- some clues to medical conditions

- year and place of marriage (or at least narrow it down)
- employment status
- exceptional circumstances, such as convicts and homeless children
- native tongue
- death dates (at least narrow down)
- other potential branches of your family living nearby

Death Records

Death certificates are among the first official records that can provide an exact place and date of death, as well as additional genealogical details, such as the date and place of birth, name of father, maiden name of mother, name of spouse, social security number, name of cemetery where buried, funeral director, and the name of the informant (often a relative of the deceased).

How to Use Death Records

The information in death records is helpful to find an approximate year of immigration or arrival in a certain locality; find an address to seek in deeds or city directories, locate on maps, or narrow your search in an un-indexed census; and identify employer records to pursue.

United States Naturalization Records

Naturalization records document that an individual was granted citizenship in the United States. Naturalization records are a way to locate arrival information for immigrant ancestors. Those issued after 1906 will have other significant genealogical information. Many immigrants become naturalized. Citizenship was required to own land, serve in public office, or to vote. Information varies greatly among documents and time period.

Pre-1906 Naturalization Records

Documents or records from before 1906 vary greatly from state to state because there were not federal standards. You should at least be able to find the following information:

- Country of origin

- Port of arrival
- Port of embarkation
- Date of arrival in the United States

Post-1906 Naturalization Records

Documents after 1906 can include information such as the following:

- Name
- Current address
- Occupation
- Birthplace or nationality
- Birth date or age
- Marital status
- Name, age, and birthplace of spouse
- Names, ages, and birthplaces of children
- State and port of emigration (departure)
- State and port of immigration (arrival)
- Name of ship or mode of entry
- Town or court where the naturalization occurred
- Names, addresses, and occupations of witnesses
- Physical description and photo of immigrant
- Immigrant's signature
- Witness names
- Immigration year
- Additional documentation, such as evidence of a name change

How to Use Naturalization Records

Use naturalization records to learn the following information for your ancestor:

- country of origin (pre- and post-1906)
- timeframe to search for a ship passenger arrival list (pre- and post-1906)
- clues about relatives or neighbors (pre- and post-1906)
- ancestor's signature (pre- and post-1906)
- perhaps another version of your ancestor's name, such as a

non-anglicized spelling (pre- and post-1906)
- exact village or town your ancestor came from (post-1906)
- immigrant's birth date and place (post-1906)
- details of arrival in the United States (name of ship, date and port of arrival, and so on) in order to find ancestor's ship arrival record (post-1906)
- names, dates, and birthplaces of wife and children (post-1906)
- occupation (post-1906)
- marriage details (post-1906)
- photograph of the ancestor (post-1906)
- evidence of a name change (post-1906)
- reference to other courts where first papers may have been filed (suggesting immigrant lived elsewhere for a while) (post-1906)

Ship's Passenger Lists

Your ancestors most likely came to America in a ship. Every ship had a record of its passengers—a passenger list or manifest. There are good chances that you will be able to find these records. The information found on these records varies over time. Below is an outline of information you can find in a ship's passenger lists from different time periods.

Prior to 1820

Most sailing ships were cargo ships, and the passenger list may be found among the ship's cargo manifest. Ships sailed only when the cargo hold was full. There is no consistency to the type and amount of information that exists. The manifests were normally deposited at the port of arrival and were originally kept at these colonial ports. Many of these early records have been lost or destroyed. If they exist, you will find them distributed among libraries, historical societies, museums, and private holders. If you are fortunate enough to find them, the type of information you may find includes the following:

- Country of origin (possibly province, or exact town)
- Date of arrival in the United States

- Family members or others who immigrated on the same ship
- Destination in the United States
- Occupation, age, and sex
- Information about the ship—its name, master, port of embarkation, and port of arrival

Between 1820 and about 1891

After immigration to America increased, ships were being built especially for passenger traffic; companies had regularly scheduled sailing dates. After the 1840s, trans-oceanic, steam-powered ships started to replace the sailing vessels, which reduced the travel time from one or two months (or longer) to about two weeks.

Customs passenger lists were prepared by the ship's captain and were filed with the collector of customs at the port of arrival. These lists were initially meant to serve for statistical purposes. Except for a few ports, most of these passenger lists have survived. Information that may be found includes the following:

- Country, province, or exact town of origin (About 10 percent of the lists may have an exact town listed)
- Date of arrival in the United States
- Family members or others who immigrated on the same ship
- Destination in the United States
- Occupation, age, and sex of immigrant

About 1891 to 1957

In 1892, Congress passed the first federal law regulating immigration. This was followed in 1891 with the Superintendent of Immigration being established, which became the Bureau of Immigration and Naturalization in 1906. The records of the Immigration and Naturalization Service (INS) are called Immigration Passenger Lists. The 1891 list consisted of one page of information. Further information was added in following years and the list became two pages in 1906. Information found on these lists includes the following:

- Ship's name and date of arrival in America
- Family members or others who immigrated on the same ship
- If going to join a relative, the relative's name, address, and relationship
- Birthplace, including country and city (added in 1906)
- Name and address of the immigrant's nearest relative in the country from which they came (added in 1907)

Look closely for notes marked on the passenger lists. For example, some annotations indicate the passenger was naturalized (possibly leading you to find the naturalization record), other notes indicate they were detained. (**Note:** The detained passengers—with the reason for detention and other information—are generally listed on the last sheet of the ship's manifest.)

Available Immigration Passenger Lists

The implementation of the new forms depended on many factors, including who was in charge of the port. Some ports were regulated by federal immigration officials while, for other ports, federal officials contracted the administration to local officers. Usually any lists created under the authority of the Immigration Bureau are considered Immigration Passenger Lists. The following table identifies these major ports. Other ports with significant Immigration Passenger Lists on microfilm include Key West, FL, and Providence, RI.

Immigration Passenger Lists in the National Archives		
Ports	Lists	Indexes
Baltimore, MD	1891–1957	1897–1952
Boston, MA	1891–1943	1902–1906, 1906–1920,
	1903–1945	1899–1940
New Orleans, LA	1897–1948	1900–1952
New York, NY	1883–1945	1897–1902, 1902–1948
Philadelphia, PA	1893–1953, 1954–1957	1883–1948
San Francisco, CA	1890–1957, 1949–1954	1893–1934
Seattle, WA		Un-indexed

How to Use Passenger Lists

You can use ships passenger lists to do the following:

- Discover when your ancestor arrived in the United States
- Find out which country your ancestor was from
- Learn roughly when he or she was born
- Find the occupation of your ancestor
- Uncover family relationships
- Find evidence of chain migration
- Perhaps find the name of a county, town, or other place more specific than a country
- Learn the dividing time period of when to focus your research in the United States and when to focus on the country of origin
- Learn marital status
- Learn place of origin in the "old country"
- Find names and addresses of other family members
- Find clues to initial (perhaps temporary) settling places in the United States
- Learn of previous stays in the United States (leading to other arrival records)
- Determine literacy
- Get a feel for economic status
- Help reconstruct the immigrant journey and experience
- Seek clues for motivation of emigration (poverty, possibly avoiding draft in home country)
- Learn of health problems
- Learn of family members who may have been turned back or who died before formally entering the United States (at sea or in a hospital)
- Learn of ancestors born at sea
- Discover an ancestor's physical appearance
- Learn the birth place
- Learn of other places the ancestor may have lived before emigrating
- Obtain information to lead to emigration records

Passport Applications

Since 1789, the Department of State has issued passports to US citizens traveling abroad, and passport records for individuals are available from 1795. Foreign-born applicants were required to provide documented proof of naturalization to secure a passport. For children, the name of the father, his date and place of birth, and naturalization were listed. Passports were issued for three years. (They are now issued for ten years.) Photos have been attached to passports since WWI, and physical descriptions were then added, including height, hair color, and eye color. Until 1941, passports were not always required for travel to most foreign countries. Passport applications can help in locating your ancestral home. Naturalized immigrants may have applied for passports when they returned to visit their native countries. If they did apply for a passport, their passport records would generally provide information regarding the following:

- Family status
- Date and place of birth
- Naturalization
- Occupation or business
- Physical characteristics

Other Immigration Lists

When our ancestors immigrated to America, especially from Europe, a number of lists were generated, including those listed below. Be sure to look for these lists, as they can give additional help to your research efforts.

- Lists made at the original port of embarkation
- Lists may have been prepared if the ship stopped at another port along the way
- Lists at the port of arrival in the United States
- Lists in newspapers tell the ships arriving and departing and type of cargo
- Lists by a sponsoring organization such as an emigrant aid society, or if the ship was quarantined when it arrived in the United States

Probate Records

Probate records (which document the process of passing property, both land and various goods, on to one's heirs) are one of the major types of records used in genealogical research. Heirs may be anybody the testator (the person who made the will) chooses to name, including servants, in-laws, friends, and others. Wills and other papers created during the probate process are often the best possible source to document relationships between family members, particularly parent to child. Persons often identified themselves according to the place (often a town) they came from or were born in. Some (but certainly not all) wills and other probate papers may provide a key link between an immigrant in the new world and his family in the old. For example, American wills may mention a family's origins in the old country. Foreign wills may bequeath property (goods or money) to relatives who had emigrated.

Many of the colonial probate records up through the early 1800s have been published.

How to Use Probate Records

Use probate records to learn the following information about your ancestors:

- death date and place
- residence
- names (and addresses) of descendants
- details to aid in search for land records
- other places where the ancestor may have held property
- relationships, including clues to help sort out adoptions, guardianships, and other unclear relationships
- economic standing
- clues about ancestor's feelings toward family members
- clues to the deaths of other family members
- names of stores and vendors frequented by your ancestor
- your ancestor's signature
- occupation
- citizenship
- marital status

Land Grants and Transfers

Land records are not a great source for learning the origins of immigrants. While they are often used in other aspects of genealogy research, they seldom mention an immigrant's home. They are used most effectively to establish residency and relationships. During the colonial period, land records may be used to establish immigration.

Many immigrants came to America because of the availability of land, and these immigrants were often the first settlers in many areas. Many of the early lists of settlers are based on land grant records. In some of the southern states, these settler lists come from headrights—documentation that helps establish the number of people transported to settle on and improve tracts of land.

How to Use Land Records

Use land records to learn the following about your ancestors:

- death date and place
- residence
- names (and addresses) of descendants
- other places where the ancestor may have held property
- relationships, including clues to help sort out adoptions, guardianships, and other unclear relationships
- economic standing
- clues about ancestor's feelings toward family members
- clues to the deaths of other family members
- names of stores and vendors frequented by your ancestor
- ancestor's signature
- occupation
- citizenship
- marital status

Social Security Applications

As a result of the Great Depression that began in 1929, destroying the finances of millions of Americans and creating widespread suffering, President Franklin D. Roosevelt pushed for the passage of the Social Security Act of 1935. In that legislation, employers and employees were taxed for the purpose of providing pensions to workers who reached the age of sixty-five. In order to get into the program, people were required to complete a short application form, the SS-5, to receive a Social Security number.

If the person you are researching lived from 1937 on, you will most likely find an application on file for male ancestors (unfortunately, this is a less useful resource for women until recent decades, when virtually everyone started to get a Social Security card). Because the application was filled out by the person themselves, the information is fairly reliable. The Social Security application is so valuable because the names of the parents were provided by the very person being researched. The SS-5 application can be used to point to other sources.

The form included sixteen questions, which have varied over time and include the following information:

- Applicant's first, middle, and last names
- For women, the maiden name or previous married name
- Applicant's address
- Applicant's employer and employer's address
- Applicant's age at last birthday
- Applicant's date of birth
- Applicant's place of birth
- Full name of applicant's father
- Full maiden name of applicant's mother
- Applicant's gender
- Applicant's race
- Applicant's signature
- Date the application was filled out

It may also include information such as the following:

- Applicant's work name, if different than name above
- Applicant's marital status
- Wife's maiden name, if applicant is male
- Beginning or ending date of employment
- How applicant was paid

In order to obtain a copy of an SS-5, you can contact the Social

Security Administration. For more information on requesting forms and information from the Social Security Administration, visit www.ssa.gov/foia/html/foia_guide.htm.

Social Security Death Index

Immigrants are included in the Social Security Death Index (SSDI). Not all names are included in the SSDI, even when there was a Social Security number (SSN). A name probably will not appear in this database if relatives or the funeral home did not report the death to the Social Security Administration or if the individual died before 1962 (when the records were computerized).

The omission of name from the index does not indicate the person is still living. It does mean that no report of the person's death was provided to Social Security Administration.

When using the Social Security Death Index, in addition to the date of birth and date of death, the following three places may be included as well:

- State of issuance (where a person then lived and applied or the state in which the office that issued their social security number was located).
- Residence at time of death (this is really the address of record, but not necessarily where they lived or died).
- Death benefit (where the lump sum death benefit [burial allowance] was sent).

Societies

Lineage or Hereditary Societies

A lineage society is an organization whose membership is limited to persons who can prove lineal, documented descent from a qualifying ancestor. Hundreds of these organizations exist in America, such as for descendants of those who fought in the American Revolutionary War (Daughters of the American Revolution, DAR), who came as Mormon Pioneers (Daughters of the Utah Pioneers, DUP), or those who arrived on the Mayflower (Society of Mayflower Descendants).

Many lineage societies publish books of interest to their members and to other researchers. These books are found in most major genealogical libraries and can help you determine if a society might have information about a possible ancestor.

Immigrant and Early Settler Societies

Dozens of societies have been established focusing on specific immigrant groups or early settlers of a particular locality. While these societies have an interest in immigrants, they do not always know where any particular immigrant came from in the old country. Their objectives do not include establishing the immigrant's or settler's ancestry, only their descent to current persons. Examples of these societies include the following:

- Society of the Descendants of the Founders of Hartford (Connecticut)—requires the ancestor be living in Hartford by early 1640
- Order of Descendants of Ancient Planters—descendants of people who arrived in Virginia before 1616
- General Society of Mayflower Descendants—descendants of the Mayflower passengers
- The Order of the Founders and Patriots of America—pre-1657 founders who established families in America, among whose descendants, of the same surname line, were persons who fought for American independence in the Revolutionary War.

Some examples of immigration collections include the following:

- The Balch Institute for Ethnic Studies at Temple University in Philadelphia—transcribes many of the passenger arrival lists of ethnic immigrants.
- The Immigration History Society at the University of Minnesota—has collected thousands of ethnic newspapers and other sources dealing with eastern European ethnic groups. Their Immigration History Research Center is one of the most significant repositories of research materials for those groups in North America.

European Ancestry Societies

Some lineage societies focus on ancestors who were notable long before the American colonies were established. Therefore, descendants who wish to join need to trace their ancestry back to the immigrant (called the "gateway" ancestor), and then trace that immigrant's ancestry back to the qualifying ancestor in the old country. Usually the qualifying ancestor was part of British royalty or nobility. Examples include the Order of the Crown of Charlemagne in the United States of America, which requires documented descent from that early emperor. This means tracing your ancestry back more than one thousand years. Another example is the Descendants of the Illegitimate Sons and Daughters of the Kings of Britain.

Nationality or Ethnic Lineage Societies

These are societies that focus on an entire ethnic group. They gather information; teach their members; and publish stories, findings, and sources about that group. A small number of such societies—and some of the oldest such societies in America—are true lineage societies. Membership is limited to those persons who can prove descent from an early settler of a specific ethnic group. Examples include Dutch settlers in New York, Germans in Pennsylvania, and Scots-Irish in the Carolinas.

Genealogical Societies

Genealogical societies exist throughout the United States and Canada in every state or province, most counties, and many major cities. The people in these societies share the same interest you do: individually discovering their heritage. They gather together, usually monthly, to learn from each other about how to trace their ancestry. They recognize that together they are much more knowledgeable about the ins and outs of family history research than they are individually.

Society Publications

Society publications can be a significant aspect of immigrant research. Any local record may be the subject of a publication by a local society. Whenever you contact a genealogical or ethnic society, be certain to inquire about their publications. Even when such publications do not identify an immigrant's hometown, they may provide further identification about your immigrant ancestor or instruct you on additional sources specific to a locality or ethnic group.

Military Records

For immigrants in all time periods, military records are very important because they often document the soldier's birthplace and birth date or their age at enlistment. Records exist for many of the military engagements taken by the United States from the Revolutionary War forward. There are three types of military records: service records, pension records, and history records. The most important for immigration records are enlistment or discharge records and pension records.

The following is an overview of all three types of records.

Service Records

Service records cover the time an ancestor was actually in the service. These records almost always include the following information:

- Name
- Dates of enlistment, attendance, and discharge
- Beginning and ending rank
- Military unit

Service records may also include the following, but it is not as common as the information listed above:

- Date and place of birth
- Age
- Physical description
- Occupation
- Citizenship
- Residence
- Mentions of injuries or illnesses
- Reference to time as a prisoner of war (POW)
- Date and cause of death
- Cemetery of burial

How to Use Service Records

Use service records to learn the following about your ancestor:

- military service
- necessary details to locate a pension file or military history
- place and date of birth
- other details such as residence, occupation, or citizenship
- physical description
- death and burial information
- medical information
- insights into ancestor's personality and performance (promotions, AWOL notations, and so on)
- if and where they were held as a POW

Pension Records

Pension records cover the post-service period when your ancestor (or their next-of-kin) may have received benefits. They usually include the same information as service records listed above:

- Name
- Dates of enlistment and discharge
- Beginning and ending rank
- Military unit

They may include the following information, as well:

- Date and place of birth
- Physical description
- Occupation
- Citizenship
- Residence
- Marital status
- Name of spouse
- Names (and possibly birthdates) of children
- Marriage date and details
- Names of parents
- Affidavits by friends, associates and others
- Letters written by the veteran, his kin, or his attorneys
- Signature

- Medical examination findings
- Date and cause of death
- Cemetery of burial
- Photo or sketch

How to Use Pension Records

Use pension records to learn the following information about your ancestor:

- military service
- necessary details to locate a military history
- place and date of birth
- dates and places of other life events
- names of spouse and children, as well as their birth dates
- other details such as residence, occupation, or citizenship
- physical description
- death and burial information
- medical information
- insights into ancestor's personality and performance (through his letters, affidavits filed by others who knew him, and so forth)
- literacy
- signature
- post-war years and life
- what he looked like

Military History

Military histories (often referred to as regimental or unit histories) can add historical background to help you understand the conflict and your ancestor's participation in it. They usually include a roster of those who served in the unit and dates of major engagements.

They may also include descriptions of battles, personal details about individuals (especially officers), references to personal diaries and letters of those who served in the unit, and photos of those who served in the unit or regiment.

How to Use Military History Records

Use military history records to learn more about your ancestor, such as the following:

- More fully appreciate the military experience of your ancestor
- Learn who he served with
- Learn which engagements he was involved in
- See what he looked like

Cemeteries

Cemetery records have their own limitations as sources for immigration information. While it is not common for a foreign birth town to appear on a cemetery headstone, there are literally thousands of cases where such is the case. Such circumstances seem to be more common where there are many immigrants in a cemetery, such as in Pennsylvania German communities or the cemeteries near the Catholic missions in California.

While locating a burial site can be difficult, people are usually buried where they die. Begin your search for a cemetery where your ancestor "drops out" of the records.

In any given area, there are usually many cemeteries, which include all or most of the types listed below. The records of these various cemeteries are often in many different places and not easily accessible. The records are often organized in chronological order or by plot, and therefore, not alphabetical. If public records exist for your ancestor, they will usually denote where the burial occurred. For deaths occurring after 1870, the community may have required a burial permit from the local health department. These are not death certificates, but they do identify the cemetery.

Many directories are available to assist you in locating a specific cemetery or even a list of all possible cemeteries in a certain locality. In large cities, begin with the city directory for the time period when the immigrant died. Directories include the following:

- Cemeteries of the United States
- United States Cemetery Address Book
- The Geographic Names Information System (GNIS)—The

nation's official repository of domestic geographic names information, including cemeteries.

If you still have trouble locating the cemetery, you may want to check current directories of mortuaries (available from your local mortician). A local mortuary in the area where an immigrant died will at least be aware of the active cemeteries and may be able to refer you to a local cemetery association. Once you have located the cemetery, you will seek the following information:

The inscription on the stone. Tombstone inscriptions are as different as the individuals they commemorate. In most cases you will find some element of value. For example, a tombstone can show a relationship with an inscription: "Beloved wife of . . .". You will find logos or markers that indicate service in the military or organization. Depending on the time period and the area of the country (such as in an immigrant-rich community), you might find a birthplace. Some tombstones contain photos, favorite saying, writings, music, or images that relate to a hobby or profession. Tombstones can also carry lineage, such as names of the children or "Daughter of . . .". You will most likely find the true given name of the person or even a nickname that can help you find information.

The Records of the Sexton

Note: Many cemeteries have paper records of persons who are buried there. These records are kept with the sexton and come in many formats. They usually include the name of the person buried, death date, and owner of the cemetery plot. The first place to find sexton's records is the cemetery itself. If you come across a cemetery that is "inactive" or "full" because there is no more room for additional burials, contact the local sexton to begin your search to see if they have records.

When you combine the tombstone and sexton's record, you can build a profile that unusually includes the name of the deceased (from tombstone and sexton record), years of birth and death (from tombstone), and date of burial (sexton record).

Your profile may also include any or all of the following information:

- Address of deceased (sexton record)
- Age of death (tombstone and sexton record)
- Birthplace (tombstone)
- Cause of death (tombstone and sexton record)
- Cost of the plot or burial (sexton record)
- Date of death (tombstone and sexton record)
- Full name, including maiden name for women (tombstone and sexton record)
- Full dates of birth and death (tombstone and sexton record)
- Information linking the plot owner to other plots, such as disinterment, reburial, and so forth (sexton record)
- Information about military service, such as unit (tombstone)
- Inscription (a poem or Bible quote, for example) providing insight into the ancestor or those left behind (tombstone)
- Logo of organization that the deceased belonged to (ethnic, religious, military, and so on) (tombstone)
- Name of doctor and hospital (sexton record)
- Name of officiating minister (sexton record)
- Names of other people or institutions involved—funeral home, officiating clergyman, memorial company (sexton record)
- Owner of the plot (sexton record)
- Relationship clues ("Beloved wife of . . .) or who else is buried in the plot (tombstone and sexton record)
- Marriage date (rare) (tombstone and sexton record)
- Where the deceased died, if other than where he or she lived (sexton record)

Types of Cemeteries

The four types of cemeteries are religious, community, private, and commercial. A brief overview of each type is given below.

Religious Cemeteries. Religiously devout immigrant ancestors were most often buried in religious cemeteries. These cemeteries are usually located next to the group's church or synagogue. Qualification for burial was often reserved for burial of the faithful (and sometimes the not-so-faithful, as well). In some religions, such as

Roman Catholic, burial in sacred, consecrated ground was vital for salvation. Other religions consider burial to be a sacrament and it needed to be conducted by a spiritual leader. If a burial was conducted by the church, the local church was the most likely place for it to occur. Records for the religious cemeteries are usually found at the church and not with the sexton.

Community Cemeteries. Most of our immigrant ancestors during the 1800s were buried in cemeteries established by a local community (a city, town, township, or county). Community cemeteries attracted immigrants whose devotion to their religion had waned during their years in North America. If there was not a local church in the area for a deceased person, they were usually buried in the community cemetery. If you suspect your ancestor was buried in a community cemetery, contact the sexton who is responsible to keep the records of burials in that cemetery. The sexton's job is to coordinate, and often actually handle, the burial duties, usually in concert with an undertaker (mortuary) and often a church as well.

Private Cemeteries. In early America, many families established private, family cemeteries. These are most often found in New England and the Southern states, but really can be anywhere. Fraternal or social groups, such as the Masons and Odd Fellows, created private cemeteries. Private cemeteries are usually found in rural areas.

Commercial Cemeteries. Commercial cemeteries, usually run by a local mortuary or company, are common and have replaced community cemeteries. You won't find your ancestor in this type of cemetery unless they lived after 1900.

How to Use Tombstones and Sexton Records

Use tombstones and sexton records to learn the following information about your ancestor:

- dates of life events for further research
- names of family members, neighbors, and others who are buried in the same plot and are therefore likely connected to your ancestor
- maiden name for female ancestors
- organizations to which your ancestor belonged

- cause of death
- military service
- insight into the personality of your ancestor
- a sense of the economic standing of the family

Obituaries

For many of our immigrant relatives, the obituary is the only biographical sketch ever written. Men and women both are likely to have obituaries written about them. Those who died young may be fully profiled in an obituary, especially if the death was the result of an accident. You will often find information written about your ancestor that you will not find anywhere else, thus making the obituary a very important resource.

When you think of newspapers to use in your research, remember that in addition to community papers, there are also two other common categories: ethnic and religious.

Ethnic Newspapers. Additional newspapers to consider are papers that focused on a particular ethnic group. For example, it was common in most midwestern cities for German-language newspapers to exist side-by-side with general, English-language newspapers. Occasionally they were published by the same company on the same presses. Ethnic newspapers are usually printed in the language of the community. Remember that while you may not be able to read the language, the name of the deceased is usually in the headline. Find what seems to be a relevant article, then have the article translated if you don't speak the language.

Religious Newspapers. Often our immigrant relatives were more religious than their descendants. They often participated in their church's activities on a regular basis. Therefore, the death would be major news within the religious community. Most denominations supported one or more newspapers in the nineteenth century. Larger denominations, such as Catholics and Lutherans, often had newspapers in every major city and in several minor ones. Religious newspapers were often published for denominations such as Baptists or Methodists.

Obituaries can be found in newspaper journals, magazines, and even yearbooks. Obituaries started to be mentioned in local newspapers during the 1870s. You should be able to find the following information in most obituaries:

- Name
- Age
- Date of death (sometimes only giving the day of the week)
- Family information
- Names of survivors
- Church or mortuary holding the service or cemetery

In addition, it wasn't uncommon to find biographical information, so you might be able to find information such as the following:

- Names of parents
- Occupation
- Military service
- Affiliations with local clubs
- Fraternities or associations
- When person settled in the area
- Birth information (for example, "came from Ireland in 1849" would tell you that the person was likely born in Ireland)
- Clues to locating documents such as passenger lists

It's not uncommon to find obituaries in several papers in the area the person lived. It is important to review obituaries from all the newspapers that you can find. It is not uncommon for obituaries to contain slightly different or additional information.

If you don't know the death date of an ancestor, consider the following ideas to narrow the scope of where and when to search:

- Check the census records to see if 1) the person even appears in the locality or 2) if the spouse appears as widow or widower.
- Check probate records from the last known residence.
- See if your state has online vital record databases to search for death records.

Once you have a date, then you can continue your search with the following steps:

- Check with local libraries and historical societies to see if obituaries have been clipped and put on file.
- Check with local libraries and historical societies about newspapers that served your area during the time period of your ancestor's death. It's not uncommon to have newspapers go in and out of business.
- Check to see if the local paper has been microfilmed, which can then be exchanged through library loan.
- Check online. It's not uncommon to have obituaries abstracted and posted to the Internet.
- Check to see if local indexes have been published that will tell you if and where obituaries were published.

Many libraries offer the services of looking in microfilm for an obituary. Of course, for them to do this search, you will need to provide the date of death. The cost of service is usually less than $10.00.

Don't overlook ethnic, religious, or professional papers. If these papers are not part of the local library collection, libraries should be able to tell where to locate them.

Depending on the region of the country, you may find several postings for the person's death: an obituary within a few days of the person's death, a profile of the person's funeral a week later, and a thank-you card from the family expressing appreciation to family and friends.

Your chances of finding an obituary will increase depending on the size of the town. The larger cities did not usually print the obituaries of every person's death.

Immigrant Church Records

American church records are often overlooked, yet they provide important information for our ancestor origins. Immigrants as a whole were religiously devout and connected closely with one another through church. The American churches, called "ethnic" churches, catered to a specific ethnic group (Germans, Irish, and

Norwegian). The two most common immigrant churches were the Roman Catholic and the Lutherans. The Roman Catholic church is mostly found in the larger cities such as New York, Chicago, Cincinnati, and Detroit serving the ethnic communities of the Germans, Italians, Irish, Poles, French and others. Lutheran churches are usually found in rural areas serving the Germans and Scandinavians. For both of these denominations, the minister was trained in the old world, and they often held services in the native language of the congregation.

Like the churches in the old world, detailed records of parishioners' sacraments—such as baptisms, confirmations, weddings, and burials—usually contain significant information about the people. These records are usually written in the native language.

When you search church records, look for records of the entire family and their relatives. Your chances of finding places of birth will vary depending upon the recordkeeping of the church. As a general rule, the more immigrants that were served by a church, the more information you'll get about the individuals, such as birthplace in the country of origin.

In order of priority, the following are the American immigrant church records that are most likely to have the immigrant's birthplace mentioned:

Burial. Immigrants usually chose a church burial, as that is how it was done in the old country, and thus their burial record will be found in the local church records. From these records you can learn the following:

- ancestor's death date and place
- ancestor's last residence
- date (or at least year) of birth
- name or surviving relative
- maiden name of a woman
- cemetery of burial for further research or visit
- date for obituary or death notice search

Wedding. If you are able to find a public record of an ancestor's marriage, you will note who performed the marriage. If you see the title of the officiator listed as Pastor, Reverend, Father, or any other as minister of the gospel, your ancestors probably had a church wedding. You can determine which church the individual belonged to and search for records there. From these records you can learn the following:

- ancestors' marriage date and place
- ancestors' place(s) of residence
- year of birth for the bride and groom
- previous marriages
- groom's occupation
- clues to family relationships (through names of witnesses and so on)
- names of the preceding generation
- ascribe children to appropriate marriage, if a parent has married more than once
- other possible religious affiliations
- handwriting of an ancestor
- time period for the death of the first spouse in the case of the widow(er) remarrying
- other family connections through dispensation remarks

Confirmation. Most church records simply list those that were confirmed on a specific day. On rare occasions you might find information such as their birth dates, parent's names, and place of birth. Information will vary somewhat by religion, with Scandinavian and Lutheran, for instance, generally providing more details.

Minutes or Communicant Lists. These records can be helpful in reconstructing family history. The disappearance of a couple from the list may signify their departure from the community. The disappearance of one but not the other may indicate death, an important clue if the death records no longer exist. These lists may also provide insight as to where persons have moved or immigrated. These records also help to build a picture of what your ancestors were like and how they worshiped.

Baptism. Since baptisms usually were recorded in America, they generally do not provide information about the country of origin.

From these records, you can learn the following:

- ancestor's birth date
- names of the preceding generation
- family's place of residence
- clues to family relationships (such as through names of sponsors)
- previously unknown children who died young
- parental association in the case of multiple marriages by one of the parents, to determine which one a particular child came from
- changes in church affiliation

Where to Find Archives for Major US Religious Denominations

The following are locations for finding the archives of various US religious denominations:

Adventists—Washington, DC
American Baptists—Rochester, NY
Southern Baptists—Nashville, TN
Brethren in Christ Church—Grantham, PA
Church of Christ, Scientist—Boston, MA
The Church of Jesus Christ of Latter-day Saints (Mormons)—
    Salt Lake City, UT
Churches of Christ—Memphis, TN
Congregational—Boston, MA
Disciples of Christ—Nashville, TN
Greek Orthodox—New York, NY
Jewish—Cincinnati, OH; Waltham, MA
Evangelical Lutherans—Chicago, IL
Missouri Synod Lutherans—St. Louis, MO
United Methodists—Madison, NJ
Pentecostal—Tulsa, okay
Presbyterians—Philadelphia, PA; Montreat, NC
Episcopalian—check local parishes
Reformed Church—New Brunswick, NJ
Roman Catholic—Notre Dame University, South Bend, IN;

Catholic University, Washington, DC

Quakers (Society of Friends)—Swarthmore, PA, for Hicksite records; Haverford, PA, for Orthodox records

United Church of Christ—Boston, MA; Lancaster, PA

Unitarian and Universalist—Harvard Divinity School, Cambridge, MA

Starting Points for Further Research

Start with the local congregation. Usually one of the workers will know about the early records and where they are stored. They may even know of descendants of your family that still attend that church. Often the records are no longer stored at the local church. Many Catholic records have been collected by the diocese. Lutheran records may be in synodical archives. If you cannot locate the local church or they no longer exist, then turn to the appropriate diocese or synod. The effort to find the records will be worth your time.

Township, City, County, and State Histories and Biographies

Local, county, and state histories detail the events that occurred in a particular region and the people who played a part in them. These histories detail the early settlements, who held what offices, who founded various towns, when different churches were started, and other valuable information. It is common to find histories that were written between 1870 and 1920 with biographical sketches of the individuals and families. The majority of these histories were written in the west, in those states bordering the Great Lakes, and in the Midwest states. These histories give insight and are helpful to the researcher since this is the region where most of the immigrants settled.

As you look for the local, county, and state histories, also look for books or volumes that focus solely on biographical sketches of people from the locality. Most of the sketches are written about men and generally include information about their family, education, and occupation. These sketches will also tell the subject's date of birth, parents' names, and wife's and children's names. Usually there is some comment about where they were born. If the subject was an immigrant, the foreign country was always mentioned, and perhaps the town of birth.

Colonial Town Records

Colonial towns had regular meetings, at least once a year, where various inhabitants (often freemen) were elected to a number of different positions. Many of the same local (town or county) government services used today (such as road repair, property registration, and so forth) were accomplished by local townsmen, often in lieu of taxes. Over the course of several years, most adult males who remained in one town had the opportunity to serve in some capacity, and their names will be listed. Town records will include a record of births, marriages, and deaths occurring in that town, as well. Town records usually do not mention a resident's country of origin. If you find your ancestor's name among the records, you gain insight into their residences and status, giving you additional clues for your research.

The lists of Freemen are the best for immigrant origins. Freemen were inhabitants of towns who were qualified to vote and participate fully in town affairs. This included the use of a town's common areas, such as fishing ponds, and distribution of new lands acquired or subdivided by the town. The Freemen usually were required to be of legal age (usually twenty-one), own land, be a member of the established church (usually, but not always), and be a resident.

The early lists of Freemen were heavily populated with immigrants. If you find the individual you seek on one of these lists, it testifies that they were an adult and an accepted member of the community. The next step would be to search records—such as church, land, or court records—that might give more information.

If the list names others who were neighbors, friends, and relatives of the ancestor, they may have emigrated together or at least are from the same locale.

Using Maps and Gazetteers to Help Find Ancestor Origins

Maps and gazetteers help us trace the migration paths our

ancestors took. More detailed maps will show what routes were available at the time, including railroads, waterways, early roads, and so forth. The following are a few ideas of how you can use maps to assist your research:

Determine Record Locations. By pinpointing where your ancestors lived, you are able to locate records that contain addresses—directories, vital records, court records, military, and naturalization records. By plotting these addresses on a map, you are able to locate where records might be kept—such as in churches, civic districts, and so on—or where to look in the census, such as ward, township, and street.

Identify Changing Boundaries. Maps help locate boundary changes that occur over the years that will put your ancestor in a different city, county, state, or country during a given time period.

Recognize Changes in Place Names. It's not uncommon for the places your ancestors lived to no longer exist, have name changes or be spelled differently in the country of origin. The following are examples of other major cities whose English name does not match the native spelling:

Native Spelling	English Spelling
Braunschweig	Brunswick
Kobenahvn	Copenhagen
Lisboa	Lisbon
München	Munich
Napoli	Naples
Praha	Prague
S'Gravenhage	The Hague
Warszawa	Warsaw
Wien	Vienna
Zaragoza	Saragossa

Topographical Features

In your records, you may find references to mountains, roads, rivers, or other topographical features. You can use these features to help find the exact location of a city or town on a map when you have multiple options to choose from. Don't be surprised to find the names of cities different at various times. Also, having some history of the area can be helpful in understanding what you are seeing on the map and understanding what parishes or districts the town belonged in.

By studying the topographical features, you can see places your ancestors may have gone because they were easier to access. For example, I was able to find a wedding certificate in the state in which my ancestor lived. The couple lived on the border of the next state, but upon searching the town that was just across the border, I found no records. After researching the topographical map, it became clear that while those towns were close, there was not a practical access point at the time the family lived. By following the roads, I was able to narrow the search to two possible locations, and the marriage record was found.

PLOT THE MIGRATION PATTERNS OF ETHNIC GROUPS AND ANCESTORS

As you research the migration patterns of ancestors, you are able to see the flow of an entire group and then map the individual path of your ancestor in relation to the group they belong to. If you are able to find more detailed maps, you will be able to find the roads, railroads, and waterways they would have traveled, which are important to locate records and associated family with specific groups. The following are a few examples:

Records may be scattered. The naturalization process may have been started at the port of entry, and the records may be scattered in stops along the route to the final destination. Ethnic and religious groups often traveled together, and your ancestors' travels can be traced by tracking others in their group. Also, on the long journey west in the United States, babies were born, people married, and people died. There may have been records of events created along the way.

City or town names can give clues to country of origin. The origins of new immigrants can be observed through names of the cities they lived in. For example, the Quakers from Wales tended to flock together in what was called the Cambry or Welsh tract. The village names of this district define the region of origin in the mother country—Flint, Montgomery, Bala, Tredyffrin, Radnor, Haverford, and Denbign. The East Anglian origins for the settlers of Massachusetts before 1660 can be confirmed by the names they gave to their New England towns. Examples of New England towns named after their counterparts in England are Ipswich, Groton, Boxford, Sudbury, Hadley, Wrentham, and Framingham from towns of the same name in Suffolk County, England. Town names taken from Norfolk, England, were Lynn, Newton, and Hingham. Other towns from East Anglia were Cambridge, Dedham, Springfield, Topsfield, Braintree, Billerica, Chelmsford, and Malden (Essex).

How to Find Your Ancestor when You Hit a "Brick Wall" and You're Out of Clues.

Do you have an ancestor that your family has been looking for and simply can't find the clues to where they came from? In his book British Origins of American Colonists, 1629–1775, William Dollarhide describes a methodology for "finding the needle in the haystack." I have several ancestors who have been difficult to locate, and I have found the following very insightful for organizing and conducting a difficult search.

1. What do you know about your family?

- What is their country of origin?
- What are the surnames of the family and possible variations? (For example, "Ewell" could also be spelled "Yuille," "Yule," or "Uhl.")
- Do you know if they belong to a specific group? (such as Puritans, Scots-Irish, Huguenots, and so on)
- About when do you think they came to America?
- Where did they settle in America?

2. Find out what has been written about the migration of your ancestors' country men. Start with a Google search. For example, if your family came from Germany, start your search with

"German Immigration," or if they were Puritans you could start with "Puritans" or "English Immigration." Be patient—there are hundreds of sources. I usually find what I need in the first three pages of an Internet search. **Hint:** As you review information on the Internet, look to see what sources are used in providing the information, such as books and other Internet sites. These provide valuable clues of where else to look if you need more information.

3. Learn what you can about immigration patterns of the group or people your family belonged to. Read and take notes. With even the most limited information you were able to gather in step 1, you will start building your knowledge base and narrow the place in the "haystack" of where to look. As you read, ask yourself questions, such as the following:

- What was the time period your ancestors arrived in America?
- Why did they come (regions, counties, states)?
- What regions in the country did the group or people come from?
- What ports did they leave from and arrive at?
- Where did they settle and why?
- What were the names of the cities where they settled in America?
- What were their social tendencies when they came to America?
- What roads did similar immigrant groups take in their travels?
- What maps or charts are included with the information you read to help explain what is being written?
- What types of records were kept at a given time period by related groups, countries, or agencies?

From my own experience: I had one ancestor for whom I had very little information. All I knew about them was they were from England. By reviewing English immigration, I came across a group called the Scots-Irish. The information I found about this group helped answer many questions about the family, from why they lived where they did to where they may have come from.

4. Compile what you have learned. You are now starting to eliminate parts of the "haystack" where you don't need to look and are narrowing your scope as much as possible.

Organize your notes, questions, and clues that you found.

Identify on a map the places or regions where the people came from and settled. Types of maps that provide help include the following:

- maps that show cities today.
- maps of the time period if available.
- maps that outline the country, counties, and states. If possible, color in the counties or states, if provided, where specific groups come from.

5. Start a Systematic Search. Based on what you have learned, start sifting through the portions of the "haystack" that are left, one straw at a time. The narrower the place you're searching is, the better your chances of finding ancestors. Keep a log of where you have been, what you reviewed, and what you found. Frequently update your notes and questions with your findings.

Start your search in America.

Search the records in the state, county, and city where your family lived in America. Chances are good that you will find key information about your family there. Don't overlook searching and reviewing the records of people that lived in the area with your family at the same time, since they probably came from the same town or region as your family.

You can begin searching published county records. These may be published online, in book format (often available for interlibrary loan), or on microfilm. Microfilm is available through family history centers of The Church of Jesus-Christ of Latter-day Saints and through interlibrary loan. Since family history centers are located in LDS chapels, you can use a phonebook to locate the nearest LDS chapel and inquire if they have a family history center They are all open to the general public.

American genealogical research is often keyed to the land a

person lived on. Land ownership in America before 1850 was as high as 90 percent of all adult white males. As a result, United States land records are nearly universally helpful for finding clues. Also, central state transactions are recorded at the county level for most US states. Indexes to deeds provide an excellent historic overview of the residents of the county in virtually every state.

Another advantage to American research is that nearly every federal census taken since 1790 lists the last names of immigrants or their descendents.

When ready, start your search in the country of origin.

Before you start, understand the type of records that were kept during the time of your ancestor and what types of books and online sources are available. For example, if you are doing British research for the seventeenth century, you should know that, unlike American research—where land records and census records are effective tools—British land was mostly limited to the elite society of landlords, and nation-wide census records were not kept until 1841.

A good source of information in the British records comes from the parish records. An English parish is a jurisdiction where vital statistics such as births, baptisms, marriages, deaths, and burials are recorded. In your research, you may have found the counties a group came from; this information will be useful in searching parish records. You can be even more effective by tying a surname to specific regions or parishes.

If a name or group can be connected to just a few English villages, parishes, or counties, your search in parish records will become narrowed. Having the surname of the male is required; having the maiden surname of the wife simply expands the opportunities to find the county. If you have a general name like Lee/Leigh, remember your American research. What were the names of the ancestor's neighbors? You can use the surnames of your ancestor's neighbors to find possible counties to start searching if you also find the names of your ancestors in the same area. The neighbors of your ancestors likely traveled with them—or at least from the same area—to America.

Let's take the example one step further—what if you don't have a particular location for a surname? Several sources are available that may help in tying a surname to possible locations. Some sources you can use include the following:

Phonebooks and Directories: A phonebook is a good source for locating a name in a certain place. Current directories can confirm if surnames are in the same area, village, parish, or county. Privately published directories are available on CD (such as the Bret-phone directory) or through an online telephone search. These resources can also be found in larger libraries.

International genealogical Index (IGI): The IGI is a great tool you can use simply online. The IGI index of surnames is divided by country and contains millions of names. For example, in the case of British records, much of the available information was extracted from parish records. You can enter the surname and will be able to find specific places where that surname is found. Even though you may not have a direct relationship to the persons listed, you will at least be able to narrow your search to the counties where the surname occurs.

Genealogical Research Directory (GRD): This is an international directory in which genealogical researchers from around the world apply the names of people they want to find. The directory lists names in alphabetical order, along with the names and addresses of the persons who submitted the names. The GRD is an annual publication with a least 150,000 name entries per year. Since 1980, the GRD has published over 2 million name entries. The GRD is a great tool for place finding. If a person back in time is listed in the GRD, the place of the person's residence, birth, marriage, or death is also listed. Even if the name is not your ancestor, the connection of the name to a place, such as a parish or county of England, is of great value. The GRD is published in Australia and has submitters from countries all around the world. Simply do a Google search for "Genealogy Research Directory" for more details.

British Isles Genealogical Register: This is a list of surnames submitted by researchers all over the world who sent in their surnames for inclusion. The register lists the surnames being researched, including the place[s] and time periods. When you locate your ancestor's surname, you can obtain the name and address of the person researching your family. Created in 1994, the Big R lists over 300,000 names submitted over the past twenty years by genealogists with a focus in British ancestry. Many of the names came from earlier publications of the Society of Genealogists.

Boyd's Marriage Index: This index to English marriage records was compiled by Percival Boyd, one of England's most acclaimed genealogists. It contains over seven million name entries taken from parish registers, bishops' transcripts, and marriage licenses. The index does not cover every county of England; however, it is virtually complete for all marriages which occurred between 1538 and 1837 in all parishes within the city of London and counties of Cambridgeshire, Cornwall, Cumberland, Derbyshire, Devonshire, Durham, Essex, Gloucestershire, Lancashire, Middlesex, Norfolk, Northumberland, Shropshire, Somerset, Suffolk, and Yorkshire. The printed, countywide volumes of Boyd's Index are available in the United States at the Family History Library in Salt Lake City, Utah. Microfilm versions are available through your local family history center.

Family Origin Name Survey (FONS): This is a two-part computerized genealogical research database. The first part contains abstracts of all known surviving British record material since 1600, with the exception of Parish baptisms and marriages, 1538–1600 (which should eventually be covered by the International Genealogical Index). The Pre-1600 Record Sources include administrations, ancient deeds, assize rolls, bishops' registers, cartularies, charter rolls, ecclesiastical courts, eyre rolls, feet of fines, fine rolls, heraldic visitations, hundred rolls, inquisitions, lay subsidies, liberate rolls, pipe rolls, poll taxes, proofs of age, star chamber, state papers, treaty rolls, and wills.

The second database, the Non-Register Archives, contains archives of will abstracts, will lists, and other name lists such as poll books, land tax assessments, muster rolls, and so forth for 1600–1838. In both databases, the information consists of abstracts of the original records, along with the name index of any person mentioned in any way. The two databases were compiled from existing computer databases as well as manual indexes that have been computerized and incorporated into the system. The FONS databases originated as the search sources specific to the study of the origins and distribution of surname groups in England from 1086 to 1858. Either database is an outstanding source for locating a surname, perhaps in the obscure record. The research will lead a genealogist to a particular county or parish location in which a surname occurs. This is a private database, and you must become a member of the organization to access it. For more information, contact:

Family Origin Name Survey (FONS)
67 Chancery Lane
London, England, WC2A 1AF.

The best information I was able to secure at the time of this writing was as follows: A registration and life membership applies to each of the databases and costs $10.00 (in US dollars) for one membership, or $20.00 for both. Members can pre-pay for five to one hundred entries for a surname search in either database. There is a fee of $5.00 per entry found in the database. As additional information is added to the databases, the FONS group will search for your surnames on a continuing basis until the pre-paid limit is reached. Additional searches can be added at any time in the future without paying the registration fee again.

Migration Patterns: Revealing Clues to Finding the Origin of Your Immigrant Ancestors

Migration Patterns for Genealogists: Think Like a Historian

One of the most important considerations in finding your ancestor is immigration research.

Look at immigration from a historian's point of view by trying to understand what your ancestors did and why.

As a genealogist, you wonder why your ancestors migrated. You look for clues that might direct you to the birthplace in the country of origin. As genealogists, the first thing we do is start searching through deeds, wills, bible records, and other such documents. Documents can tell that your ancestor sold his property from one person to another, but it does not tell why he moved from Virginia to Tennessee.

When you seek to understand immigration patterns from a historian's perspective, because you begin to understand what your family was thinking, what other individuals were doing, where they were going, and where they came from, your chances for success expand dramatically.

By learning about your ancestor's ethnic group's immigration patterns for the time period they lived, you see trends that correlate to your family, such as the ports they arrived at, the counties and cities from which they came, where they settled, the reasons for decisions that were made, the types of records they left behind, and where to find these records.

Start by answering questions, such as "To what ethnic background or group do you think they belonged? Were they Puritans? Welsh? Germans?

Now begin to answer the following questions:

- Why did they come to America?
- When did they come?
- Where did they settle?
- What were their social and work conditions?
- What was their religious background?

America: People on the Move

When you step back and begin looking at the "big picture"— that your ancestors are part of an ethnic group at a given time and in a specific place—you quickly see that America is a land of people on the move. Our ancestors were part of groups that felt a "push" to move, whether to escape political or religious oppression, wars, violence, or major natural disasters. The reasons include, but are not limited to, the following:

- War or other armed conflict
- Famine or drought

- Disease
- Poverty
- Political corruption
- Disagreement with politics
- Religious intolerance
- Natural disasters
- Discontent with the natives, such as frequent harassment, bullying, or abuse
- Lack of employment opportunities

These factors generally do not affect people in developed countries; even a natural disaster is unlikely to cause out-migration in such places.

When you are pushed, where do you go? You can sense the "pull" that America had on our ancestors. Economic and professional opportunities were by far the leading reason for our ancestors coming to America. The availability of lands for farming, an abundance of jobs, and higher salaries were enticing. Other reasons for migration to America include the following:

- Higher incomes
- Lower taxes
- Better weather
- Better availability of employment
- Better medical facilities
- Better education facilities
- Better behavior among people
- Family reasons
- Political stability
- Religious tolerance
- Relative freedom
- Weather
- National prestige

Perhaps the only major group of immigrants in early American history who did not respond to push or pull factors was the Africans, who were captured and traded into slavery in the Americas against their will.

As I have researched the immigration patterns of my ancestors, I have developed a format that allows me to capture the most important facts and helps me better understand my ethnic heritage. It acts as a guide for my research. The following is an example of the profile I created for Scottish and Scots-Irish ancestors. Note the type of information I gathered and the clues provided.

Scottish and Scots-Irish Immigration

What are some of the important immigration facts?

- The first Scottish immigrants to America were prisoners of war, sent (or transported) to the colonies by English ruler Oliver Cromwell (1599–1658) after he defeated Scotland in 1650.

- After the Battle of Culloden in 1746, the British placed the Act of Proscription upon the Highland Scots, which prohibited them from almost every aspect of practicing their traditions: wearing their tartan kilts, bearing arms, and even playing their traditional bagpipe music. The act completely destroyed the Highlands clan system.

- In the early 1600s, British King James I (1566–1625) decided he wanted a Protestant population in Northern Ireland. From 1608 to 1697, about 200,000 Presbyterian Scots from the Lowlands immigrated to Ulster in Northern Ireland. Later, when these immigrants relocated once again to North America, they would be known as the Scots-Irish.

- In the American Revolution (1775–83), Scots-Irish Americans generally joined the rebel cause while Scottish Americans tended to side with the British crown.

Scottish

When and why did they come?

- The first Scottish immigrants to America were prisoners of war, forcibly sent to the colonies by Cromwell after he defeated Scotland in 1650. They served out their sentences by laboring in the English colonies of North America.

- In 1707, the Act of Union made Scotland, together with England and Wales, part of the United Kingdom, sharing a single parliament. Scots were given the same freedoms as English citizens.

- After the 1707 Union of the Parliaments, trade between Scotland and America increased. Scottish emigration at that time was mostly to Virginia, where tobacco was high in production and was a financially rewarding business.

- In the early eighteenth century, more Scots were transported to America as political prisoners of England in 1715 and 1745. More than fourteen hundred defeated Jacobite rebels (Scots who wanted to return a Stuart monarch to the throne of Britain) were sent to America. They were forced to become indentured servants—people who contracted to work for an agreed-upon period of time with someone in the New World in exchange for payment for their passage.

- Another large group of involuntary immigrants were Scottish soldiers who had been brought to America by the British to fight in the French and Indian War (1754–63). The French and Indian War was a war between France and England over territory in America where Indians fought as allies to the French. At the end of the war, when the soldiers were discharged, the majority of Scottish soldiers elected to remain in America. The British offered them land in western Pennsylvania as an alternative to being shipped home. Of the twelve thousand Scottish soldiers discharged, only seventy-six returned to Scotland.

- Voluntary Scottish immigration to America picked up in the years between the union with England (1707) and the American Revolution (1776–83). Conditions were already difficult for Highland Scottish farmers, with a cold, rainy climate, short growing season, and rocky ground. In the Highlands, one method of earning a living had been armed raiding of the more prosperous Lowlands. In the mid-eighteenth century the British prohibited the Highlanders from bearing arms. Without being able to raid, there was not enough work to support the clans.

- Landlords began to raise the rents for Scotland's tenant farmers

(farmers who rented their land), also seizing grazing grounds and evicting tenants in order to squash Scottish uprisings.

- Wealthy landowners in America advertised for indentured servants. A number of Scots jumped at the opportunity and hired on.
- Others sold their farms and livestock to pay for their own passage.
- Some Highland clan leaders organized mass migrations to the New World. Whole communities would pack up and emigrate.

Are there any clues to family naming patterns?

Many Scots' families follow the custom of naming their children after the grandparents in the following manner.

- First-born son named for the paternal grandfather.
- Second son named for the maternal grandfather.
- Third son named for the father.
- First-born daughter named for the maternal grandmother.
- Second daughter named for the paternal grandmother.
- Third daughter named for the mother.

Notes on Scottish naming patterns:

This practice can cause families to have two children with the same name if the grandparents had the same name. The process also started over if the parent remarried, so it is common to find half brothers or sisters with the same names.

Not all Scottish families followed this pattern, but many that did continued it long after leaving Scotland.

One variation of the pattern above was for the eldest son to be named after the mother's father and the eldest daughter after the father's mother.

JUST IN CASE: IMPORTANT RESEARCH NOTES AND PRACTICES FOR FINDING IMMIGRANT ANCESTORS

I would like to add a few more thoughts that can be valuable in giving you more ideas to assist in your search for immigrant ancestors and in helping to sort out information as it relates to researching women ancestors and naming patterns.

How to Increase Your Success in Finding the Ancestor's Maiden Name

It's not uncommon for immigrant ancestors to marry outside of their culture. In my case I have Great-Great Grandmother Dahle, a Norwegian, marrying into my Welsh Jones line. In these situations the key is being able to locate the maiden name of the female ancestor. In my own research I have found that female maiden names are not included in the records of our male ancestors. For example: Females were not allowed to vote until the twentieth century and seldom owned land. Even in church records, we often find the full name of the husband or father, but then only the first name is listed for the female.

When I am faced with the need to find the maiden name of an ancestor, I will search the following record types:

Marriage records. I find marriage records to be the best place to find a maiden name. Marrige records refers to a group of records that are created at the time of marriage. Types of marriage records include a marriage license, marriage certificate, marriage announcements, marriage banns and bonds. To secure a marriage certificate, you will need to know the:

- Full name of the groom
- First name of the bride
- Approximate date of the marriage
- State or county of where the marriage took place

Church records. Church records usually include recordings of church marriages, baptism or christening. You will need to know the:

- Individual name
- Church where ceremony or ordinance was performed
- Name of clergy that appears on the certificate

Newspapers. The most common articles that yield maiden names are wedding announcements or obituaries. You will need to know the following:

- Approximate date of event
- Name of the groom for the wedding announcement

- Full name of deceased person
- State and city where the event occurred

When I can't find the obituary of a female ancestor, I will look for obituaries of their siblings and other family members, which usually provides clues I can follow in the census and other records.

Land records. I have found a few land records that were transferred from father to daughter. Examine deeds for your ancestor or her husband which include the Latin phrases "et ux." (and wife) and "et al." (and others). Land records may include the names of family members. Make sure you check who was selling land to your ancestors. It was common for these persons to be related to your family. If the parents of a female ancestor are the sellers, you may be able to find her maiden name.

Bible records. If you suspect there was a family bible, but it's no longer in the family's possession, you can sometimes find them through message boards or database searches. Many bibles have been digitized and are searchable on the internet. You will need to know the following information:

- Woman's full married name
- State and county in which she lived

Death records. If your ancestor died within the last century, chances are there is a death certificate. The certificates often list a maiden name. You will need to know the following:

- Woman's full name
- State and county in which she lived
- Approximate date of death

Death certificates can often include inaccurate information. Make sure you review who provided the information and the relationship to assess the potential for accuracy.

Military pension records. If the husband of the ancestor I am researching was in the military, there is a good chance there is a pension record. You will need to know the following:

- Veteran's name
- Branch of service (Army, Navy, Air Force, or Marine Corps)

- State where the veteran enlisted
- War in which the veteran served. (**Note:** If service was after 1916, you must also know entry and release dates, military ID number, Social Security number, whether an officer or enlisted, and date of birth.)

Cemetery records. Tombstones may reveal female's maiden name through

- The inscription: "wife of so and so"
- The inscription: Maiden name as a middle name or initial
- Checking nearby plots for possible family members

Census records. Follow your ancestors through the census. Consider the following:

- Young couples may be found living with the wife's parents
- Elderly parent may have been added to the household
- Brothers, sisters, or other family members may be found living with the ancestors' family
- Clues may also be found in the names of families living nearby

Probate records and wills. If I have an idea of who the parents might be, I will check the probate records and wills for the name of children. To find the maiden name in probate records, you will need to know:

- Woman's full name at time of death
- Approximate date of her death
- County or town in which she lived at the time of her death

In Search of a Name: A Few Helpful Reminders

Finding Clues in Family Naming Patterns

As you search for your ancestor, one of the clues to help identify family is when you see the same names used again and again. Many cultures have long made it a practice to honor their elders by naming their children after them. Just when one suggests that you can find family based on a naming pattern, that's when your family won't follow the pattern. You will, however, see names of parents and grandparents, siblings, aunts and uncles repeated, but not in any strict order. While over half of the names in a family will probably appear to be repeats, there always seems to be a few totally different ones. A child might be named after a good friend or a popular hero of the times.

In Western Europe, there were four ways of acquiring a surname:

1. **Occupation**—Names which are derived from trades and occupations—mostly found in towns. Occupational surnames are self-explanatory: Taylor (tailor) Baxter (baker) and Cooper (barrel maker).

   Some apparently obvious occupational names aren't what they may seem, however. A Farmer did not work in agriculture but collected taxes, and Banker is not an occupational surname at all, meaning "dweller on a hillside."

2. Locality—Surnames representing localities are easy to spot if they come from a specific geographical area or part of land: Marsh, Middleton, Sidney, or Ireland, for example. The evolution of language from other localities are less obvious: Cullen ("back of the river"), and Dunlop ("muddy hill").

3. Nickname—Names which could refer to color or size, (White, Black, Small, Little). Nicknames are perhaps the most fascinating surnames—but not always very flattering to one's ancestor. Gotobed, for example, stemmed from someone who was very lazy, and Kennedy is Gaelic for "ugly head."

   As a general rule of thumb, the following naming patterns were used in the eighteenth and nineteenth century. (Check your individual ethnic group for variations.)
   Male
   • First son: named for his paternal grandfather.
   • Second son: named for his maternal grandfather.
   • Third son: named after father or father's paternal grandfather.

- Fourth son: named after father's oldest brother or mother's paternal grandfather.
- Fifth son: named after mother's eldest brother or father's material grandfather.
- Sixth son: named after father's second oldest brother or for mother's maternal grandfather.

Female

- First daughter: named for maternal grandmother.
- Second daughter: named for her paternal grandmother.
- Third daughter: named after mother or for mother's maternal grandmother.
- Fourth daughter: named after mother's oldest sister or for father's paternal grandmother.
- Fifth daughter: named after father's eldest sister or for mother's paternal grandmother.
- Sixth daughter: named after mother's second oldest sister or for father's paternal grandmother.

Notes:

With people being what they are, there were all sorts of variations, some covered by rules and some by family decision.

It was customary to name the next daughter or son born within a second marriage for the deceased husband or wife.

If a father died before his child was born, the child was often named for him. If a mother died in childbirth, that child, if a girl, was usually named for the mother.

Another child was commonly named for a child who had died within the family.

Searching for the origins of immigrant ancestors is among the most challenging yet rewarding research I have conducted as a genealogist. It requires an eye for detail and the ability to see your ancestors in the times and seasons in which they lived. As you gain the skills to conduct this research, you will be able manage with confidence your ancestral research.

Lesson 14: The Oral Interview Is the Most Valued Research

Of all the various opportunities I have had in genealogy to research my ancestral lines, the most important and productive research was the oral interviews I began to conduct shortly after the death of my mother and in the ensuing six years.

Often when we talk about the oral interview in genealogy, we closely associate the topic with writing individual and family histories. In this chapter, I will present the oral interview and oral history as one topic under the umbrella of oral history. The difference between a mediocre and a great history is planning, researching, and carefully stitching the memories and artifacts into a cohesive blend of resources to tell the story that will inspire generations to come.

Mary Jones: The First Ten Interviews

During my mother's funeral and memorial services, I had many people tell me about their experiences with Mary as a youth, as an adult, and at work; they told me about her service and offered their thoughts about her children. I longed to know more about my mother. Whenever I asked Mom about her life, she simply replied that it was hard and nothing more needed to be said. Within the first several months of Mom's death, I began conducting oral interviews.

The first ten interviews were more than people simply answering my questions. They were individuals who had respect, love, and insight into Mary Jones as a mother, friend, and sister. I was discovering the Mary Jones I was never privileged to fully know. I loved my mother before, but I loved her even more following the interviews. This group of ten people held the keys to every stage of my mother's life. They answered my questions honestly, directly, and without any reservation. As a result of the interviews, I learned about the following aspects of my mother's life:

- Cherished experiences they shared with Mary.
- Traits they admired about Mary.
- Innermost thoughts Mary shared with them about her life and family.
- Her dreams that were dashed by choices in marriage.
- Dark, troublesome times of pain and sorrow that were triumphantly overcome.
- My heritage and roles of progenitors in preparing a path for me.
- Family rifts that were three generations deep.
- Identification of photos and other artifacts.
- Individuals and families from my heritage whom I should learn more about.
- "Skeletons" that were long since buried.
- Precious artifacts (photos, cards, letters, scrapbooks, journals) that were given to me to keep or to scan.
- Artifacts that existed and where I could find them.

Interview your immediate family members. Take time to interview and compare your memories with those of your siblings, parents, cousins, grandparents, and others. Genealogy is not just names and dates; it is about people, who they were, and the stories of their lives. What is keeping you from talking to your family? Get over it. Don't wait until after a relative passes on to find information. Someone in the family has excellent information on the line, and you have to find them. Rest assured that your family will provide answers to your questions and insights that will be invaluable to writing your history and searching for your roots. In this chapter, I want to share with you the important lessons I have learned when interviewing immediate family members:

Interviews provide opportunities to locate family records. Interviews also provide opportunities to locate, identify, catalog, and preserve items that are important to the family and why they are important. Items can include heirlooms (such as furniture, small collectibles, and photographs), manuscript materials (diaries, letters, and family bibles), and copies of public records (certificates of birth, marriage, death, land, patents, and wills.)

Of the more than 60,000 artifacts I have gathered relating to my ancestral lines, 75 percent have come as a result of conducting interviews with family. Once I was made aware of available information, I was permitted to scan or photograph the artifacts. In several instances, I was given the life-long research of the person I was interviewing.

EVERY LIFE IS A STORY

As we live our lives, we become a very special, one-of-a-kind, cherished set of memories. Stories about the family's past may include immigration or emigration, old neighborhoods, military service, marriages, births, deaths, famous or infamous family members, culture, religion, political endeavors, education, and social and economic status.

Without an autobiography or a personal or family history, these memories become nothing more than a footprint in the sand, a name on a headstone, and a precious opportunity lost. This chapter is about what we can "tell the children."

Family histories provide valuable insight into the lives of our ancestors. They tell us information about their daily lives, such as the following:

- the who, what, and (most important) why—the motives and attitudes of the participants, their actions and reactions to the world around them.
- memories of other times, places, and events, such as

the Great Depression, world wars, and the Civil Rights movement.

- patterns of living—how the household was organized, how the family money was spent, who sat where at the dining table, and what types of meals were served.

- information from traditional sources such as the family bible, school diplomas, letters, photo albums, and scrapbooks which provide preliminary research for the interview.

- stories of feuds or other stressful incidents that may be painful to revisit, but that are vital for understanding family dynamics and ongoing or ended relationships. Family members experience the same events, yet react and remember them quite differently from each other, depending on their age, attitude, placement in the family, and expectations overall.

FIVE QUESTIONS WE ALL ASK ABOUT WRITING FAMILY HISTORIES

1. What is a personal history?

Personal histories are a documented, detailed record of a person's life—the thoughts, feelings, events, people, and places of an individual's past. Histories are usually arranged chronologically and have a blend of one or more of the following elements:

Topical. Focus on a particular historical event, such as World War II; a special family event, such as a wedding; or a place associated with the family over the years, such as a farm or neighborhood.

Autobiographical. One person's life history, usually starting from infancy and progressing chronologically through their life.

Genealogical. A record of a person's ancestors and lineage.

Skills or occupations. Descriptions and demonstrations of how things were done in the past.

Social history. Includes ethnic culture, religious practices, gender roles, everyday life, and so forth.

Folklore. Includes favorite stories, songs, and poems; local legends; and games and other pastimes.

2. Why should I write a personal history?

The most important reason to write a personal history is because "I want to." Then couple that desire with other reasons, such as the following:

- To provide a gift to your posterity to do any or all of the following:
  - Ensure that you or the one you write about is not forgotten
  - Share personal stories
  - Share incidents of one's life that teach a lesson
  - Tell of your triumphs over adversity
  - Provide inspiration to others facing a challenge
- To discover who you are, search for your own identity, and understand the forces that have shaped you.
- To have a story to go with those old photos.

Every life is important and unique. It's about the people known, the places visited, the decisions made, the opportunities lost or gained, and the spiritual, physical, and mental exuberance and folly. If for no other reason, your life is important to you, and that is reason enough to write a personal history.

Do not underestimate your value and how incredibly important your history will be to your loved ones. How many times have you said, "I wish that my grandparents had written a personal history"? We have many questions about those who have gone before us. The history (or histories) you write will be among the most prized possessions you give to others.

3. What can I write about?

Don't worry too much about what to write. With a gentle nudge—the right question, a photo, stories, lessons learned—you will find the memories, and ideas will be begin to flow. This chapter will provide many helpful tools to aid in your rediscovery of a life story. In most cases, you will organize your thoughts chronologically through life's stages. One thought leads to the next. Tip: Once you start to write the personal history, keep a pocket notebook or recorder with you to capture the thoughts or memories that will come to you at any moment.

4. How and where do I begin?

Why not start today? You don't have to be an accomplished writer. The end goal is to produce a story written in your own words reflecting your own thoughts and feelings. The writing happens one memory, one lesson, and one line at a time. Find a quiet, comfortable place to sit. Define a specific time each day, week, or month when you won't be disturbed. Think about your life, your memories, and find the one experience you most want to write about. Start there.

Like any project, there is a beginning and an end. The focus of this chapter is to outline the phases of writing a personal history and to provide detailed resources for preparing a personal history. The process includes three phases:

Phase I: Setup and Organization
Phase II: Gathering, Interviewing, and Research
Phase III: Writing and Publishing

There are many paths, options, and approaches to writing and organizing a personal history. This is an important step and decision. The following are several options that are available. Any of these options will work well; the decision comes down to what you want to accomplish with your personal history.

How-to Books and Articles. How-to books are a great way to get started. You can find these books and articles online with a simple search. The following is a list of some of the details included in how-to books and articles:

Organization and helpful hints that will guide you through the process of writing a personal history.

- How to organize your project

- How to conduct an interview, including what questions to ask
- How to write and publish your completed work

Fill-in-the-blank book. This is a common method used by individuals writing autobiographies. It is probably the easiest method, since it provides you a list of questions to answer that cover the basic chronology of your life. The disadvantages to this approach include the following:

- Rarely will your life fit neatly into a bound book.
- Usually not much space to talk about your life.
- Lots of irrelevant questions.
- Limited to writing longhand.

Fill-in-the-blank binder. A common approach that combines the ease of a bound fill-in-the-blank method with the flexibility of a three ring binder. With a fill-in-in-the-blank binder, you are able to do the following:

- Freely write the wide variety of life stories you have accumulated.
- Include photo and zipper pockets for heirlooms and other memorabilia.
- Choose to handwrite onto a prepared page or type onto a computer and print the completed document, or a combination of the two.

Professional Personal Historians. You can choose to work with a professional personal historian who can help to coordinate the process. With the help of a professional personal historian, you will complete your personal history project faster than by any other method. Professional historians bring a unique perspective to the process and can be helpful in organizing and packaging a final product, whether that means you end up with a written, oral, or video presentation, or a combination of the three. There are a wide variety of organizational styles depending on the professional.

It is not always easy to find a professional personal historian in all areas, but one excellent source of information is the Association of Personal Historians. Remember that you are hiring a professional; you are paying for someone else to help complete the task. Sticker shock should not be an issue. You can have them complete the entire project or work with you on different aspects. References are always expected. And make sure you interview several historians before you make your final choice.

Oral and Video Personal Histories. Oral and video systems are somewhat more complex than writing or typing a personal history or hiring a professional. You will need to purchase, hire, or otherwise use audio or video equipment. Most often, you need to involve another person to help you though the process. Consider contracting the services of a professional personal historian to help coordinate the process, since do-it-yourself audio and video programs usually turn out to be "easier said than done."

A benefit of making an oral or video personal history is that you gain both audio and video, so people are able to hear and watch your personal history. However, expect cost or complexity of duplicating this type of personal history to limit the number of people who will be able to view your personal history. Consider transcribing and copying the content of the recording for wider distribution to your family and friends.

Online Systems. Online web templates are very popular at the moment. Normally you pay an annual membership fee or a one-time fee to gain access to an online template containing fill-in-the-blank type questions. Membership provides you a password to log into the online template whenever you please and fill in your answers from your own computer. You can type in as little or as much information as you want.

It's convenient to log in anytime and from wherever you are. The real drawback is data safety. Most online autobiography template providers cannot guarantee your data is safe, secure, and kept completely private.

How long will it take?

It could take a few days, months, or years to compile your personal history. It really depends on what you want to accomplish.

The sooner you start, the sooner you will finish. One of the most important lessons learned by those before you is to start with a general chronically of the life you are writing about. Then set up achievable goals (such as one memory a day or two pages a week) so that you will keep moving forward and not lose interest. Many of your goals will come once you have had a chance to ponder, organize, and scope the project. For example, if your goal is to write a 250-page autobiography, you could complete the project in four months by writing two pages a day or in two months by writing four pages a day. If your goal is to interview five siblings of your mom, do one interview per week for five weeks.

Enjoy the experience. At times you will be like Sherlock Holmes, searching for the answers to expand upon a topic, uncovering answers to questions you have asked for years, and experiencing a full scope of human emotions.

Phase I: Setup and Organization

Define the Life Stages. The hardest part of creating a personal history is deciding where to start. I suggest you begin by simply breaking down the person's life or experience into an outline consisting of key blocks of time. As you discover, uncover, and learn more about your subject, you will fill in the outline and organize your thoughts so that writing the history will be a choice and enriching experience for you.

I created the following outline for my mother, Mary Jones:

Mary Jones Personal History	
Life Stage	*Years*
Childhood (0-11)	1933-1944
Adolescence (11-18)	1945-1951
Early Adult (18-25)	1951-1958
Prime Adult (25-45)	1958-1978
Middle Adult (45-65)	1978-1998
Senior Adult (65+)	1998

Prepare a Filing System to Organize and Preserve Research and Artifacts. Throughout your research, you will collect and gather information that needs to be organized, documented, and preserved for later retrieval. You should be able to find any piece of information or artifact in your file in thirty seconds or less.

Create a Personal History Profile Storage Container: "The Box." The purpose of the container is to provide one central location where you will file and protect your research and artifacts to write the history. For a list of materials needed for organizing a paper file, see Lesson Two: Start Organized, Stay Organized.

Organizing Folders and Files. Once materials have been assembled, you are ready to set up the file. Choose one color to represent each life stage. I organized "Mary's Box" as follows:

- Insert five hanging files, one of each chosen color for each life stage
- Create and label one folder for each life stage
- Use two-inch expanding file jackets
- Print and color code labels
- Add folders as needed or desired

Note: As I interviewed and researched Mary's life, I added additional files.

Mary's Box—Initial Set-up				
Life Stage Category	*Color Code*	*File*	*Timing*	*File Folder Label*
Index and Misc.	White	1A	Set-up	Jones, Mary Index
		1B	Added	Jones, Mary Miscellaneous: Spanish Fork
		1C	Added	Jones, Mary Miscellaneous: Las Vegas/ Horseshoe Club
		1D	Added	Jones, Mary Miscellaneous: Acts of Kindness and Service
		1E	Added	Jones, Mary Miscellaneous: Favorite Memories

Life Stage Category	Color Code	File	Timing	File Folder Label
(Index and Misc., cont.)	(White)	1F	Added	Jones, Mary Miscellaneous: Oral Interviews and Transcripts of Friends
		1G	Added	Jones, Mary Miscellaneous: Oral Interviews and Transcripts of Family
		1H	Added	Jones, Mary Miscellaneous: Personal Artifacts
Childhood (0-11)	Red	2A	Set-up	Jones, Mary (1933-1944) Childhood: Infancy, Grade School
		2B	Added	Jones, Mary (1933-1944) Childhood: Family
		2C	Added	Jones, Mary (1933-1944) Childhood: (Cared for by extended family)
		2D	Added	Jones, Mary (1933-1944) Childhood: Family
Adolescence (11-18)	Blue	3A	Set-up	Jones, Mary (1945-1951) Adolescence: Jr. High, High School
		3B	Added	Jones, Mary (1945-1951) Adolescence: Family
Early Adult (18-25)	Yellow	4A	Set-up	Jones, Mary (1951-1958) Early Adult: Marriage
		4B	Added	Jones, Mary (1951-1958) Early Adult: Children
Prime Adult (25-45)	Green	5A	Set-up	Jones, Mary (1958-1978) Prime Adult: Marriage
		5B	Added	Jones, Mary (1958-1978) Prime Adult: 2nd Marriage
		5C	Added	Jones, Mary (1958-1978) Prime Adult: Children

Life Stage Category	Color Code	File	Timing	File Folder Label
		5D	Added	Jones, Mary (1958-1978) Prime Adult: Cards and Letters
		5E	Added	Jones, Mary (1958-1978) Prime Adult: Sisters
Middle Adult (45-65)	Purple	6A	Set-up	Jones, Mary (1978-1998) Middle Adult: 2nd Marriage
		6B	Set-up	Jones, Mary (1978-1998) Middle Adult: 3rd Marriage
		6C	Added	Jones, Mary (1978-1998) Middle Adult: Cards and Letters
		6D	Added	Jones, Mary (1978-1998) Middle Adult: Sisters
		6E	Added	Jones, Mary (1978-1998) Middle Adult: Travel and Pleasure
		6F	Added	Jones, Mary (1978-1998) Middle Adult: Cancer
		6G	Added	Jones, Mary (1978-1998) Middle Adult: Best Friend
Senior Adult (65+)	Orange	7A	Set-up	Jones, Mary (0August 1998) Later Adult: Funeral
		7B	Added	Jones, Mary (1998) Later Adult: Probate/Will

Phase II: Gather, Interview, and Research

Gather, Catalog, Clues, and Questions. Once you have the file set up, gather together what you currently have associated with the person.

Assume you know nothing. You are the detective seeking to understand what you have and what your next steps will be. You are simply gathering information. This is not a time to edit and decide what is or is not important. It is the first round; as you move beyond this stage and begin to interview others, you will uncover new artifacts, other individuals to interview, and places to visit. Start by doing the following:

Gather artifacts you have in your possession that belonged to or reference the individual. (These could be photos, letters, receipts, journals, and so forth.)

Develop a spreadsheet to catalog each artifact and identify persons of interest. The spreadsheets will become more and more important as you conduct your research, because it tells where you've been and where you're going and supplies the details for providing necessary citing and documentation when writing your history.

Review and catalog each artifact. Look for any clues and write them down. You can decide later whether to do further research. Conduct a "Good Glance." Look at the artifacts close enough to know what you have. The following list is an example of what to look for in various types of artifacts:

- Photos: Inscriptions, people, signs, and dates
- Unpublished (cards, letters, and journals): To and from names, topics, and dates
- Memorabilia (brochures, tickets): Places, events, dates, and notes
- Newspaper Clippings: Names, associations, and dates

Write down any questions or thoughts that come into your mind as you review the material. You can organize later.

File the artifacts in the appropriate folder.

Make a list of family, friends, and acquaintances who you think knew the person. List the person's name, address, telephone, and relationship to your person of interest. The list will come both from your personal knowledge and from clues you gain from reviewing the artifacts.

Gathering Information and Materials. Start finding pertinent information and material to support your writing of the personal history by looking for and evaluating the following:

Diaries: A regularly kept diary is the most valuable source of personal history.

Letters and emails: Letters go two ways—to and from. Letters to you provide important information because the writer often responds to things you told them. As you interview family, friends, and acquaintances, ask to see if any correspondence has been kept that was sent to them from your person of interest.

Documents and artifacts: Papers and objects that are important in our lives ought to be saved, such as birth certificates, marriage licenses or certificates, missionary certificates, awards, diplomas, drawings, paintings, poems, and talks. More bulky but still important are artifacts like sewn items, carvings, jewelry, and other handicrafts. Official government records are valuable, as are church records.

Photographs: Beyond simply showing the faces of ancestors, pictures ought to capture typical work and play situations. Labeling dates and names on our photographs is a must. The same goes for our digital files too.

Tape and video recordings: Recording voices of children year by year is a great way to chronicle their lives. Dictated life stories preserve not only the story but the voice of the storyteller.

Recollections of others: Written or tape-recorded, other people's memories of your subject can provide a wealth of insight. People to contact for the person of interest can include parents, children, brothers and sisters, teachers or students, employers, employees, neighbors, close personal friends, local church leaders, visiting teaching partners, doctors, and former classmates or roommates.

Life sketches and autobiographies: I have come across a number of life sketches and autobiographies about my ancestors that range from a few pages to ten pages. I find them to be very shallow, missing feelings and experiences. Full chapters could be written on their stages of life and topics such as parenting, work experiences, religious work, family roots and background, influential people, life philosophy, and humorous episodes. These small life sketches provide a great starting point for further research and interviews to get a fuller, more complete picture of the person's life.

Your memories: Use photos, documents, and so forth to jar the memories of those you will be interviewing. If you are researching your own history, look through the family photo album with a tape recorder in hand and record the thoughts and stories as you think about who is in that fuzzy picture and why they're important. What do you remember about the place and time? Jar your memory with other things: visit your old school, listen to old records or tapes, see movies that were filmed about the years you grew up, or brainstorm with siblings or old friends.

Gathering and Cataloging Example:
Mary Jones's Sack of Odds and Ends

After Mom's passing, I received some of her personal affects. I remember finding photos, articles, brochures from a trip, past checks and receipts, and so forth in the bottoms of drawers, tops of closets, and every place imaginable. I put those items in a sack, brought them home, and forgot about them.

When I was ready to start my research, I rediscovered the sack I had put away and spread the contents out on the kitchen table. I made two spreadsheets to help me sort through the material. The spreadsheets helped me organize the early phases of my research. I was able to begin building a mental picture of activities and experiences by time periods, identify people who might have insights and artifacts relating to my mother's life, identify topics and questions I wanted to discuss with different individuals, identify gaps for which I did not have information, and identify areas where I could conduct background research to help tell the story.

Once I finished going through the sack, I reviewed other artifacts I had gathered, such as our family photo album, items in shoe boxes, and so on. The following are examples of the spreadsheet I set up. **Note:** When I develop the spreadsheets, I like to pose questions as column headings.

Mary's Artifacts List—Sample			
What do you have?	*Describe what you have.*	*What clues or questions do you have? (Inscriptions, people in picture, and so on)*	*Are any further actions needed?*
Photo	Mom and Dad's wedding photo.	On back of picture, list of persons in picture (Name 1, Name 2, Name 3, Name 4, Name 5, Name 6, Name 7)	Find name and address of persons in photos. Set up time to interview.
Photo	Wanda and Mom standing next to life preserver with name of ship.	Mom is on cruise.	Ask Wanda about photo and trip.
Photo	Unknown boy with dog in early 1900s.	Who is this? Family?	Show and ask Mom's sisters if they know about the photo.
Birthday Card	Birthday card given to Mom by (name).	Relationship? Shared thoughts?	Follow up with person to learn more of the relationship between person and mom.
News article	Obituary of Mom's dad (name)	Lists surviving family, residence of children and brothers and sisters.	Find name and address of Grandpa's brothers or sisters or surviving spouses. Set time to interview.
US Passport	Mom's passport from 0000-0000	Where Mom traveled and dates.	Look for brochures, tickets, photos of trip. Ask friends who went with Mom and if they have photos.

Mary's Family, Friends, and Acquaintances List			
Who is the person?	*What is their relationship?*	*Address and telephone*	*Notes for follow-up*
Name	Friend	Las Vegas	Ask (name) about photo and trip.
Name	Sister	Spanish Fork	Show old photos and see if they can help identify. Ask about other family artifacts.
Name	Sister	Las Vegas	Show old photos and see if they can help identify. Ask about other family artifacts.
Name	Sister	Springville	Show old photos and see if they can help identify. Ask about other family artifacts.

WHAT ARE ORAL INTERVIEWS?

The real record of history is found in the lives of ordinary people who lived it.

Before you start conducting an interview, it's important to understand the advantages and disadvantages of an oral interview. Oral history is the collection and recording of personal memoirs as historical documentation. It emphasizes the significance of human experience.

Oral history interviews are *not* the best method for obtaining factual data—such as specific dates, places, or times—because people rarely remember such detail accurately. You will need to use more traditional historical research methods—courthouse records, club minutes, newspaper accounts, and so forth—to help fill in these gaps.

Oral history interviews *are* the best method to use to get an idea of what happened, what those times meant to people, and how it felt to be a part of that time. Oral interviews are great for capturing eye-witness accounts and reminiscences about events and experiences which occurred during the lifetime of the person being interviewed and for gathering narratives passed down verbally from generation to generation beyond the lifetime of any one individual. This includes stories, songs, sayings, memorized speeches, and traditional accounts of past events.

Oral histories provide an added dimension to historical research. An oral history project can aid your research in the following ways:

- Foster appreciation for little-known or rapidly vanishing ways of life.
- Verify the historical nature of events that cannot be determined by traditional methods of historical research.
- Correct stereotypical images of life, ways, and people.
- Recover and preserve important aspects of a human experience that would otherwise go undocumented.

Types of Oral History Interviews

There are four basic types of oral history interviews, which are outlined below.

Life histories. These are interviews with individuals about their backgrounds from childhood to adulthood. Most follow a chronology. Life histories provide an opportunity to discuss a variety of subjects based on the interviewer's interests and the interviewee's remembered experiences and perspectives. They are ideal for family research, as well as for certain aspects of community and social histories.

Topical histories. These interviews are often used for focused studies of particular events, eras, or organizations. Examples include an interview about the Depression Era in Utah County or about the Thistle mudslide in Spanish Fork Canyon in 1983. An oral study about World War II in a specific locale, for example, might include interviews about military involvement, civil defense preparedness, the home front, rationing, bond and scrap metal drives, war industries, and myriad related topics.

Thematic histories. These studies focus on broad patterns and concepts. These themes could include topics such as love, conflict, hope, religion, education, competition, success, or art. Thematic oral histories are not common, but they present opportunities worth considering.

Histories to document specific artifacts or sites. Oral history may be used, for example, to explain items within a museum collection— how to churn butter, how to operate a Farmall F-12 tractor, how to use a Victrola, how to dress for travel in the 1940s. Another method is to have a subject orally document the history of an individual home, a particular street, an old schoolhouse, a vacant field or an overgrown cotton patch.

Oral History Legal Issues

Copyright issues may become a factor, even if you're just conducting an informal interview with immediate family. Legally, both the interviewer and interviewee share the copyright to an oral history interview (an exception occurs when an interviewer is conducting the interview as a work for hire). While copyright may never come into question, you should still protect yourself from potential copyright infringement by having both the interviewer and the interviewee sign release forms at the time of the recording.

Sample Oral History Interview Agreement

Below is a sample of an oral history interview agreement, which is available for download on my website.

This interview Agreement is made and entered into this _____ day of _____, by and between _____ hereinafter called "Interviewer" and _____, hereinafter called "Interviewee."

Interviewee agrees to participate in a tape-recorded interview, commencing on or about _____, with Interviewer in association with his or her research on

_____

_____.

This Agreement relates to any and all materials originating from the interviews, namely the tape recordings of the interviews and any written materials, including but not limited to transcripts or other finding aids prepared from the tapes.

In consideration of the mutual covenants, conditions, and terms set forth below, the parties hereby agree as follows:

Interviewee irrevocably assigns to Interviewer all his or her copyright, title, and interest in this work.

By virtue of this assignment, Interviewer will have the right to use the interview for research, educational, and other purposes, including print and electronic reproduction.

Interviewee acknowledges that he or she will receive no remuneration or compensation for either his or her participation in the interview or for the rights assigned hereunder.

Interviewee understands and agrees that Interviewer may donate any and all materials to _____ upon completion of his or her research.

Interviewer agrees to honor any and all reasonable interviewee restrictions on the use of the Interview, if any, for the time specified below, as follows:

Interviewer and Interviewee have executed this Agreement on the date first written above.

INTERVIEWEE   INTERVIEWER

_____   _____
(Signature)   (Signature)

_____   _____
(Typed or Printed Name)   (Typed or Printed Name)

_____   _____

_____   _____
(Address)   (Address)

Date_____   Date_____

Do Background Research

It is natural to want to rush out and start the interview process, but no project should begin without some basic investigation of available resources. I found that by gathering and organizing material, I was able to gain a very good insight into which direction I should go and what questions I needed to ask. As you prepare, you may need to review other artifacts, such as old newspapers, county histories, archival records, cemeteries, and photographs.

Involve Family and Friends

Involving your family and friends in the process of creating your personal history will not only make the process easier (and the end result more interesting), but it will also help ensure that you have an audience of interested readers who are connected to the completed work. Start the process of involving family and friends by sending them a letter signed by the subject of the project, if available. These letters are most effective if, at a minimum, they accomplish the following:

- Introduce the project and explain the desired time frame for completion.
- Ask the recipients to collect photos, stories, and memorabilia that might be appropriate for use in the book.
- Offer to pay for any copies and other costs they incur in assisting you.
- Ask family members to contribute their favorite stories concerning the subject.
- Describe the word processing software being used so that the material submitted (either by disk or in an email attachment) is in the correct format.
- Include a self-addressed, padded envelope, and a dollar or two "advance reimbursement" for the out-of-pocket costs they will incur in assisting you.

WHO TO INTERVIEW: ORGANIZE A FAMILY, FRIENDS, AND ACQUAINTANCES LIST

A list of family, friends, and acquaintances is a good way to brainstorm people to interview. I began by organizing Mary's list of family, friends, and acquaintances into the following three groups:

- **Group One:** Family and friends she spoke with often during the last five years of her life.
- **Group Two:** Family, friends, and acquaintances that appeared (in artifacts) at key moments in her life (for example, bridesmaids at her wedding).
- **Group Three:** Family, friends, and acquaintances that were in everyday activities with her, such as a friend's birthday or a group picture in the cafeteria.

I began with Group One, which consisted of ten people. I prepared for the interviews by developing a few general, broad questions that would help uncover information about each of the periods of my mother's life and by calling each person to set up the interview.

ORAL INTERVIEW CONSIDERATIONS

Do I conduct a telephone or a personal oral interview? When you have an option, choose to interview the person in their own home. It is by far the best option, as the interviewee will be much more relaxed. A one-on-one interview is best. Privacy encourages an atmosphere of trust and honesty. A third person present, even a close partner, can inhibit and influence free discussion.

Audio versus video taping. Should you audiotape or videotape an interview? The choice may not be yours—sometimes a person who is comfortable sitting and talking into a tape recorder will cringe at the thought of being videotaped (if you're uncertain, ask the interviewee). Regardless of whether audio or video is more convenient for you, you'll get the most from an interviewee who is comfortable with the environment.

Choosing recording equipment. Because you can't write

down everything that someone tells you, it is a good idea to use an audio or video recorder. Your recordings will be unique historical documents that other people need to be able to hear and understand easily, so it's worth getting a good-quality recording.

Audio recorders (digital versus analog). There are many different makes of portable audio recorders. Digital recordings are not necessarily better than analog recordings. A good quality tape recording is better than a second-rate digital one. With both kinds of equipment, you will need to be aware of the following important considerations:

Digital recording equipment.

If you are unsure of the capacity of your digital recorder in this regard, check your equipment manual or ask a technician. Minimum recording requirements for all digital media, including computers are as follows:

- 44.1 kHz—minimum sampling rate
- 16 bit—minimum bit depth

Not all digital recorders are suitable for interviewing. Avoid those that use proprietary software—for example "personal recorders" that create files that can only be used with the manufacturer's software. You are dependent on such software for listening to the sound and copying it. The typical price range for digital recorders is from $150 to $500.

Working with digital files. Keep the raw material from a digital interview recording for archiving exactly as you have recorded it. Make a copy of the file to use for any editing that needs to be done. In order for material to be preserved for the future, you need to use standard formats that computer systems recognize. Save the original as a .wav file or an AIFF, not as an MP3. WAV (or WAVE), short for Waveform audio format, is a Microsoft and IBM audio file format standard for storing audio on PCs. AIFF, short for Audio Interchange File Format, is a standard audio file format used on Amiga and Macintosh computers. Both WAVs and AIFFs are compatible with Windows and Macintosh operating systems. WAV and AIFF file formats take up considerably more space than MP3.

Tape (analog) recording.

If you buy equipment, the size of your budget will determine the quality of the equipment you are able to get. Ideally, a professional-quality tape recorder with an external microphone and high-quality cassettes should be used. The price range is typically from $50 to $150 for a mini-cassette or cassette recorder. If you have a suitable tape recorder that has not been used for a while, take it to a technician for a maintenance check.

Features to look for in a tape recorder include the following:

- Controls which allow you to play the tape (PLAY), wind back the tape (REWIND), wind the tape forward quickly (FAST FORWARD), RECORD, STOP and EJECT
- A tape counter, which allows you to find your place within the tape by denoting a numerical location
- A jack socket for an external microphone
- A recording-level volume control which allows you to adjust the volume at which you record
- A recording-level meter
- The option of using either a wall socket or battery power
- A jack socket for headphones
- A built-in speaker

Cleaning your tape recorder—Isopropyl alcohol, which is 91 percent pure, applied with Q-Tips, will eliminate debris from all recorder parts that come in contact with the magnetic tape. Standard "rubbing alcohol," which may contain some undesirable lubricants, should not be used, because the ingredients may damage the rubber pinch-roller if applied regularly.

Microphones. Whatever recorder you decide to use, it is important to use an external microphone. If you are buying microphones, go for the best quality you can afford. An external microphone is preferred over one built into the recorder. A built-in microphone will record all sounds indiscriminately, including the noise made by the recorder itself. It is difficult to position a tape recorder with an inbuilt microphone so that all voices are recorded clearly.

If you are buying only one microphone, you will need one with a stand, not one that has to be held. Hand-held microphones record any sound of the mic itself moving. Free-standing or table-top microphones are generally quite unobtrusive and record both the interviewee and interviewer clearly if they are placed carefully. However, they often pick up an undesirable level of background noise.

Microphones pick up a range of noise in four patterns. The different types are as follows:

- Unidirectional or cardioid, which picks up sound in a heart-shaped pattern in one direction. They generally record sound around them but not directly behind them. These are the best type to use.
- Omi-directional, which pick up sound coming from all directions.
- Bi-directional, which pick up sound from two opposite directions.
- Hyper-directional, which pick up sound from one direction only and have a very narrow field.

For indoor recording: For one-on-one interviews indoors, the best microphone is a small tie clip or lapel microphone. Lapel microphones tend not to record as much background noise as free-standing ones because the body of the wearer helps to absorb unwanted noise. Their only disadvantage is that most recorders do not have an input for more than one microphone, so while the interviewee is recorded clearly, the interviewer sounds very distant. There are two solutions to this problem: buy a recorder with two microphone input jacks, or buy a "split cord" which allows you to plug two microphones into one cord and then into the recorder. If your recorder is stereo and has two microphone sockets, you can get two microphones—one for your interviewee and one for yourself. They can be attached discreetly to your clothing and give excellent results.

For Outdoor Recording: For interviews done outdoors, a unidirectional (or cardioid) hand-held microphone is best, as it will pick up less unwanted noise. The ideal for interviews is to use two lapel microphones that clip onto the clothing of the interviewer and the interviewee. Electric condenser or dynamic microphones are particularly good. Talk to someone at your local electronics shop (such as Radio Shack) or contact a manufacturer to find out what model would be best for your requirements. Tell them you will be recording voices, not music.

Video. Many interviewers (including me) prefer audio over video recordings for its ease of use, portability, and intimacy; but video equipment has fallen in price and size in recent years and formats such as digital video are becoming affordable options. Video has its benefits—for example, apart from the interview itself, photographs can also be filmed for later use—but video done badly is perhaps best not done at all. Oral historians have mixed views about the impact of a video camera on the intimacy of the interview relationship.

Cassettes

The following are some tips to keep in mind when considering cassette tapes for recording your interviews:

- Use 60-minute cassettes for recording your interviews. They are physically thicker than the longer-playing ones, and so are less likely to stretch (and thus distort the sound) or break. Do not use 90-minute tapes or larger. Longer tapes are too thin and tend to bleed, stretch, or tear.
- Buy normal tapes, not metal or high-bias ones. The latter are designed for recording music and are too expensive for this purpose.
- It is a good idea to use cassettes that are put together with tiny screws in each corner instead of glue, because if the tape jams or breaks, the case can be opened, the tape repaired, and the case put back together again. If you are using tapes without screws, you have to destroy the case to get to the tape if it jams or breaks.
- Use only name-brands of cassettes, such as Sony and TDK.

Other equipment

Batteries are expensive, so use a wall adaptor, allowing you to plug your tape recorder into an outlet. If you have to use batteries for your recorder, you will need a battery tester to ensure they are fully charged. If they are not fully charged when you are recording, the tape will wind through the machine slowly. When you play the tape back at normal speed the voices will be distorted. Battery testers can be bought cheaply from electronic stores.

For tape recorders, you will need some cotton swabs and isopropyl alcohol, readily and cheaply available from a pharmacy, for cleaning the heads (the bit the tape runs over in order to record). This method is more efficient and cheap than using commercial head-cleaning cassettes.

A padded bag, such as a camera bag, is useful for carrying your equipment and protecting it from damage.

Preparing for the Telephone Interview

Because I lived a great distance from most of these contacts, I conducted most of the interviews via telephone. Each conversation was taped. Over the years that I have conducted interviews, I have found that taping the interview leaves me free to focus on the discussion. The only notes I took were thoughts that came during the discussion about further questions to ask or expand upon. I used the following equipment for the interview:

- Micro-cassette player with fresh batteries.
- Three fresh 60-minute cassette tapes.
- Radio Shack recording device that connected the phone to the recorder.
- Backup micro-cassette player in case the player failed or the tape became entangled while recording.
- List of questions for interview.
- Note pad to record thoughts, requests, and promises.
- Envelope to enclose tape immediately following interview.

Prior to each interview, I made sure the tape recorder worked and lines were clear. If you haven't used a tape recorder for interviews before, it is imperative that you practice recording and asking questions so you know your equipment and questions. That way, if you have any problems, you will have time to research and make corrections.

Recording an Interview via Telephone. The FCC protects the privacy of telephone conversations by requiring notification before a recording device is used to record interstate (between different states) or international phone calls. Interstate or international telephone conversations may not be recorded unless the use of the recording device meets the following requirements:

- Preceded by verbal or written consent of all parties to the telephone conversation; or
- Preceded by verbal notification that is recorded at the beginning, and as part of the call, by the recording party; or
- Accompanied by an automatic tone warning device, sometimes called a "beep tone," that automatically produces a distinct signal that is repeated at regular intervals during the course of the telephone conversation when the recording device is in use.

Also, a recording device can only be used if it can be physically connected to and disconnected from the telephone line or if it can be switched on and off.

Call Recording Options. You have several options for recording personal history interviews via phone.

Telephone recording controls are used to connect your phone to a recording device of some kind. Radio Shack sells two options, which are both under $30. Results are mixed, but of all the options these are potentially the worst audio sound quality if used improperly. However, I have used these types of devices for years and been satisfied with the quality.

A second option is using Skype or iChat. These free Internet telephone applications are a great way to conduct remote interviews and conference calls. There are many options of how to use Skype to record telephone conversations. I have not personally used this option, but I know many individuals who use Skype or iChat to record podcasts.

Setting up the Interview

The best way to approach someone you want to interview is by personal contact, rather than by letter, and often the initial contact will be by telephone. This gives you an opportunity to introduce yourself, explain your project, and outline the sort of topics you might cover in your conversation. The person you have approached may be uncertain or might feel they have nothing interesting to say, so you sometimes have to do a bit of persuading. The key is to talk in terms of "a chat about the past" or a "story" rather than an "interview," which can sound intimidating.

Once you have chosen the individuals with whom you would like to interview, telephone them and do the following:

- Introduce yourself.
- Explain why you are doing the project. If the interviewee is a member of your family or someone you know very well, you will still need to explain the project, get their agreement to record an interview, gather biographical information from them, and explain the other details listed here.
- Explain what you will be covering in the interview.
- Explain that you would like to tape the interview.
- Explain what will happen to the interview once you have finished it.
- Make an appointment to conduct the interview and record it, preferably within a week.
- Explain your desire to find photos, documents, and so forth to help tell the story.
- Request their address or email address so you can write to them after they've had a few days to ponder your questions.
- Give the interviewee your name and phone number to contact in case they need to clarify anything else.

Note: If the person does not wish to be interviewed, thank them for their time. Do not try to persuade them to change their mind. Every time I have coaxed someone to interview when they first said no, I have had a less-than-acceptable interview.

Preparing for the Interview

Preparing for any interview—whether it's ten minutes or all day in length—requires careful planning, research, familiarity with your equipment, and establishing a good rapport with the interviewee. Consider the following as part of your preparation:

Practice a couple interviews before the real thing. Before you start recording, make at least one practice interview, preferably with someone you know so that you are not afraid to make mistakes. This will give you practice in interview techniques and help you become confident in using your equipment. Practice setting up your equipment quickly and efficiently.

Take the time to experiment with different recording levels on your machine and with changing the distance of the microphone from the interviewee, so that you know the optimum positions for recording. You are aiming to make recordings in which both the interviewee and the interviewer are clearly audible, with little unwanted background or tape noise.

Tip: Take some time to watch or listen to how professional interviewers conduct interviews on TV and radio.

Correcting Recording Noise Problems

As I have interviewed, I have been disappointed when I play back the recording that sounds muffle and distort the voices. Listed below are some common noise problems and suggestions for their solution.

Hiss. This problem may be caused by recording at too low of a level. Turn up your recording-level volume. Alternatively, the recording heads of the tape player may need cleaning or de-magnetizing. The latter can be done by a professional, or it is possible to buy special de-magnetizing tapes. Read the instructions carefully.

Hum. The microphone may be too close to the machine and be picking up the mechanical noise of the recorder. Move the microphone away from the machine. Alternatively, the machine and microphone may be too close to a power source or near another electrical appliance. If so, move the machine and microphone. The wiring on your machine or microphone may be faulty. Have them serviced if you think this is the problem.

Whistle. This can be caused by a television, radio-telephone, or radio-paging system. The only way to stop it is to turn off the apparatus causing the problem.

Distortion. Having the level set too high when recording digitally can cause clipping, which is unwanted distortion of the audio. While distortion happens in analogue recording as well, the artifacts caused by digital distortion can be more severe.

- A popping noise when people say "p," a whistle when they say "s," or a sizzling noise when they say "t" occurs because either they are speaking too close to the microphone or the recording volume is too high. To fix these problems, simply change the angle of the microphone, move it further away, or turn down the recording level.

- If you are recording someone with a high-pitched voice, you may need to adjust the recording volume.

Echo. This is the result of recording in a room that has few soft furnishings and no carpet, such as a kitchen. Because there is little to absorb it, the sound bounces off the hard surfaces and is re-recorded.

You can get around this problem by moving the microphone closer to the interviewee, placing it on a cushion to absorb the echo, drawing the curtains, or moving to another room. A lapel microphone is helpful because the interviewee's body will absorb a lot of echo.

The effect will prevent broadcast-quality recording but is acceptable for research purposes.

Microphone cable noise. This is crackling or clicking noise on the tape caused by the movement of the microphone cable, which usually happens if you are holding the microphone.

It is best to use a microphone stand while recording. Alternatively, place the microphone on some magazines or a cushion. If you have to hold the microphone while recording, wrap the cable around your hand.

Cable noise sometimes occurs when you use a clip-on microphone and the interviewee fidgets with it. If this happens, explain politely that this will muffle their voice on the recording and ask them to stop. You may wish to give them something else to play with; a rubber band is an ideal toy for restless fingers, as it makes no noise.

Recording outside. You should avoid interviewing outside, because it is almost impossible to control the recording of background noise.

If you cannot avoid recording outside, you will need some sort of windshield for the microphone, either a foam-rubber one that you can buy or something like a handkerchief or a few layers of muslin secured with a rubber band.

Try to place the recorder on the ground or on a wall, as the motor speed may vary if it is hanging from your shoulder, causing the sound to be distorted when you replay the tape.

Other sounds to avoid include rustling paper, clicking pens, fluorescent lights humming, clocks ticking, traffic noise, caged birds, dogs barking, and open fires. To avoid the first two, use a pencil and write your questions and notes on a notecard rather than paper. There is little you can do about the others except to notice them at the preliminary meeting and suggest recording the interview in another room.

If you deliberately record some of the above effects when you are practicing with your equipment, you will hear how irritating they sound when the tape is played back. You will then realize why you need to make clearly audible recording for interviews, particularly if you are collecting for an archive.

Preparing Interview Questions

Some of the best things you find out will be unexpected. Once you get started with the interview, you are likely to be told some things you had not previously thought about, so it is essential to give the person you are recording plenty of space to tell you what they think matters. But you should not let the interview drift: it is your job to guide it. For this, you need an overall plan. Group the topics you want to cover in a logical way. I really like the chronological structure, such as talking through life stages in order. I have provided examples of questions, organized by life stages, that you can review and download from the companion website.

Below is a sample outline of an interview about two different life stages:

Married Life and Children

Children:

- Names
- Dates and places of birth
- Health of mother before and after
- How father fared
- Characteristics and differences
- Talents and hobbies
- Smart sayings and doings
- Growing up (daily routine in home)
- Humorous episodes
- Problems
- Joys and sorrows
- Accomplishments

Child rearing psychology:

- Role of yourself, spouse, children in the home

Family traditions:

- Holidays
- Birthdays
- Graduation
- Deer hunting
- Funerals
- Mother's Day, Father's Day
- Weddings

Family vacations:

Grandchildren:

- How many
- Where they live
- How their parents raised them
- Things done together
- Trips to visit them and vice versa

Middle Age and Toward Retirement

General life pattern changing:

- More time on hand
- Financial situation
- Different and new interests
- New friends and associates
- New hobbies (genealogy, golf, reading, music, art, books)

Health:

- In general
- Operations
- Allergies
- Physical disabilities

Decided preferences: favorite foods and so on

Civic and political activities:

- Positions held
- Services rendered
- Politics
- Political issues you were involved in
- Memorable campaigns
- Red Cross or other volunteer work
- Church positions

New business ventures:

Memorable travels:

New and different homes:

Retirement and its impact: financial, family, leisure time, volunteer activities

Personal Philosophy about Life in General

Your ideal: What personal trait do you admire most and why?

Regrets: if you had your life to live over again, what would you do differently?

One of the most important days of your life and why?

Greatest joy and biggest sorrow

Biggest lesson in life you found to be true

Most important lesson, message, or advice you've learned that you would like passed on for others to profit by

One word on how to live successfully

Your secret for living a long, healthy, happy, prosperous life

Does the Lord answer prayers?

How you would like to be remembered

Funeral arrangements: music, speaker, ceremony, special instructions, headstone inscriptions, selection of burial clothes

Special words of counsel to:

- Children
- Grandchildren
- Other kin

As you develop your questions, use plain words and avoid suggesting the answers. Rather than saying, "I suppose you must have had a poor and unhappy childhood," instead ask, "Can you describe your childhood?"

You will need some questions that encourage precise answers, such as "Where did you move to next?" But you also need questions that are open, inviting descriptions, comments, and opinions. Some examples of open questions include "How did you feel about that?" "What sort of person was he?" "Can you describe the house you lived in?" and "Why did you decide to change jobs?"

There are some points to cover in every interview, such as date and place of birth and what their parents' and their own main jobs were.

Before You Leave Home

It's now the day before your interview. Take time to do a quick check of the material, equipment, and artifacts you will take with you to make sure you're all set. A simple checklist might help make sure you have all the equipment you need. Ensure that everything is in good working order. Check that you know how to operate all your equipment properly and that you have enough cassettes, and fresh batteries or an adaptor. Put together a folder that includes maps, extra questions, a note pad, pencils or pens, and interview agreements (if you are using them).

Review the questions you have developed and choose which would be most appropriate for each person, as well as whether there are other questions you should be asking specifically about the family line the person belonged to (such as about grandparents, times in which they lived, and so on). Then send each person a letter or email with the following information:

- Your name, address, email, and telephone number
- A brief overview of the project
- Questions you are going to ask
- A request to share artifacts

Conducting the Interview

Choose a quiet place. Try to pick a room that is not near a busy road. If you can, switch off radios and televisions, which can sometimes make it difficult to hear what someone is saying.

Interview introduction. Before you actually begin the interview, explain to the person that not all of the information provided will be used in the family history. They will have an opportunity to see and approve it before it is published or distributed to other family members. Explain that you will ask questions to prompt ideas, but they do not have to answer all the questions. If a question seems too personal, have them let you know and then move on to the next question. If they tell you something they later regret, simply have them tell you and let them know that you will exclude it from being used.

Equipment set-up. It's really important to make sure your equipment is set up right. Plug the recorder into the wall or put in the batteries. Switch it on. Put a battery in the microphone if it needs one, and plug it into the microphone jack socket. Turn the microphone on. Always check the microphone battery before going to an interview, and carry spare batteries at all times. I always put in fresh batteries for an interview. All you need to make you a believer is one experience where the recorder becomes slow or stopped and you have to do the interview over.

If using a tape recorder, make sure you have the tape in the right way, and remember that nothing will be recorded on the clear plastic lead-in at the beginning, so wait until it has wound through before you start talking. Alternatively, wind the lead-in tape through manually so that you can begin to record as soon as you press the "record" button.

Check that you have your recording volume adjusted to the correct level and your playback volume turned off. If you don't, you may experience a shrieking noise called feedback. Check to see that you have copies of your questions and other material that are pertinent for the interview. Place the microphone on the table or clip it to the interviewee. Press the "record" button or the "record" and "play" buttons, depending on your machine.

Remember that if your recorder has only a playback volume control, this does not control the recording level, which you can adjust only by moving the microphone or speaking more loudly or softly.

If you have only one clip-on microphone, place it on your interviewee and speak up yourself. While it is more important to record their voice than yours, it is useless if the listener to the tape is unable to hear your questions, so make sure that your voice is also audible.

For a unidirectional tabletop microphone, the optimum position is for the two of you to speak over it at a 90-degree angle.

Get close. Generally, the closer the microphone is, the better the results will be. If possible, use a clip-on microphone and put it about nine inches from the person's mouth. With a hand-held microphone, place it as near as possible but not on the same surface as the recorder nor on a hard surface, which gives poor sound quality.

Record a "tape identification" at the beginning of side one. Do this at the beginning of every cassette in case it is ever separated from its case. The following is a typical tape identification:

> Side A. Interview with [Say name and spell it.](say—Susan Longhurst, spelled S-U-S-A-N, New word L-O-N-G-H-U-R-S-T) 25 May 2011. Interviewed by Barry Ewell. [State purpose of interview]

Be reassuring. You are their guest, and if they are elderly, you may be the first person they have spoken to for several days. They will be as nervous and apprehensive as you are, so it is essential to be cordial and patient.

The interview is not a conversation. The point of the interview is to get the narrator to tell her story. Limit your own remarks to a few pleasantries to break the ice, then brief questions to guide her along. It is not necessary to give her the details of your great-grandmother's trip in a covered wagon in order to get her to tell you about her grandfather's trip to California. Just say, "I understand your grandfather came around the Horn to California. What did he tell you about the trip?"

One on one is best. Interviews usually work out better if there is no one present but you and the interviewee. Sometimes two or more interviewers can be successfully recorded, but usually each one of them would have been better alone.

If you are using interview agreements, ask your interviewee to review and sign the agreement form before you start the interview.

Begin the interview with straightforward questions. Start with questions that are not controversial; save the delicate questions, if there are any, until you have become better acquainted. A good place to begin is with the interviewee's youth and background. For example, ask questions about the following topics:

- Date of birth and birthplace
- Names of parents
- Names of spouse and children
- Names of siblings
- Occupation, schooling

Ask questions that requires a detailed answer. Early in the interview, ask a question that requires a very detailed answer. After having gained the trust of the person you are interviewing, have some question ready to signal to the person that you want details. Sometimes asking for a tour of a place, such as a house or place of work, helps to gain much information. Ask follow-up questions with each "step" through the structure.

Getting the best answers.

Throughout the interview, the questions that will give you the best information are those that start with *how, who, why, what, where,* or *when.* Ask specific questions to get specific answers, and open-ended ones to get longer, more detailed answers.

Avoid simple yes-or-no questions. For example, ask "What were your living conditions like?" rather than "Did you have cramped living conditions?" Ask open-ended questions if you want description or comment: "What can you remember of the trip over to England?" or "Can you tell me more about what swimming in the Great Salt Lake was like?" Don't ask more than one question at a time.

Get past stereotypes and generalizations. This is one of the most challenging aspects of interviewing people. As well as a mere descriptive retelling of events, try to explore motives and feelings with questions like "Why?" and "How did you feel?"

Ask for concrete illustrations and examples. If someone says, for example, "Aunt Marjorie was a great cook," then ask, "Could you give me an example of that?" Not only does this add depth and illustration to the material you are collecting, it also requires the interviewee to be specific and to qualify sweeping statements.

Use "reversals" to gain more in-depth information. As you interview, the interviewee will give general sentences, such as, "I thought it was a great experience" or "Mom made a great stew" or "That was a trying time." Reversals are statements that say, "please tell me more" It keeps the flow of the conversation moving. The following are examples of reversals:

General Comments	Example of reversal:
"I thought it was a great experience."	What do you mean by 'great?'
"Mom, made a great stew."	What made it so great?
"That was a trying time."	In what way?

Sometimes you will need to use reversals multiple times for the same questions. For example, consider the following exchange:

Comment 1: I admired Mr. Jones.
Reversal 1: Tell me more.
Comment 2: He was a kind man.

Reversal 2: Meaning?

Comment 3: Whenever he went to town, he would always stop by our house and give my widowed mother extra food, coal, and so on. Whatever he purchased for his family, he purchased a little extra for us.

You are not the one being interviewed. You are there to find out information. Your aim is to get them to talk, not to talk to yourself. Don't tell them the answer to a question: "So you milked the cows by hand?" Allow them to explain how they did things. Listen carefully and maintain good eye contact. Don't contradict and don't get into heated debate. Respond positively—body language like nodding and smiling is much better than "ers" and "ums" and "really." Try not to say "yes" or make encouraging noises, and don't wriggle about or shuffle your papers.

Good interviewers don't shine. Don't use the interview to show off your knowledge, vocabulary, charm, or other abilities. Good interviewers do not shine; only their interviews do.

Be sensitive and always respect confidences. There are some topics that may be sensitive or very personal. Be respectful of the interviewee's feelings and sense of privacy.

Don't interrupt. Be relaxed, unhurried, and sympathetic. Make sure that your interviewee has finished answering before you ask the next question. Don't interrupt a good story because you have thought of a question, or because the interviewee is straying from the planned outline. If the information is pertinent, let her go on, but jot down your questions on your notepad so you will remember to ask it later. Do not fill every pause they take. Most people will need to think about answers, especially if they are remembering things that happened long ago. Don't worry if you seem to be straying from your prepared questions, as long as the information you are hearing is relevant. Listen carefully and maintain good eye contact.

How to manage a stray. It's not uncommon for an interviewee to stray on a subject that is not pertinent to the discussion. Common areas to stray include family medical problems and what family children are doing. Try to pull the interviewee back as quickly as possible. For example, say "Before we move on, I'd like to find out how the closing of the mine in 1935 affected your family's finances. Do you remember that?" It is often hard for a narrator to describe people. An easy way to begin is to ask her to describe the person's appearance. From there, the narrator is more likely to move into character description.

Use your paper for notes. Jot down names or other details that you need to clarify before leaving. If the interviewee is telling a story and you think of another question, don't interrupt; jot down your thought and come back to it. Don't sit and transcribe all of the interviewee's answers.

Keep your questions short and clear. If your interviewee doesn't understand what you're asking, repeat the question or rephrase it.

Don't expect people to remember dates. Most people won't remember exact dates. Instead ask, "How old were you then?" or "Was that before or after [Regensburg or Munich]?" If you have done your background research well enough, the answer should allow you to pinpoint the year.

What to do when stories are different than what you've heard. What do you do when the interviewee is telling a story that is contrary to what you have heard? Tactfully point out to the interviewee that there is a different account of what she is describing, if there is. Start out by saying, "I have heard . . ." or "I have read . . ." This is not to challenge her account, but rather an opportunity for her to bring up further evidence to refute the opposing view, or to explain how that view got established, or to temper what she has already said. If done skillfully, some of your best information can come from this juxtaposition of differing accounts.

When in doubt, don't. If you feel awkward or uncomfortable in asking for sensitive or potentially damaging information, don't ask. Your hesitation reminds you that there is a human being with feelings sitting right across from you. Details are important, but maintaining a respect for privacy is even more important. Sometimes, interviewees simply need a moment to compose themselves for sensitive discussions, or they may actually be evaluating your behavior as a decision-making factor in whether to talk openly about specific individuals or events.

Try to avoid "off the record" information. At times the interviewee will ask you to turn off the tape recorder while they tell a good story. Ask the person to let you record the whole thing and promise that you will erase that portion if he asks you to after further consideration. You may have to erase it later, or he may not tell you the story at all, but once you allow "off the record" stories, he may continue with more and more, and you will end up with almost no recorded interview at all. "Off the record" information is only useful if you yourself are researching a subject and this is the only way you can get the information. It has no value if your purpose is to collect information for later use by other researchers.

Ask interviewees to spell out measurements. "It was about this wide" will mean nothing to a listener. Try to get the interviewee to give a verbal estimate of size—"Oh, about three feet"—or give it yourself: "Is that about three feet?"

Don't challenge accounts you think might be inaccurate. Try to develop as much information as possible that can be used by later researchers in establishing what probably happened. Your interviewee may be telling you quite accurately what he saw or heard. As Walter Lord explained when describing his interviews with survivors of the Titanic, "Every lady I interviewed had left the sinking ship in the last lifeboat. As I later found out from studying the placement of the lifeboats, no group of lifeboats was in view of another and each lady probably was in the last lifeboat she could see leaving the ship."

When a negative is better than a positive approach. Ask about the negative aspects of a situation. For example, in asking about a person, do not begin with a glowing description. "I know that Uncle Larry was a very generous and wise person. Did you find him so?" Few interviewees will quarrel with a statement like that even though they may have found the uncle a disagreeable person. You will get a more lively answer if you start out in the negative. "Despite Uncle Larry's reputation for good works, I hear he was a very difficult man for his employees to get along with." If your interviewee admired Uncle Larry greatly, she will spring to his defense with an apt illustration of why your statement is wrong. If she did find him hard to get along with, your remark has given her a chance to illustrate some of the uncle's more unpleasant characteristics.

Keep the recorder running. While you are recording, try not to turn off the recorder. You will obviously not want to keep it running if you are interrupted by something such as a telephone call, but leave it running during pauses while people think. It is much better to waste a little tape on irrelevant material than to call attention to the tape recorder by a constant on-off operation. For this reason, I do not recommend the stop-start switches available on some microphones. If your mic has such a switch, tape it to the "on" position—then forget it.

The last two questions you should ask. In concluding the interview, ask, "Is there anything I haven't asked that you think I should know?" and "Do you have any questions for me?"

Say thank you. At the end of an interview, it is helpful to say thank you while still recording so that listeners know the interview has finished.

AFTER THE INTERVIEW

After the interview is finished, don't rush away. Take time to thank them and talk about yourself. It is also the time to discuss the copyright and clearance form (if you're choosing to use one) and have them sign the form. You will often be shown some interesting old photographs or documents. Before you leave, provide an address or phone number where you can be contacted and make clear whether you will be returning for a follow-up interview or not. This can avert any unnecessary worry. Remember that your visit will often have a major impact on someone who has perhaps never told anyone their memories before.

When you arrive home, write a letter of thanks to the interviewee and enclose a copy of the agreement form (if used) for their records. Think critically about your interview. Consider what was good about it and what could be improved next time. Prepare a listing of proper nouns, places, and jargon words or phrases for each interview tape. Examine an authoritative source to double-check spellings.

Taking Care of the Recorded Interview

Digitize the interview. If you are using a cassette or mini-cassette recorder to record the interview, seriously consider digitizing the interview. Digitizing the interview will allow you to do the following:

- Back up the interview on CD.
- Use audio editing software (like Audacity) to cut your favorite stories from the interviews and use them to augment family histories that are placed online or on CD.
- Cut out problems like phones ringing, dogs barking, or small talk.
- Easily transcribe and edit the interview.
- Easily share interviews. For example, I recently interviewed a person for a personal history. Shortly following the interview, the individual passed away. This was the only voice recording the family had of the person. It was easy to make an MP3 file of the recording and share it with the family.

Save cassette tapes. If you are using a cassette or mini-cassette recorder, make sure that you make a copy before using them. You will then have an original copy, which should be put aside and used for no purpose other than making further copies. When you wind and rewind your tapes, especially if you are transcribing them, this can stretch the tape and result in distorted sound. Snap out the plastic tabs on the top of the cassette to prevent the tapes from being recorded over. Do not reuse the tape on other interviews. Place it in an envelope and store it in a safe place. I write on the envelope the date and who was interviewed. I also include the equipment used, date, place, time, and any additional notes.

Transcribe your interviews. A transcript or transcription is a word-for-word written copy of a taped interview. Transcribing an interview provides several important benefits, including that there is no misunderstanding what was said in an interview. You have the ability to see where clarification is needed for the interview.

Creating a word processing document allows you to search for key words and cut and paste sections of interviews with other relevant information under topics you have designated for your life history. Transcription saves the wear-and-tear of the audiotapes and videocassettes, provides for easy searching on a key word in word processing, provides an easily accessible reference substitute for the recordings, and requires no special play-back equipment or listening booth.

Tip: Highlight the best potential quotes in another color (such as blue, red) by using the highlighting icon on the formatting toolbar or by highlighting with a highlighter on the hard copy. It will save you time later on.

How complete should the transcript be? The purpose of the transcript is to provide you access to key details from the interview. On an average I will transcribe from 40 to 70 percent of the interview. I will focus on the question and the key answers to the questions. In my transcription, I will list the name of the interviewee; equipment used; date, time, and place of interview; and key highlights of the interview.

There are portions of the interview where "abstracting" is a great choice. Abstracting is where you will briefly tell what is being discussed and then insert word for word transcription as needed. For example, "Recalls where he was when WWII was declared. Describes atmosphere at home. [Now transcribe detailed explanation of feelings and so forth.]"

Use words like *explains, describes, mentions, recounts,* and *recalls* to give the researcher an idea of what is included and how much material there is on a particular topic. "Mentions how traveled to school," for example, means that there is less information than if you had written "Describes how traveled to school." It is important to choose your words carefully.

How much time does it take to make a transcript? Word processing software and other computer programs have made the task easier than before, but it can still be a long process. I average a ratio of about 1:3, or three hours of transcription work for every one hour of recorded interview.

Some Tips for Creating and Editing Transcripts:

- Listen to about ten minutes of the interview before starting to transcribe.
- Transcribe what you hear. Do not put words or phrases into the interviewee's mouth, even if what they say is awkward or ungrammatical. Do not change word order.
- It will help if you have special transcribing equipment, such as good headphones and a transcribing machine that can be operated by foot pedals so you can stop and rewind the tape during playback, freeing the hands for transcribing. They also play at variable speeds to enable muffled or garbled portions to be intelligible. Using an ordinary recorder will take longer. If you have access to a personal computer, it will be easier to correct mistakes, although making a first draft by hand works quite well. Manufacturers of transcribers include Sony and Panasonic, among others.
- At the beginning of the transcript, identify who transcribed the tape, who edited the transcript, and the date(s) these tasks were done.
- Include a title page with the name of the interviewee, the interviewer, and the date of the interview. State clearly whether restrictions have been placed on any parts of the interview.
- When formatting the text on the page, use one-inch margins on each side of the paper, number the pages, and double-space the text.
- Identify all speakers at the start of their comments by typing their name in bolded capital letters, followed by a colon—for example, **SMITH:**
- Create a verbatim transcript, but omit such expressions as "um" or "ah." Include expressions such as "umhum" or "huh-huh" when used to mean "yes" or "no" in response to specific questions.
- Put in periods at what seem to be natural sentences breaks. Transcripts with little punctuation are very difficult to read, let alone understand.

- Do not revise the narrator's words to force them into standard written prose. Leave any sentence fragments, run-on sentences, and incorrect grammar untouched. Commas and dashes may be used to reflect pauses in the spoken words.
- Punctuate so that the transcript makes sense of the words as they were spoken. Be consistent in your punctuation; don't, for example, indicate a pause by a dash (—) in some transcripts and three dots (. . .) in others.
- If changes are made, clearly indicate when and how the transcript differs from the original tape recording.
- Use "stage directions" with care. Some may be useful to help understand what is happening, for example, "[reading from newspaper]" or "[interruption for telephone call]" may be useful, but those which make interpretations—such as "[laughs sarcastically]"—should be used with caution.
- Include word contractions as they occur, such as "don't" and "wouldn't."
- Place a question mark before and after a word or phrase to indicate any uncertainty about it, such as "?destroyed?."
- Indicate the end of a side of the tape in capital letters—END OF SIDE ONE, TAPE ONE; BEGIN SIDE TWO, TAPE ONE.
- Identify garbled or inaudible portions of the tape. If one word is inaudible, indicate the gap with an underscore (___). When multiple words are inaudible, insert "___+" or estimate the elapsed time using a time indicator, such as "___ . . .. (3 seconds)."
- When you are satisfied that what is on the page accurately reflects what is on the tape, type a final copy and assemble the interview file.

Personal History Documentation

As the individual writing the personal history, it becomes your responsibility to collect documentation that is complete, accurate and reliable, especially if you intend to incorporate the information into a book or article for distribution.

If pieces of written and oral information contradict each other, then you must go deeper to determine which is more accurate, unless contradiction is the key to the issue.

Sometimes, interviewees will recall events in the form of past conversations ("she said to me . . ."). People reconstruct dialogue not only in oral histories, but also in letters and diaries and the results can be treacherous for those wanting to publish the "truth." When you, as the researcher and interviewer, hear such dialogue, measure the conversation with what they already know (or don't know) about the subject and even the interviewee. Most often, you are going to need to do further research.

Sorting Fact from Hearsay

The interview is the cornerstone to writing personal histories, yet it's an opinion, a perception that is presented as fact. As a genealogist and family historian, I understand the importance of documentation and doing the extra research to confirm and effectively tell the story.

Adding Background Information to Your Personal History

During the research and writing of your personal history you will have the opportunity to expand and provide background to help make the history richer and inviting. Depending on your needs, consider the following:

- Take advantage of your public library and libraries in the areas where your ancestors lived. Many libraries have extensive genealogical departments with staff knowledgeable about the history and people of the region or state.
- Join genealogical societies and historical associations in the locales you are researching. Even if you live too far away to participate in local meetings, you can access valuable records and dedicated genealogists who are familiar with the history of the region.
- Use online resources—archives of source documents, places to search for ancestral information, discussion forums to

share with other researchers, and blogs that offer advice, links to other resources, and opportunities to make contacts.

- Be as eager to share information as you are to obtain it. You may have a piece of information that fills a gap for someone else, and the more gaps that are filled in genealogical records, the more information is available to everyone.
- Gather enough information to work with before you start writing, but expect to continue to research throughout the writing process.

Lesson 15: Write and Publish Your Story

Writing personal histories takes planning, time, and effort to stitch the research into a cohesive blend of resources that tells the story that will inspire generations to come.

A Story Worth Writing
Begins with an Outline

"Why do you need an outline? I already know what I want to say." These are the words I remember saying in tenth grade as I started my English creative writing course. As I discussed the first writing assignment with my teacher, I assured her that I could finish the story without writing the required outline. She allowed me the opportunity to prove her wrong. After several drafts, I reluctantly told the teacher I was not able complete the story in the assigned time. I found myself writing and rewriting. I found myself expanding and deleting sections of each paragraph. It was never completely what I wanted to say.

The teacher offered me a second chance. This time, I was to use an outline and then write the story. With a new topic, I wrote the outline and finished the story. I don't remember my grade, but I remember the lesson: a story worth writing begins with an outline.

An outline is a blueprint of your final product—in this case, your personal history. It represents the content of your story, organizing your memories, lessons learned, and supporting details. The outline is all about organization and providing a visual and conceptual design of your writing.

How does an outline help? The outline helps you expose gaps in your story early in the process and gives you time to fill them in, so you don't leave out any important events, stories, and ideas that you want to tell. You will understand the full breadth of the story you write, have a clear focus on the detail you want to include with each topic, and always have a reference point from which to add, rearrange, and delete.

How to Use the Outline to Write Your Story

Remember, the outline is a blueprint. Just as blueprints help a builder create a structure, your outline can form the foundation or frame for the first draft.

Writing experience by experience, topic by topic: If your outline is on a computer, you can just click your cursor at any part of the outline you have created and fill in the details. This can help you overcome writer's block. That is, you can write the third section first, if you want. Then simply go back and fill in sections one and two. When you revise, you can make sure all the pieces fit together.

Modifying the design. Outlines are not set in stone. As you write, you may discover that you've left out essential information. If you keep a printed copy of your outline handy, you can figure out where in your outline the new information belongs and insert it (don't be formal about it—just pencil it in). That way, you can see how the addition alters the rest of the story.

Starting again. Sometimes your original outline simply needs to be restructured. If you are careful, this is not a problem and you can rework the original outline. When you create the new outline (even if it's simply a sketch), focus on your purpose and who you are writing to.

Using the outline to crosscheck the final draft. Finally, if you update your outline as you work, rather than abandon it after it has been created, you'll have a handy reference to double-check the organization of the final story. For a larger story, the outline can also provide your section headings and subheadings and can become the table of contents.

Structure of a Personal History Outline

Like any good story, a personal history has three sections: introduction, body, and conclusion. The outline is designed to indicate levels of significance using major and minor headings. You will organize your information from general to specific. For example, the general headings could be as follows:

- Childhood (0-11)
- Adolescence (11-18)
- Early Adulthood (18-25)
- Prime Adulthood (25-45)
- Middle Adult Years (45-65)
- Senior Adulthood (65-present)

And subordinate headings or topics could include:
- Memories of your children
- Community Service
- Health Record
- Physical Characteristics
- Social Life
- Religion
- Memorable World Events
- Military Service
- Education
- Vocation
- Counsel to Posterity

As you create your subheadings, make sure there is a clear relationship between the subheadings and their supporting elements. Consider the following example:

Mary Jones Attends High School
- High School Attendance
- High School Activities
  - Drill Team
  - Sr. Prom
- Mary Jones Summer Work
  - Picking fruit (Cherries, Peaches)
  - Working at the Spanish Fork Cannery

The most important rule for outlining is to be consistent! An outline can use topic or sentence structure, which are explained below.

Sentence Structure. A sentence outline uses complete sentences for all entries and uses correct punctuation.

> **Advantages:** presents a more detailed overview of work, including possible topic sentences, and is easier and faster for transitioning to writing the final paper.

Topic Outline. A topic outline uses words or phrases for all entries and uses no punctuation after entries.

> **Advantages:** Presents a brief overview of work and is generally easier and faster to write than a sentence outline.

There are two simple formats that seem to work well with creating a personal history outline—roman numeral and decimal. They are explained below:

Roman numeral

I. Major Topic
    A. Main Idea
    B. Main Idea
        1. Detail of Support
        2.
            a. Broken down further
            b.
                (1) More details
                (2)

Decimal

1.0
1.1
1.2
1.2.1
1.2.2
    1.2.2.1
    1.2.2.2

Regardless of simplicity or complexity, an outline is a prewriting tool to help you organize your thoughts and create a roadmap for writing your personal history.

Remember, the outline is for you. It exists to help orient you within the personal history and to help ensure a full answer. You can deviate from it if you wish, and as you write, you may find you have more and more ideas. Stop and take the time to brainstorm and write them down, then reassess and adjust your plan.

Creating the Personal History Outline

If you took the time to create the Profile Storage Container or "The Box" (discussed in Lesson Two), you will find the outline is very easy to create. Start with the first folder and move your way back through the folders, whether you have them in chronological or topical order. If you didn't take time to create "The Box," start at the beginning and outline the major events of your life. Start with your childhood years and continue through to the present. For example, the following is a very rough outline, using the roman numeral format, of the "childhood years" life stage for Mary Jones:

I. Childhood (0-11) (Years covered)
  A. Birth
      1. Detail
  B. Death of Mother
      1. Detail
          a. Detail of Detail
          b. Detail of Detail
  C. Life with Uncle Irv and Aunt Minn
      1. Detail
      2. Detail
          a. Detail of Detail
  D. Remarriage of Ora to Faye
      1. Detail
          a. Detail of Detail
          b. Detail of Detail
      2. Detail
          a. Detail of Detail
          b. Detail of Detail

Some individuals prefer to use the method of picking topics or life stages and simply answer a set of predetermined questions from each stage of life to help prompt them through.

OVERVIEW OF WRITING THE PERSONAL HISTORY

Get a "second opinion" or several other opinions after you've written part of the story—from people you interviewed to be sure you understood their meaning, from people who don't know anything about your family to see if they understand, and from people who know something about writing to see what they think of your work.

Decide whether you agree with the feedback you get from early readers; use the input you find helpful to improve the story as you continue writing.

Make any needed revisions, then, in the final edit, read the manuscript aloud—preferably with someone else. You'll be amazed at how many problems show up when you're reading aloud that you missed when reading silently.

Put the name of the history's subject on each page and number each page (such as "page 1 of 10"). This keeps each history in order and ensures that all pages are accounted for. For example, if the history is scanned, pages may get out of order or different histories may get mixed together.

WRITING THE PERSONAL HISTORY—DRAFT ONE

By now, you should be ready to start writing. Whether you are writing about yourself or someone else, be honest. I have read many histories over the years, and those that have the most meaning include true stories about real life. The stories range from the sad and tragic to the exciting, funny, and simple day-to-day.

Gather your resource materials and find a place to write. Gather your outline and any other resource materials, such as "The Box," near you for easy reference. Now that you are ready, sit down and start writing. When you open the doors of memory, you will probably be eager to capture everything just right. Sit in a comfortable place, relax, and take it one page at a time.

Write your first draft as fast as you can, without concern for style and grammar. You may think this contrary to practical writing style, but write your first draft as rapidly as you can. The focus of the first draft is to put your thoughts to paper (or keyboard) as quickly as you can. Be yourself—you'll write faster and more naturally. Don't think that the first draft has to be perfect—you'll probably think it's awful, but if you worry about writing a great first draft, you'll never finish.

Don't spend too much time thinking about style and grammar; just write. Let yourself explore the ideas as you go. If you change your mind about how to say something, don't stop to cross it out, just write an improved version. You may have a lot of repetition in your first draft. That's fine. Only if you find you've veered far off-course should you revise what you've written before moving on. Otherwise, wait until the second draft to make changes in the first part of the book.

Where should you begin? Remember: you have an outline, so start wherever you like. Start in the beginning, middle, or end. Just start writing. Start writing with the intent of getting some ideas down on paper.

Use memory triggers. A memory trigger can be a question, photograph, letter, or a discussion with a friend with whom you shared an experience. Think about the times you have looked through the photo album and come across pictures and were able to experience a time past as though it was just yesterday. All your memories are still in safekeeping; it's simply a matter of finding them.

Write your first draft in the way that's best for you. If you are a good typist, you will probably use the keyboard. If you write long-hand, you can write with pen and paper. If you have a computer and you are using voice-recognition software (like Nuance Naturally Speaking), then use this software to write your first draft. It is important to write your first draft as quickly and easily as possible, focusing on the words but not the way you produce the words. Assume you will be revising anyway.

Use descriptive words. Think about the who, what, where, when, how, and why of each memory. Use your senses to help describe your stories. These details will help bring your stories to life.

Make note of any and all ideas. One experience you will have as you are writing about one topic is that you will receive inspiration and ideas. Your thoughts will range from a new topic to add to the outline or a piece of information to add to a topic that you just finished. You may get an idea to call Aunt Peggy to ask a specific question or to go look for a photograph in the scrapbook. Whatever the thought, write it down or capture it electronically. When I am writing, I will keep a digital recorder (or a notebook and pen) with me so I don't miss those moments.

Put brackets around sections that are tough to write or require further information. When you are writing your first draft, it's common to either not have all the information you need or simply be stumped. You may be writing about a specific memory and think to put in a text from an obituary. Simply use brackets to denote that more information is needed and keep moving. For example: [Need text from Mary Jones Obituary] or [Need to confirm statement made by Uncle George on Spanish Fork city project during Depression.] By using brackets, you will save a lot of time and keep your train of thought moving. When you move on to the revision phase of the writing, you can go back and work through the bracketed sections one at a time.

Need help writing? If you are not confident of your writing ability, join a local or online writers group to learn about the craft of writing, or take a writing class at a community college.

NEED MORE HELP WITH THE OUTLINE OR STORY? TRY THE MAPPING TECHNIQUE

Whenever I need a little bit—or a lot—of extra help developing ideas that I am going to write about, I use what is called "mapping." Mapping refers to organizing your ideas visually by connecting one thought with another. Eventually, mapping will lead you to a list of ideas and a sequence to use them in.

How to use mapping to generate ideas.

1. Write the topic in the middle of the page.
2. Draw lines that branch out from that topic to other key words or phrases that you associate with that topic.
3. As needed, draw more lines that branch out from each of the key words (subtopics) that help to develop these ideas.
4. Now that you have created a few subtopics, evaluate which, if any, of the subtopics go together and can be linked. Connect the ideas that work together with lines.
5. If you need to regroup your ideas, write the topic in the middle of the page again and go through the first steps again with the new groupings.
6. Continue this process as many times as needed until you can form the topic groupings into the parts of your story or experience. With the bubbles and branches, you can see how they interrelate and work together as a whole.

How to use mapping to sort out stories, experiences, or paragraphs.

1. Write your topic in the middle of a large piece of paper.
2. Take your brainstorming list and circle the central ideas.
3. Which of those ideas link to other ideas on your page? What would be the main idea? What would be subsidiary or linked ideas?
4. Now transfer the main ideas to the mapping page. Draw a circle (bubble) around the idea and then link the ideas with lines, like branches of a tree.
5. By connecting the ideas with braches you show concepts and ideas interrelate. Continue to add bubbles and branches as the ideas continue to expand. Use lines and branches to show how any of the large or linked ideas interrelate. Don't be afraid to add bubbles or branches that weren't in your original preparation writing. Keep those ideas growing!
6. When you have completed the exercise, you can see how the ideas fit together. Once you see how the ideas work together,

you are ready to make a list of which ideas to use in your writing.

Need help writing the paragraph?

Sometimes the paragraph you are writing doesn't seem to want to flow. The following is a simple look at the construction of a paragraph, which may help you grow your ideas and write better, easier paragraphs.

A well-written, cohesive paragraph communicates one complete thought. In order to organize your subtopics into clear, concise thoughts, the following outline of paragraph structure is helpful.

A paragraph begins with the topic sentence, followed by supporting details, and ending with a closure.

- **Topic sentence.** The topic sentence states the main idea of the paragraph. The topic sentence is usually the first sentence of the paragraph but can be in the middle or at the end.
- **Supporting details.** Once you have the topic sentence, it needs to have supporting details, which can be in the form of explanation, examples, stories, facts, or a combination of these things. The supporting details will develop your topic statement and show your idea.
- **Closure.** This is where you bring your ideas to a close and link your ideas to the next point or paragraph.

Planning your paragraphs. You have plenty of ideas, you kind of know what to say, and you know the basic structure of your writing. What do you do now? You need to work out what goes where. Look at all your ideas and identify logical sequences. Consider the following points when planning your paragraphs:

- Choose which idea the reader should know first. If all of the ideas seem equally relevant, choose the one you feel will provide the best "hook" for the reader. Choose the idea that will bring your reader into the story and guide them to what you're thinking and answer. Choose one that will pull the reader in and orient them to your thinking and your answer.

Don't put the most dramatic ideas first. If the idea is the most dramatic, you should build up to it.

- After choosing the first idea, decide which idea should go second. Which one would naturally come after? Is there an idea that belongs to or is an extension of that first one?
- If you have an idea that needs to be explained in order to be understood, save it until the end so that the sentences leading up to that idea can explain your meaning more clearly.

Making the actual plan

1. Make a list of the order in which you want the ideas to flow. This can be as simple as one word for each idea.
2. Look at your list and ask yourself if the ideas flow naturally. If not, rearrange your thoughts until you have a plan you like.
3. Double-check that there are enough ideas written down to fully support your topic sentence.
4. If you want a more detailed plan, include smaller ideas next to each idea (subtopic or heading). You'll use these smaller ideas to expand your thoughts. Also include any examples you may want to use.

Revising the First Draft

Your first draft is done—congratulations! That's a good beginning. Now it's time to revise and edit. The difference between a mediocre personal history and a great personal history often comes in the revising and editing stage. I can't stress this phase of writing enough! I have had the sad experience of writing and printing a newsletter, brochure, or flyer where thorough editing was not done, and an error (such as a misspelling) slipped by. No matter how great the work, a simple error is like a splash of mud on clean windows. Editing is like hoeing the garden: it may not be pleasant at the time, but the end result is wonderful. It's also much cheaper to catch the error now rather then after you have printed and bound your work.

Toward the end of my father's life, he began to reflect upon his life and write his memoirs. He wrote well over one thousand pages in longhand. It was his desire to have his writings published for all of his family to read. As I read over the lines and pages, I found many wonderful stories, examples, and lessons learned, but the writing was very, very rough. I was willing to work with my dad to edit and prepare the writings for publication, but it was no use; he was adamant that the first draft is the way it should be because it was his story. The 1000-plus handwritten pages are now filed away and on my to-do list.

Plan on at least two edits for your personal history.

In the first edit, concentrate on the organization and content. Is the story in the right order? Did you include all the characters and events you intended? Is it clear to readers who these people are and why they do what they do? Flesh out the characters, descriptions, and dialogue (if you have included it).

In the second edit, work on grammar, punctuation, sentence structure, and transitions to polish the story. Edit the story as many times as necessary to make it the best you can, but realize that it will never be perfect. You have to stop editing your work and finish it at some point. You may not achieve the "perfect" personal history—there will always be something to add and tweak—but you will be able to have the story you want. Remember, you can always add additional volumes. Complete the personal history and share it.

After you've edited the manuscript several times, ask other people to read it. A professional editor can make a big difference; if you plan to publish for an audience larger than your family, professional editing is essential.

Who does the editing? Editing is a team exercise. You will probably do most of the writing and editing, but also plan on at least two other people to review and assist with the editing. If you are not interested in or don't have the skills for editing, then definitely enlist the help of others. Editors can also be for hire.

The next section will explore some important techniques associated with editing a personal history. These techniques will dynamically improve your writing and help create a history your ancestors will want to read.

Three types of edits

During the revision and editing process, you will engage in the following three types of editing:

- Restructuring or reorganizing—this involves reflecting on what has been written and making major improvements in the way parts fit together.
- Acquiring new information—adding photos, maps, or exhibits, or doing further research on topics to provide a better understanding of topics discussed or eluded.
- Sharpening—adding clarity by going over what is written and smoothing it out.

Restructuring and reorganizing is the most important part of the revision stage. It requires that you step back and look at your writing with a fresh eye, as if you were a person fifty years from now, reading your history for the first time. The following are a few ideas that will help you in the editing and revising process.

Read your personal history aloud and make notes.

One of the hardest things you will do as a writer is try to see your work from an outsider's perspective. "Being too close to the forest to see the trees" is a good idiom to describe what is taking place. When I read my own writing, I have misspellings and usage errors that I simply gloss over or don't see. When my wife edits my work, I'm surprised that I missed the errors she finds. I overlook a lot of errors because I remember what I meant to say and don't necessarily look at what I wrote. There are three techniques that will help you to focus on words you have written.

Read your writings aloud at every stage of revision. Read what you have written aloud so you can hear the words. When I read what I have written aloud, I force myself to focus on what I am reading and the flow of my sentence structure. I will often catch grammatical errors or flawed writing style when I read it aloud. When you first begin your revision, read through the whole draft of a section—start to finish—before you start to revise the parts.

Print out a draft of your personal history before you start

editing. If you wrote your first draft on the computer, print it out before you start editing on the screen. By printing out what you wrote, it is much easier, for example, to evaluate the lengths of paragraphs and overall flow. You can write directly on the draft, make notes, and list changes that need to be made. You are able to circle sentences and draw a line to where it might fit better. With a printed copy, you can physically note which passages sound weak, need more evidence, or could benefit from more examples.

Read your essay aloud with a pencil or pen in hand. As you read aloud, make notes about what you think might need to be changed. When you read the draft the first time, make notes in the margins. If you see spelling mistakes or grammatical errors, simply circle them so you can come back to them when you start your revision and editing.

Look at your writing through a reader's eyes.

When I first started writing, I found myself becoming very defensive when someone made an edit or comment about the writing. I took it very personally. That "filter" was keeping me from seeing how my writing was being received by others. Often the editing and suggestions others made were minor, but they really made a difference in how the writing would be received. Even if I didn't agree with the recommendation, it gave me a chance to rewrite a sentence or paragraph and make it much clearer. Thus, when you read your writing, it is very important that you try to see the writing through the reader's eyes. The following are a few techniques to consider:

Read your writing from the perspective of someone who has no interest in what you wrote. Writing the personal history is something *you* care about. Your first draft is essentially writing to yourself. It's easy to skip important facts simply because you already know them. When you read your writings from the point of view of someone who has no interest in the subject, you start asking questions or making comments—"Where's the proof?" "That's a lame statement." "Why is that important?" "What was the date?" "What was it like to live in the city at that time?" You are able to more easily see any omissions, and this process gives you a direction of what to do to strengthen your writing.

Read your writing from the perspective of a doubter. Our personal histories are filled with experiences that are personal, spiritual, and sensitive in nature. When you read your writing from the perspective of a doubter, you find areas where you can add more proof and expand on details. If you wrote something negative about someone, when you read as a doubter you take on the opinion of defending the person who was not shown in the greatest light. I have found myself "toning down" or simply leaving out my own opinion in some instances, and instead just presenting the facts.

Have someone who will give you honest feedback read your writings. The two techniques above are based on you pretending to be the audience. This technique focuses on giving your writing to someone else and having them give you honest feedback. The first level of feedback that is most important is their reaction to your writings. Were they bored? Intrigued? What did they like the most and why? What do they wish you would have expanded on or simply left out? When you ask people for their real, honest feedback, do so with the understanding that you will take their feedback seriously. You may not agree with what will be said, but you will listen, not be offended, and view it as an opportunity to write a great personal history that generations will cherish.

Personal History Structure

Your first draft was an exercise of getting your thoughts on paper. One of the first tasks you will address when reviewing your writing is to look closely at the body of the personal history and decide if the reader will be able to see and follow the flow. A good personal history is not simply a collection of good paragraphs, it doesn't start and stop at random—it moves in one direction. Good structure comes about through restructuring—moving, deleting, and adding sentences, paragraphs, or even whole sections. When you focus on the structure of your writing, you are not too concerned about transitions before and after the paragraph or even about detail in spelling and grammar, because you're not sure if that word, phrasing, sentence, or paragraph will even be in the final draft.

Reorganize and rewrite personal histories from the top down. Look at the overall organization of your ideas first, and then work your way down to the details. If your paragraphs need to be moved around, settle on the order you are going to put them in before you rewrite them. If you need to add new material, decide where it will go before you begin to write it. Do not waste your time revising and inserting sentences until you know where every paragraph for a section of your personal history belongs. It is easier to start revising by inserting a sentence where you see you need one and correcting errors in your paragraphs.

Look at how the main parts of the body are connected. Whether you developed an outline or simply started writing, look at your writing to see how the information flows. One way to analyze the flow of your writing is to write down the topic sentence and see how the information flows and holds together from one topic to the next. The main task of this exercise is to see if your paragraphs are in a reasonable order. Does one paragraph lead to the next, or do you seem to be jumping around? Are you missing material? Are questions left unanswered?

Look at the way your paragraphs begin and end. Once you have the overall flow of your writing figured out, then examine your paragraph transitions. Does one paragraph lead to another? Are you answering the questions that were discussed in the previous paragraph or providing needed information? Or are you just changing subjects at random? Look for accidental or unintended breaks in the flow that are distracting and confusing for the reader.

Look for gaps. Look for those places where your thoughts seem to jump from one point to another without linking information. As a researcher, I find that I leave gaps in writing when I chose not to explain or expand an idea that I already understood and knew the background information for. I have to remember that my reader doesn't know the detail behind the story and that I need to include the information so the reader can have the same understanding that I have gained.

Support Your Claims

When you write personal histories, most individuals will take your word on what you write concerning experiences and stories or about instances that are "common knowledge." If your personal history is going to be interesting, you should tell the reader something they don't already know. When you write about other people, you will need backup—beyond your own word—to help develop and support what is being said. This type of backup would include newspaper articles, photos, certificates, letters, and history books. Evidence is information that tells how you know about the claim you have made. It is important that you take this very literally. It is often hard to tell the difference at first between telling readers what you know and telling them how you know it. An effective personal history establishes its credibility by the answers you give, both about what you know and your sources for that knowledge.

Discover what claims in your history need supporting evidence. It is fair to assume that readers will accept claims about your own experiences—assuming they sound reasonable—without further evidence. If, however, you make a claim that is not common knowledge and is not from your own experience, it requires that you add supporting information. As a researcher, keep in mind that not everyone knows everything you know.

Tell your readers how you know the claim is true. Your personal history is devoted to answering the question "How do you know?" When revising your history, take that question very literally. You need to let your reader know why you believe a claim is true. This can be done by letting them know what you saw, read, or heard. If you believe that a claim you are making is true, let your readers know what you saw, read, or heard that convinced you it was true. Sometimes you are going to have to do further research to confirm what you believe to be true. The following are a few examples of ways I have told readers how I know something to be true:

- *The experience is based on personal experience.* Tell your experience in a way that your readers will understand how you learned what you know. When I was writing about the physical abuse my mother received during her marriage to my father, I simply described what I observed. If I was simply to make the statement that my father abused my mother, there would be no reason for the reader to accept my statement or conclusion.

- *The experience you relate is not your own direct experience.* When you write a history, many of the experiences you relate will be those shared by others in oral or written format. Simply tell the reader how you found out about the experience and how it illustrates your point and how you found out about it.

- *The experience and claims you are making are about a larger group of people or a family.* If you are making claims about a group of people, it is important to provide more than one experience to support the point you are trying to make. For example, if I was to make a claim that my Jones ancestry came from a rich history of raising cattle, I would then show examples of how members of the Jones ancestry raised cattle from several generations, gather proof of brands, articles from newspapers, photographs of the family with cattle, and so forth.

Explain your sources and cite them where necessary. In order to tell us how you know something, you need to tell us where the information came from. If you personally observed the case you are telling us about, you need to tell us that you observed it, including when and where. If you read about an experience, tell us where you read about it. If you are accepting the testimony of another person, you need to tell us who the person is and why or how she has the information you are providing.

Remember, the question your readers will always be asking is whether what they are reading is true. Your history will be a compilation of your personal experiences and those of others. You are always answering the question, "How do you know?" When you tell the experiences and stories of others, you are answering the question, "How do they know?" If you care about the truth you are writing about, readers need to have some way to check the reliability of your sources.

Use examples. The easiest—and usually the best—way to keep your readers interested in your writing is to use examples. All other things being equal, examples are more entertaining and involving than generalizations.

In almost every case, what readers remember best from a personal history is an example, usually a detailed and fully developed one. In such an example, we see and hear something that really happened; it shows us people (or animals or machines) acting as we see them act all the time. When I read a detailed example story, it's like being there. It relates a personal experience that I haven't had but that I might have had if I had been in the right place at the right time.

Dates and places don't have to be dull. You can increase the interest in dates and places by adding a little description. Rather than saying, "Grandpa Jones had an eighty-acre farm," you could say, " When he was just 25 years old, Grandpa Jones bought an eighty-acre farm located four miles from town, next to the Spanish Fork River." Dates can tell stories, but when they are used with out description, few readers will stop to notice. When you have an important day you want to draw attention to, add definition. For example: "At the age of 32, his wife died from a black widow bite, leaving him four small children under the age of 7," or "At the age of 17, just three months shy of his eighteenth birthday, he joined the Navy as a radio man at the beginning of WWII." These phrases are much more interesting then "His wife died in 1933," or "He joined the Navy in 1942."

Including Artifacts, Photos, and Images

As you write, edit, and prepare your personal history for publication, you will continually be referring to or wanting to include images in your writing. The following is an overview of the types of artifacts, photos, and images you will want to consider in helping to write and tell the personal history.

Adding photos and scanned images to your personal history

As part of the process of preparing your writing for publication and distribution, adding photos and scanned images is a very important consideration. What images will you choose to help tell the story? In addition to photos of people, include photos of significant buildings or other locations, including homesteads, churches, family cemeteries, or places of business. Images of certificates (such as birth, marriage, and death certificates), letters, and other personal documents will add great value in telling the personal history.

I have found that the most difficult part of using images is choosing which one to use. It is a common desire to want to use as many images as possible, but you should choose the images that are the best to help you tell the story. If you are talking about a family, try to find a photo of the family rather than individual photos of each person. Consider the following list of suggestions when choosing images for your family history:

1. With your personal archive or the archive you created (such as "The Box") in front of you, review each folder in relation to the story you have written. I personally organize all my images into electronic folders that match up to my physical box and sort the images to consider for use in my personal history.

2. Place a sticky note on each photo that fits the text of the history you have written. Mark on the sticky note the section title and paragraph that you believe the image would be good for.

3. Review each item you have tagged with a sticky note and ask the following questions:
   - Would I find that item useful or interesting if it were in someone else's history?
   - Would it be as effective to simply describe the item rather than include it in the book?
   - Is the item representative of the time period in which it will be included?

Note 1: If the answer to any of the above questions is "no," remove the sticky note and place the item back into the personal history archive. Only those items that still have a sticky note will be considered for use in the final history.

Note 2: If you are using photos of persons who are still living, it is important to gain their permission for use.

Note 3: At no time is it permitted to include vital record certificates (birth, marriage) or any related types of records of living persons.

4. Choose the best quality and most typical images to use in a personal history. Often you won't have the opportunity to choose the photo because it's the only one you have, but if you do have a chance, consider the following when choosing photos:

   - *Get Close.* Choose photos that get close. Photos where the subjects fill the frame with only the most important image are just better.

   - *Are Not Centered.* Choose photos that do not have your subject right in the center of the photo. Photographs are uninteresting and static when they are centered, so having an un-centered photo lends more interest to the subject.

   - *Aren't rushed.* Choose from photos where you have a series to choose from. You can choose where the photo will be on the page and then look for the one that best fits the space and is composed well.

   - *Explore all angles.* Choose photos that give you a change in perspective (such as a photo shot up from an angle or down from a higher angle). The photos help to eliminate distracting backgrounds, telephone poles, or other obstacles that would otherwise have a negative affect on your photo.

   - *Focus on the eyes.* If possible, choose photos that have the subject looking directly at the camera. There is nothing more inviting then looking into the eyes of our friends and loved ones.

   - *Use the richness of the sunrise and sunset.* Some of the best photos are taken during the first and last hour of sunlight each day. During these times, the light is warm and soft, lending a beautiful quality to the photograph. Choose photos that are taken during these hours.

   - *Shoot photos on overcast days.* Photos taken on overcast days are great to use because you don't have harsh shadows and the colors are overall better.

   - *Don't use direct flash.* Choose photos taken without flash.

Direct camera flash often causes flat lighting and red-eye.

- *Use window light.* Choose photos that take advantage of soft, natural light.
- *Don't have the midday look.* Midday photos are among the worst photos because the sun is bright, which creates harsh shadows on faces and objects, squinting eyes, less appealing skin tones, and overall muted colors.

5. Stay away from the scrapbook look. This is where you trim images and documents with special cutting scissors, add stickers, and write on the photo, or any such related activities. While it might look cute, it simply destroys the artifact and is not seen as providing any real value to what you are trying to display. Instead of scrapbooking your artifacts, spend your time writing a good and descriptive caption.

6. When you have more than one photo for a specific section and you can't decide which one to use, ask others for their opinions about your final selections.

Using maps, documents, letters, and other artifacts in your personal history

In addition to photographs, you can effectively use a wide variety of artifacts to help expand and bring meaning to your writings. For example, you can do the following in your personal history:

- Use maps to show current boundaries for counties, states, or other areas and the boundaries that existed at the time your family lived there. Use a map to show the migration path of your ancestors. Use different styles of lines and a legend to show historic and current boundaries and routes of migration. When using photocopies of actual historic family documents, also include a typed transcription.
- The use of documents and maps usually fit into the same grid format (explained below) that you use for your photographs.
- In addition to historic documents you may find it valuable to include drawings or handwritten stories from youth, as

well as newspaper clippings, or notations about current activities of living family members.

- Add a few blank or lined pages for future family members to make additional notes as the family grows.
- Scanned signatures (taken from wills, letters, and so forth) placed next to photographs can be a nice addition.

Note: Any works published more than seventy-five years ago are no longer covered by copyright, so you can use the pictures, but you should give credit. Be aware of copyright issues when using maps, illustrations, and other materials that are not your own.

Image Layout for Personal Histories

As you begin to combine your writings with images, the following lessons that I have learned will help improve the layout and readability of your personal history:

- Develop a layout grid for your personal history. A layout grid denotes where you will put images and text on the pages to help maintain visual consistency through the book. Where possible, place photos near the text (narrative or charts) describing the individuals in the picture. Accompany narratives with photos of the key people in that story.
- Group photos from the same branch of the family tree on the same page or group of pages.
- Create a photographic timeline, such as a series of group shots from family reunions taken over successive years. For example, pair a wedding photo of a couple with a photo from their fiftieth anniversary.
- Enhance an otherwise dull chart with a headshot of the "head" of each primary branch of the family.
- Instead of an initial drop-cap (a large, two- or three-line tall capital letter at the beginning of a chapter), place a photo at the start of a narrative rather than placing it "tombstone" style over the top of the story.

Preparation of Photos and Images

You will most likely be using digital images in the final preparation of your family history. Take the time to enhance your photographs using editing software. The following are a few thoughts about photo editing. I encourage you to seek more detailed how-to advice for your specific needs.

Remember: your original photos are your negatives. Never make changes to these—always work with a copy of the photo. When you load a photo into your image manipulation program, *always* do a "save as" to make a copy of the photo, and then work with that copy. If you make a mistake, you can always go back to the original and try again.

What to do with photo-editing software. Most common photo-editing tasks you will perform include the following:

- Reassemble large documents that have been photographed in sections.
- Correct the effects of poor lighting conditions or remove shadows from your photos.
- Compensate for distortion of the document photo caused by a poor shooting angle or curled pages.
- Enhance the quality of document photos suffering from low contrast or hard to read text.

An example of editing a document. Below I've outlined the steps I go through in editing an image with poor lighting. This is a simple process that has worked well for me. (I use Adobe Photoshop or Elements.)

1. Import image.
2. Create a duplicate image.
3. Rotate image, if necessary.
4. Use a cropping tool to trim the image.
5. Use auto level, auto color, and auto contrast. Use the manual versions of these tools if needed.
6. Save as a new file with a different name.

Other Elements to Include in Your Personal History

Ancestry or family tree charts. Ancestry charts show family relationships. Careful consideration should be used when deciding to include them in your personal history because they can take up too much space or their format might not fit the layout of the book. Most individuals will start with a common ancestor and show all descendents, or start with a current generation and show linkage to the common ancestor. Charts do not have to be extensive. A two- to five-generation chart can be a nice addition. There really is no right or wrong way to include ancestry charts, as long as they fit the format of your book. As a rule of thumb, use standard, commonly accepted genealogy formats. While genealogy publishing software may automatically format charts and other family data in a suitable fashion, when formatting data from scratch consider these tips:

- When listing generations and descendents, it's a good idea to indent bullets and numbering because it makes the information more readable.
- Use the same formatting throughout the book when you are listing dates such as birth, marriage, and death.
- When continuing information to another page, end on one individual and start the next page with a new individual.
- Be consistent with the way you connect family lines with boxes and lines.

Chronology sheets. These sheets allow you to detail, in date order, the schools you attended, the jobs you have had, homes you've lived in, and so forth, as well as any other details you may wish to include. Remembering exact dates can be difficult, so indicating the year is usually sufficient.

Dedication. You may have decided before you start writing your personal history who you want to dedicate your work to. I would advise that you wait until you have completed it until you decide this. Working on your personal history will stir up many old memories, feelings, and emotions, and you may change your mind about your dedication by the time you are finished.

Documentation. The first rule of genealogy is to document your resources. Should you use documentation in your personal history? Many prefer not to use footnotes or endnotes because they find them distracting. However, it is my belief that you should include documentation in your personal history.

You include documentation because it provides the reader with important information about your source and credibility in your writings. If readers have conflicting information, it becomes very easy for them to compare their notes with yours and correct their data. When you are talking about families and what they did or did not do, having the source of the information makes the truth easier to understand. When you expand your research about separate topics, you give readers a place to go for further reading, such as a book, website, or article. Documentation will save you a lot of argument and time.

Epilogue. Once you have completed writing your personal history, take some time to reflect on the completed project. Write down your thoughts and feelings about the experience in an epilogue.

Preface. The preface is a place for you to put a few of your thoughts before you start your personal history, such as why are you writing your autobiography, what you hope to achieve by writing it, what you hope others will get out of it, any worries, fears or concerns about reliving the past, and so forth.

Index. The index is the most important addition to your personal history. An index provides the listing of where to find mentions of topics, people, and images. If you are using a genealogy program to assist with the production of your book, you can also do indexing or use your word processing program to develop and edit it.

Note: It's a good idea to index a woman under her maiden as well as married name.

Table of contents. Next to the index, the table of contents is a necessary element of your writing. The table of contents helps others understand how the writings are organized and provides a map of your work. Use the table of contents to show general sections, such as chapters and subheadings.

Vital statistics. A listing of your vital statistics—such as your name, address, and age—is the information needed to identify the work as your own and serves as a point of reference later on. Anyone who reads your history will also know who the writer is.

How to Organize the Sections of Your History

The following is an example of how to organize your history into chapters and sections for a cohesive presentation.

Title page: This is the first page after the cover, and it contains the title (and sub-title) in as few words as possible. It may also include the edition number if there is more than one edition. The title page is the place to list your name and the names of other authors and editors, as well as the place and date of publication.

Copyright statement: The copyright statement is usually on back of the title page. It includes information about the publication, such as the publishing date and who to contact for more information.

Example: Copyright 2012 by Barry J. Ewell. All rights reserved.

Table of contents: This is a list of chapters and sections with accompanying page numbers. It provides an outline and guide for readers to find sections that are of most interest to them.

Dedication: The dedication contains the name of the person or people to whom you are dedicating the history and why. It is usually written on the page after the copyright page.

List of illustrations: This contains the name and page number of each picture, map, or illustration in the personal history.

Foreword: A foreword is a statement about the history, written by someone other than you or the editor.

Preface: This statement, written by you, describes why you wrote the history; provides an overview of the history's scope, content, and organization; and outlines the research methods you used. It also provides an address for readers who wish to contact you.

Acknowledgments: An acknowledgments page is a place to show gratitude to people or institutions who helped you in researching, compiling, editing, or otherwise putting together your personal history.

List of abbreviations: This reference contains the abbreviations you have used in your family history and their meanings.

Introduction: An introduction contains background or historical information that may be needed to understand the family history.

List of contributors: This lists the names of people who helped write the family history.

Chronology: A chronology provides dates and descriptions of key events in a family history. It give readers an overview of the events that shaped the person's life and provides a quick reference to important events. Including a chronology is particularly useful if your history is not arranged chronologically.

Main body: The main text of your personal history is usually divided into several sections or chapters, and can also be divided according to time period. You can use divider pages to separate the chapters. The text may contain footnotes, endnotes, and so forth, as well as illustrations, photographs, maps, or copies of records and certificates.

Appendix or appendices: An appendix contains information that is not essential to the main body of text but may be useful to readers who want more specific information about a topic. An appendix can also list the sources used in writing your history.

Examples: family group sheets, pedigree charts, and similar items

Bibliography: A bibliography lists the sources you used in compiling your personal history.

Index: This is a list of individuals, place names, and subjects mentioned in your history, with page numbers of where the topic is mentioned.

PUBLISHING YOUR HISTORY

When you write your history, there are many options of how to publish the writings. However, before you start talking about publishing, you need to ask yourself a few questions, such as the following:

How good is my material?
- How thorough has your research been?
- Are you satisfied with the accuracy of the information you have acquired, and have you documented your sources?
- If your research contains hypotheses or conclusions that are based only on conjecture, are you willing to state them as such? This will help other researchers put your work in context and, hopefully, encourage additional research.
- If there are gaps or if there is questionable data, you should probably conduct additional research to make your publication the best it can be.

Does the information present a cohesive picture of the family?
- Are there large chronological gaps in your research, missing individuals, or missing vital dates?
- Do the family stories relating to historical events fit with documented historical facts? Can you prove them?

Are you a good writer?
- You may want to enlist the writing or editorial assistance of someone who is good with words, sentence construction, punctuation, and writing engaging text.

Are you sure you want to share your research with others?
- If you plan to publish material on the Internet (see below), are you ready to extend your research range and invite other researchers and family members to contribute more material or challenge what you are publishing?
- You are always certain to receive feedback in some form or another. If you receive corrections to your data or additional data, are you prepared to publish a revised edition of your work?

All of these issues influence your decision about when to publish. As you proceed with the desire to publish, you will have multiple options for publication, including the following formats:

Blog. Individuals will sometimes use a blog to publish their history or the histories of their family. The format is much like that of an online journal. The process of posting to a blog is fairly simple. It becomes an easy and inexpensive way of sharing your history. A typical blog includes the following elements:

- Short, informational entries—generally arranged in reverse chronological order
- A time or date for each post
- Links to other blogs or websites for additional content
- Archives of all previously posted content, sometimes arranged into categories

If you decide to use a blog to publish your family history, focus on telling stories about individuals. You can include photographs, video, audio, and scanned images such as a newspaper article or letter. You have the ability to organize your posts into individual or family groupings. Include your documentation where appropriate. If you are in the process of researching a family line, you can tell the stories as you discover them.

Family newsletter. Family newsletters usually focus on happenings of the family that are usually spread far and wide. Many family newsletters also become a medium to share family histories and include documents, stories, photos, and newly discovered facts with all interested researchers. Newsletters are usually published two to four times a year by printing, photocopying, or electronically posting.

Family history CD or DVD. A family history CD or DVD has the ability to hold large amounts of data in a small space, and can include photos, sounds, scanned document images, and even video—something a printed family history can't do. And since a CD is compact and relatively inexpensive, you can easily share it with other family history researchers at family reunions, genealogical conferences, or through the mail. One of the biggest challenges in creating a family history CD is to decide what information you'd like to present and how to organize the information. If you've spent years studying the genealogy of a particular family or surname, you probably want to include the results of that research in the form of lineage-linked family trees or register reports. You may also want to include a written family history or photographs of your ancestors, their houses, headstones, and so on. Or perhaps you have video or sound recordings of ancestors or family members that you would like to showcase.

Printing and Publishing

Of all the options, printing and publishing is usually the first option you think about when it comes to sharing your research and history. Self-publishing your history is a relatively simple process with the available technologies. Options range from a simple print-out of a word-processing document to a book layout in a desktop publishing program. If you chose to do a book layout, you can then print your book at a quick-copy and bind it with a spiral ring, or print at an offset press and have it professionally bound. You can print a few copies and distribute them to a few families or publish and sell many copies to the public. The following are a few lessons learned by others pertaining to publishing your personal history.

Quick copy versus book publisher. If you are planning to print under two hundred copies, you are probably better off to go to a quick-copy, although there are specialty publishers that take on "short run" projects. Most commercial publishers prefer a print "run" of more than five hundred books. Printed books are usually well designed and of good quality.

If you're publishing a few copies of the book for your family only, you can lay the book out in a word processor and have it printed at a local printer or even print the pages on your home printer and insert them in loose-leaf binders.

If you're publishing for a wider audience, you'll need to hire professionals for the interior and cover design and printing. You can contract with individual vendors for the various services you need or hire someone to handle everything. Be wary of publishing companies that charge you large fees to publish your family history and then require you to purchase the copies of the book. Check the credentials and references of professionals you use and interview them to be sure you're comfortable working with them.

Talk to publishers before you start. Start talking to publishers when you start writing your history. They will help walk you through options that include design and formatting that will affect what you write and format.

Review other histories to gain ideas. Take the time before you start writing your book to browse through other family history books to see how others have done it. Photocopy pages from the book that you like so you have them as a reference when planning your own book. Factors to consider include paper type and quality, print size and style, number of photos, and binding. A little extra time and money can go a long way toward making your book as attractive as possible—and keep it within your budget parameters.

Compare costs. Call a few potential publishers and printers to compare costs and quality of service and to find out their requirements for publishing a personal history. To obtain an estimate for a full life story, plan for a book of two hundred pages, including images, with enough copies to distribute to your parents, siblings, children, and grandchildren (and a few extras). If you want to be more exact, provide the publisher exactly how many pages are in your manuscript. It is always a good idea to take your finished manuscript with you which includes the mockup of picture pages, introductory pages, and appendixes. If you want to spend more, you can have your history printed by an offset publisher. The quality will be better, but the additional quality may not be justified by the significant additional cost.

How to fund publishing. It is not necessary to spend a lot of money completing a personal history, but if you are going to do it, it should look good and read well. It's not uncommon for individuals writing family histories to have the total project funded by family members, provided you are doing the work.

Ask for samples. Ask your publisher to see samples of the types of binding they offer. Most publishers will show you a variety of bindings. Having your history hard bound with a sewn binding is not a requirement; however, it will last longer than other types of binding. Your goal is to publish and distribute your history, regardless of how it is bound.

Work with the publisher. If available, have your publisher archive your history for you. Many publishers will offer a one-time storage fee and keep it for you in digital form, which you may use later to make additional copies. Or, if you prefer, save it to a CD and store in a safety deposit box.

Use electronic files. Use a publisher that prints copies from a file you've saved to a disk. Each copy will then be as good as the original. Contact your publisher to find out what file format they prefer. Most publishers will accept files in recent versions of Microsoft Word, Corel WordPerfect, and other widely used word processing programs. Extra care should be taken to ensure that the end product is acceptable and correct.

Paper makes a difference. 20 lb. paper is acceptable (but too thin to print on both sides of the page), but 24 lb. is better and 60 lb. is best. Double-sided printing is preferable. Standard paper will discolor and become brittle within fifty years, so always have your history printed on acid-free paper.

Black-and-white photos are best. All photographs and images should be copied into black and white images. Black and white images will preserve much longer than color images, and printing black and white images is much cheaper than printing full-color photos.

Layout considerations and options. There will be many details to remember when defining how your history will appear on the page. For example you will need to think about the book's size. The standard paper size is 8.5 by 11 inches and will be the most cost effective to duplicate. Smaller page sizes may be more attractive, but will require more pages and will be more expensive as the pages will have to be cut to the smaller size. Other layout considerations include the following:

- Stay away from trying to use a fancy type face. Use fonts like Helvetica, Times New Roman, Arial, or members of serif text families. These fonts are easy to read.
- It's always a good idea to use a large type face such as 10 to 12 point type with normal margins for one or two column format.

- When you align your text, you can left justify your text (aligning your text on the left side of the page with ragged right) or you can justify the text with a flush left and right.
- There are many different types of binding available for your personal history. Search the one that best fits your budget and at the same time fulfills the purpose you have in mind for the book.
- Remember, when you are laying out the page, it is important to make the side you will bind to be $1/4$" larger than the outside edge. For example, if your outside edge is $1/2$", your binding edge will need to be $3/4$" wide.
- Take great care in writing the captions in your book. For example, try to the best of your ability to include the name of every person in the photograph. When you have large groups of people and you are not able to identify everyone, at least give the date when the photo was taken.

Sharing Your History

Throughout the preparation of your history, keep your eyes focused on the completion and distribution. The following are a few ideas to consider:

Publish several extra books for future generations. Posterity should have easy access to your history.

- Sell it.
- Donate copies to libraries or other institutions.
- Post it on the Internet.
- Donate a copy to the Salt Lake Family History Library.
  - Give permission to microfilm using the Family History Library's "Permission to Duplicate" form.
  - Send a letter of permission with your manuscript.
  - Send an unbound copy as it's easier to microfilm.
- Plan ahead for the publishing and marketing of your book.
- Be alert for contacts and opportunities for promotion as you research and write.

Keep good records of anyone who has been contacted or helped with the book. You will be able to contact them as potential buyers or persons who will be able to help publish and distribute the family history book.

When I first started researching and writing a personal history—be it my own or about my mother, my family, or my ancestors—I wanted to record the profound and thought-provoking experiences that could last for generations. Instead I found the history to be about life and how choices determine our course and how our course provides us an opportunity to become the individuals we are and to create the legacy we leave with our ancestral lines. No matter how great or small, every story has value because a life was lived, and every life is a gift. The story is what we did with the gift.

Epilogue: Genealogy, Prayer, and Inspiration

I have thought a lot about the topic of prayer and genealogy and just how to approach the concept without offending or preaching. Prayer is the most important tool I have as a genealogist. I remember one of my very first experiences as a genealogist, where I had chosen to work on one family line with very little success. I felt the need to include prayer but didn't. As time went on, I became more and more frustrated. Finally one day, now at a dead end, I knelt in prayer and poured out my heart and pleaded for help. Within days, information began to pour in and has been almost continuous for ten years.

Is it coincidence? No! I have had many personal experiences associated with genealogy that are divine in nature. I have felt like the hand of the Lord has literally guided me to find information, meet people, and soften hearts, making it possible to find what I needed. Prayer is the cornerstone upon which I build my genealogical research. I have spoken with many people who included prayer as part of their research, and they have had similar experiences. It's hard for me to believe that genealogy work is anything but divine. Personal revelation is available to anyone who is willing to pray, serve, and listen. Include prayer in your work; experience the difference it will make in your success and happiness in your genealogy research. Pray for which lines you should follow, for help in finding the information you seek, for help in softening the hearts of those who have information you need, and for guidance of where to search. Pray for anything and everything you do in research.

And be sure you show your gratitude for the blessings you receive. May you have the blessings of a loving Father in Heaven in your work and all else you pursue.

I would like to share one final experience with you that I hope will help to explain my belief in the power of this work we call genealogy.

"I'm here. Look again."

I had been researching my Danish ancestry for several months and had progressed several generations back to the early 1700s. I had reached a brick wall and couldn't seem to locate a descendent who had been born and had raised a family in the area I was researching.

The family had lived in the community for generations and then they were suddenly gone, leaving no trace of where they might have gone. I searched the military, community, and church records with no success. My next step was to systematically search all the neighboring communities and parishes in a twenty-five-mile radius. After several weeks of research, I was down to the last several microfilms for the search area. I arrived at the family history library at 8:00 a.m. and began searching a rather large parish record carefully—line by line, page by page—for most of the day. As I finished the film and was on my way back to return the film to its original location, I audibly heard the words, "I'm here; look again."

The voice pierced my very soul. I knew I had to return and research the film the next day. When I returned to the family history library the next day, I anxiously retrieved the film to embark on what I hoped would be a successful search. Again I searched each line and page. I went through the film forward and backwards. Sadly, at the end of the day I was no closer than I was the day before. As the library was closing, I was returning the film to its location and, again, I heard the words, this time with greater force "I'm here. Look again." Were the words wishful thinking or actual direction to once again search the film?

I privately agreed to give it one more look on the following day. As I had on the previous two days, I retrieved the film. This time I somehow knew that I would find the ancestor I had been searching for.

I spent several hours searching the same pages. This time, I searched every word, letter, and line with focused precision. I was being very detailed in my research notes. I marked off page 56, decided to take a break, and rested my head to take a short nap. When I awoke twenty minutes later, before me on the screen was the name I had been searching for. The microfilm reel had been advanced more than one hundred pages. I can't explain why or how the film had been advanced. I do know that I heard and obeyed the prompting I had received: "I'm here. Look again."

This, like so many other experiences, has taught me that my ancestors want to be found. I have come to believe, in my pursuit of researching each of my family lines, that my ancestors do take an active role in helping me join the generations.

Final thought

As a genealogist, I have many opportunities to mentor other genealogists both in a conference and a one-on-one setting. Whether you are a beginning genealogist or a seasoned researcher, I hope that this book has in some way helped you become a better genealogist by being more focused and productive with the time you have available. Enjoy this experience we call genealogy. What will you do with the time you have available? Remember, you are just one link in a chain that extends generations, but you are the link that binds the present with the future and the past.

About the Author

B arry J. Ewell is the founder of MyGenShare.com, a comprehensive digital library for the genealogist, providing a dynamic collection of companion resources used to advance learning, sharing, and discovering family history.

His professional career has been in advertising and public relations strategy for technology companies such as IBM and 3M.

Since being introduced to family history in 1998, he has researched his family roots in the United States, United Kingdom, Scandinavia, Germany, and Russia. His focus has been to preserve the record of his family by doing oral and written histories, artifact preservation, and genealogy research.

Barry is an advocate of "Sharing Information to Join Generations." He is a writer, presenter, researcher, and mentor of genealogists. Barry has authored articles, eBooks, videos, and podcasts about his experience in Internet and field family history research, plus digital and software resources. He has presented and shared his knowledge and experience at local, regional, and national conferences.

Barry and his bride, Colette, are the parents of six children.

Notes

Notes

Notes

Notes